Mark Twain: an American Prophet

Books by Maxwell Geismar

THE NOVEL IN AMERICA

Writers in Crisis: The American Novel, 1925–1940
(*Studies of Ring Lardner, Ernest Hemingway, John Dos Passos,*
William Faulkner, Thomas Wolfe, John Steinbeck)
The Last of the Provincials: The American Novel, 1915–1925
(*Studies of H. L. Mencken, Sinclair Lewis, Willa Cather,*
Sherwood Anderson, F. Scott Fitzgerald)
Rebels and Ancestors: The American Novel, 1890–1915
(*Studies of Frank Norris, Stephen Crane, Jack London,*
Ellen Glasgow, Theodore Dreiser)
American Moderns: From Rebellion to Conformity
Henry James and the Jacobites
Mark Twain: An American Prophet

EDITOR

The Ring Lardner Reader
The Walt Whitman Reader
The Portable Thomas Wolfe
Sherwood Anderson: Short Stories
Jack London: Short Stories

MARK TWAIN
AN AMERICAN PROPHET

Maxwell Geismar

Houghton Mifflin Company Boston
1970

A selection from this book appeared in the March 1970 issue of
Scanlan's Monthly, copyright © 1970 by Scanlan's Literary
House, Inc.

Thanks are due to Harper & Row, Inc., Publishers, for permission to quote illustrative passages from the following books:
"The Mysterious Stranger" from *The Mysterious Stranger and
Other Stories* by Mark Twain. Copyright 1916 by Harper &
Brothers; copyright renewed 1944 by Clara Clemens Gabrilowitsch. *Europe and Elsewhere* by Mark Twain. Copyright
1923, 1951 by The Mark Twain Company. *Mark Twain's Autobiography,* Vol. I and Vol. II, edited by Albert Bigelow Paine.
Copyright 1924 by Clara Gabrilowitsch; copyright renewed
1952 by Clara Clemens Samossoud. *Mark Twain in Eruption,*
edited by Bernard DeVoto. Copyright 1922 by Harper & Brothers; copyright renewed 1940 by The Mark Twain Company.
Letters from the Earth by Mark Twain, edited by Bernard De-
Voto. Copyright © 1938, 1944, 1946, 1959, 1962 by The Mark
Twain Company. *The Autobiography of Mark Twain,* edited
by Charles Neider. Copyright © 1917, 1940, 1958, 1959 by The
Mark Twain Company. Copyright © 1959 by Charles Neider.

Thanks are due also to Hill and Wang, Inc., Publishers, for
permission to quote from *Mark Twain and the Russians, An
Exchange of Views* by Charles Neider. Copyright © 1960 by
Charles Neider.

To my wife Anne

In tribute to Mark Twain's Eve,
edenic divine native artist

"Fiat justitia ruat coelum"
— *The Noble Savage*

CONTENTS

Mark Twain: an American Prophet

ONE

FACTUAL

THIS IS a critical study of Mark Twain's literary career in which I have used autobiographical material to clarify certain issues of Twain's work, certain works of his in which personal background was relevant, or certain phases and periods of his work in general. Since I have used this material for the purpose of clarifying his "real life" (that is to say, his literary work) rather than for its own sake, and have used it partially in places, and in other places perhaps familiarly, in the sense of taking it for granted, it occurred to me that it might be helpful to present some kind of factual summary of Twain's life at the outset.

He was born Samuel Langhorne Clemens on November 30, 1835, in Florida, Missouri. His family came from the good southern stock which emigrated westward in those days; his father was a man of cultivation and dignity (and a certain aloofness) who was always on the edge of material comfort and always falling below it. The family was poor but respectable; the mother was a central influence to whom Sam Clemens paid ample and affectionate tribute. In 1839 they moved to Hannibal, Missouri, the scene of Twain's enfabled romances of western childhood and of a later violent and black despair as to both his own dreams and frontier democracy.

In 1847 the father died (just when he was about to achieve some worldly success again), and Sam Clemens left school, which he never much praised, to become a printer's apprentice in the shop of his even more grandiose but ill-fated brother Orion. From 1855 to 1856 he wandered around the country as a journeyman printer in St. Louis, New York, Philadelphia, Keokuk, and Cincinnati, and he began some journalistic work. (His career so far was typical, and paralleled that of another orphic spirit of his own day, Walt Whitman, whom Twain in effect never knew or mentioned.) The years from 1857 to 1860 were the years of piloting on the Mississippi which formed another central strand of Twain's early experience, and which were molded into the chronicle of frontier river life, following after and not unrelated to Herman Melville's epic of the whaling trade.

The Civil War destroyed Mississippi shipping; at the war's start Clemens was a Southern volunteer who promptly resigned, along with his regiment, when news of General Grant's presence was rumored. In July, 1861, he left with his brother Orion for the Nevada territory where he prospected on and off for silver, struck it rich, lost his money, and became a reporter for the Virginia City *Territorial Enterprise* and then, moving west because of a duel which he had no heart for, for the San Francisco *Morning Call*. In 1866 he made a fateful visit to the Sandwich Islands, now Hawaii, which proved his vision of an earthly paradise, provided another central theme for his writing, and started him out on the lecture platform. In 1867 he traveled to Europe and the Holy Land as correspondent for the San Francisco *Alta California,* and just two years later, using the material from this trip, he published his famous travel book, *The Innocents Abroad*, which established his literary reputation and sold one hundred thousand copies.

This was the apprenticeship of a genius in the annals of world literature; from being in effect a proletarian vagabond Sam Clemens overnight became a culture hero to which he promptly added a legendary marriage to an American coal heiress from upper New York state.

In 1870 he married Olivia Langdon and they moved to Buffalo, where their first son, Langdon, was born. (He died in 1872.) They were planning and building the Hartford mansion which was to be their true home; in 1871 they moved there; and their daughter Susy was born in 1872, and Clara in 1874. Meanwhile Clemens was publishing a series of famous early books, *Roughing It, The Gilded Age, The Adventures of Tom Sawyer*.

Their third daughter, Jean, was born in 1880. They were always taking trips to Europe, and in London Twain was lionized. The eighties brought forth more big books, among them *Life on the Mississippi, The Adventures of Huckleberry Finn*, along with that curious chronicle, *A Connecticut Yankee in King Arthur's Court*. By then, however, Clemens, who always gambled, who was a child of the nineteenth century and lived to regret it, was involved in the business and scientific ventures which broke his life in half. At first it was his publishing house which made a fortune on General Grant's *Memoirs*, and gradually went broke. And then there was the fabulous Paige typesetter, reputedly the most expensive machine ever made, on which Twain squandered every cent he had made, and Livy's fortune too. (They were living to the tune of one hundred thousand dollars a year, about half of which Clemens spent on his "inventions.") At fifty, at the peak of his fame, he went bankrupt in a society where most men of his age never made it back again.

Mark Twain did, by the grace of God and a Standard Oil tycoon named Henry H. Rogers. Fortune's favorite child was not abandoned yet — though the terrible financial crisis led indirectly perhaps (or so the Clemenses may have believed) to the death of their beloved Susy while they were away from her on a lecture tour, and to Livy's own nervous collapse, lingering illness, and death. With the end of Mark Twain's domestic idyll, his private garden of innocence and love and play (Twain's favorite ancestors were Adam and Eve), he entered the second and most severe trauma of his mature life. But that is enough for you to know about the facts of the situation; here let the book take over the story. And what a remarkable story it is: of success and failure, of innocence and corruption, of good and evil, of the great spiritual peaks and deep abysses which accompanied Mark Twain's life and career.

But he lived it through; he survived it all. Like the great book of his old age, the *Autobiography* — one of the great books of our letters — he would have many editions, and perhaps the final one is yet to come. In his affinity with the animal world, Mark Twain's behavior was sometimes catlike; but he did not really have nine lives. He had something better, the double soul of a great artist.

That is to say, he did not have the split personality which is commonly attributed to him, nor all the frustration and repression and mental conflict which goes along with that. He had a soul both pagan and civilized, but a civilizational soul which did not repress or replace the pagan one, but lived together with it, harmoniously or acridly, as it may be, but together, always fused and joined in Clemens' central artistic vision: the double aware of its loss and rejoicing in its heritage. (Among depth psychologists Freud knew this, but it was Otto Rank who pursued it to final meanings — and Mark Twain was Rank's favorite writer.) All writers have this to some degree; it is the special province of art and the artist. But few have had it so openly, freshly, and actively as Clemens, and it is the secret of his whole achievement.

That is why, literally, he is such a pleasure and a delight to read; because to him life and art *were* pleasure, or at least art was, at its best. That is why the early Sam Clemens refused to work any more than he had to, and why the later Clemens refused to write when he did not enjoy the writing. He is one of the great "daylight writers" of the world, as you'll see, who transcended all the torments, horrors, fears, pain, and illness in the black night of our existence.

It will become clear, too, that I do not accept certain other fixed concepts of Mark Twain criticism extending from the twenties to the seventies. It is obvious that the grand historian of our literature, Van Wyck Brooks, did not understand Twain's humor and falsely used this great artist as an example of native genius being broken and destroyed by American materialism. The remarkable thing about Mark Twain is that his great financial and social success never touched his heart or temperament. Nor was he seriously affected by the Victorian censorship to which he yielded ironically on occasion; but rather the reverse. The underground sexuality of his nature, sometimes hidden or suppressed, emerged in full force in his later work, and in the *Autobiography* itself.

Was he also a writer, broken in mid-course, who will be remembered only for those idylls of frontier youth, and who turned away from the society of his period to live in some historical fantasy-land? (Justin Kaplan, in the latest biography of

Mark Twain.) On the contrary, a whole area of Twain's social criticism of the United States has been repressed or avoided by Twain scholars precisely because it is so bold, so brilliant, satirical, and prophetic. He was one of the most mature American artists precisely because he had, so to speak, such a long, deep childhood. Those whose childhood is cut short or is never lived through fully: those are the ones who never fully mature, and remain caught in the pubescent or adolescent emotional states throughout their lives. To become old, one has first to be young; and to be truly young is never to become completely old. It was not mere whimsy that led Livy to call Clemens "Youth," but the recognition of a deep strain in his temperament.

Was Twain just a personal, anecdotal, intimate "humorist," as was said at the start of his career and as Charles Neider says again in the most recent edition of Twain's last book? Never was a writer more interested in the whole world around him, or more involved in every detail of it. The "I" of Whitman and Twain alike was not the "Big Me" of the autistic personality. It was the primitive and animistic "I" (to a large degree that of Eastern and Asiatic religious philosophy) of an organism which does not even recognize its own separation from the world around it, which *is* that world, while being most clearly itself. Just as nothing human is alien to it, so it is immersed in everything which is human. Curiosity — and what he called the "unobstructed eye" — is a dominant feature of Twain's temperament. He could never stop looking at the world, and at the "damned human race" which he viewed with such ridicule, wrath, and laughter. Because he too belonged to that race, and worse he could say of no man.

Two concluding notes. I have used the names of Mark Twain and Samuel Clemens almost interchangeably throughout this book, but that of Sam Clemens when I am talking of the man behind the artist, or when talking of him more personally, perhaps, or affectionately. Upon a few occasions I have used the name "Sam" by itself, but rarely, or never, I think, have I used the name "Mark" by itself, perhaps for some curious reason of personal taste which I have not myself been able to understand.

And finally: I know I have quoted from Clemens in great detail in terms of a formal literary study. I did this because I never thought it was excessive, and I could never bring myself to stop quoting some passages. (Though what is printed here I have pruned sharply, much to my private regret, from the original block of quotations.) It is not just that when Mark Twain is good, he is too good *not* to quote. But also, much of the material reprinted here has been buried in his more obscure books, some of it appearing in almost unknown books. And I thought it better to rescue and to collect here all those prose passages, from whatever source, which seem today as sharp and fresh and pristine; or as appropriate and brilliant and penetrating, as sophisticated and satiric and entertaining as when the ink first flowed from such a pen, divine and diabolical.

TWO

A PAGAN PURITAN

Even the beginning was auspicious. His early short story "The Celebrated Jumping Frog of Calaveras County" was printed and became the title story of a volume of Twain's newspaper sketches published in 1867.

The story was a typical example of the frontier tall tale, but what marked it off was that it was already a parody of a parody. Twain was interested in the form of the sketch, and that is to say, in the garrulous narrator whose stream of consciousness is continuously nonselective. The "Frog" is still entertaining and a good example of its genre, but the young author, coming across a translation of it in the *Revue des Deux Mondes,* felt a need to translate the French back into English in a new version called "The Frog Jumping of the County of Calaveras."

"It there was one time here an individual known under the name of Jim Smiley . . ." Who was the man "the most fond of to bet which one have seen, betting upon all that which is presented, when he could find an adversary; and when he not of it could not, he passed to the side opposed. All that which

convenienced to the other, to him convenienced also; seeing
that he had a bet, Smiley was satisfied. And he had a chance!
a chance even worthless; nearly always he gained." The revised
version of the "Frog" went on to Smiley's animals: the queer
birds, dogs, horses of the original tale, and the frog himself. "Eh
bien! this Smiley nourished some terriers and rats and some
cocks of combat, and some cats, and all sorts of things; and
with his rage of betting one no had more of repose. He trapped
one day a frog and him imported with him [*et l'emporta chez
lui*] saying that he pretended to make his education. You me
believe if you will, but during three months he not has nothing
done but to him apprehend to jump [*apprendre à sauter*] in
a court retired of her mansion [*de sa maison*]."

Already Sam Clemens, this "rude frontier genius," was displaying his wit, his verbal play, and that kind of humor, both
in the original "Frog" and the revised "Frog," which had no
counterpart (until the days of Ring Lardner) in the national letters. And barely two years later, with his first travel book, *The
Innocents Abroad,* in 1869, he was suddenly catapulted into a
national prominence beyond his wildest dreams. He had wanted
to be a journalist, a lecturer, an entertainer who would make
people laugh; now he was suddenly a popular writer on the
way to money, fame, and social position.

In New York Clemens attended Henry Ward Beecher's
Plymouth Church less for religious reasons than to observe the
platform style of the famous minister; and it was Beecher's
church that initiated the "pilgrimage" to the Holy Land which
Twain covered as the *Alta California*'s foreign correspondent
before writing his book. The enduring secret of *The Innocents
Abroad,* of course, lies in the fact that it was the first American
travel book, realistic, satirical, homely, debunking, to set itself
off against a whole tradition of foreign "romance" in this

genre; a romance literature of travel exemplified at that very moment by the Jamesian "dream of Europe." Conversely, Twain was at his best just when he quoted and parodied the conventional travel books about the scene he was visiting; this was a very cosmopolitan, a highly sophisticated country bump- kin from the wild west who paid mock homage to the hallowed shrines of Old World culture.

On these excursions, he was trying to write not what he ought to feel, as he said, but what he did feel. To be sure, *The Inno- cents Abroad* contains many sections of padded material or plain filler, of more or less conventional gambits of comedy, of dragging and belabored narrative. As in almost all Twain's work from start to last, the quality is uneven; and it is precisely in this rough literary terrain that you fall upon the priceless literary episodes and prose passages.

For all the semblance of a genial old-fashioned American tale of travel entertainment, too, the *Innocents* was at base a radical document which presaged the future career of Mark Twain. It was perhaps even more radical in its "innocence" than some of the middle Twain would be, though not the later or the last Twain at all. As usual, after the trip was over, Sam Clemens started with the thing that was closest to him: in this case the "Old Travelers," whom he met in France. "But still I love the Old Travelers. I love them for their witless platitudes; for their supernatural ability to bore; for their delightful asi- nine vanity; for their luxuriant fertility of imagination; for their startling, their brilliant, their overwhelming mendacity!" In France there was the description of the cancan. "I placed my hands before my face for very shame. But I looked through my fingers. They were dancing the renowned 'Can-can.' A handsome girl in the set before me tripped forward lightly to meet the opposite gentleman — tripped back again, grasped

her dresses vigorously on both sides with her hands, raised
them pretty high, danced an extraordinary jig that had more
activity and exposure about it than any jig I ever saw before,
and then, drawing her clothes still higher, she advanced gaily to
the center and launched a vicious kick full at her *vis-à-vis* that
must infallibly have removed his nose if he had been seven feet
high . . . That is the Can-can. The idea of it is to dance as
wildly, as noisily, as furiously as you can; expose yourself as
much as possible if you are a woman; and kick as high as you
can, no matter which sex you belong to."

Along with his insistence on factuality and materiality, Clemens had a natural affinity for the flesh; this astute realist was
close to the primitive bases of life. Thus the *Innocents* pays its
tribute to pretty women everywhere, to animal life always; and
here too Clemens initiated a lifelong admiration, at once
esthetic, moral and social, for the dark-skinned peoples of the
earth. Yet in all his moments of worship and devotion there
was always a satiric sting. "Ah, the grisettes! I had almost
forgotten. They are another romantic fraud." In Paris Twain
noted directly that "all through this Faubourg St. Antoine, misery, poverty, vice, and crime go hand in hand, and the evidences
of it stare one in the face from every side. Here the people live
who begin the revolutions. Whenever there is anything of that
kind to be done, they are always ready. They take as much
genuine pleasure in building a barricade as they do in cutting a
throat or shoving a friend into the Seine. It is these savage-
looking ruffians who storm the splendid halls of the Tuileries,
occasionally, and swarm into Versailles when a king is to be
called to account."

Wasn't there a note of veiled admiration here, too, when compared, say, with the mincing nightmares of "anarchism" in *The
Princess Casamassima*? In Genoa, Clemens was impressed by

the ladies again. "I scanned every female face that passed, and
it seemed to me that all were handsome; I never saw such a
freshet of loveliness before." He noticed the female attendants
at the Italian public baths. "I am an unprotected male, but I
will preserve my honor at the peril of my life!" — and here
came the highly charged and controversial commentary on
the Old Masters and the Catholic religion. The gory paintings
of the Savior were repugnant to Twain's democratic esthetics,
and he disdained the huge, coarse frescoes of suffering martyrs.
"It could not have diminished their sufferings any to be un-
couthly represented. We were in the heart and home of priest-
craft — of a happy, cheerful, contented ignorance, superstition,
degradation, poverty, indolence, and everlasting unaspiring
worthlessness."

But it is interesting that he blamed the people themselves —
"How can men, calling themselves men, consent to be so degraded and happy?" — as much as their institutions. (And
he was still unaware of the paradox contained in their "happiness.") In Venice, indulging in a deliberately deadpan low-
browism which produced fine pages of satire on the conventional art-snobbery of his period, he confessed his own taste for
the Renaissance art which dealt with the affairs of men in this
world. Considering Clemens' lack of background, of formal
education, of knowledge of Old World culture, there is already
a remarkable sense of history in these sections of *The Innocents
Abroad,* just as there is a nice analysis of the Catholic clerical
organization. "As far as I can see, Italy, for fifteen hundred
years, has turned all her energies, all her finances, and all her
industry to building up a vast array of wonderful church edifices,
and starving half her citizens to accomplish it. She is to-day
one vast museum of magnificence and misery . . . It is the
wretchedest, princeliest land on earth."

In his early mood of nineteenth-century materialistic progress, no doubt Clemens stressed the achievements of Morse,
Fulton, Jenner, and Daguerre at the expense of "Roman sloth,
Roman superstition, and modern Roman boundlessness of ignorance." But the first volume of *The Innocents Abroad* was an
eloquent defense of the American democracy which, abandoning its own roots, corrupting its own aspirations in the
Gilded Age, was just then turning toward that dream of European nobility and "culture" which Twain attacked. Reading
over this classical travel book today, we notice how steadily it
builds its power from a mild and genial tone at the opening to
its closing satire on the Old World's social misery, princely castes,
and religious superstition. "From the sanguinary sports of the
Holy Inquisition; the slaughter of the Colosseum; and the dismal tombs of the Catacombs," said he, "I naturally pass to the
picturesque horrors of the Capuchin Convent." And how skill-
fully Clemens mixed these passages of social satire and parody
with a brilliant kind of personal humor. "I never felt so fer-
vently thankful, so soothed and tranquil, so filled with a blessed
peace, as I did yesterday when I learned that Michael Angelo
was dead." So much for Europe — in which Clemens, however, was destined to spend more of his mature life than he did
in America; and the second volume of *The Innocents Abroad*
turned to the East and the Holy Land itself.

In Constantinople he was even more appalled at Eastern
misery and disease. "A beggar in Naples who can show a foot
which has all run into one horrible toe, with one shapeless nail
on it, has a fortune — but such an exhibition as that would not
provoke any notice in Constantinople. The man would starve
. . . Who would pay any attention to attractions like his
among the rare monsters that throng the bridges of the Golden
Horn and display their deformities in the gutters of Stamboul?"

The Mosque of Saint Sophia was the rustiest old barn in hea-thendom; the Turks were dirty pagans, and if Clemens was in-cited by European Catholicism, he was not greatly impressed by Mohammedanism. "Mosques are plenty, churches are plenty, graveyards are plenty, but morals and whiskey are scarce. The Koran does not permit Mohammedans to drink. Their natural instincts do not permit them to be moral. They say the Sultan has eight hundred wives. This almost amounts to bigamy." This was tongue in cheek, of course, and he was aroused by the "incendiary" travel books on the Mideast, along with the food. "When I think how I have been swindled by books of Oriental travel, I want a tourist for breakfast." There is another hilarious diatribe against the celebrated Turkish baths as a malignant swindle; in the ruins of Sebastopol, they took home the fragments of a Russian general for a souvenir. Yet, received by the Czar at Yalta, this democrat was rather taken in by the charm of Russian royalty — at least when com-pared with ordinary life in Asia, in Smyrna. "Everywhere there is dirt, everywhere there are fleas, everywhere there are lean, broken-hearted dogs; every alley is thronged with people; wher-ever you look, your eye rests upon a wild masquerade of ex-travagant costumes" — while the muezzin's cry called the "faith-ful vagabonds" to prayer, and superior to everything was the com-bination of Mohammedan stenches.

He was struck by the Armenian women, though, as he had been by the peasant girls in Yalta, and as he was by the ancient history of Ephesus. "We speak of Apollo and of Diana — they were born here; of the metamorphosis of Syrinx into a reed — it was done here; of the great god Pan — he dwelt in the caves of this hill of Coressus; of the Amazons — this was their best-prized home; of Bacchus and Hercules — both fought the war-like women here; of the Cyclops — they laid the ponderous marble blocks of some of the ruins yonder — of Homer — this was one of his many birthplaces . . ." The *Innocents* is a diary of what the early Sam Clemens hated and liked; and if there was much more of the former than the latter in his book, it was also true that the intensity of his admirations made up for their lack of range.

In the approach to the Holy Land itself, the women of Beirut added an interest to Twain's travels by covering their faces and exposing their breasts. And here again he spoke of animals as though he was one. How does a camel look? "When he is down on all his knees, flat on his breast to receive his load, he looks something like a goose swimming; and when he is upright he looks like an ostrich with an extra set of legs . . . They are not particular about their diet. They would eat a tombstone if they could bite it . . . I suppose it would be a real treat for a camel to have a keg of nails for supper." The holy traveler also had a horse by the name of Jericho. "He is a mare. I have seen remarkable horses before, but none so remarkable as this. I wanted a horse that could shy, and this one fills the bill. I had an idea that shying indicated spirit. If I was correct, I have got the most spirited horse on earth . . . He has only one fault. His tail has been chopped off or else he has sat down on it too hard, some time or other, and he has to fight the flies with his heels" — and so on until Jericho is one of the characters taking the trip.

Battered old parodies of animals that they are, they are usually in better shape than their masters.

Clemens found the Syrians to be naturally goodhearted and intelligent but horribly poor and ground down by their rulers. "If ever an oppressed race existed, it is this one we see fettered around us under the inhuman tyranny of the Ottoman empire. I wish Europe would let Russia annihilate Turkey a little —

not much, but enough to make it difficult to find the place again without a divining-rod or a diving-bell."

Ancient and nostalgic evils vanished to make place for new and future evils in the prophetic strain of Mark Twain; and there are times in the *Innocents* when one is torn between the social injustices and the pleasure evoked by Clemens' denunciations of them. The Ottoman Empire was his special peeve here, but he had enough spirit left to turn upon something much closer: his fellow Christian pilgrims who were beating their horses to death in a frenzied attempt to reach Damascus before the Sabbath day. "Nothing could move the pilgrims. They *must* press on. Men might die, horses might die, but they must enter upon holy soil next week, with no Sabbath-breaking stain upon them. Thus they were willing to commit a sin against the spirit of religious law, in order that they might preserve the letter of it. I am talking now about personal friends; men whom I like; men who are good citizens; who are honorable, upright, conscientious: but whose idea of the Saviour's religion seems to me distorted."

Meanwhile he had come across a whole new vein of comic writing. The retelling of Biblical legends in Twain's ironical, poker-faced, flat western country style is another feature of the *Innocents* which a whole line of American humorists, and perhaps particularly Ring Lardner, would use and adapt to their own needs. In the holy shrines of Jerusalem, Clemens erupted into passages of irony and parody:

> The great feature of the Mosque of Omar is the prodigious rock in the center of its rotunda. It was upon this rock that Abraham came so near offering up his son Isaac — this, at least, is authentic — it is very much more to be relied on than most of the traditions, at any rate. On this rock, also the angel stood and threatened Jerusalem, and David persuaded him to spare the city. Mohammed

was well acquainted with this stone. From it he ascended to
heaven. The stone tried to follow him and if the angel Gabriel
had not happened by the merest good luck to be there to seize it,
it would have done it. Very few people have a grip like Gabriel
— the prints of his monstrous fingers, two inches deep, are to be
seen in that rock today . . . This rock, large as it is, is suspended
in the air. It does not touch anything at all. The guide said so.
This is very wonderful . . .

But notice that this pantheistic Mark Twain could endow
even a stone with a remarkable personality. Then there is the
central aphorism of *The Innocents Abroad*. "There are some
things which, for the credit of America, should be left unsaid,
perhaps; but these very things happen sometimes to be the very
things which, for the real benefit of Americans, ought to have
prominent notice."

And then there was the final blast — scandalous at the
time — at the whole boatload of Christian pilgrims; the folly
of the entire trip to the Holy Land. Very early, Sam Clemens
started out to bite the hand that fed him. Yet it made for an exciting end to a book which still remains, in these high spots, a
vital, fresh and interesting kind of travelogue, one which is
still popular and still read today. For Twain had already become
a master stylist without appearing to know it. Here was that
natural, personal, simple, informal western "country-style" of
prose — appearing just like the "conversation" or table talk
it never was — which as early as 1869 had transformed the
American language. While in the same years both Howells and
Henry James were trying to "refine" the English language, and
while a full century later our contemporary academic prose was
full of lingering anachronisms, Twain, after Thoreau, had
dealt formal English a mortal blow. How sharp and fresh and
brilliant is the prose style of *The Innocents Abroad* as you read

it now. In fact Twain's next book, *Roughing It,* published in 1872, if entirely different in scene and tone, was another such travelogue as the *Innocents,* with the language even more native and homelier. Starting out to be the recital of Clemens' first trip west into Nevada and California, about nine years earlier, *Roughing It* was also, in its best moments, a classical account of a frontier society.

After the prefatory note in *Roughing It,* where Twain lamented the fact that information poured out of him "like the precious ottar of roses out of the ottar," the chronicle launched into a handsome description of the western stage coaches. The book's opening note, which Twain was to develop on that celebrated Mississippi raft, was one of pagan pleasure; the pure enjoyment of life.

> The stage whirled along at a spanking gait, the breeze flapping curtains and suspended coats in a most exhilarating way; the cradle swayed and swung luxuriously, the pattering of the horses' hoofs, the cracking of the driver's whip, and his "Hi-yi! g'lang!" were music; the spinning ground and the waltzing trees appeared to give us a mute hurrah as we went by . . . and as we lay and smoked the pipe of peace and compared all this luxury with the years of tiresome city life that had gone before it, we felt that there was only one complete and satisfying happiness in the world, and we had found it.

Very early, Twain sounded this note of escape and asylum from the burden of the nineteenth-century civilization whose commerce and science he elsewhere appeared to celebrate. This was already a flying womb, so to speak, in whose "cradle" Sam Clemens lolled and luxuriated. And here he mixed the marvelous descriptions of the western frontier with the profiles of the heroic Overland stage drivers. These "great and shining digni-

taries" were early prototypes of the Mississippi pilots; this favorite son of the wild west was the envy of hostlers and station-
keepers alike. "When they spoke to him they received his
insolent silence meekly . . . when he opened his lips they all
hung on his words with admiration . . . when he discharged
a facetious insulting personality at a hostler, that hostler was
happy for the day; when he uttered his one jest — old as the
hills, coarse, profane, witless, and inflicted on the same audience, in the same language, every time his coach drove up there
— the varlets roared and slapped their thighs . . . And how
they would fly around when he wanted a basin of water, a gourd
of the same, or a light for his pipe! — but they would instantly
insult a passenger if he so far forgot himself as to crave a favor
at their hands. They could do that sort of insolence as well
as the driver they copied it from — for, let it be borne in mind,
the Overland driver had but little less contempt for his passengers than he had for his hostlers."

There are the crude scenes of the Overland stations; the barren settings, the rough and coarse human types, the bad food
mixed with dead flies: scenes of human desolation to contrast
with the portraits of the Overland coach drivers and of the
western animals. To the jackrabbit, Clemens added the ante-
lope, the wolf, the prairie dog, the coyote. These were the
western democratic souls too, along with the frontiersmen; our
very own domestic animals, and how well Twain knew them.
"The coyote is a long, slim, sick and sorry-looking skeleton with
a gray wolf skin stretched over it, a tolerable bushy tail that forever sags down with a despairing expression of forsakenness and
misery, a furtive and evil eye, and a long, sharp face with
slightly lifted lip and exposed teeth. He has a general slinking
expression all over. The coyote is a living, breathing allegory of
Want. He is *always* hungry. He is always poor, out of luck and

friendless. The meanest creatures despise him, and even the
fleas would desert him for a velocipede. He is so spiritless and
cowardly that even while his exposed teeth are pretending a
threat, the rest of his face is apologizing for it. And he is *so*
homely!" This was prose again, and, since the coyote's only
answer to life was to run, there is a comic description of the
coyote pretending to let a dog catch up with him.

The trick was the personifying and the "humanizing" of the
animals whom Twain described with a sense of perfect familiarity, but in this western paradise — this western inferno — animal and human life existed in a kind of natural equality. (But
there is a distinction between the "civilized" town animals and
the wild animals.) Like Melville before him and Dreiser after
him, Clemens had the primitive writer's sense of physical grace
and vitality, of pure animal dignity even when, as in the coyote's
case, it was notable for its absence. And to these early frontier
heroes *Roughing It* added the division agents of the western
Overland. There were only eight of these division kings who
ruled supreme by law of club and pistol over the station-keepers,
hostlers, outlaws, and fugitives of the west; and, moving from
the pony express of four hundred gallant horses and eighty rid-
ers delivering the United States mail to the black hills of Fort
Laramie where the Indian raiders still persisted, *Roughing It*
reached an early peak of eloquence with the advent of the outlaw Slade. (But the whole opening section of the book is lyrical, hilarious, brilliant; as fresh and interesting today as when
it was first written.) Slade was another of the division managers
— "A high and efficient servant of the Overland, an outlaw
among outlaws, and yet their relentless scourge, Slade was at
once the most bloody, the most dangerous, and the most valuable citizen that inhabited the savage fastnesses of the mountains." As an outlaw, he had been picked by the Overland to

protect the company against the other outlaws. And "we had gradually come to have a realizing sense of the fact that Slade was a man whose heart and hands and soul were steeped in the blood of offenders against his dignity; a man who awfully avenged all injuries, affronts, insults or slights of whatever kind — on the spot if he could, years afterward if lack of earlier opportunity compelled it; a man whose hate tortured him day and night till vengeance appeased it."

Working directly, and openly, from a local history of the desperadoes which he recreated in his own vein, Clemens wrote a chapter on this type of democratic hero-villain; villains whose villainy captivated their western chronicler. Slade with his "history-creating revolver" and his energetic administration of the Overland became the absolute ruler of a "very paradise of outlaws and desperadoes. There was absolutely no semblance of law there. Violence was the rule. Force was the only recognized authority. The commonest misunderstandings were settled on the spot with the revolver or the knife. Murders were done in open day and with sparkling frequency and nobody thought of inquiring into them . . ." Nor did Mark Twain himself have much thought here as to what kind of future culture would emerge from "this hive of horse thieves and assassins," or what imprint this frontier violence would leave upon the American character. If violence and force, without semblance of law, were at the root of the frontier code, the early Clemens was more concerned with their esthetic color than with their cultural implications. So, too, while Twain's early fictional portraits are not complex, his first two travel books proved his talent for reporting and documentaries, his sense of scene and atmosphere, his capacity to take in the world around him sharply and fully. This was a fusion of journalism, philosophy, poetry, and drama, of mixed emotions ranging sharply from lyricism to satire, comedy and broad farce, in which Twain was really modeling an altogether new literary form: the prose epic of travel, or the American picaresque.

The eventual death of Slade at the hands of a group of Montana vigilantes, the condemned outlaw's hunger for his wife, his mixed nature of childlike courage, savagery, tears, and passion — this was meat for the primitive bard in Clemens, while his pen flourished again on the Rocky Mountain passes and peaks. "These Sultans of the fastness were turbaned with tumbled volumes of cloud, which shredded away from time to time and drifted off fringed and torn, trailing their continents of shadow after them; and catching presently on an intercepting peak, wrapped it about and brooded there — then shredded away again and left the purple peak, as they had left the purple domes, downy and white with new-laid snow." This "plain style" managed to achieve its complex effects in language not altogether unlike that of Hemingway's famous Gulf Stream descriptions some sixty years later.

There were skeletons of mules, oxen, and men along the western route of *Roughing It,* monuments of the huge emigration of the past, and during a great rain Clemens' coach lost the road and almost fell into a gully. "I have always been glad that we were not killed that night. I do not know any particular reason, but I have always been glad." There is a chapter on the Mormons, newly established at Salt Lake City. Clemens was fascinated by their society, their history, their peculiar institutions, and their power, as by the Mormon Bible which was so pretentious, slow, and sleepy, such an insipid mass of inspiration. "It is chloroform in print. If Joseph Smith composed this book, the act was a miracle — keeping awake while he did it was, at any rate." But this satire was as nothing compared with the venom of Twain's attack on the Goshoot Indians who were, if anything,

worse than the Digger Indians. As a disciple of Fenimóre
Cooper, he said, and a worshiper of the Red Men, "even of the
scholarly savages in the *Last of the Mohicans,*" he found the
Goshoots so repulsive as to make him question all his former
ideas about the American Indians. "It was curious to see how
quickly the paint and tinsel fell away from him and left him
treacherous, filthy, and repulsive — and how quickly the evidences accumulated that wherever one finds an Indian tribe he
has only found Goshoots more or less modified by circumstances and surroundings — but Goshoots after all." Was this
plain realism on the part of Clemens, or plain ignorance and
prejudice on the part of an artist who in the course of the very
same book would be outraged by the treatment of the Chinese
in California and intoxicated by Polynesian beauty? For a
writer like Twain, who was so early attracted by the Negro slaves
and their descendants, was there even an element of frontier
guilt in his hatred of the Indian? *

But such ambiguities hardly concerned the young Sam Clemens who simply wrote as he felt, and whose western travelogue
had now reached the end of its journey to Carson City, Nevada.
In literary terms, too, one notices there are no "central characters" in *Roughing It,* and no central human relationships, just
as there is no plot line except the trip itself, and no narrative
structure except that of the picaresque. There is barely a mention of Clemens' brother Orion under whose tutelage the original trip was taken. There is only a narrator — but a narrator

* The whole frontier thesis in American culture, as first expounded by Frederick
Jackson Turner in the 1920s, and endlessly discussed by academic historians
ever since, is obviously false, since the "Frontier in American History" was the
white man's frontier which expanded itself only by the destruction of the Indian
culture which it replaced — which was established, that is to say, and, as
D. H. Lawrence pointed out, through the genocide on which American culture
rested.

whose vision has entered so completely into that of the narrative scene itself as to erase even the sense of a narrator. This
was Mark Twain's primary narcissism; a total identification of
ego and world in which the ego, as with Walt Whitman's mystic
"I," was primitively submerged into the world and part of it,
without any bounds of separate personality. This is the art of
Roughing It.

In what is really the central part of the book, the silver-mining
life in Nevada, the logic of the pistol is a primary fact and the
description of Carson City amounts to a nightmare. No wonder
Clemens discovered Lake Tahoe as another watery Eden far
from "civilization," and this episode has overtones of a western
Walden, surrounded by all the vice and corruption and violence
of the mining town. Typically, however, it was Samuel Clemens who set fire to his island retreat, and typically this satanic
spirit voiced no guilt for his crime in these pages. In 1858 the
silver lodes had been discovered, the Californians had flocked
in to become a majority over the original Mormon government, and President Lincoln had sent out Governor Nye. But
what is curious about the time of Clemens' visit there in 1863
is how remote the Civil War was from Carson City and Clemens' mind alike. He had deserted from his southern regiment
without compunction; the regiment itself had "disbanded" upon
hearing that General Grant was in the vicinity; and in *Roughing It,* while he was mildly pro-Union, the great moral issues of
slavery and abolitionism were never touched upon. The stupidity and corruption of the Nevada legislature were much closer
to his heart.

The first volume of the travelogue closed with the description
of the moment when the silver mines were discovered. "Plainly
this was the road to fortune. The great 'Gould and Curry' mine
was held at three or four hundred dollars a foot when we ar-

rived; but in two months it had sprung up to eight hundred. The 'Ophir' had been worth only a mere trifle, a year gone by, and now it was selling at nearly *four thousand dollars a foot!*" There followed a list of other fabulous mines being opened up. "I would have been more or less than human if I had not gone mad like the rest." And he did. "I confess, without shame, that I expected to find masses of silver lying all about the ground." And it became a raging fever. "Of all the experiences of my life, this secret search among the hidden treasures of silver-land was the nearest to unmarred ecstasy . . . It was a delirious revel." And with what irony Clemens relived the fabulous fortune-hunting of his youth. "We had not less than thirty thousand feet apiece in the 'richest mines on earth,' as the frenzied cant phrased it — and were in debt to the butcher. We were stark mad with excitement — drunk with happiness — smothered under mountains of prospective wealth — arrogantly compassionate toward the plodding millions who knew not our marvelous canon — but our credit was not good at the grocer's. It was the strangest phase of life one can imagine. It was a beggars' revel."

Between the descriptions of such fevered frenzy, Twain felt obliged in *Roughing It,* as he had in *Innocents Abroad,* to insert a series of western tall tales, some of them funny and some not. They are a form of padding in the book which mainly must be endured or skipped until we realize that Clemens has abandoned mining in favor of milling. "That is to say, I went to work as a common laborer in a quartz-mill, at ten dollars a week and board." But he never worked any longer than he had to, inheriting what he called "the nomadic instinct" from distant Arabian ancestors. Experiencing, as Jack London did, the "pit" of manual labor, Clemens was determined never to work at all unless he had to. The whole meaning of life was just this

sense of *escape* from work, of leisure and pleasure as the goal of
life. Like Whitman who, perhaps unknown to Twain, had invited
his readers to "loaf" with him; like Dreiser "mooning about" in
the days of his youth, Clemens also remembered "my slothful,
valueless, heedless career." These great anti-puritanical writers
all agreed on the value of no value in their experience; the direction of no direction, in a childlike voyage through life for
the sake of life — in a hapless mood of discovery, excitement,
and enjoyment very different from that of stern dedication to
discipline, toil, responsibility, and "maturity."

Mark Twain was perhaps the clearest example of them all,
and he had an element of the Dostoevskian Gambler in him
too. Out there in Carson City they did find their blind lead
and Clemens was worth a million dollars for ten days, while his
mind was obsessed by visions of much wealth — until they forgot to work their claim, as required by law, and lost it. Destiny
was saving this artist for other purposes.

But taking her time about it. Moving away from the narrator's speculative insanity, the second volume of *Roughing It*
gives a lurid picture of the "flush days" in Nevada, a unique picture of what was surely one of the gamiest periods of frontier
"culture." "Virginia had grown to be the 'livest' town, for its
age and population, that America had ever produced. The
sidewalks swarmed with people . . . The streets themselves
were just as crowded with quartz-wagons, freight-teams, and
other vehicles. The procession was endless. So great was the
pack, that buggies frequently had to wait half an hour for an
opportunity to cross the principal street. Joy sat on every countenance, and there was a glad, almost fierce, intensity in every
eye, that told of the money-getting schemes that were seething
in every brain . . . Money was as plenty as dust; every individual considered himself wealthy, and a melancholy counte-

nance was nowhere to be seen. There were military companies, fire companies, brass-bands, banks, hotels, theaters, 'hurdy-gurdy houses,' wide-open gambling-palaces, political pow-wows, civic processions, street-fights, murders, inquests, riots, a whiskey-mill every fifteen steps . . ." Here, too, surrounding the fabulous Comstock lode, were all the frauds and tricks, the wildcat claims, the doped mines. The North Ophir was salted with melted half dollars; while the renowned tragedian, McKean Buchanan, quit the stage for a mining fortune which turned out to be nil. Again there was a reign of violence where not merely the editors of local newspapers but the printers carried guns. "The first twenty-six graves in the Virginia cemetery were occupied by *murdered* men," as Clemens reported, and nobody was respected until he had shot his man. Death was by the visitation of God, and "to attempt a portrayal of that era and that land, and leave out the blood and carnage, would be like portraying Mormonism and leaving out polygamy." But this was a society of equality in Nevada where for a time "the lawyer, the editor, the banker, the chief desperado, the chief gambler and the saloon-keeper occupied the same level in society." And "to be a saloon-keeper and kill a man was to be illustrious."

Clemens stressed the violence of this primitive frontier more than the sexual mores.* "The saloons were overburdened with custom; so were the police courts, the gambling dens, the brothels, and the jails — unfailing signs of high prosperity in a mining region," while "vice flourished luxuriantly during the

* What is most curious for a writer so essentially autobiographical and confessional as Clemens is the absolute taboo he succeeded in throwing around his early sex life in this free frontier world. There are stories and rumors about his heavy drinking during this period, but despite all of Clemens' self-descriptions, and his obvious affinity for women, his pagan sense of pleasure and the flesh, and despite massive Twain scholarship, there is, as regards his sexual experiences or lack of them, a complete silence, and blank. Later on too, Clemens was very open about his physical affection for Livy, and there are certain strains of apparent sexual guilt, but this area remains highly secret, closed off.

heyday of our flush times." But here he was flat in tone and noncommittal.

Not so, however, about the Chinese inhabitants of Nevada and California whose cause like that of the Negroes Clemens espoused very early. Unlike the Indians, the Chinese were quiet, peaceable, tractable, industrious — and a great convenience to everybody, even to the worst class of white men. "For the Chinaman bears the most of their sins, suffering fines for their petty thefts, imprisonment for their robberies, and death for their murders. Any white man can swear a Chinaman's life away in the courts, but no Chinaman can testify against a white man. Ours is the 'land of the free' — nobody denies that — nobody challenges it. (Maybe it is because we won't let other people testify.) As I write, news comes that in broad daylight in San Francisco, some boys have stoned an inoffensive Chinaman to death, and that, although a large crowd witnessed the shameful deed, no one interfered."

Making a modest fortune out of the silver mines at last, it was to California that the narrator of *Roughing It* moved in order to enjoy his wealth, his ease, his luxury. "After the sagebrush and alkali deserts of Washoe, San Francisco was Paradise to me. I lived at the best hotel, exhibited my clothes in the most conspicuous places, infested the opera, and learned to seem enraptured with music which oftener afflicted my ignorant ear than enchanted it, if I had had the vulgar honesty to confess it . . . I had longed to be a butterfly, and I was one at last. I attended private parties in sumptuous evening dress, simpered and aired my graces like a born beau, and polka'd and schottisched with a step peculiar to myself — and the kangaroo."

All, that is, until the silver-mine bubble exploded; the stocks which Clemens held were not worth the paper they were printed on. He went to work again on a newspaper, but lost heart, faltered, had the symptoms of a nervous breakdown. He became adept at "slinking" and suddenly found himself (as a correspondent for the Sacramento *Union*) on the Sandwich Islands. Typical of *Roughing It* is the abrupt alternation of mood and place and theme; the travelogue's form was simply the form which Sam Clemens' younger life had taken. And if the trip on the western Overland ended up on an enchanted tropical isle, what mattered after the surprise of the changing scene was what Mark Twain wrote about it. Just as in Herman Melville's case, the South Sea Islands left a lasting imprint on Sam Clemens. The hardened chronicler of a frontier civilization, overcome again by his "vagabond instinct," was entranced by the Polynesian natives.

"In place of roughs and rowdies staring and blackguarding on the corners, I saw long-haired, saddle-colored Sandwich Island maidens sitting on the ground in the shade of corner houses . . . instead of wretched cobblestone pavements I walked on a firm foundation of coral . . . instead of cramped and crowded street-cars, I met dusky native women, sweeping by, free as the wind, on fleet horses and astride, with gaudy riding-sashes, streaming like banners behind them; instead of the combined stenches of Chinadom and Brannan Street slaughterhouses, I breathed the balmy fragrance of jasmine, oleander, and the Pride of India; in place of the hurry and bustle and noisy confusion of San Francisco, I moved in the midst of a summer calm as tranquil as dawn in the Garden of Eden . . ." These natives, said Clemens, were almost as dark as Negroes in the main; and there were "women with comely features, fine black eyes, rounded forms inclining to the voluptuous, clad in a single bright red or white garment that fell free and unconfined from shoulders to heel, long black hair falling loose, gypsy hats, encircled with wreaths of natural flowers of a brilliant carmine

tint; plenty of dark men in various costumes and some with
nothing on but a battered stove-pipe hat tilted on the nose, and
a very scant breech-clout; certain smoke-dried children were
clothed in nothing but sunshine — a very neat-fitting and picturesque apparel indeed.

"It was trance luxury," he said, "to sit in the perfumed air
and forget that there was any world but these enchanted islands" — and here indeed all the sensuous, pagan, and edenic
elements in both *Innocents* and *Roughing It* found a natural
climax. Just like Melville too, Clemens had some doubts as to
the virtue of the Christianity which had been conferred upon
these ignorant savages. "How sad it is to think of the multitudes
who have gone to their graves in this beautiful island and never
knew there was a hell." In the dark ages of Hawaii, that is,
"long, long before the missionaries braved a thousand priva-
tions to come and make them permanently miserable . . ."
And to show the poor native "what rapture it is to work all day
long for fifty cents to buy food for next day with, as compared
with fishing for a pastime and lolling in the shade through eternal summer, and eating of the bounty that nobody labored to
provide but Nature." Working hand in hand indeed, Christianity and civilization had all but finished off this handsome playful race with our ameliorating and purifying influence.

"But doubtless this purifying is not far off, when we reflect that
contact with civilization and the whites has reduced the native
population from *four hundred thousand* (Captain Cook's estimate) to fifty-five thousand in something over eighty years!"
This was the real price of the white man's "triumph" in the
South Seas and of Hawaii's acquisition of American statehood
almost a hundred years after *Roughing It;* and to the line of
American writers from Melville and Twain and Eugene O'Neill
the benefits were dubious. The conclusion of the western trave-

logue recorded Twain's fascination with primitive Hawaiian culture; while *The Gilded Age* (1873), written with Charles Dudley Warner, was a different and puzzling work.

It will be better to divide this book up into its two volumes, and for all its renown, the first volume of *The Gilded Age* is poor as literature and disappointing as a historical document. (The second volume is a very different story.) As Clemens himself noted, according to Justin Kaplan's *Mr. Clemens and Mark Twain,* while he and Warner were working together in the supposition that they were writing one coherent yarn, they were in fact writing "two *in*coherent ones." Nor is it very difficult, from Clemens' records and from the internal evidence of *The Gilded Age,* to separate the work of these two different writers — if it is worth it. The pre-Civil War opening in the east Tennessee town of "Squire Hawkins" is a crude parody of Twain's western material in *Roughing It* as well as a curious prelude to the mythical boyhood in Hannibal. This barren landscape and "these groping dumb creatures" constitute another view of that romantic western frontier which Sam Clemens had described. (Was he in such ambiguous conflict?) But the poverty, want, ignorance, the village types, and the language are overdone and unconvincing; just as the family slave of the Hawkinses, Uncle Dan'l, is a typically "comic" view of the ignorant and superstitious "darkie."

This was the first attempt at fiction proper by Clemens, and it marks the early Twain at his poorest. The passages on the river steamboats, intimations of *Life on the Mississippi,* are a relief since they are also bearing us away from the opening scenes of the book; and we notice here the "eager hands" and "warm Southern hearts" of the chronicle. Writing what was an obviously satirical survey of the most corrupt period in the national history, Clemens and Warner were not averse to using

some patriotic ploys. With the advent of "Colonel" Beriah Sellers — his plan for a monopoly of the wildcat banks and his "Infallible, Imperial Oriental Optic Liniment" among a series of
other such grandiose schemes — we come to the famous central
figure in *The Gilded Age*. But Sellers, symbol of the get-rich-
quick spirit of the time, is also, to this critic, something of a
bore. In what seems to be Warner's part of the novel, we get
two eastern heroes, Philip Sterling and Henry Brierly, a Quaker
heroine, Ruth Bolton, and her financier father; and there are
times in the course of this confused and uneasy narrative when
we may think that Warner is writing another story altogether
which the Twain shall never meet — but hold on. With the advent of the "Salt Lick Pacific Extension," as another example
of congressional corruption, both in respect to the Reconstruction era in the South and the development of the western frontier, *The Gilded Age* begins to take on focus and form, and
even more, a historical content. In the narrative, Washington
Hawkins (based on Sam's hapless brother, Orion) takes on a
fictional prominence, while his sister Laura emerges as a hard,
glossy, cunning financial and political operator. She is the curious princess of this whole group of scoundrels, rascals, quacks,
and dupes who are all obsessed by the vision of sudden and
fraudulent wealth. What is interesting in Laura's portrait is
the frank sexuality which she uses to gain power over the men
who will further her own self-interest. Here *The Gilded Age*
has created an American heroine who is far different from the
whole line of "innocent maidens" and "nice girls" and all those
sweet, passive ladies fainting (when not having the vapors),
who generally dominated the literary scene of the Victorian
epoch in the United States.

At the beginning of this sexual career, Harry Brierly, Laura's
first victim, is completely destroyed by her. (She is just practic-

ing.) "She excited his hopes and denied him, inflamed his passion and restrained it, and wound him in her toils day by day. To what purpose? It was a keen delight to Laura to prove that she had power over men" — and to use that power for financial gain. In Washington, in Congress, this scheming, plotting, and manipulative heroine, in the age of virtuous and spotless literary ladies, finds a natural field for her sexual wiles and her acquisitive instincts.*

She takes up her role in Senator Dilworthy's life and affairs very much in the style of Dreiser's Jennie Gerhardt, if for different reasons. She is the link between the Senator (based on the notorious Samuel Pomeroy) and Sellers in their scheme for a Negro college on the unsalable Tennessee lands. Both Dilworthy and Sellers are concerned about the condition of the emancipated race, although the Colonel has certain reservations. "You can't do much with 'em . . . They are a speculating race, sir, disinclined to work for white folks without security, planning how to live by only working for themselves. Idle, sir, there's my garden just a ruin of weeds. Nothing practical in 'em . . . You educate the niggro and you make him more speculating than he was before. If he won't stick to any industry except for himself now, what will he do then? He would only have a wider scope to injure himself. A niggro has no grasp, sir. Now a white man can conceive great operations, and carry them out; a niggro can't." But when the Senator argues for multiplying the Negro's chances for the hereafter, Sellers promptly agrees. "I'd elevate his soul — that's just it;

* It is amusing to compare Laura with the charming and innocent young American maidens of Henry James, virgins all, who are also "making their way" in the circles of James' Washington aristocracy, since their unspeakable, unrecognized bourgeois families were useful only for their financial support. As in "Pandora," James was still writing these stories more than a decade after *The Gilded Age.*

you can't make his soul too immortal, but I wouldn't touch *him*, himself. Yes, sir! make his soul immortal, but don't disturb the niggro as he is." And beneath the satire of Twain's description of the "speculating race" that wants to work only for itself lies the grim truth of the white man's version of true Negro religion.

Beneath his own clownishness indeed, Sellers has no heart of gold; this "comic" figure is often brutally cruel, and just as corrupt, in his idiocy, as is the successful Senator Dilworthy. Now the grand scheme for improving the navigation on the Columbus River begins to bear fruit. "An appropriation was a tangible thing, if you could get hold of it, and it made little difference what it was appropriated for, so long as you got hold of it." The physical panorama of Washington itself, the raw, cheap, and ugly capital of this sordid socio-economic system, and the account of Washington's daily political life are described in brilliant pages of satire. Harry and Sellers become "rich" with their Columbus River Slackwater Navigation Company; the appropriations come out of Congress nicely; the visionary western town of Napoleon starts to boom with land lots and a newspaper — until the actual money is held up in the New York brokers' office. "Beautiful credit! The foundation of modern society. Who shall say that this is not the golden age of mutual trust, of unlimited reliance upon human promises? That is a peculiar condition of society which enables a whole nation to instantly recognize point and meaning in the familiar newspaper anecdote, which puts into the mouth of a distinguished speculator in lands and mines this remark: 'I wasn't worth a cent two years ago, and now I owe two millions of dollars.' " Like Dreiser's odes to gold in the Cowperwood novels, and his descriptions of money behaving like a hysterical woman, *The Gilded Age* is very sharp on the cash nexus of a morally distraught society.

The two hundred thousand dollars appropriated by Congress is divided about equally between Congress itself and the New York bankers. Both Sellers and Harry Brierly are duped, while being assured that the first congressional appropriation is simply to pave the way for future appropriations. And again Clemens used his familiar pagan comparison. "We send missionaries to lift up the benighted races of other lands. How much cheaper and better it would be if those people could come here and drink of our civilization at its fountainhead." Thus, if *The Gilded Age* is an inferior literary work, it is still, in these sections of the novel, a rough, tough, honest, and ironical source book of crucial areas of the American life of its time, from the vicious political corruption in Washington to the dreary, sordid, depressing frontier boomtowns. It is an ugly picture of the manners and habits of a supposedly great nation and a fortunate people; it describes the Washington mud literally, financially, politically, socially. It is a hardbitten view of the American frontier and the development of the west, and of the Robber Baron epoch and the politicos whom Matthew Josephson described. It shows the political treatment of "the emancipated race" directly after the high moral crusade of Abolitionism. It is a sharp, clear, ironical picture of a rich and powerful continent, an energetic people, all duped and corrupted by an obviously false, greedy, and dishonest social system of finance and politics. And it is an almost impossible book, *The Gilded Age,* to evaluate by ordinary critical standards.

For this is hardly a novel at all in technical terms, and yet it is a unique chronicle in the national letters; and without it our literature would be immeasurably impoverished. Laura, too, her heart filled with Christian piety, is willing to sacrifice her "landed estates" to the spiritual uplifting of the downtrodden Negro; and here we have the description of the parvenu Washington aristocracy which now wielded the real power in the nation. "Great wealth gave a man a still higher and nobler place . . . than did official position. If this wealth had been acquired by conspicuous ingenuity with just a pleasant little spice of illegality about it, all the better. This aristocracy was 'fast,' and not averse to ostentation." *The Gilded Age* is not kindly to any of the three circles of aristocracy which it describes, and one notices that long before Veblen the key words here are "conspicuous" and "ostentation."

It is not impossible that Veblen garnered some of his observations about American society from this early and original source book. "The Hon. Higgins had not come to serve his country in Washington for nothing. The appropriation which he had engineered through Congress for the maintenance of the Indians in his territory would have made all those savages rich if it had ever got to them." And here Twain's hatred of the noble savage was equaled only by his savage ridicule of American civilization. The Washington profiles in the second volume of *The Gilded Age* are brilliant, and no punches are pulled. "Petroleum was the agent that had suddenly transformed the Gashlys from modest hard-working country village folk into 'loud' aristocrats and ornaments of the city . . . The Hon. Patrique Oreille was a wealthy Frenchman from Cork. Not that he was wealthy when he first came from Cork, but just the reverse." And there follows the description of a typical Irish contractor-politician who is a friend of New York's Boss "William M. Weed" of Tammany Hall.

Just as in Lincoln Steffens' *The Shame of the Cities,* there is a certain grudging admiration in *The Gilded Age*'s portraits of these colorful and corrupt figures. In Clemens, at least, there was nothing of the self-righteous moralist. Crime, as a principle, attracted him more than conformity. What a panorama of "democracy," of capitalism at its peak of primitive power is here, down to the Lardnerian dialogues among the wives of these fantastic crooks. *"Hon. Mrs. Higgins* — 'Is François's health good now, Mrs. Oreille?' *Mrs. O. (Thankful for the intervention)* — 'Not very. A body couldn't expect it. He was always delicate — especially his lungs — and this odious climate tells on him strong, now, after Parry, which is so mild.'" It comes as small surprise that "François" is the Oreilles' canine pet, while the authors added: "As impossible and exasperating as this conversation may sound to a person who is not an idiot, it is scarcely in any respect an exaggeration of one which one of us actually listened to in an American drawing room."

The note of hypocritical moral virtue on the part of all these political knaves expands proportionately as the financial corruption increases. In this "wearing, sordid, heartless game" of American democracy at work, a chronicle of political improbabilities is made entirely plausible — and factual. And already, barely beyond the bloody wound of the Civil War, there is the smell of a new empire. " 'Don't you think we want Cuba, Mr. Hawkins?' 'I think we want it bad . . . And Santo Domingo. Senator Dilworthy says we are bound to extend our religion over the isles of the sea. We've got to round out our territory.' "

The atmosphere in Washington is almost identical with that of the silver boom in *Roughing It* as Sellers reaches the peak of his prominence. "He was now at the center of the manufacture of gigantic schemes, of speculations of all sorts, of political and social gossip. The atmosphere was full of little and big rumors and of vast, undefined expectations. Everybody was in haste, too, to push on his private plan, and feverish in his haste, as if in constant apprehension that to-morrow would be Judgment Day." But when Laura reaches the height of her own career as a congressional lobbyist, promoter, intrigante, sexual tease, and even blackmailer, and when, still consumed by her jealous passion for Colonel Selby, she kills him, *The Gilded Age* expires on the same note of melodrama upon which it started; or rather, the slow, aimless, confused opening of the book is resolved by a far-fetched ending.

Realizing what a wealth of marvelous social satire still resides in the almost unreadable ending of *The Gilded Age,* we see finally that Clemens, at least, used the improbable romance as a kind of native surrealism upon which to drape the brilliance of his artistic vision. He has not the least concern with the credibility of his "plot" — to the point of often not even having, or simply reversing the plot. He has immense concern with the credibility of his moral and social commentary — just as the absurd "trial" of Laura for an absurd murder presents, in the end, a beautiful panorama of "justice" in the democracy. Poorly written, tedious to read, false and artificial in both human and literary terms as is much of *The Gilded Age,* it still discloses hidden veins of satire in retrospect. Our early annoyance at the literary quality of the novel is replaced by a growing admiration for a large part of the novel's content. This was Sam Clemens' natural literary "form," or lack of form very often, which one must understand and accept in order to grasp the secret of his greatness.

Sketches Old and New, in 1875, followed *The Gilded Age* and preceded *Tom Sawyer.* This was the volume from which earlier I quoted the Jumping Frog's metamorphosis into the French and then back again into the English language, and perhaps this tour de force was the headiest item in the collection of Clemens' newspaper sketches and essays. Casual, minor pieces — but in Mark Twain's writing the golden nuggets of humor appear in the unlikeliest places; it was a matter of inspiration rather than intent. There was the fable of the good little boy who got punished for all his virtues and the bad little boy who was rewarded for his sins; a parody of the Sunday school morality and the exhortatory juvenile fiction of Clemens' time. In the line of Josh Billings, Petroleum V. Nasby, and other American humorists who all worked for James Redpath's Lecture Bureau in Boston along with Twain, he helped to initiate these inverted western fables and perverse "fairy tales" which, as we noticed elsewhere, later on, George Ade and Ring Lardner would develop even further. In the early *Sketches,* even more clearly, Sam Clemens was out to break all the Victorian taboos of his period, while the main thrust of his satire was directed against American puritanism and the developing middle-class ethos of materialism, mediocrity, conformity.

Very early, Clemens was in direct revolt against the salient features of his own society. His answer to the Moral Statistician, written as early as 1865, was clear.

> Money can't save your infinitesimal soul. All the use that money can be put to is to purchase comfort and enjoyment in this life; therefore, as you are an enemy to comfort and enjoyment, where is the use of accumulating cash? It won't do for you to say that you can use it to better purpose in furnishing a good table, and in charities, and in supporting tract societies, because you know yourself that you people who have no petty vices are never known to give away a cent, and that you stint yourselves so in the matter of food that you are always feeble and hungry. And you never dare to laugh in the daytime for fear some poor wretch, seeing you in a good humor, will try to borrow a dollar of you; and in church you are always down on your knees, with your eyes buried in the cushion, when the contribution-box comes around; and you never give the revenue officers a full statement of your income. Now you know all these things yourself, don't you? Very well, then, what is the use of your stringing out your miserable lives to a lean and withered old age?

Now wasn't this a sort of prose variation on Whitman's description of those who, "smartly attired, countenance smiling, form upright," had still suffered a spiritual death under the breastbone:

> Under the broadcloth and gloves, under the ribbons and artificial
> flowers,
> Keeping fair with the customs, speaking not a syllable of itself,
> Speaking of anything else but never of itself.

Speaking never of Clemens' joy and pleasure in this life, or later, of Henry Miller's love and laughter, while inside of the respectable dresses and ornaments, "Inside of those wash'd and trimm'd faces, behold a secret silent loathing and despair." Yes, surely, no major American writer has had much sympathy for the walking skeletons of broadcloth puritanism or the subsequent middle-class materialism. Following this essay, there is Clemens' even more vehement attack on Ben Franklin's abstemious morality. (Here D. H. Lawrence trod directly in Clemens' footsteps, in his *Studies in Classic American Literature*.) "The subject of this memoir was of a vicious disposition, and early prostituted his talents to the invention of maxims and aphorisms calculated to inflict suffering upon the rising generation of all subsequent ages. His simplest acts, also, were contrived with a view of their being held up for the emulation of boys forever — boys who might otherwise have been happy . . . With a malevolence which is without parallel in history, he would work all day, and then sit up nights, and let on to be studying algebra by the light of a smoldering fire, so that all other boys might have to do that also."

In this pernicious biography of Franklin, Clemens said, "his maxims were full of animosity toward boys. Nowadays a boy cannot follow out a single natural instinct without tumbling over some of those everlasting aphorisms and hearing from Franklin on the spot . . . If he does a virtuous action, he never gets anything for it, because 'Virtue is its own reward.' And that boy is hounded to death and robbed of his natural rest because Franklin said once, in one of his inspired flights of malignity: 'Early to bed and early to rise/Makes a man healthy, wealthy, and wise.' As if it were any object to a boy to be healthy and wealthy and wise on such terms. The sorrow that that maxim has cost me, through my parents, experimenting on me with it, tongue cannot tell. The legitimate result is my present state of general debility, indigence, and mental aberration."

One notices how Clemens stressed Franklin's malignity and malevolence — strong words used not altogether comically — and here, of course, we are back to that state of childhood freedom from which Mark Twain viewed caustically all modes of morality and "education," not to mention the repressions of civilization itself. This was an early and clear view of the born rebel against the duress of whatever code threatened the fullest expression of the natural life; one who affirmed all the pleasures of "this life" against all the penny-pinching reservations and restrictions of the living dead on earth. This was another early revolt of the flesh in American letters; of the instincts and of the dominant pleasure principle without which there was no full existence; and these western "boys" of Sam Clemens sprang from this deep source exactly as did the marvelous outbursts of the "reversed" — that is to say, natural — humor of a pagan vision. Clemens was of course in the whole tradition of wild western journalism and irreverent native humorists, but in this tradition, how divinely original he was!

Sketches New and Old has many other sections of trivia; casual, hasty little familiar essays as that on raising poultry: "When you wish to raise a fine, large, donkey-voiced Shanghai rooster, you do it with a lasso, just as you would a bull." Or on the raising of children: "Love, it is notorious that pine is the least nutritious food that a child can eat." Or on ladies' fashions: "She wore a pink satin dress, plain in front but with a good deal of rake to it — to the train, I mean; it was said to be two or three yards long. One could see it creeping along the floor some little time after the woman was gone. Mrs. C. wore also a white bodice, cut bias, with Pompadour sleeves, flounced with ruches; low neck, with the inside handkerchief not visible, with white kid gloves. She had on a pearl necklace, which glinted lonely, high up the midst of that barren waste of neck and shoulders. Her hair was frizzled into a tangled chaparral, forward of her ears, aft it was drawn together, and compactly bound and plaited into a stump like a pony's tail, and furthermore was canted upward at a sharp angle, and ingeniously supported by a red velvet crupper, whose forward extremity was made fast with a half-hitch around a hairpin on the top of her head. Her whole top hamper was neat and becoming."

This was Clemens writing in heat again; this was a kind of verbal pyrotechnics dazzling out of Clemens at any point when the genie seized him — this was another example of native Dada in the mid-seventies. Somewhat as in the "Jumping Frog," there were examples here of Clemens' trick of starting an open sentence, and letting free association take over the direction and the subordinate clauses until the prose reached the complexity of, say, *The Golden Bowl*.

Distressing Accident — Last evening, about six o'clock, as Mr. William Schuyler, an old and respectable citizen of South Park, was leaving his residence to go downtown, as has been his usual custom for many years with the exception only of a short interval in the spring of 1850, during which he was confined to his bed by injuries received in attempting to stop a runaway horse by thoughtlessly placing himself directly in its wake and throwing up his hands and shouting, which if he had done so even a single moment sooner, must inevitably have frightened the animal still more instead of checking its speed, although disastrous enough to himself as it was, and rendered more melancholy and distressing by reason of the presence of his wife's mother, who was there and saw the sad occurrence notwithstanding it is at least likely, though not necessarily so, that she should be reconnoitering in another direction when the incident occurred, not being vivacious and on the lookout, as a general thing, but even the reverse, as her own mother is said to have stated, who is no more, but died in the full hope of a glorious resurrection, upwards of three years ago, aged eighty-six, being a Christian woman and without guile, as it were, or property, in consequence of the fire of 1849, which destroyed every single thing she had in the world . . .

In the *Sketches* there was also a strange, dark tale of a graveyard whose inhabitants decide to move one night (an early sample of Clemens' mortuary humor), and the famous item called "A True Story." This was the story, told in the Negro dialect of the period, of a black "mammy" whose son, sold off in a slave auction, returns to her in a Negro regiment during the Civil War. But despite Clemens' sympathy for his heroine, who anticipates the Roxanna of *Pudd'nhead Wilson,* and despite much praise through the years for this touching picture of slavery, the story is sentimental and the cadences of the Negro dialect, despite Clemens' usually accurate ear, are stylized here and questionable. There were other pieces in *Sketches New and Old* that went back to Clemens' mining experience as well as his early journalism, and back to his own youth, which was the setting for the first epic of boyhood, *The Adventures of Tom Sawyer,* a year later, in 1876.

Whether this was a children's book for adults, as Clemens first believed, or for children, as it turned out at the time, and not too successfully either, it is certain that when Mark Twain went back to his memories of childhood the deepest preoccupations of his temperament emerged more clearly. If Twain traced his own ancestry to the Garden of Eden in fact, this was an edenic vision of frontier life in which the young hero was both an orphan and a devil. "He's full of the Old Scratch," says Aunt Polly, "but laws-a-me! he is my own dead sister's boy, poor thing, and I ain't got the heart to lash him, somehow." And if there was one thing in the world that Tom Sawyer hated more than anything else, it was *work*. In its underlying satire, this paradise of playtime was also a travesty not merely of American society but of civilization's basic values. It was an outwitting, through art, of the adult world which all "mature" adults could approve of, just as it praised freely the variations of childhood's gangsters, thieves and crooks in its antisocial revolt. In Tom's first battle with the new boy "in the little shabby village of St. Petersburg," Clemens showed up the mixture of cowardice, bluffing, verbal bombast, and chicanery which all the animals indulge in, and only man deplores. In this heavenly arena, too, there were happy slaves and a racial intermingling.*

In the opening scene of the novel, the whitewashing of the fence, Tom remembers the company of children at the town pump. "White, mulatto, and Negro boys and girls were always there waiting their turns, resting, trading playthings, quarreling, fighting, skylarking . . ." And we are told that Work consists of whatever a body is *obliged* to do, and Play consists of whatever a body is not obliged to do. While Ben, forsaking

* Since the English critic, F. R. Leavis, uses the word "nigger" with almost obscene pleasure in his absurd introduction to *Pudd'nhead Wilson,* it is interesting to note that the first mention in *Tom Sawyer* is of "Negro boys and girls." The point here is that Clemens himself, with a few rare exceptions, used "Negro" this early when speaking in his own voice, and "nigger" when it is used as the common usage of the period. Both Mr. Leavis and the NAACP, for different reasons, do not seem to grasp this distinction.

his "Mississippi steamboat," takes over the coveted job of whitewashing, Tom, the "retired artist," sits in the shade, dangles his legs, munches his apple, and plans "the slaughter of more innocents." By the middle of the afternoon, Tom, a poverty-stricken boy in the morning, is literally "rolling in wealth" — having been given a kite in good repair, a dead rat on a string, twelve marbles, part of a jew's-harp, a piece of blue bottle-glass, a spool cannon, a key that wouldn't unlock anything, a tin soldier, a couple of tadpoles, six firecrackers, a kitten with only one eye . . . Just as Tom's infantine wickedness is cast in the comic mode, so is the parody of the "acquisitive society," or of capitalism's spurious wealth gained by such devilish manipulation and double-talk on the part of the novel's hero.

Tom Sawyer is certainly a boyhood entrepreneur of the highest order, and carries over his trickery (and vanity) into the field of adolescent love affairs. But the emotions of real love are centered in the relationship between him and Aunt Polly. And what is curious is the intensity and the *flow* of such affection under the mask of orphanhood and half-brothers (the suffering Sid of the novel) and mother surrogates and missing (dead) fathers. All of Tom's ostentatious moods of guilt, martyrdom, suffering, remorse are designed to attract Aunt Polly's eye and to solicit her attention; here the cunning mockery of love leads into the genuine article. In terms of Aunt Polly's "punishments" too, and of the harsh moral and religious tradition of the frontier, one is reminded of those cannibalistic savages in Melville's *Typee* who worshiped their savage deities — and beat them up when they were angry at them. The chapter on Sunday school is hilarious in *Tom Sawyer*. There is the boy of German parentage (Twain is careful not to say "German boy") who once recited three thousand verses from

the Bible without stopping, "but the strain upon his mental
faculties was too great, and he was little better than an idiot
from that day forth."

What is apparent in the blissful atmosphere of frontier boyhood in *Tom Sawyer* is that the sense of evil is comic too. The
"diabolism" of the hero, however deep this strain ran in Sam
Clemens himself, and despite what might come of it later, is itself a form of playful parody; and life is basically innocent and
loving.* If *Tom Sawyer* is, on one level, a parody of an adult
society of power and manipulation, of property and place, of
trading and acquisition — the parody itself is divine, is innocent, is wistful and comic. (That is the real secret of the book's
lasting appeal.) Beneath all the humor is the deeper rhythm
of Sam Clemens' affinity with animal life and a natural sense of
pleasure. Monday mornings always found Tom Sawyer miserable
"because it began another week's slow suffering in school," and
school, like church, is human nature in fetters, in the prison of
civilization. Just here we have the advent of Huckleberry Finn,
son of the town drunkard, even more idle, lawless, vulgar; and
culture hero that he is to all the "respectable children" who are
envious of his gaudy outcast condition.

"Huckleberry came and went, at his own free will. He slept
on doorsteps in fine weather and in empty hogsheads in wet;
he did not have to go to school or to church, or call any being
master or obey anybody; he could go fishing or swimming when
and where he chose, and stay as long as it suited him; nobody

---

* In view of so much stress in contemporary thought (in a period of social and
historical reaction) on the evil sources of life, or on evil itself as the life force,
it is important to note this. And the related fact that — despite so much personal tragedy later on, and so much criticism which stressed this tragedy, and
the "failure" or "frustration" of Twain's life and career — this edenic strain remained constant in Mark Twain's temperament to the end. Compare, for
example, the amoral children of Richard Hughes' *The Innocent Voyage* or the
evil ones in William Golding's *Lord of the Flies*.

forbade him to fight; he could sit up as late as he pleased; he was always the first boy that went barefoot in the spring and the last to resume leather in the fall; he never had to wash, nor put on clean clothes; he could swear wonderfully. In a word, everything that goes to make life precious that boy had. So thought every harassed, hampered, respectable boy in St. Petersburg . . . Tom hailed the romantic outcast." Thus, in this boyhood idyll of freedom from civilization in a frontier town, we come finally to the symbol of absolute freedom. In this radically democratic antisocial chronicle of youth, we have at the climax the outcast hero who is the antithesis of all ethical, moral, social, worldly, or financial patterns of "maturity," of human "betterment" or success. Even in the comic mode of childhood.

It is from the ignorant Huck also that we get the dominant use of "nigger" in this story, as though already in the reaches of his unconscious Clemens was evolving his parable of Huck's education. Through Huck also we get the sense of that darker stream of Negro superstitiousness, of African witchcraft, of voodoo charms and cures and curses which runs, like a submerged Mississippi current, through the pages of *Tom Sawyer*. (I mean the worship of that ancient and primitive "White Goddess" of fertility and sexuality, in short, who is here quite obviously a Black Goddess.) Does this classical work of childhood also hinge upon a ridiculous melodrama: the murder of Dr. Robinson by Injun Joe, who blames the murder on his partner in crime, Muff Potter? We realize again that Clemens was supremely careless about the plot structure of his narratives — or supremely confident that any improvised, twisted, shaky narrative structure could be used to convey his own vision of experience . . . and that what counted was not the improbable structure of his tale but what he could do with

it. The episodes of calf love between Tom and Becky Thatcher
take up more space in the story, too, than they are worth, and
Clemens was slightly uneasy in this area of emotions.* And
the subplot of the boys escaping to the island, while the whole
town and their parents and relatives believe they are dead
and prepare a mock funeral, has a sadistic undertone which the
comedy of the trick barely obscures.

But then there is the description of the first raft scene in these
frontier idylls. Clemens' evocation of the womb theme, or of
the (lost!) plenary state of man, or of that childhood garden
of innocence which is man's deepest myth, is done so naturally,
surely, accurately. There is the water fighting of the naked boys,
not altogether in accordance with the Victorian proprieties, and
the sumptuous island breakfasts of fish and bacon while these
social exiles loaf and contemplate their souls. There are the
brilliant passages on frontier education and the "moral and
religious mind" (partly reminiscent of Edward Eggleston's *The
Hoosier Schoolmaster,* published some five years earlier). There
are those pages in *Tom Sawyer* where Clemens indulged himself
with some of his satire on school compositions, schoolchildren,
and schoolmasters — and on provincial poetry:

> And cold must be mine eyes, and heart, and tete,
> When, dear Alabama! they turn cold on thee!

In these Twainish notes from an older world, recalling the
vanished democracy of the raw western towns in the mid-

---

* It was William Dean Howells who made Clemens tone down the scene of
Becky's discovering the schoolteacher's hidden book of anatomy and coming
across "a handsomely engraved and colored frontispiece — a human figure,
stark naked" which she Freudianly rips while trying to hide the book from Tom
Sawyer.

nineteenth century, before the Civil War and before the establishment of the great American fortunes which changed the whole texture of American life, we realize that the poor, the idle, the vagrants are much more prominent in a village life which has not yet been altogether converted to the rationale of work, social respectability, and material success. The boys pay a visit to the innocent Muff Potter at the town jail, where he is lodged without guards, to bring him tobacco and matches. And indeed, as in his attack on Ben Franklin in *Sketches New and Old,* Clemens makes this point very specifically. "Huck was willing. Huck was always willing to take a hand in any enterprise that offered entertainment and required no capital, for he had troublesome superabundance of that sort of time which is *not* money." You might say that Clemens was the spokesman for that central line of American writers who were at variance from the outset with the materialistic hypocrisy of Franklin.

The end of this childhood classic revolves upon the melodrama of the nightmare vigil of Tom and Becky lost in the island cave — and the "happy ending" of Tom and Huck dividing up the cash loot of twelve thousand dollars which they have discovered in the cave. A happy ending of easy money which is apparently the complete antithesis of the central vision of *Tom Sawyer,* until we realize that Mark Twain was just as adroit as Henry James, say, in the use of literary decoys. For Huck was now rich, and being "educated" into civilized ways by the Widow Douglas.

"He had to go to church; he had to talk so properly that speech was become insipid in his mouth; whithersoever he turned, the bars and shackles of civilization shut him in and bound him hand and foot." And he can't stand the process and throws it all over. "Don't talk about it, Tom. I've tried it, and it don't work, it don't work, Tom. It ain't for me; I ain't used to it. The widder's good to me, and friendly; but I can't stand them ways . . . Tom, I wouldn't ever got into all this trouble if it hadn't 'a' been for that money; now you just take my sheer of it along with your'n, and gimme a ten-center sometimes — not many times, becuz I don't give a dern for a thing 'thout it's tollable hard to git — and you go and beg off for me with the widder." Or at least Huck wants to throw it all over, since the novel ends on an ambiguous note, just as Clemens does later on in another childhood romance.

In the western speech rhythms of *Tom Sawyer,* we may notice that apparently casual, and yet very skillful use of repetition, and repetition with variation, which Twain brought into our national literary style, which later on, Sherwood Anderson, among others, would cultivate, and which Ernest Hemingway refined into a kind of fixed perfection that was almost too perfect, too fixed. Meanwhile, shortly after *Tom Sawyer* and while working on another children's tale, *The Prince and the Pauper,* and reading the diary of Samuel Pepys, Clemens tossed off a celebrated tour de force called *1601: or Conversation as It Was by the Social Fireside in the Time of the Tudors.* A few copies of this were privately printed in 1880, and reprinted in 1882, and then reprinted ever since. This pamphlet, hardly so much pornography as erotica, showed a remarkable virtuosity in Clemens' use of an earlier, franker English language; and, despite a stress on anal-erotic as well as genital humor, it is an entertaining satire.

Howells had already commented on Clemens' "Elizabethan breadth of parlance" in those letters which he could not bear to burn, yet, after the first reading, could not bear to look at again. The script of *1601* was written to Clemens' other close friend, the robust divine, Joseph Twichell of Hartford.

It was an afternoon's entertainment for Clemens; it was a private protest against Victorian censorship, as he said. At any rate Elizabeth the Queen, Ben Jonson, Lady Helen, Walter Raleigh, Lord Bacon, and "Shaxpur" — and "ye child Francis Beaumonte" and "ye Duchess of Bilgewater" among other court ladies — are the principal figures in this social conversation, and there was an opening reference to Twain's own epoch.

"Then spake ye damned windmill, Sir Walter, of a people in ye uttermost parts of America, ye copulate not until they be five and thirty yeres of age, ye women being eight and twenty, and do it then but once in seven years." While the little pamphlet was centered around the inciting of young or precocious sexuality, as the Queen verbally seduces the child Beaumonte — "With such a tongue as thine, lad, thou'lt spread the ivory thighs of many a willing maid in thy good time, an thy codpiece be as handy as thy speeche" — Clemens could not forbear a literary thrust at "that poor ass, Lille himself." He had little in common with the Euphuists of an older time or his own. And one notes the beautiful rhythmics, reminiscent of John Donne's love poetry, in the last line of *1601* which, like Howells, I cannot bear to ignore, yet cannot quite bring myself to quote here.

In our own period it hardly needed the Kinsey laboratory or a Steven Marcus, or a bulky and tedious "masterpiece" like *My Secret Life,* privately printed for a century, and first published in 1967, to remind us not only of *The Other Victorians* but that the great Victorians had other selves, since they were after all barely removed from the early nineteenth century verve for life. Yet *1601* does raise some interesting questions about the private and public personalities of Samuel Clemens that we will keep in mind. In 1877, "A True Story" was the Negro mammy tale reprinted as a separate item from *Sketches New*

and Old; and *Punch, Brothers, Punch,* in 1878, contained
some jingle verses which achieved popularity at the time. But
the *True Story* volume contained a more interesting tale of
Twain's which was called "The Recent Carnival of Crime."

Reprinted in Twain's collected works as "The Facts Concerning the Recent Carnival of Crime in Connecticut," this
story was actually the prelude to a dark line of surrealistic parables which would include *Pudd'nhead Wilson,* "The Man That
Corrupted Hadleyburg," and *The Mysterious Stranger,* in a different and more complex vein of Clemens' talent. Here we
meet "the shriveled, shabby dwarf" who is about forty years
old and no more than two feet high — this little person who
is a deformity as a whole, "a vague, general, evenly blended,
nicely adjusted deformity." And yet, "this vile bit of human
rubbish seemed to bear a sort of remote and ill-defined resem-
blance to me!" He knows everything that goes on in the narrator's (Clemens') mind and spirit; he knows all his lies, vices,
and sins, his arrogance, dishonesty, faithlessness, disloyalty,
fits of violent anger, remorse. Clemens paints a very low view
of himself here, and it is recognizable, until the narrator suddenly accuses his tormentor of being the devil, of being Satan
himself. In this dubious shifting light, Clemens stresses his lifelong affinity with the fallen angel. But the odious and moldy
dwarf turns out to be not the devil or Satan at all, but Twain's
conscience.

And while the autobiographical narrator of the story is being roundly abused by his Conscience, he in turn abuses his
Conscience and is intent upon capturing and killing the malignant dwarf. "Dwarf," as the dwarf explains, because while
originally he started out precisely as tall as Clemens, his being
neglected and abused through the years has steadily reduced
his stature and power.

What abuse and self-abuse abounds in this curious parable; what violence of language in Clemens' charges and counter-charges. "My good slave, you are curiously witless — no, I mean characteristically so. In truth, you are always consistent, always yourself, always an ass," says Clemens' Conscience to Clemens, addressing him in his own "s-n-i-v-e-l-i-n-g d-r-a-w-l — baby!" while the outraged victim of this impudence is plotting the sudden demise of the insolent demon. "If I only had you shrunk down to a homeopathic pill, and could get my hands on you, would I put you in a glass case for a keepsake? No, sir. I would give you to a yellow dog! That is where *you* ought to be . . ." Now was the "aunt" of this story — always reproaching the Clemens narrator for his smoking, among other vices, rather like the Aunt Polly of *Tom Sawyer* — a mother surrogate or a wife surrogate? It is her intrusion, at any rate, which allows the dualistic and divided hero to achieve his deadly purpose. "My breath was coming in short, quick gasps now, and my excitement was almost uncontrollable. My aunt cried out: 'Oh, do not look so! You appal me! Oh, what can the matter be? What is it you see? Why do you stare so? Why do you work your fingers like that?'" While the aunt pleads hysterically with the hero to drop the vices which lead to such fits, Clemens' Conscience "began to reel drowsily and grope with his hands — enchanting spectacle!" and droops languidly to the floor "blinking toward me a last supplication for mercy, with heavy eyes," when

With an exultant shout I sprang past my aunt, and in an instant I had my lifelong foe by the throat. After so many years of waiting and longing, he was mine at last. I tore him to shreds and fragments. I rent the fragments into bits. I cast the bleeding rubbish into the fire, and drew into my nostrils the grateful incense of my burnt-offering. At last, and forever, my Conscience was dead!

This was the history of the narrator's "freedom" in "The Recent Carnival of Crime," as his aunt, with all her charities and mercies, flies from him in terror; and in "bliss, unalloyed bliss" he embarks upon a criminal career.

Now in orthodox Freudian terms this story is just what it sounds like, and orthodox Freudians can shake their heads sadly and commiserate ad nauseam over poor Sam Clemens' burden of sin and guilt. In Rankian cultural terms, however, what this story marks (as Clemens must have felt and known in his depths) is the hero's *liberation* from the repressive burden of civilizational discontents, his defiance of conventional morality, his determination to be himself at all costs (every artist's design) — and hence, the "bliss, unalloyed bliss," of Clemens' natural spirit, and the carnival of crime which is the organism's realization it is enjoying itself despite the dictates of society. — A kind of vestigial guilt, yes, which is laughing at itself. This curious parable, so much harped upon by conventional depth psychology, proves to be the exact opposite, or the true rationale of art and the artist. This was Sam Clemens exorcising his Puritan past.

And why not? Clemens was riding high in those days. And yet the mixed tone of the fable, and the curious confusion of Satan, who is the obvious symbol of pagan life, with his own conscience, rather than, as elsewhere, with his true temperament, indicated certain strains in Eden.

With the popular success of *The Innocents Abroad* and *Roughing It* — his first two books selling one hundred thousand copies each — Mark Twain became something of a phenomenon in American literature. In its purely worldly aspects, his career surpassed anything before it, and probably almost everything after it. His royalties were immense; his lecture tours and magazine articles brought in a large income besides — and he had

married an heiress. Their first house in Buffalo was presented
to them by Livy's father as a wedding gift; it included the cook
Ellen and the Irish coachman, Patrick McAleer, who became
their lifelong servant and Clemens' confidant. Even more successful in the middle of the seventies, the Clemenses planned
and built the great mansion in Hartford, adding a corps of new
domestics, and living in the grand style of millionaires — all of
which Clemens, so desperately poor, searching, unknown, a
working-class ruffian of sorts just a few years before, accepted
with the equanimity of genius.

Yet Hartford life was exhausting to them both; the early years
of their marriage were full of tension. There was the steady
presence of house guests, the parties and lunches and dinners,
all the elaborate trappings of wealth, and the large expenses.
They lost their first son, Langdon, named after Livy's father
(who had died shortly after their marriage), at the age of two,
and Clemens blamed himself for this death. Susy and Clara were
delicate children physically and precocious in spirit; Livy drove
herself into a series of physical and nervous ailments. The
European trip of the seventies was in reality a flight from their
grandiose American existence in a home they loved and a
social sphere they hated. Clemens was also worried about
money; toward the decade's end the sales of his books had de-
creased sharply. The Hartford mansion would become a monster to him; and the beginning of his career, so grand, so magnificent, so fortunate, had already changed sharply for the
worse in what was to be a lifelong pattern of ups and downs.

He was exhausted and depressed by a decade of glory and
feasting, and he hoped to find both solitude and freedom to work
in Europe — the peace of death as he said. But, struggling
with the manuscript of *A Tramp Abroad* in Heidelberg, Mu-
nich, and Paris, after having invited Twichell to join him on

his tour, after having "lost" one of the notebooks for his manuscript and then, unhappily, discovering it again, Clemens found little zest either in his tramping abroad or in writing the book itself. Although this was another travel book, returning to the first success of *The Innocents Abroad,* Clemens' mood was dark. "I *hate* travel, and I *hate* hotels, and I *hate* the opera, and I *hate* the old masters," he wrote to Howells from Italy, as recorded by his first biographer, Albert Bigelow Paine. "In truth I don't ever seem to be in a good enough humor with anything to satirize it. No, I want to stand up before it and curse it and foam at the mouth, or take a club and pound it to rags and pulp. I have got in two or three chapters about Wagner's operas, and managed to do it without showing temper, but the strain of another such effort would burst me."

Even this outrage and anger was not evident in the sluggish prose of *A Tramp Abroad,* in 1880, while Howells himself was just then publishing a dreadful novel called *The Lady of the Aroostook,* which Clemens dutifully praised. (It was on the same trip abroad, in London, just before returning home, that Mrs. Clemens had her chat with Henry James; while Clemens mentioned only his visit with the great Darwin.) In the travel book itself there was, to be sure, the western tall tale of Jim Baker's bluejays, another brilliant animistic legend. But this piece of "padding" had little to do with Twain's torpid descriptions of student life in Heidelberg, say, and the dueling clubs of the young German officers whom he found so gently bred and kindly natured. There are still good lines, of course. "One day we took the train and went down to Mannheim to see 'King Lear' played in German. It was a mistake." And there is a section of hilarious farce on *Lohengrin* and the other Wagnerian operas.

There is a comic episode of Clemens' insomnia; there are his brilliant drawings, and his reflections, always funny, on the German language: "I can *understand* German as well as the maniac that invented it, but I *talk* it best through an interpreter." There is a parody of the Lorelei legend as "translated" by Twain from the German:

> I believe the turbulent waves
> Swallow at last skipper and boat;
> She with her singing craves
> All to visit her magic moat.

But still these are the exceptions to the prevailing sense of tediousness in *A Tramp Abroad*. It was one of the two Mark Twain books not reprinted by the year 1970, and this publishing verdict was probably sound.

Yet even as I say this I come across another comic passage on Baden-Baden, and let us record at least some other good things in this generally subdued book. As art critic, Clemens was hilarious about Turner's *Slave Ship*, in his "vulgar" western lowbrow mask. What a red rag is to a bull, said he, Turner's painting was to him before he studied art. "Mr. Ruskin is educated in art up to a point where that picture throws him into as mad an ecstasy of pleasure as it used to throw me into one of rage last year, when I was ignorant. His cultivation enables him — and me, now — to see water in that glaring yellow mud, and natural effects in those lurid explosions of mixed smoke and flame, and crimson sunset glories; it reconciles him — and me, now — to the floating of iron cable-chains and other unfloatable things; it reconciles us to fishes swimming around on top of the mud — I mean of the water. The most of the picture is a manifest impossibility — that is to say, a lie; and only rigid cultivation can enable a man to find truth in a lie. But it enables Mr. Ruskin to do it, and it has enabled me to do it, and I am thankful for it. A Boston newspaper reporter went and took a look at the Slave Ship floundering about in that fierce conflagration of reds and yellows, and said it reminded him of a tortoise-shell cat having a fit in a platter of tomatoes. In my then uneducated state, that went home to my non-cultivation, and I thought here is a man with an unobstructed eye. Mr. Ruskin would have said: This person is an ass. That is what I would say, now."

It was the "unobstructed eye" which Clemens brought to so many shams of life beyond those of European travel and the fashionable taste of the time. This remarkable writer looked at everything with the candid, unblinking and clear gaze of the "innocent." Even though he may have sometimes clowned up the frontier spirit, though he was full of notions and obsessions which he did not try to hide, the source of everything good in Mark Twain lies in this transparently honest, open, and full human vision, so rare, even in art, as to be priceless. And what is interesting in the development of *A Tramp Abroad* itself, is that the second volume, as Clemens overcame his initial resistance to the writing of the book, is so much better than the first. As in the case of *The Gilded Age,* the mediocre esthetic entity is saved by the brilliance of the parts. If *A Tramp Abroad* is a poor narrative, it still contains some of the best items of classical Clemens humor, nonsense and Dada; and it reminds us that very rarely can a Mark Twain book be wholly written off. Take the example of the clothing of the Swiss waitresses. (Though this was a familiar gambit of Twain's comedy.)

"The table d'hote was served by waitresses dressed in the quaint and comely costume of the Swiss peasants. This consists of a simple gros de laine, trimmed with ashes of roses, with overskirt of sacre bleu ventre saint gris, cut bias on the off-side, with facings of petit polonaise and narrow insertions of pâté de foie gras backstitched to the mise en scène in the form of a jeu d'esprit. It gives to the wearer a singularly piquant and alluring aspect . . ." One of these waitresses, a woman of forty, "had side-whiskers reaching half-way down her jaw," but nevertheless Clemens is one of the few American writers with an eye for women's clothes (and for women). And there is the later episode when the hotel laundry returns the wrong underclothing. "I did not get back the same drawers I sent down, when our things came up at six-fifteen. They were merely a pair of white ruffle-cuffed absurdities, hitched together at the top with a narrow band, and they did not come quite down to my knees. They were pretty enough, but they made me feel like two people, and disconnected at that. The man must have been an idiot that got himself up like that to rough it in the Swiss mountains."

He was almost savage about a young American maiden (and her young American boy) whom he encountered on this trip; just as he was the only writer of his time to question the cultural dominance of the innocent virgin, which Howells grumbled at but accepted; which led to the fatal flaw in all the Henry Jamesian ladies. (Though he appeared to relent about the American youth by saying that you could not keep a grudge against a vacuum.) In Venice, Clemens found he had more pleasure in contemplating the Old Masters than on his previous trips. "But still it was a calm pleasure; there was nothing overheated about it." And yet, describing Tintoretto's three-acre picture in the Doge's palace, he could write:

The movement of this great work is very fine. There are ten thousand figures, and they are all doing something. There is a wonderful "go" to the whole composition. Some of the figures are diving headlong downward, with clasped hands, other are swimming through the cloud-shoals — some on their faces, some on

their backs — great processions of bishops, martyrs, and angels
are pouring swiftly centerward from various outlying directions
— everywhere is enthusiastic joy, there is rushing movement everywhere. There are fifteen or twenty figures scattered here and
there, with books, but they cannot keep their attention on their
reading — they offer the books to others, but no one wishes to read,
now. The Lion of St. Mark is there with his book; St. Mark is
there with his pen uplifted; he and the Lion are looking each other
earnestly in the face, disputing about the way to spell a word —
the Lion looks up in rapt admiration while St. Mark spells . . .

When it came to painting he liked, this so-called frontier ig-
noramus was writing art criticism of a high order. He came also
to feel pleasure in the completely perfect and soothing ugliness
of Saint Mark's Cathedral. Too many famous buildings were
comprised of both ugliness and beauty, Clemens said, and left
you confused and uneasy. "But one is calm before St. Mark's;
one is calm within it, one would be calm on top of it, calm in the
cellars; for its details are masterfully ugly, no misplaced and impertinent beauties are intruded anywhere; and the consequent
result is a grand harmonious whole of soothing, entrancing, tran-
quilizing, soul-satisfying ugliness. One's admiration of a perfect thing always grows, never declines; and this is the surest evidence to him that it *is* perfect. St. Mark's is perfect. To me it
soon grew to be so nobly, so augustly ugly, that it was difficult
to stay away from it, even for a little while. Every time its squat
domes disappeared from my view, I had a despondent feeling;
when they reappeared, I felt an honest rapture — I have not
known any happier hours than those I daily spent in front of
Florian's, looking across the Great Square at it. Propped on its
long row of low thick-legged columns, its back knobbed with
domes, it seemed like a vast warty bug taking a meditative
walk."

For prose passages like this, the whole ordeal of reading the central narrative of *A Tramp Abroad* is justified; and indeed one must read the book just to discover passages like this. But then there are those sections, also on Italian art, which reveal such curious ambiguities in this "Puritan in Paradise." Twain noticed with indignation the advent of the fig leaf on ancient statuary. "It makes a body ooze sarcasm at every pore, to go about Rome and Florence and see what this last generation has been doing with the statues. These works, which had stood in innocent nakedness for ages, are all fig-leaved now. Yes, every one of them. Nobody noticed their nakedness before, perhaps; nobody can help noticing it now, the fig-leaf makes it so conspicuous. But the comical thing about it all, is that the fig-leaf is confined to cold and pallid marble, which would be still cold and unsuggestive without this sham and ostentatious symbol of modesty, whereas warm-blooded paintings which do really need it have in no case been furnished with it." There was an odd turning in Clemens' thoughts within a single passage here; a curious sensitivity to the nature of the medium. And of these "warm-blooded paintings" which could use a touch of censorship, there was no doubt that Titian's Venus was among the worst (or best?).

"At the door of the Uffizzi, in Florence, one is confronted by statues of a man and a woman, noseless, battered, black with accumulated grime — they hardly suggest human beings — yet these ridiculous creatures have been thoughtfully and conscientiously fig-leaved by this fastidious generation. You enter and proceed to the most-visited little gallery that exists in the world — the Tribune — and there, against the wall, without obstructing rag or leaf, you may look your fill upon the foulest, the vilest, the obscenest picture the world possesses — Titian's Venus. It isn't that she is naked and stretched out on a bed —

no, it is the attitude of one of her arms and hand. If I ventured to describe that attitude, there would be a fine howl — but there the Venus lies, for anybody to gloat over that wants to — and there she has a right to lie, for she is a work of art, and Art has its privileges. I saw young girls stealing furtive glances at her; I saw young men gaze long and absorbedly at her; I saw aged, infirm men hang upon her charms with a pathetic interest. How I should like to describe her — just to see what a holy indignation I could stir up in the world — just to hear the unreflecting average man deliver himself about my grossness and coarseness, and all that . . ."

Clemens continued these animadversions on "Titian's beast," just as he had already pointed out that Fielding and Smollett "could portray the beastliness of their day in the beastliest language," when compared with modern propriety. "Art retains her privileges, Literature has lost hers." But what was the meaning of all this hocus-pocus where Clemens was (apparently) wavering between censorship and obscenity, between pleasure and puritanism? Was it put on, with a straight face, for the edification of his audience, or did it reflect the contradictions in his own temperament? Was he honestly shocked by Titian's Venus or secretly enjoying it; defending or attacking the principle of censorship and fig-leafing? Was his writing, marked at the outset with such frankness and openness about so many Victorian taboos, already coming under the prudish sway of his period; or did these passages reflect deeper contradictions in Clemens' own temperament? Or was he "putting on" the whole show of mock-virtue? Written so directly after *1601,* moreover, these sections of *A Tramp Abroad* create a curious impression of ambiguity — or of suppressed irony. And these later sections of the book conclude with the first of Clemens' descriptions of "The Awful German Language." There is, for example, the parenthesis disease and the separable verb. "The trunks being now ready, he DE —— after kissing his mother and sisters, and once more pressing to his bosom his adored Gretchen, who, dressed in simple white muslin, with a single tuberose in the ample folds of her rich brown hair, had tottered feebly down the stairs, still pale from the terror and excitement of the past evening, but longing to lay her poor aching head yet once again upon the breast of him whom she loved more dearly than life itself, PARTED."

There are the different declensions and cases in the German language. "For instance, if one is casually referring to a house, *Haus,* or a horse, *Pferd,* or a dog, *Hund,* he spells these words as I have indicated; but if he is referring to them in the Dative case, he sticks on a foolish and unnecessary *e* and spells them *Hause, Pferde, Hunde.* So, as an added *e* often signifies the plural, as the *s* does with us, the new student is likely to go on for a month making twins out of a Dative dog before he discovers his mistake; and on the other hand, many a new student who could ill afford loss, has bought and paid for two dogs and only got one of them, because he ignorantly bought that dog in the Dative singular when he really supposed he was talking plural — which left the law on the seller's side, of course, by the strict rules of grammar, and therefore a suit for recovery could not lie."

This was grammar as never before taught on land and sea; and what a student of languages was this maker of the plainest and homeliest native American prose. In the closing pages of *A Tramp Abroad,* in the "Appendix" in which Clemens poured such handsome "asides," there followed the "reduction" from German into English of the fable called "Tale of the Fishwife and its Sad Fate." "It is a bleak Day. Hear the Rain, how he pours, and the Hail, how he rattles; and see the Snow, how he

drifts along, and oh the Mud, how deep he is! Ah the poor
Fishwife, it is stuck fast in the Mire . . ." (He was capitaliz-
ing the nouns, Clemens added, in the German and ancient
English fashion.) "It has dropped its Basket of Fishes; and its
Hands have been cut by the Scales as it seized some of the
falling Creatures; and one Scale has even got into its Eye, and it
cannot get her out. It opens its Mouth to cry for Help; but if
any Sound comes out of him, alas he is drowned by the raging
of the Storm. And now a Tomcat has got one of the Fishes
and she will surely escape with him. No, she bites off a Fin, she
holds her in her Mouth — will she swallow her? No, the Fishwife's brave Mother-dog deserts his Puppies and rescues the
Fin — which he eats, himself, as his Reward. O, horror, the
Lightning has struck the Fish-basket; he sets him on Fire; see
the Flame, how he licks the doomed Utensil with her red and
angry Tongue; she attacks the Fishwife's Leg and destroys *it;*
she attacks its Hand and destroys *her;* she attacks its poor worn
Garment and destroys *her* also; she attacks its Body and con-
sumes *him;* she wreathes herself about its Heart and *it* is consumed; next about its Breast, and in a Moment *she* is a Cinder;
now she reaches its Neck — *he* goes; now its Chin — *it* goes;
now its Nose — *she* goes . . ."

In this discourse on the shifting sexuality of the German language, Clemens also caught all the latent sadism of a whole
tradition of German "fairy tales" for children. And so we see it
is almost impossible to ignore any book of Mark Twain's without the risk of missing some remarkable prose episodes. Yes,
the decade of the seventies foreshadowed the alternation of Sam
Clemens' life between peaks of splendor and depths of despair, failure, and frustration — financial, domestic, personal.
But he loved two things: his wife Livy and their home life, and
his own literary work. Beneath all his comic poses he knew deep in

his heart he was destined to be a great writer. Life would betray him as it betrays all things except death; but his art, his writing, would sustain him to the last. He would survive; he would survive and flourish and throw off his splendor until the end of his days.

THREE

THE RIVER
AND THE RAFT

THE PRINCE AND THE PAUPER, in 1882, was a blessed relief for Clemens to write, as Paine tells us, after the nightmare of composing *A Tramp Abroad*. "I am as soary (and flighty) as a rocket to-day, with the unutterable joy of getting that Old Man of the Sea off my back where he has been roosting more than a year and a half," Clemens wrote to Howells. He took a jubilant delight in writing this children's book, even if it never sold, and Mrs. Clemens pursued him to continue it like a "horse-leech's daughter."

The point was, of course, that Clemens was momentarily abandoning his "comedy," or his rebellious satire, and writing a typical romance melodrama of sixteenth-century England for that audience of "good little children" (and good parents) which he had previously mocked. Escaping from his status as a mere "humorist," thinking not even to publish the book under his own name, he had become a juvenile moralist. No wonder Livy admired and pressed him; or that his own children reported this was his finest work, a new and more elevated stage of literary development. Clemens had come to terms, apparently, with his own society, and Howells, too, was delighted, as were the Hartford clergy, the critics of the time, and Harriet Beecher Stowe. The New York *Herald,* the Boston *Transcript,* the *Atlantic,* the *Century* used such words as pure, noble, subdued, delicate, and "refined."

The fit of repentance was not for long, however, since directly after the publication of *The Prince and the Pauper,* Clemens began work on his "demonic" biography of the villainous Whitelaw Reid. But meanwhile the damage had been done. In the parable of Edward Tudor, the young Prince of Wales, and Tom Canty, outcast child of a thief and a beggar, it is difficult to know whether Tom is more tedious as the false king of England, or Edward more affected as the real one. The Prince of Poverty meets the Prince of Plenty in a dreamworld of artificial romance and, for Clemens, quite execrable language. As he would again toward the close of the century, in *Joan of Arc,* Clemens apparently lost his head when encountering these adolescent figureheads of antique royalty. This is silly stuff, this is Twain at his worst, as we realize when we meet Lady Elizabeth, or Mary Stuart "with her gloomy mien," or when the Prince's eyes begin to flash — and we rather yearn for *1601.*

In the scenes of London poverty and crime, there is a kind of Dickensian pathos, but even Clemens' central view of the "good king Edward VI," based mainly on Hume's history, was contrived and inadequate.* The central plot was hokum, the im-

* Beset by internecine wars and religious persecution, by the rivalry among the children of Henry VIII, by court intrigues of the most terrible and obscene nature in this period of Elizabeth and Mary of Scotland, the brief reign of young Edward VI was really not distinguishable from the bloody nightmare of English history which surrounded it. This panorama of "noble" savagery, crime, passion, the use of raw power, evil, cunning, of debauchery and bloodshed, easily matched that of the Russian Czars (the only difference was one of historical time) and was sufficient, as Clemens came to realize, to make the English, the French, and the Russian revolutions appear as benevolent interludes of social progress.

plausible narrative proceeded by a sequence of improbable scenes related in a fancy, stilted, and "noble" manner. When the young Edward is thrown out of the palace because he had unwittingly allowed Tom Canty to try on his clothes — "There followed such a thing as England had never seen before," Clemens said, "the sacred person of the heir to the throne rudely buffeted by plebian hands, and set upon and torn by dogs." And "plebian hands" is very un-Twainish Twain. When Tom Canty assumes the royal place for which he has been unwittingly training himself in his earlier fantasies of nobility, it is Lady Jane Grey, all innocent grace and goodness, who notices his discomfort. "Oh, what aileth thee, my lord?" When the dying Henry wants Norfolk's head to take with him — "Warn my parliament to bring me Norfolk's doom before the sun rise again, else shall they answer for it grievously!" he cries in ringing tones. This is the feudal age in feudal prose, in a very dreamy dream of the past.

The central fantasy of the barefoot boy become proxy king was Sam Clemens' own dream, no doubt, and in his case a fact. But it was also a racial myth from the time of Moses — the illegitimate origins of the great prophet — as well as, in America, a national materialistic obsession. In *The Prince and the Pauper* we notice also the converse of this proposition: the young king who *loses* his royal status, power, and prerogatives. This double and conjoined fantasy embraced both Clemens' youth and his maturity, his dream of success and his fear of losing it which was indeed prophetic, and the loss imminent. This fantasy was in a sense two sides of the same coin, and here we are back to the double personality intrinsic in Sam Clemens' nature . . . But a double personality which has been, for his juvenile audiences, purged of the demonic and satanic elements. Which indeed was the "dream self" in Mark Twain, or which the impostor, in this continuously shifting psychic dualism of such intertwined and interchanging phases of his personality? The ambitious dream of the pauper prince became the horrid nightmare of the outcast and persecuted king. But make no mistake — despite the literary failure of *The Prince and the Pauper,* the inadequate form, the surrender to the conventions, the whole pious fraud which Clemens was attempting to put over, even on himself — the central vision of the book was one of royalty.

For the orphan and pauper, Tom Canty, took on his newly assumed nobility with remarkable ease, just as though he had been indeed "rehearsing" for it. And Childe Edward is definitely still a king when unacknowledged and in rags. What we have here is *two* kings; and what we have been discussing is only the narrow Freudian concept of the early Mark Twain's fears and anxieties, from which in a sense he was also purging himself in this oblique parable. The true issue of Twain's "Double" can be understood only on a larger scale more closely identified with the Rankian *cultural* psychology, where ego is entwined with the social process, and the history of evolutionary development. And when young Edward is kidnapped by John Canty and meets up with a gang of dispossessed yeomanry in the book, Clemens begins to hit his stride again. Made poor, shiftless, and violent by the land enclosures, these outcast English farmers are "controlled" by the barbaric criminal code of sixteenth-century England. "They begged, and were whipped at the cart's tail . . . till the blood ran, then set in the stocks to be pelted; they begged again, and were whipped again, and deprived of an ear; they begged a third time — poor devils, what else could they do? — and were branded on the cheek with a red hot iron, and then sold for slaves; they ran away, were hunted down, and hanged." * And set against these dark

* There were as many as sixty thousand convicts at one time in Henry VIII's prisons, and over seventy thousand thieves and robbers were executed, according to Hume's *History of England,* quoted by Clemens.

scenes of social victims, outcasts, criminals, with the accompanying undertones of witchcraft and the devil-cult, there is the scene where the suffering Edward, released from these customs of "civilization," sleeps with a calf. After these horrible glimpses of English life under the Tudors, the innocent child and the innocent animal find a brief happiness together. "He was free of the bonds of servitude and crime, free of the companionship of base and brutal outlaws; he was warm, he was sheltered . . . He merely snuggled the closer to his friend, in a luxury of warm contentment, and drifted blissfully out of consciousness into a deep and dreamless sleep that was full of serenity and peace. The distant dogs howled, the melancholy kine complained, and the winds went on raging, whilst furious sheets of rain drove along the roof; but the majesty of England slept on undisturbed, and the calf did the same, it being a simple creature and not easily troubled by storms nor embarrassed by sleeping with a king."

Even the rats are innocent in this familiar evocation of the plenary state, the womb feeling, the Garden of Man, and the Twainian raft — and do not bother to bite the peacefully sleeping child-prince. There are elements in the juvenile novel which may remind us in part of the Mark Twain who wrote *Tom Sawyer* and *Huck Finn*, though the ending of *The Prince and the Pauper* is as ridiculous as the beginning, and most of the middle is also. Perhaps it need only be added that Albert Bigelow Paine, Clemens' first and official biographer, considered this book as having an "imperishable charm" and the two heroes, twins in spirit, ranking "with the purest and loveliest creations of child life in the realm of fiction." And that the pauper theme had not only a mythic and biopsychic origin in Samuel Clemens' life, but, living as he was at a scale of one hundred thousand dollars a year, almost half of this being invested in mystical patents and inventions which never paid him back a cent, the other half of his income, very large for that time, expended on the Hartford mansion — the pauper theme was also to be encountered in fact and lived and realized in the flesh.

"The Stolen White Elephant," published in the same year as *The Prince and the Pauper*, was an elaborate parody, in a vein repeated later in "A Double-Barreled Detective Story," both of the conventional mystery tale of the time and of police graft, inefficiency, and stupidity. But now Clemens was on the edge of his two great (and related) works of the 1880s, and perhaps the two best books of his early, though not of his mature and late career. He had in fact been brooding over *Life on the Mississippi*, in 1883, for seven years, ever since he had published the series of sketches in the *Atlantic* called "Old Times on the Mississippi," which formed the core of the first half of the book. In 1882 he took a trip back to the river to refresh his memories, and this account forms the disappointing last half of *Life on the Mississippi*. For all practical purposes it is better to divide the book into two volumes, the first one, ending with that famous twentieth chapter, a great imaginative work;* the second volume another one of Twain's lesser travelogues.

At this period of his life he was already revealing dark speculations about the future in his letters to Joe Twichell. Delighted

* Thomas Hardy believed that *Life on the Mississippi* was the best of Clemens' books, and added, "Why don't people understand that Mark Twain is not merely a great humorist. He is a very remarkable fellow in a very different way." Clemens was already an international figure, celebrated in Germany as well as England, and yet at the *Atlantic* dinners he was not seated on the dais with Emerson, Longfellow, Holmes, Whittier, Howells, and Aldrich — all of these writers, except Emerson, and in some respects Howells, being of the second rank. Perhaps this explains Clemens' particular admiration for and gratitude to Howells, who, after all, did understand his talent and was Clemens' link to New England's decaying pantheon. Both Emerson and Longfellow died while Clemens was writing the Mississippi book.

with the birth of his daughter Jean, he was beset by anxious visions of failure, pain, illness, and death. But who could guess this when he swung into the introduction to *Life on the Mississippi* which gave the background of the great river itself: its age, size, grandeur, and the early history of that mighty stream which the ignorant Captain Marryat had called "the great sewer."

Typically, Clemens almost forgot his own prejudice against the American Indians in the account of their persecution. "For more than a hundred and fifty years there had been white settlements on our Atlantic coasts. These people were in intimate communication with the Indians: in the south the Spaniards were robbing, slaughtering, enslaving, and converting them; higher up, the English were trading beads and blankets to them for a consideration, and throwing in civilization and whisky, for lagniappe . . ." Indeed, as Clemens drew freely from Parkman's history, while making this material his own, the Mississippi River Indians are described almost uniformly as gracious, dignified, hospitable; peaceful victims of the white man's conquest. "Then, to the admiration of the savages, La Salle set up a cross with the arms of France on it, and took possession of the whole country for the king — the cool fashion of the time — while the priest piously consecrated the robbery with a hymn. The priest explained the mysteries of the faith 'by signs,' for the saving of the savages; thus compensating them with possible possessions in heaven for the certain ones on earth which they had just been robbed of. Nobody smiles at these colossal ironies."

Very early, Clemens viewed the whole process of empire building and colonialism with a savage irony of his own. "France stole that vast country on that spot . . . and by and by Napoleon himself was to give the country back again —

make restitution, not to the owners, but to their white American heirs." (It is interesting, incidentally, to notice Clemens' contempt for the Sultan of Versailles — "Louis the Putrid" said this vulgar democrat — and his early admiration for the French Revolution.) The history of the Mississippi moves into the period of commercial great barges and keelboats. "Hordes of rough and hardy men; rude, uneducated, brave, suffering terrific hardships with sailor-like stoicism; heavy drinkers, coarse frolickers in moral sties like the Natchez-under-the-hill of that day, heavy fighters, reckless fellows, everyone, elephantinely jolly, foul-witted, profane, prodigal of their money, bankrupt at the end of the trip, fond of barbaric finery, prodigious braggarts; yet in the main, honest, trustworthy, faithful to promises and duty, and often picturesquely magnanimous." And wasn't this a passage straight out of the Democratic Vistas of that fellow bard whose work Mark Twain never mentions?

Clemens was often, in fact, a prose Whitman; or Whitman a poetical Clemens. These two writers often say the same things in almost identical language, just as the dark endings of their entwined visions of democracy were curiously similar. The river steamboats marked the end of keelboating, while *Life on the Mississippi* describes the annual procession of mighty rafts that used to glide by Hannibal when Clemens was a boy. And he threw in here a chapter of a book he had been working on for the past five or six years, the story of an outcast village boy named Huck Finn. Clemens' literary "form" was that of pure association, or inspiration, or of simple padding when inspiration was lacking. The value of the form, at polar opposites from the cunning and calculated Jamesian esthetics of "effects," was determined by the value of the content — never forgetting the beautiful natural form of Clemens' mind and his prose alike.

This chapter was the famous raft episode from *The Adven-*

tures of Huckleberry Finn where, en route to Cairo, Huck sneaks aboard a river barge and is captured by the boisterous but good-natured crew. The two boys are heading to where "the negro will seek freedom in the heart of the free states," as Clemens said in his own voice. "Jim had a wonderful level head for a nigger," says Huck in his natural dialect.

These pages in *Life on the Mississippi* are unusual in that one great book in American letters makes the first historical mention of another great book. Sam Clemens himself tipped us off about the imminent arrival of Huck Finn. And then in what was poetry the young hero of the present chronicle announced his own determination to become a river pilot. "So, by and by/ I ran away./ I said I never would come home again/till I was a pilot/and could come in glory." The opening description of the frontier town of Hannibal, Missouri, would also echo through American literature; but upon his leaving it, the river has already given the hero a special eminence. "I was in such a glorified condition that all ignoble feelings departed out of me, and I was able to look down and pity the untraveled with a compassion that had hardly a trace of contempt in it." As a youth Clemens was never great on details, and he had had a vague plan of sailing to explore the mouth of the Amazon. But he was instantly smitten by the mate of the river steamer. "It was not in (young) human nature not to admire him. He was huge and muscular, his face was bearded and whiskered all over; he had a red woman and a blue woman tattooed on his right arm . . . and in the matter of profanity he was sublime."

Since *Life on the Mississippi* is ostensibly another of Mark Twain's travel books, it has not been sufficiently realized that it is also a work of literary imagination. The young hero of the chronicle — who is the autobiographical Clemens looking back on the early Clemens with such wistful and nostalgic humor —

is surely an older brother of Huck Finn, and a more complex figure. But the mate rebukes young Clemens' advances and the night watchman, the humblest personage on the boat, is the only one who will talk to him. "What was it to me that he was soiled and seedy and fragrant with gin?" Or what to Clemens that, as he would discover, he was "a low, vulgar, ignorant, sentimental, half-witted humbug"? The point is precisely that *Life on the Mississippi* presents all the lower depths of river life with unflinching truth, and yet, through the worshipful eyes of its young apprentice, with a glowing and even heroic glamor. It is social realism, yes, to the utmost; but it is also, definitely, epic realism.

It is as though the great river itself, in the days of Mark Twain's youth, cast an extra dimension upon everything around it. Just as in Clemens' world of childhood the sordid is not quite sordid, in these glowing pages drunks are not drunk, dirt is not dirty, lies are romantic illusions — though there will be horrors and nightmares to come. It was just then that the ambitious and wily Clemens persuaded Horace Bixby to teach him piloting in return for five hundred dollars payable later on — and we reach the central relationship in the book. Bixby is a hard master who will "learn" his apprentice the river or kill him. But the river is a hard master too. There is the chapter on Clemens' first experiences as a cub pilot, and what is remarkable again is not merely the total recall of this artist, but the complete candor, the entertaining honesty in the self-confessions and self-descriptions of this temperament — this altogether Open Ego. Clemens' personality is totally unarmored, as may be seen by now, and the direct opposite of his contemporary, the autistic Henry James, who was in turn close to Bruno Bettelheim's concept of "the empty fortress," in the book by that name.

The youthful Clemens, in all his naive presumptuousness, was subjected to the worst forms of ridicule and abuse by the implacable Mr. Bixby; and there is Clemens' rage at his master, and his fantasy of revenge when the great pilot is landing at Jones' plantation on a dark night. "My exultation began to cool and my wonder to come up. Here was a man who not only proposed to find this plantation on such a night, but to find either end of it you preferred. I dreadfully wanted to ask a question, but I was carrying about as many short answers as my cargo-room would admit of, so I held my peace. All I desired to ask Mr. Bixby was the simple question whether he was ass enough to really imagine he was going to find that plantation on a night when all plantations were exactly alike and all of the same color. But I held in. I used to have fine inspirations of prudence in those days."

Notice Twain's classic answer to Bixby's catechism on the "points" in the river. "I was gratified to be able to answer promptly, and I did. I said I didn't know." There are Bixby's rages at Clemens, since the young hero of *Life on the Mississippi* had something of Tom Sawyer's verbal insouciance. "Oh, but his wrath was up! He was a nervous man, and he shuffled from one side of his wheel to the other as if the floor was hot. He would boil awhile to himself, and then overflow and scald me again." And there is the grand episode in *Life on the Mississippi* when a whole group of visiting pilots attend upon Mr. Bixby's feat of running Hat Island by night:

> Now the engines were stopped altogether and we drifted with the current. Not that I could see the boat drift, for I could not, the stars being all gone by this time. The drifting was the dismalest work; it held one's heart still. Presently I discovered a blacker gloom than that which surrounded us. It was the head of the island. We were closing right down upon it. We entered its

deeper shadow, and so imminent seemed the peril that I was likely
to suffocate; and I had the strongest impulse to do *something,* anything, to save the vessel. But still Mr. Bixby stood by his wheel,
silent, intent as a cat, and all the pilots stood shoulder to shoulder
at his back.

A remarkable, almost mythic scene of the Freudian "son-
horde," grouped behind the parental figure. Only not in a cunning death struggle and parricide, but in admiration and support of individual daring and collective survival.

There is Pilot Bixby teaching the young Clemens the different kinds of darkness on the river, and the changing shape of
the river — and the "exact spot and the exact marks the boat
lay in when we had the shoalest water in every one of the five
hundred shoal places between St. Louis and New Orleans." To
which the young apprentice rejoins: "When I get so that I can
do that, I'll be able to raise the dead, and then I won't have to
pilot a steamboat to make a living. I want to retire from this
business. I want a slush-bucket and a brush; I'm only fit for a
roustabout. I haven't got brains enough to be a pilot; and if I
had I wouldn't have strength enough to carry them around, unless I went on crutches." To which Bixby replies: "Now drop
that! When I say I'll learn a man the river, I mean it. And you
can depend on it, I'll learn him or kill him." And there is Bixby
teaching Clemens a lesson on water-reading and boat-reading.

Now watch her; watch her like a cat, or she'll get away from you.
When she fights strong and the tiller slips a little, in a jerky, greasy
sort of way, let up on her a trifle; it is the way she tells you at night
that the water is too shoal; but keep edging her up, little by little,
toward the point. You are well up on the bar now; there is a bar
under every point, because the water that comes down around it
forms an eddy and allows the sediment to sink. Do you see those
fine lines on the face of the water that branch out like the ribs of

a fan? Well, those are little reefs; you want to just miss the ends of them, but run them pretty close. Now look out — look out! Don't you crowd that slick, greasy-looking place; there ain't nine feet there; she won't stand it. She begins to smell it; look sharp, I tell you! Oh, blazes, there you go! Stop the starboard wheel! Quick! Ship up to back! Set her back!

Here of course the ship has become a living creature in this prevailing animism of Clemens, or a pantheism where the pilot of the watery universe projects his spirit into every faintest surface ripple, slick, and point. Then there is that nightmarish sequence when Clemens, piloting at night, encounters a wind reef. "Once I inspected rather long, and when I faced to the front again my heart flew into my mouth so suddenly that if I hadn't clapped my teeth together I should have lost it. One of those frightful bluff reefs was stretching its deadly length right across our bows! My head was gone in a moment; I did not know which end I stood on; I gasped and could not get my breath; I spun the wheel down with such rapidity that it wove itself together like a spider's web; the boat answered and turned square away from the reef, but the reef followed her! I fled, but still it followed, still it kept — right across my bows! I never looked to see where I was going, I only fled." And there is Bixby's serenity as he rescues the steamer from crashing into the forest woods. "Just then Mr. Bixby stepped calmly into view on the hurricane-deck. My soul went out to him in gratitude. My distress vanished; I would have felt safe on the brink of Niagara with Mr. Bixby on the hurricane-deck. He blandly and sweetly took his tooth pick out of his mouth between his fingers, as if it were a cigar — we were just in the act of climbing an overhanging big tree, and the passengers were scudding astern like rats — and lifted up these commands to me ever so gently . . ."

And Bixby asks Clemens just why he had brought the ship

into the forest woods because of a rippling wind on the water, the water whose face Clemens does get to know so intimately. "It turned out to be true. The face of the water, in time, became a wonderful book — a book that was a dead language to the uneducated passenger, but which told its mind to me without reserve, delivering its most cherished secrets as clearly as if it uttered them with a voice . . . There never was so wonderful a book written by man, never one whose interest was so absorbing, so unflagging, so sparklingly renewed with every reperusal." And that "knowledge" of the water, as Mark Twain realized, also meant that he could never more enjoy the river so purely for its own sake, since all the river's beauties now held the hint of treachery. "Since those days, I have pitied doctors from my heart. What does the lovely flush in a beauty's cheek mean to a doctor but a 'break' that ripples above some deadly disease? Are not all her visible charms sown thick with what are to him the signs and symbols of hidden decay? Does he ever see her beauty at all, or doesn't he simply view her professionally, and comment upon her unwholesome condition all to himself? And doesn't he sometimes wonder whether he has gained most or lost most by learning his trade?"

On the river, too, "reason" and knowledge replace, and suppress the original state of innocent pleasure and enjoyment — though of course it is just that state of feeling which sets off *Life on the Mississippi* as a primitive epic, and those primary emotions of pleasure, admiration, awe, worship, and affection which pervade its pages. This work of art records the inevitable suppression of feeling by the intellect while it simultaneously evokes the suppressed emotions that reason or civilization must deny.*

* For these insights and indeed for the whole view of Mark Twain, in terms of Rankian cultural psychology rather than the much narrower concepts of Freudian psychological blockage and trauma — an ideology of personal neurosis

In the close study of the *trade* of piloting, *Life on the Mississippi* reminds us of the hard economics of whaling in *Moby
Dick,* and both these great works of the watery domain, soaring
up to the heights of art, still rest securely on a firm basis of material factuality. And just here occurs another fine section of
Twain's epic — that which describes the big rise in the river,
the river life at floodtime, when all the farmers and merchants
who live along the banks take to their keelboats and barges in
an enormous flotilla of nautical riffraff. "During this big rise
these small-fry craft were an intolerable nuisance" — and these
pages of *Life on the Mississippi* are a gaudy pageant of American lowlife casually afloat on the great southern river.

The flooding river has changed its shape again.

We were shaving stumpy shores, like that at the foot of Madrid
Bend, which I had always seen avoided before; we were clattering
through chutes like that of 82, where the opening at the foot was
an unbroken wall of timber till our nose was almost at the very
spot. Some of these chutes were utter solitudes. The dense, untouched forest overhung both banks of the crooked little creek,
and one could believe that human creatures had never intruded
there before. The swinging grape-vines, the grassy nooks and
vistas glimpsed as we swept by, the flowering creepers waving their
red blossoms from the tops of dead trunks, and all the spendthrift
richness of the forest foliage, were wasted and thrown away there.

Slipping through these newly formed chutes, they came
across families of poverty-stricken poor-white farmers huddled

---

which hardly can encompass Samuel Clemens' outgoing soul and his cosmic
empathies — I am greatly in debt to a massive and illuminating, though as yet
unpublished, study of modern depth psychology by the brilliant American cultural historian Jack Jones . . . For the reader who may be puzzled by a certain
inversion, or subversion, of commonly accepted psychological notions, I can
only beg patience until the development of the present book makes them
clearer with reference to Mark Twain himself.

together on improvised rafts and boats, waiting for days or
weeks until the floodwater would subside — or crazy fences
with "one or two jeans-clad, chills-racked, yellow-faced male
miserables roosting on the top rail, elbows on knees, jaws in
hands, grinding tobacco and discharging the result at floating
chips through crevices left by lost teeth." In such flood changes
the monster river, like the great white whale, was a triumphant
and irresistible force of nature, beyond good and evil, unchecked
and untamed except by those bold pilots who rode its back with
such human grace and skill and style. And here we reach another crucial statement in *Life on the Mississippi* when Clemens
adds: "If I have seemed to love my subject, it is no surprising
thing, for I loved the profession far better than any I have followed since, and I took a measureless pride in it. The reason is
plain: a pilot, in those days, was the only unfettered and entirely independent human being that lived in the earth. Kings
are but the pampered servants of parliament and people; parlia-
ments sit in chains forged by their constituency; the editor of a
newspaper cannot be independent, but must work with one hand
tied behind him by party and patrons, and be content to utter
only half or two-thirds of his mind; no clergyman is a free man
and may speak the whole truth, regardless of his parish's opinions; writers of all kinds are manacled servants of the public.
We write frankly and fearlessly, but then we 'modify' before we
print. In truth, every man and woman and child has a master,
and worries and frets in servitude; but in the day I write of, the
Mississippi pilot had *none*."

He had seen a boy of eighteen, "taking a great steamer se-
renely into what seemed almost certain destruction," while the
aged captain stood by powerless to interfere. And: "I think
pilots were about the only people I ever knew who failed to
show, in some degree, embarrassment in the presence of travel-

ing foreign princes. But then, people in one's own grade of life are not usually embarrassing objects . . . By long habit, pilots came to put all their wishes in the form of commands. It 'gravels' me, to this day, to put my will in the weak shape of a request, instead of launching it in the crisp language of an order." Thus the freedom of primitive nature along the banks of the Mississippi River and the freedom of the natural life are matched by the sense of human freedom in the spirit of the Mississippi pilots. Then the book adds further portraits of these sublime beings, of whom Bixby was the supreme example, and following is the account of the pilots' guild — "perhaps the compactest, the completest, and the strongest commercial organization ever formed among men."

The formation of this guild becomes another folk epic in these pages. After so many early failures and disasters, and so much patient cunning on the part of the guild organizers, in the moment of its success "the organization seemed indestructible. It was the tightest monopoly in the world" — until, with the Civil War and the advent of the railroads, and then the development of the Mississippi River tugboats, the whole steamboat industry collapsed in a few brief years. In the closing pages of the first part of *Life on the Mississippi,* Clemens described the famous river races which were in fact less dangerous than an ordinary run with a careless engineer; he listed the names of the famous steamers and their record trips — and he introduced the nemesis of his story, a certain Captain Brown of the steamer *Pennsylvania.* "He was a middle-aged, long, slim, bony, smooth-shaven, horse-faced, ignorant, stingy, malicious, snarling, fault-hunting, mote-magnifying tyrant." There was obviously no love lost between the evil pilot, who concludes this triumphant chronicle of innocence in life, and Horace Bixby's cub. Indeed all of young Clemens' pleasure in his newly acquired craft seems to crash upon the rock of Brown's conniving sadism and ridicule; and he spent his spare time inventing ways of killing his new master.

"That was the thing I used always to do the moment I was abed. Instead of going over my river in my mind, as was my duty, I threw business aside for pleasure, and killed Brown. I killed Brown every night for months; not in old, stale, commonplace ways, but in new and picturesque ones — ways that were sometimes surprising for freshness of design and ghastliness of situation and environment." Was the demonic element in Mark Twain, so long repressed, absent and wanting in the chronicle of youth and the great river, rising to the surface at the book's conclusion? It was unthinkable in the river code to strike a pilot in the performance of his duty, and Clemens believed there was a penitentiary law against it. It was only when Captain Brown physically attacked Sam's brother Henry that his rage erupted. "The boy started out, and even had his foot on the upper step outside the door, when Brown, with a sudden access of fury, picked up a ten-pound lump of coal and sprang after him; but I was between, with a heavy stool, and I hit Brown a good honest blow which stretched him out." Once Clemens had committed the crime of crimes, he concluded there was nothing to stop him from continuing, and he added to his blows a long-delayed tongue-lashing of Brown's character. And this episode, which did not turn out so fatally in itself, was the prelude to the final tragedy in the book. For Clemens was forced to leave the *Pennsylvania,* while Henry remained on it, and the *Pennsylvania* blew up, and Henry was fatally wounded. If Clemens, who always blamed himself for the twist of fate which led so ironically to his brother's death, showed little concern for conventional literary form as such, he had a deeper sense of organic form. For here the epic chronicle of innocence and goodness and the wondrous natural life, these blessed notes from an older world, still ends on the tragic theme of guilt, death, and a blighted career. After chapter twenty, the second half of *Life on the Mississippi* describes the western trip of Mark Twain to see Hannibal and the great river once more; it is an inferior travelogue which really forms the prelude to *The Adventures of Huckleberry Finn,* published a year later, in 1884.

This was Clemens' most celebrated book, although not by any means, as so often claimed, his single great book; nor was this redoubtable genius of our native literature confined, in my view, to the world of childhood, or to the "natural boy" of a Rousseauism which Mark Twain had never heard of. Indeed it was most clearly Clemens' deep sense of the early world of childhood and of natural pleasure which made his view of maturity and of society so penetrating, so caustic, so comic, and so wise.

It was around this famous juvenile that the issue of censorship — what was proper fare for young American children — came out most sharply both within the bosom of the Clemens family and in the outraged reviews and editorials which first greeted a classic of world literature. "Ever since papa and mama were married papa has written his books and then taken them to mama in manuscript and she has expurgated them," so Susy Clemens declared in her autobiography. "Papa read *Huckleberry Finn* to us in manuscript, just before it came out, and then he would leave parts of it with mama to expurgate, while he went off to the study to work, and sometimes Clara and I would be sitting with mama while she was looking the manuscript over, and I remember so well, with what pangs of regret we used to see her turn down the leaves of the pages, which meant that some delightfully terrible part must be scratched out. And I remember one part pertickularly which was perfectly fascinating it was so terrible, that Clara and I used to delight in and oh, with what despair we saw mama turn down the leaf on which it was written, we thought the book would almost be ruined without it . . ."

But in this account (Paine's) the censorial process itself carries the note of childhood delight. This was a nice moment in the Clemens family idyll of domestic bliss. Livy was hardly as severe on her husband as were Howells and other literary friends; Sam used to put in the "offensive words" deliberately in order for them to be scratched out. Olivia Langdon's notorious censorship of Mark Twain's writings was not really very serious. It was not in what his family condemned about his work, but in what they approved of, that his trouble lay. During this period Clemens was also in a frenzy of playwriting; within weeks he had done dramatizations of *The Prince and the Pauper* and *Tom Sawyer* which never reached the stage; with Howells he was writing *The American Claimant,* as a sequel to *The Gilded Age.* On a lecture tour, which he had originally envisaged as including Howells, Thomas Bailey Aldrich, George Cable, and himself traveling over the country in their private railroad car, he was paying Cable $450 a week and expenses, plus the commission for his agent J. B. Pond. Perhaps the humorless and prissy English writer Matthew Arnold was "the only literary Englishman left," as Paine adds, "who had not accepted Mark Twain at his larger value." *

But did *The Adventures of Huckleberry Finn* actually mark the climax of his career, and a decline in his creative powers as suggested by his most recent biographer, Justin Kaplan? Was Twain caught up in his idyll of western adolescence to the point

---

* "And is he *never* serious?" so Howells quotes Arnold as asking about Clemens, while "his hand laxly held mine in greeting." In this connection, it is interesting to remember that Matthew Arnold was Lionel Trilling's early "master" and influence, and to a large degree it was Arnold's respectability, conventionality, "good taste," and all-around esthetic mediocrity that the young Trilling brought over to his criticism of the modern American writers whom he found so vulgar and tasteless (and radical).

of retreating from all contemporary reality, or even, let us say, from artistic maturity itself? This curious vein of Mark Twain criticism was also propounded in various ways by such critics as Van Wyck Brooks in the twenties, Bernard DeVoto in the forties, Mr. Kaplan and Charles Neider in the fifties and sixties. What nonsense, really! *Huck Finn* did indeed take eight years and seven other books before it was finished; but was this a mark of deep inner conflict or perhaps of Clemens' deep intuitive sense of craftsmanship — or of both, as occurs usually with such great books? Was the publication of the book "jinxed from the start," and accompanied by more than usual of Clemens' emotional tantrums and rages, as we are told? — though it is a classic work which finally sold over ten million copies in almost every language, as Mr. Kaplan does finally concede. The reviewers' silence at the time of publication, and then the abuse, the attacks, the attempted censorship of this masterpiece of "vernacular naturalism," this most revolutionary children's book for that time which was described as "gutter realism," as degrading, immoral, improper, irreverent, flat, coarse, trash that was "suitable only for the slums" — all this which redounds so clearly to the credit of an original work of art, of a great and original artist, hardly serves to lift Mr. Kaplan's Freudian gloom.*

---

* In *Mr. Clemens and Mark Twain* (New York, 1966). Mr. Kaplan's biography is an essential supplement to Albert Bigelow Paine's standard three-volume work published in 1912. I have used both biographies throughout this book, but Paine's, despite its obvious Victorianism and omissions, with an increasing admiration, and Mr. Kaplan's with an increasing reserve. To use, as Kaplan continually does, orthodox Freudianism on Twain's talent and work alike is simply to reduce all that was original, bold, and best in him to some kind of trivial personal maladjustment. We have already seen that Twain can hardly be comprehended within such a narrow framework; that a better illumination comes from Rankian cultural psychology. It is unfortunate, moreover, that Mr. Kaplan, working within the Cold War period of our literary scholarship, either ignores or detracts from just those aspects of Twain's writing which have made him universally admired and beloved.

Maybe Mark Twain's joy in the book was beclouded by its initial reception, but still there must have been some pleasure in the writing of the book, and, in his own lifetime, its growing acclaim.

There was. There were times in the writing of it when Clemens went soaring away on the wings of his tale, when he could hardly stop writing it. The narrative carries this imprint of a special pleasure and delight, from the beautiful, lyrical opening of Huck's discontent with even the civilization of the frontier towns. "I felt so lonesome I most wished I was dead." There are the undertones of primitive superstition (the black slave folklore) which surround this chronicle of native boyhood. Miss Watson has attempted to "convert" Huck, the town's bad boy, to respectability and culture and religion. "She told me to pray every day, and whatever I asked for I would get it. But it wasn't so. I tried it. Once I got a fish line but no hooks. It warn't any good to me without hooks . . . I set down one time back in the woods and had a long think about it. I says to myself, if a body can get anything they pray for, why don't Deacon Winn get back the money he lost on pork? Why can't the widow get back her silver snuff-box that was stole? Why can't Miss Watson fat up? No, say I to myself, there ain't anything in it."

Tom Sawyer had satirized, as we know, all the conventional values of "maturity," social success and social power and place. But from the very outset Huckleberry Finn *defied* all the proprieties, including also wealth, success, social position, and conventional religion of the time. It was outrageous what Clemens got away with. It is curious, too, that Twain's Freudian biographer did not stress the opening fantasy of Huck's horrid father (as projected by the outcast prince, Huck-Sam) who was the evil guardian, in Clemens' mind, of the natural child. Like any good primitive myth, the opening of *Huck Finn* is heavy with dubious and shifting oedipal imagery; it is through this drunken, outcast, scheming, cruel — also impotent, pathetic, and helpless — father figure that Huck achieves his escape from the Widow and "sivilization." (First, Huck gives up his inheritance to Judge Thatcher for a consideration of one dollar; no more cash nexus.) And Huck appeals to "Nigger Jim" in his urgent need for charms and witchcraft to help him against the villainous parent. "So the hair-ball talked to Jim, and Jim told it to me. He says: 'Yo' ole father doan' know yit what he's a-gwyne to do. Sometimes he spec he'll go 'way, en den ag'in he spec he'll stay. De bes' way is to res' easy en let de ole man take his own way. Dey's two angels hoverin' roun' 'bout him. One uv 'em is white en shiny, en t'other one is black . . ."

These two angels, these contraries, these doubles give Jim an easy out, of course, just as he foresees two girls playing contrary parts in Huck's own future. "Dey's two gals flyin' 'bout you in yo' life. One uv 'em's light en t'other one is dark. One is rich en t'other is po'. You's gwyne to marry de po' one fust en de rich one by en by. You wants to keep 'way fum de water as much as you kin, en don't run no resk, 'kase it's down in de bills dat you's gwyne to git hung." And after the fantasies (and plots) of murdering the father, Huck escapes to the woods by feigning his own murder. After this mock-primitive hero has his mock-primitive ritual of death and resurrection, we enter the primeval world of the great river and the western wilderness. Time stops; there is the immense black water at night, the first gray of dawn; the fleeing boy takes a nap before daylight. "I was powerful lazy and comfortable — didn't want to get up and cook breakfast." And there is the haunting refrain of this primitive return. "I wanted to put in the time," which is the pure spending of time, the "waste" of time according to society and civilization, the time which is not money;

but the passing of time which is "merely" living for pleasure —
according to Twain — or *living*. Huck gets the "lonesome"
feeling at night, he goes to the river again, and then he goes to
bed. "There ain't no better way to put in time when you are
lonesome; you can't stay so, you soon get over it."

But Huck discovers that Nigger Jim has run away and is also
on the island — thinking that Huck is dead. "He bounced up
and stared at me wild. Then he drops down on his knees, and
puts his hands together and says: 'Doan' hurt me — don't!
I hain't ever done no harm to a ghos'. I awluz liked dead people, en done all I could for 'em. You go en git in de river ag'in,
whah you b'longs, en doan' do nuffn to Ole Jim, 'at 'uz awluz
yo' fren'.' " They feed up together, Jim stops calling Huck
"sah," and tells him how Miss Watson has planned to sell him
down to Orleans, and how he has managed to escape.*

"She didn' want to, but she could git eight hund'd dollars
for me, en it 'uz sich a big stack o' money she couldn' resis'. De
widder she try to git her to say she wouldn' do it, but I never
waited to hear de res'. I lit out mighty quick, I tell you." Thus,
as in Thomas Wentworth Higginson's classic account of Negro
troops in the Civil War, *Army Life in a Black Regiment*, once
again these "lazy," no-account, improvident and incompetent

---

* "Nigger Jim," one of the heroic figures in American fiction against whom the
NAACP has recently been raising some academic objections, is to some degree
a stereotype of the Negro slave or even an Uncle Tom in name, behavior,
language perhaps — but he is a very ambiguous stereotype indeed. First of all,
Huck is obviously the "innocent" hero, the story is his education, and it is told
through the classical double vision of all such stories. Twain always knows more
than Huck seems to know, and very often he deliberately contrives Huck as a
deadpan comic figure in the process of his education. The double vision is
thus almost a triple vision. Moreover this "Nigger Jim" — and again "Nigger"
is Huck's natural and ignorant usage, while Twain uses "Negro" — is also
playing *his* role, as a typical slave and Uncle Tom. It is only gradually that
Huck begins to realize — and that Twain lets him realize — and that Jim lets
him realize — the true nature and temperament of the runaway Negro slave
who is the book's alternate or double hero.

African slaves could be very decisive, quick, energetic and remarkably capable when they had to be, or wanted to be. Jim's
account of his own escape testifies to this. And so much, in these
three brief sentences of Jim's, for the "good" slaveholders of
family-type slaves whom Sam Clemens himself sometimes tried
to contrast with the "evil" deep-south cotton plantation owners. Now comes Jim's plaintive and "capitalistic" comment.
"Yes, en I's rich now, come to look at it. I owns mysef, en I's
wuth eight hund'd dollars. I wisht I had de money, I wouldn'
want no mo'." And then, as these two rebels bid farewell to
the inequities of civilization, the story is suddenly saturated by
the signs and portents of primitive man and nature. When the
birds are flying low, as a sign of rain, and Huck is about to kill
them, Jim invokes all the ritualistic taboos about the sacred-
ness of animal life.

There is the episode of the snake bite where Jim again suf-
fers from Huck's practical jokes; the snake evil is overcome
but not exorcised from the story, as Jim knows. We get the
first of a recurrent series of "visits," or revisits to the civilizational restraints of the frontier towns, where Huck attempts to
personify a girl — and then the swift escape back to the raft:
the first of these great plenary-pagan womb episodes of "drifting" down the limitless void of the great river. "This second
night we run between seven and eight hours, with a current that
was making over four mile an hour. We catched fish and talked,
and we took a swim now and then to keep off sleepiness. It was
kind of solemn, drifting down the big, still river, laying on our
backs, looking up at the stars, and we didn't ever feel like talking loud, and it warn't often that we laughed — only a
little kind of low chuckle. We had mighty good weather as a
general thing, and nothing ever happened to us at all — that
night, nor the next, nor the next." The silence, the solemnity,

the grandeur, the peace of this dark, rocking infinitude are set off by Twain's wry humor. They pass a series of river towns, "nothing but just a shiny bed of lights," at night, and Huck seizes upon these occasions to slip ashore at times to "borrow" a watermelon or a muskmelon or a chicken "that warn't roosting comfortable." To "liberate" them.

In this watery Eden the "crimes" of society are indulged in with all the impunity of childhood play, and "Take it all around, we lived pretty high." Civilization comes back to them briefly, and anticipatorily, in the lurid episode of the floating river boat, the three robbers, and their own hasty, terrified escape — the ominous hint of violence in Eden — while Huck gradually comes to a truer realization of Jim's "black soul." Their conversations are grand affairs where Huck is "teaching" Jim. When Jim doesn't accept the lesson or the moral and wins the argument, Huck takes refuge in the white man's superiority. "I see it warn't no use wasting words — you can't learn a nigger to argue. So I quit." But Jim of course is teaching Huck much more about nature, life, and human beings, as Huck has the grace to admit. "Well, he was right; he was most always right; he had an uncommon level head for a nigger."

But the story's subtlety lies in the fact that Huck does not yet know how much more Jim still has to teach him. Are some of these scenes and episodes and passages to be considered "paternalistic" in the hard light of the race conflict in modern times? Perhaps; and some of them are obviously sentimental, too. Yet this narrative was remarkably open and bold for its own time and place; and it is still very fresh and touching in its fundamental human terms. Sometimes Jim's natural heroic splendor makes Huck feel so ordinary and mean that he humbles himself before the Negro — and "warn't very sorry for it afterward, neither." This is another stage in the developing relationship between what you might call the poor-white-trash boy and the runaway slave: these mutual outcasts who fashion their own world of affection, pleasure, and "underground" trust and responsibility. And the language? Clemens was very proud, technically, of the "four dialects" — or actually six, counting his modifications of the Missouri Negro and ordinary Pike County speech — in which *Huck Finn* was composed; and while it is questionable if any white writer has ever recorded black southern talk accurately, Clemens had perhaps the best "ear" of his time. The different dialects in his book are convincing and consistent within themselves as a literary achievement "based on" southern Negro language, if one can't quite attest to their social and historical verisimilitude. Despite the fact that Clemens had become, by the first decade of his mature career, the most "desouthernized" of southern writers — and would become infinitely more so — there were still lingering prejudices perhaps never, in the case of any southerner or even any white man, to be completely eliminated; and he had a curious weakness for the stylized Negro dialect of Joel Chandler Harris' Uncle Remus.

But still, accepting these modern strictures, it was a lovely language that Mark Twain fashioned to carry along the exuberant, lyrical, touching, entertaining, and deceptively "simple" narrative line in this parable of a southwestern boyhood.* Yes, there was still a false "innocence" about the whole question of slavery which Huck's mind could not be expected to entertain; and there are the familiar "fillers" of romance melodrama in this

---

* It was from this book, of course, that both Sherwood Anderson and Ernest Hemingway, among others such as Gertrude Stein, got their "plain Western rhythms" in the fiction of our own day. Hemingway even claimed, mentioning Thoreau, that American literature started with *Huck Finn,* while Anderson used the Twainian word "fan-tods" in a variety of midwestern tales of adolescence.

book of Mark Twain's, too. Clemens plays cat's-paw with his audience as the raft fluctuates around that Mississippi River "Cairo" where Jim is to find his freedom, and when Huck begins those remarkable reveries as to his own "guilt" in aiding a runaway slave. "Jim said it made him all over trembly and feverish to be so close to freedom. Well, I can tell you it made me all over trembly and feverish, too, to hear him, because I begun to get it through my head that he *was* most free — and who was to blame for it? Why, *me*. I couldn't get that out of my conscience, no how nor no way . . ." And moreover, when Jim comes close to freedom's line he begins to act (and talk) quite differently from his behavior as a black slave — he even plans to buy back or to steal back his wife and children. He begins to act like a free man, a human being. In that double view of Clemens' craft we realize, while it is quite *natural* for Huck to go through those agonized reveries about Jim's freedom, what illuminating and ironical effects Twain achieved through his "innocent" hero. For the "conscience" which so torments Huck is the Freudian superego, the voice of parents, the community, of habit and conformity, which Sam Clemens himself had already seen through.

This is a deadpan, double-edged social satire which is brilliantly entertaining and acute. For Clemens was describing the Freudian "false conscience" — or pseudo-conscience — which, alas, so many practitioners of psychotherapy still value as the only true conscience, not knowing what the human will is. And with what simplicity, irony, and grandeur prevailing over deep social taboos, does Huck finally resolve that he might as well do evil and *not* betray his friend. "Then I thought a minute, and says to myself, hold on; s'pose you'd 'a' done right and give Jim up, would you felt better than what you do now? No, say I, I'd feel bad — I'd feel just the same way I do now. Well, then, says I, what's the use you learning to do right when it's troublesome to do right and ain't no trouble to do wrong, and the wages is just the same? I was stuck. I couldn't answer that. So I reckoned I wouldn't bother no more about it, but after this always do whichever come handiest at the time." Mark Twain was on his most familiar and penetrating ethical grounds: not only attacking human morality for its general hypocrisy, but attacking a specific social "virtue" based on the deepest social crime of slavery. In the caricature of Huck resolving to do "good or bad" depending on which was most convenient, wasn't Twain reaching for a still deeper human impulse: namely, a basic indifference to morality for its own sake and a simple deference to those habits and customs, whether moral or not, which are socially acceptable — convenient — at any given historical moment.

Where was morality now? But we are projecting certain implications of Clemens' thought which were developed later on in his career, and perhaps were not even conscious in *Huck Finn* itself. In the midst of Huck's conflict, he is stricken by Jim's trust in him. "Dah you goes, de ole true Huck; de on'y white genlman dat ever kep' his promise to ole Jim." And there was still here a profound note of natural virtue in contrast with social "ethics" or civilized repression — and a sly pagan laughter. "The place to buy canoes is off of rafts laying up at shore." Now the narrative begins a long disquisition on the frontier culture of the Grangerford and Shepherdson families: on the frontier southern "nobility," on their family feuds, systems of slavery, their household furnishings, their "culture" and art — including the brilliant set piece of Clemens on the interior decoration of the Grangerford house, and the commentary on the mortuary paintings of young Emmeline Grangerford. "These was all nice pictures, I reckon," Huck says, "but I didn't somehow seem to take to them, because if ever I was down a little they always give me the fan-tods. Everybody was sorry she died, because she had laid out a lot more of these pictures to do, and a body could see by what she had done what they had lost. But I reckoned that with her disposition she was having a better time in the graveyard."

Emmeline wrote poetry, too —

Ode to Stephen Dowling Bots, Dec'd

And did young Stephen sicken,
And did young Stephen die?
And did the sad hearts thicken,
And did the mourners cry?

But despite a few saving passages, this is a laborious and dreary episode in *Huck Finn*. It is with some relief that we escape from these horrible southern "gentry" and their farcical codes of gentlemanly behavior; their "loyal niggers," their squalor, prejudices, and violence; the continuous and senseless family feuding — to return to the fullness and peace of the raft again.

This is a sordid and depressing picture of the southwestern country "gentry" which will be useful to remember when we come to a similar problem of interpretation in *The Tragedy of Pudd'nhead Wilson*. "The boys jumped for the river," Huck says, describing a frontier killing, "both of them hurt — and as they swum down the current the men run along the bank shooting at them and singing out, 'Kill them, kill them!' It made me so sick I most fell out of the tree. I ain't a-going to tell *all* that happened — it would make me sick again if I was to do that. I wished I hadn't ever come ashore that night to see such things. I ain't ever going to get shut of them — lots of times I dream about them." And for contrast there is Jim's affectionate delight at Huck's return to the raft.

"Good lan'! is dat you, honey? Doan' make no noise." It was Jim's voice — nothing ever sounded so good before. I run along the bank a piece and got aboard, and Jim he grabbed me and hugged me, he was so glad to see me. He says: "Laws bless you, chile, I 'us right down sho' you's dead ag'in . . . Lawsy, I's mighty glad to git you back ag'in, honey."

Now it was from such passages of physical affection between Jim and Huck — scandalous for their time; and there is more — and from such direct emotional tenderness that the critic Leslie Fiedler found his inspiration for the charge of "homosexuality" in *Huck Finn* — one of the most absurd statements in contemporary criticism. Mr. Fiedler, however, in hot pursuit of love-and-death in American literature, is guilty so often of an utterly misleading and purely sensational use of Freudian symbolism that one wonders if he is even trying to be a responsible critic. (The article on the homosexuality in *Huck Finn* was run by the *Partisan Review* as a hoax; only later did they discover that Mr. Fiedler was serious.) Here this critic has missed not only the whole point of the central relationship in the novel, but the meaning of the raft itself in terms of frontier "civilization." * Get off the raft, Leslie! — and return it to the natives.

While Huck and Jim eat supper they talk again. "We said there warn't no home like a raft, after all. Other places do seem so cramped up and smothery, but a raft don't. You feel mighty free and easy and comfortable on a raft." There is a description of a sunrise on the Mississippi, after two or three days and

---

* It should be obvious that the present writer also uses Freudian insights when they are relevant, and not when they are *not* relevant. In Mark Twain's case, within the Rankian cultural psychology, the Freudian symbols have a sometimes interesting but usually minor significance. They cannot define a culture hero such as Twain; while Rank pointed out that the Artist is not a cured or sublimated neurotic — but an artist. The difference is qualitative; it is a different kind of animal. Though it is chic for contemporary Freudians to pursue the mystery of "Art," they will never, I believe, be able to understand it within the limits of their methodology.

nights went by, timelessly, sliding along "so quiet and smooth and lovely." And we suddenly realize that *this* is the real form of *The Adventures of Huckleberry Finn*: a series of long, over-done, brutal and otherwise unpleasant forays into "civiliza-tion" (so-called), or forays of civilization onto the raft. And then the return into natural and altogether pleasurable existence, a natural existence on the blessed raft, with the "uncivilized" black slave and the delinquent and "uneducable" juvenile drop-out.

Here indeed the tone of the narrative grows more overtly and sensuously pagan, as Huck rejects even the clothing prepared for him by the frontier gentry. "So we would put in the day, lazy-ing around, listening to the stillness." There is the smell of Eden, the silence yes, the stillness, the timelessness. "We was always naked, day and night, whenever the mosquitoes would let us — the new clothes Buck's folks made for me was too good to be comfortable, and besides I didn't go much on clothes, nohow." (Another passage to offend the more tender or re-pressed sensibilities on the race question perhaps, just as Mel-ville opened another great epic of the water by having Ishmael share his bed with similar heathens and pagans.) There is the tremendous lyrical ode to the great river, defying description, in these pages of *Huck Finn*; and the necessary obeisance to the darker spirits of nature — just before the advent of the Duke and the Dauphin. Alas! The serenity and satisfaction of in-fancy and the more primitive stages of man alike, existing be-fore the cumulative repressions of societal sacrifice; the fullness of a presocial and more organic functioning (in the memories and dreams of man at least) — all is shattered again by the "comic" dregs of civilization, two coarse, cruel, and commercial scoundrels, attired with all the false trappings of English "nobil-ity."

How can Jim and Huck be taken in by these crude and vulgar practitioners of such farcical pretensions? Such, Mark Twain implied, laying it on heavy and thick, is the fate of all innocents caught in the web of civilization. But one notices another aspect of Twinship even in these raucous parodies of the Jamesian "Dream of Europe." If Clemens reversed the cultural myth quite deliberately here, he was not altogether immune to its appeal, or that of the larger racial, or biopsychic, myth which it rehearsed — the theme of the Noble Pretender (the American Claimant) — or of the ancient folk hero of disguised royalty who is here being satirized. Through these implausible frauds of the "Duke" and the "Dauphin" (as though Clemens, half realizing his own vulnerability to the concept, were even more savagely and brutally exorcising it), we are treated to another dose of southwestern pioneer culture. The terrible "theatrical performances" in the ugly halls of the hideous river towns which are at the center of *Huck Finn*'s narrative are the worst things yet. Here as in *The Gilded Age,* Clemens became the crude satirist of a crude frontier, and he anticipated the "Menckenian" tone of disgust for the boobs of the hinterland. There is the cruel trick played by the Duke who ties Jim up in the daytime to exhibit him as a captured slave, and Jim's weary reaction. "I doan' mine one or two kings, but dat's enough."

Yet Clemens rescues some of this overdone farce and heavy tedium by flashes of brilliant sophistication which, as in the "Shakespearian" reverie, predates a similar episode in an English musical satire, *Beyond the Fringe,* by over half a century:

To be, or not to be; that is the bare bodkin
That makes calamity of so long life;
For who would fardels bear, till Birnam Wood do come to Dunsinane,
But that the fear of something after death

Murders the innocent sleep,
Great nature's second course,
And makes us rather sling the arrows of outrageous fortune
Than fly to others we know not of.
There's the respect must give us pause . . .

There is another famous episode made familiar to modern audiences by Hal Holbrook's theatrical presentations, where a southern gentleman, Colonel Sherburn, routs a mob and indulges in some famous reflections about lynchings — even though we may not remember that this same southern colonel has just wantonly shot down a helpless drunkard.

After the failure of their "Shakespearian" revival with the "Arkansaw lunkheads," the Duke and Dauphin arrange an obscene "comedy" for the river towns where the Duke prances on all fours, nude. This is an obvious comparison with the idyllic nakedness of the raft, and Jim says mournfully, "But, Huck, dese kings o' ourn is reglar rapscallions; dat's jist what dey is; dey's reglar rapscallions." "All kings is mostly rapscallions, as fur as I can make out," says Huck. "Take them all around, they're a mighty ornery lot. It's the way they're raised." "But dis one do *smell* so like de nation, Huck." "Well, they all do, Jim. *We* can't help the way a king smells; history don't tell no way." And Huck adds: "What was the use to tell Jim these warn't real kings and dukes? It wouldn't 'a' done no good; and, besides, it was just as I said; you couldn't tell them from the real kind." And then Jim is miserable again at the memory of his wife and children. "I knowed what it was about. He was thinking about his wife and his children, away up yonder, and he was low and homesick . . . and I do believe he cared just as much for his people as white folks does for their'n. It don't seem natural, but I reckon it's so."

It was the whole concept of the Negro as subhuman, as animal /

— a concept assiduously cultivated by the slave-owning classes, and then the post Civil War south, and still insidiously established in the white man's psyche in the latter half of the twentieth century — that Huck's great innocent "discoveries" were being directed at in the mid 1880s.* And just as Twain's double-barreled use of the word "conscience" means with Huck only a tribal custom at first; so his hero's original use of the word "natural" meant cultural and societal. What the book reveals is Huck's discovery of both a true conscience, his own, and a true use of "natural" as being often *anti*social: a defiance of stale (or evil) customs.

The whole episode of the bewildered frontier village where the Duke and the King try to steal the fortune of the deceased Peter Wilks is poor and heavy again; but an interesting prelude to *The Man That Corrupted Hadleyburg.* Now in the alternating sequence of a beneficent nature and repressive civilization which forms the true plot structure of *Huck Finn,* and in the up-and-down sequence of a beautiful lyrical prose narrative and heavy romance-melodrama blocks of action — just here come the final reveries of that boyhood hero who chooses pagan damnation in preference to Christian virtue.

Huck does indeed write to Miss Watson that "your runaway nigger Jim is down here two mile below Pikesville, and Mr. Phelps has got him and he will give him up for the reward if you send." And he feels good "and all washed clean of sin for the

---

* See for example William Styron's *Confessions of Nat Turner* in 1968, where the author ignores the very solid possibility of Turner's black wife and children being sold away from him as another cause of his anger and revolutionary passion — and makes Turner into the kind of black sexual pervert, one who lusts for and murders a beautiful white southern lady, that a middle-class white audience would recognize with pleasure. But then, Styron's novel ignores or reverses many of the known facts about both Nat Turner and the long history of slave revolts in the South which have been recognized in Abolitionist and Negro history alike. It does express beautifully the typical fantasy life of a southern liberal — so to speak.

first time I had ever felt so in my life, and I knowed I could pray now. But I didn't do it straight off, but laid the paper down and set there thinking — thinking how good it was all this happened so, and how near I come to being lost and going to hell. And went on thinking . . ." So Clemens wrote in a burst of inspired irony, eloquence, insight:

> And got to thinking over our trip down the river; and I see Jim before me all the time: in the day and in the night-time, sometimes moonlight, sometimes storms, and we a-floating along, talking and singing and laughing. But somehow I couldn't seem to strike no places to harden me against him, but only the other kind. I'd see him standing my watch on top of his'n, 'stead of calling me, so I could go on sleeping; and see him how glad he was when I come back out of the fog; and when I come to him again in the swamp, up there where the feud was; and such-like times; and would always call me honey, and pet me, and do everything he could think of for me, and how good he always was; and at last I struck the time I saved him by telling the men we had smallpox aboard, and he was so grateful, and said I was the best friend old Jim ever had in the world, and the *only* one he's got now; and then I happened to look around and see that paper.
>
> It was a close place. I took it up, and held it in my hand. I was a-trembling, because I'd got to decide, forever, betwixt two things, and I knowed it. I studied a minute, sort of holding my breath, and then says to myself:
>
> "All right, then, I'll *go* to hell" — and tore it up.
>
> It was awful thoughts and awful words, but they was said. And I let them stay said; and never thought no more about reforming. I shoved the whole thing out of my head, and said I would take up wickedness again, which was in my line, being brung up to it, and the other warn't. And for a starter I would go to work and steal Jim out of slavery again; and if I could think up anything worse, I would do that, too; because as long as I was in, and in for good, I might as well go the whole hog.

This was the real ending of *The Adventures of Huckleberry Finn,* although the narrative, as usual, ran through another hundred pages of inferior plot sequence until Huck lighted out for the territory before Aunt Sally could adopt and civilize him again. "I can't stand it. I been there before." And this was also the conclusion of Mark Twain's first great burst of creative fiction in the 1870s and 1880s, including *The Innocents Abroad, Roughing It,* parts of *The Gilded Age, Tom Sawyer, Life on the Mississippi,* and *Huckleberry Finn* itself. And let us note now that "the river and the raft," the true theme of this period of Mark Twain's work, is by no means to be interpreted as the Freudian "return to the womb." It is indeed a "floating" — but a *floating through life,* unencumbered by society or civilization, just for the sake of living each moment, hour and day. It is that familiar dashing and floating so joyously and freely that Clemens invoked in the western stage coaches of *Roughing It,* as he unconsciously continued to use similar or the same symbolism throughout his work.

The common denominator of these early books is, of course, that idyll of "innocent" childhood and youth. Twain's accounts of the primitive yearnings of the frontier town boys for fame and glory, pleasure and excitement, may remind you of Jelly Roll Morton's descriptions of the gamblers, pimps, and musicians in the early days of New Orleans' jazz — the accent is the same, the accent of great art in its first flush of joy. Depicting the garden of boyhood in these books, the carry-over of this mood, so central to Mark Twain, was in the rest of the early works too and would remain constant during the rest of his career. And reducing all the "mature" values of ambition, competition, possession, material wealth, fame, and success to these boyhood fits of admiration, envy, rage, jealousy, yearning and emulation, scorn, trickery, revenge, Clemens displayed his deepest and central vein of edenic-satanic feeling. Life here was a cosmic kind of merriment — and this theme, this tone, this concept had never appeared before in the national letters so clearly and purely all its own.

Our adult strivings appear to be as ludicrous as they really are: mature achievement is a satiric joke. And here all the low, base, and sordid — or even evil — emotions can be openly described for what they are, since in this childhood context they are at the same time not "serious." This is Satan playing in the garden of innocence. And this "make-believe" world of infancy and childhood, of the primitive emotions, even of the animal life that Clemens described so intimately, is in fact, as in the parallel cases of William Blake and Henry Miller, to cite only two examples, a classic source of man's dreams, his psychology, his deep nostalgia, his myths, his art. Before the Fall, in this world of boyhood yearning, while "adventure," "glory," "fame" are primary things, sin is not sin, evil is not evil, cupidity is not cupidity nor is corruption corruption, and death is not yet death. The heroics and villainies of human nature are revealed more clearly just because their whole context and weight has been shifted in the "comedy" scene of childhood innocence; while all of human pretense could be stripped away by the un-blinking gaze of childhood candor. This is mock heroics, mock villainy, mock passion, mock pride, and mock despair, in a world of poetic mockery — just as Clemens told us, in the Mississippi book, how his own youthful ambition was formed.

Or notice Mark Twain's letter to Horace Bixby, the pi-lot-teacher of his youth whom he had met once more in his later trip to the river. "I didn't see half enough of you. It was a sore disappointment. Osgood could have told you, if he would — discreet old dog — I expected to have you with me *all* the time. Altogether the most pleasant part of my visit with you was after we arrived in St. Louis, and you were your old natural self again. Twenty years have not added a month to your age or taken a fraction of your loveliness . . ." In this touching epistle to the old river friend whom he had made the hero of a classic book was revealed all of Clemens' own sense of veneration, respect, awe, affection, an outgoing sense of love and concern for all human beings which is rare in our literature, which was perhaps even more "un-American" in Mark Twain's more inhibited period than in our own. This was simply another example of Sam Clemens' unique core of primary emotion, not to be subjected to any kind of niggardly Freudian "analysis."

Now obviously this is not to say that Clemens was a saint — since the range of human affection in his temperament would be matched by an equal range of anger, wrath, jealousy, vanity, or plain pique, yes and delicious malice, in what was simply a natural, open, organic, and notably unrepressed and "uncivilized" human being. In much of his later work Clemens would indeed appear, consciously and "rationally," to stress the baser human motives almost exclusively and dwell upon them in his central literary vision, and in his rages, polemics, and furious parodies of the "damned human race." He was obviously more sensitive to, and more affected by the baseness of humanity than humanity was. A good man is hurt more by badness; a loving man is more vulnerable to hatred; an innocent man (like almost all great artists in a special sense of "innocence") is more betrayed by evil. Right here was one element of Clemens' later periods of blackness, bitterness, and despairing cynicism, so puzzling to describe at times, but perhaps very simple to locate in the extent and degree of his basic human trust.

He was presently at the early peak, the golden day of his career. Paine's biography of Twain gives us the whole story of

Clemens' rescue of the bankrupt, disgraced, and dying General Ulysses S. Grant; of the publication of Grant's *Memoirs* by Mark Twain, and the book's huge success; of the royalty check of two hundred thousand dollars which Clemens delivered, after the general's death, to Grant's family. The characters of both Grant and Twain are illuminated in this extraordinary relationship; it was actually again a touching friendship, with a great admiration and respect on the part of both men. And whether Grant (like Horace Bixby?) was a "surrogate-father" figure, or not, according to the Freudians, is of singularly little importance. This was a meeting of two immortals in American history; and what really matters about Sam Clemens is that he extended his affection to the unknown river pilot just as fully as to the famous warrior.

His publishing house had a vista of immense success, including the memoirs of the other Civil War generals like McClellan, Sheridan, Wylie Crawford, and culminating with an "Authorized Life" of Pope Leo XIII, which had been contracted for in what amounted to a papal mission to Rome, in April, 1886. The fabulous Paige typesetting machine, in which he was investing half his annual income, was on the verge of success, it seemed; and Clemens — how like Balzac this native genius was — had involved himself in a dozen other deals to secure his fame and fortune as inventor, promoter, businessman, tycoon. Or was he closer to Dostoevski's "Gambler"?

His home life was never happier; his social life never more full and gay; even when he was not writing his days were bounteously full, and Clemens, like Huck, was never more fulfilled than when just "putting in the time." But he was ironic and superstitious and prophetic about his own good fortune. "I am frightened at the proportions of my prosperity. It seems to me that whatever I touch turns to gold." Or, as it would turn out, to false gold; but meanwhile Livy, too, was the best mother in the world, as Sam said, and one whose children adored her. Much as she never contented herself "with anything short of a perfect obedience," he wrote in the *Christian Union,* "they know her, and I know her, for the best and dearest mother that lives." The Clemens household was another kind of untouched nest of domestic fun and games for Jean and Clara; while Susy, the prodigy, embarked upon her celebrated biography which was kept under her pillow so conveniently for the infatuated parents to read it. Her father, she said, was a perfect figure of a man except for his teeth and his temper. In turn, Sam wrote a Lardnerian love song to Jean's donkey Cadichon —

> O du lieb' Kiditchin
> Du bist ganz bewitchin,
> Waw- - - -he!

> In summer days Kiditchin
> Thou'rt dear from nose to britchin
> War-- -- -- -he!

Life at Quarry Farm, in Elmira, included eleven cats, while Clemens rose at seven-thirty, according to Clara's diary, breakfasted at eight, wrote, played tennis with his daughters, and "tried to make the donkey go." Mrs. Clemens meanwhile had a strictly arranged day with her children in the study of languages, reading, history until after dinner when she played whist with Sam until bedtime. Clemens was nearing fifty; gray-haired, he was still a funny-looking and tiny-bodied smallish man, full of adoring worship for his beautiful and cultivated and wealthy wife. (Later his features became handsome, his own face beautiful to look at.) At his birthday there were verses by Oliver Wendell Holmes; Richard Watson Gilder made much of the affair in *The Critic;* Frank Stockton, Charles Dudley Warner, Joel Chandler Harris sent letters; Andrew Lang sent a poem. As with Howells and the New Englanders, Clemens welcomed the approval of all these fashionable literary figures of the time, among whom, in fact, he was the only first-rate talent.

His business agent, F. G. Whitmore, lived near the Hartford mansion; even their housekeeper for thirty years, Katie Leary, would eventually set down her reminiscences of this famous family . . . Years later, after Susy's early death, and the tragic deterioration of this whole so happily self-enclosed, talented, and mutually adoring family group, Clemens would brood over the broken sentence which ended Susy's diary of that period. "When I look at the arrested sentence that ends the little book it seems as if the hand that traced it cannot be far — it is gone for a moment only, and will come again and finish it. But that is a dream; a creature of the heart, not of the mind — a feeling, a longing, not a mental product; the same that lured Aaron Burr, old, gray, forlorn, forsaken, to the pier day after day, week after week, there to stand in the gloom and the chill of the dawn, gazing seaward through veiling mists and sleet and snow for the ship which he knew was gone down, the ship that bore all his treasure — his daughter." But that was to be another world of Mark Twain's, imminent but unsuspected in the eighties — when Clemens was still taken up in their Browning readings if he could not quite cotton to the Meredith cult. "It doesn't seem to me that Diana lives up to her reputation," he told Livy. "The author keeps telling us how smart she is, how brilliant, but I never seem to hear her say anything smart or brilliant. Read me some of Diana's smart utterances."

Here was Clemens' statement to Howells, paralleling and confirming the sections on the French Revolution he would write for *A Connecticut Yankee,* on the "catalytic influence" — in reverse — of Carlyle's *French Revolution* upon his own thinking. "How stunning are the changes which age makes in man while he sleeps! When I finished Carlyle's *French Revolution* in 1871 I was a Girondin; every time I have read it since I have read it differently — being influenced & changed, little by little, by life & environment (& Taine & St. Simon); & now I lay the book down once more, & recognize that I am a Sansculotte! — And not a pale, characterless Sansculotte, but a Marat. Carlyle teaches no such gospel, so the change is in *me* — in my vision of the evidence." Carlyle taught no such gospel indeed, and what is fascinating in this letter, to confound Mark Twain's critics and apologists alike, is the simple fact that this statement of radical conviction was written — as we see — just at the height and peak of Sam Clemens' worldly fame and success. Proclaiming himself a Marat Sansculotte, via the reactionary Carlyle, at this golden noon of Clemens' career — why, then, what becomes of the critical orthodoxy which holds that Mark Twain's "black despair" came out of his depths of frustration, financial loss, family pain, and suffering? That it was simply a "bitter old man," perhaps even a drunkard, who penned those brilliant, flaming, sardonic, pulsing revolutionary papers of his later period, and toward the very close of his life? What was most curious, indeed, was the exact opposite of this thesis — that Clemens' spirit was virtually untouched by his own fame, wealth, and popular success, or by his showy and extravagant way of life, or his friendships with men of great status in life, or even with the robber barons of the time who courted him so assiduously. By what remarkable and untoward streak of genius, what innate perversity of feeling, so to say, or originality of vision was it that the more successful Samuel Clemens was, the more rebellious, radical, or revolutionary in essence his inner spirit became!

It was actually the "river and the raft" — that sweet spirit of the garden, infancy, and childhood untouched by the temptations and corruptions of civilization — which saved him. Like Huck, he could not seem to abide conventional American civilization. He had no use for this kind of schooling and "learning," and would rather put in his time loafing and playing, searching his soul, and thinking his own private thoughts. Social fame, success, respectability were all right in their place. But he had been there.

FOUR

FAILURE AND TRIUMPH

THERE IS NO question that the decade of the nineties was one of trauma and disaster in Mark Twain's life, financially and domestically. It did indeed *appear* to split his life in two; and life for him would never be the same again. Yet he emerged on the other side of the chasm bloody and beaten in spirit, but unconquered — unconquerable. He had added a dimension of tragic experience to his unique sense of the general comedy of living. The memory of the Garden entails the knowledge of the Fall.

The life of his imagination would take on more complex, darker hues of emotion; his own judgment of his social period and country became sharper and brilliantly prophetic; in the first decade of the twentieth century he wrote one of his greatest books, *The Autobiography of Mark Twain* — one of the great books of our literature. In the last half of his life, indeed, Sam Clemens produced some of his best writing — much of it newly released to the public eye — and the whole thesis of his being a childhood writer destroyed by the pressures of maturity falls to the ground. In terms of a broad cultural psychology, rather, he was a writer who carried his edenic vision of life to the very end; and it was precisely that vision, embedded in his deepest spirit, untouchable, uncorruptible, which *created* his whole remarkable description of our human pilgrimage undertaken amidst so much laughter and so many tears.

But meanwhile the mounting financial crisis of the late eighties was reflected in the uneven writing of *A Connecticut Yankee in King Arthur's Court,* in 1889, and in its divided or even contradictory theme. Was it written as a justification of "the living, tearing, booming Nineteenth, the mightiest of all centuries"? Clemens' description of his own period was not without equivocation, as the book itself was full of ambivalence. It was interesting that he invoked his memories of the Sandwich Isles, "that peaceful land, that beautiful land" as an earthly haven and paradise which he remembered so vividly from a visit of twenty-three years ago.

> That far-off home of solitude, and soft idleness, and repose and dreams, where life is one long slumberous Sabbath, the climate one long summer day, and the good that die experience no change, for they but fall asleep in one heaven and wake up in another . . . No alien land in all the earth has any deep, strong charm for me but that one; no other land could so longingly and so beseechingly haunt me, sleeping and waking, through half a lifetime as that one has done . . .

But was it an "alien land," or was it more likely Sam Clemens' true home? — as the natural genius of the latter nineteenth century would find himself increasingly alienated from his own pushing, tearing, booming, materialistic American society.

That was the hidden conflict in the *Connecticut Yankee,* and the main reason for the book's confused structure. It is true that just before it, enraged by what he felt to be a hostile and unperceptive critical reception of his work, and increasingly torn between the glittering diversions and the mounting anxieties of his lavish career, Clemens had *said* he wanted to retire permanently from literature — and pass "to the cemetery unclodded." But that was the anger of genius, the mask of a prophet; in his heart he had known from the start that he would be a writer, and a writer he was until the last day of his life. He had written the *Yankee* in great bursts of savage energy between his other affairs at the time, and the story also showed its hasty and careless composition. Cast in the Arthurian landscape of sixth-century England, the novel was a curious hodgepodge of juvenile romance (a sort of sequel to *The Prince and the Pauper*), of a burlesque plot line often exaggerated and tedious, of heavy satire — and of great, eloquent passages of social and historical commentary which are still remarkably fresh today.

The hero was a New England mechanic-superman who had returned to the year 528 in the Arthurian court. Clemens did not bother to make this hero any more credible or sympathetic — it is a question of whether he wanted to — than the primitive feudal nobility he satirized here, and who reflected so coarsely his readings in Sir Thomas Malory's "enchanting book." "You soon saw that brains were not needed in a society like that," says the Yankee — but since when had Sam Clemens, the poet of human feeling, cared so much for the rational power of science? In real life, of course, he was in a state of momentary intoxication with his fabulous typesetter — and increasing hatred of it.

The book's opening makes much of the "childlike" nature of the Arthurian court, the dirt and coarseness of life there, the open and frank bawdiness of the conversation, while the

Yankee struggles with the magician Merlin for the supreme power in the kingdom through a series of "scientific" miracles. What is curious, of course, is that Clemens, always so much at home with primitive life and people, did not bring over this insight to Arthurian legend; he was probably too obsessed by his message of radical democracy in the *Yankee* and the evils of monarchy.

In a satanic fantasy of Twain's, his hero becomes the "Boss" of early or prefeudal England. How this artist varied between dreams of omnipotence and visions, satirical and terrifying, of total impotence, failure, and destruction! But just as we almost lose patience with the opening sections of the book, we meet those great passages of personal utterance which do indeed, in the pages of the *Connecticut Yankee,* redeem everything else in the story. The middle Mark Twain, still believing in his vision of ideal democracy, and using his radical democratic critique — far from the "socialism" that Albert Bigelow Paine deplores in hushed tones — on the feudal nobility and the church, on monarchy and the whole European social structure, was very eloquent. In a curious way he reminds us, nostalgic, heartwarming, and lyrical as he sounds today, of *our* past. Our national past.

It was pitiful for a person born in a wholesome free atmosphere to listen to their humble and hearty outpourings of loyalty toward their king and Church and nobility; as if they had any more occasion to love and honor king and Church and noble than a slave has to love and honor the lash, or a dog has to love and honor the stranger that kicks him! Why, dear me, *any* kind of royalty, howsoever modified, *any* kind of aristocracy, howsoever pruned, is rightly an insult . . . It is enough to make a body ashamed of his race to think of the sort of froth that has always occupied its thrones without a shadow of right or reason, and the seventh-rate people that have always figured as its aristocracies — a company of monarchs and nobles who, as a rule, would have achieved only poverty and obscurity if left, like their betters, to their own exertions.

Nor is it any reflection on these sentiments to add that Sam Clemens himself basked, like any provincial westerner, in the glow of the European nobility who happened to admire his work. It is imperative to realize about this special spirit, as we have just noticed, that Clemens' personal life, for good or bad, his personal fame, success, glory, or failure, his grand virtues and his flamboyant faults, hardly seemed to affect the secret, inner core of his genius living its own private, sheltered, wayward, and inspired existence. "The most of King Arthur's British nation," he added here, "were slaves, pure and simple, and bore that name, and wore the iron collar on their necks; and the rest were slaves in fact, but without the name; they imagined themselves men and freemen, and called themselves so. The truth was, the nation as a body was in the world for one object, and one only: to grovel before king and Church and noble; to slave for them, sweat blood for them, starve that they might be fed, work that they might play, drink misery to the dregs that they might be happy, go naked that they might wear silks and jewels, pay taxes that they might be spared from paying them, be familiar all their lives with the degrading language and postures of adulation that they might walk in pride and think themselves the gods of this world . . ."

Despite the uneasy narrative line in the book, the broad and often flat farce, the somewhat paranoid fantasy of the superman mechanic in a world of feudal oafs, the improbable characters who were fashioned out of the Arthurian legends, and the cheap humor of their depiction — Sam Clemens was beginning to wake up in *A Connecticut Yankee,* was gradually rousing his talent and his temper. Just as he had intuitively sensed the restrictive and exploitative purpose of the Christian missionaries in the South Sea Islands (and how much more so, he would discover, in Africa, Asia, China, where the figure of Jesus became the sign of racial oppression), so now he knew the historical role of the medieval Church.

> In two or three centuries it had converted a nation of men to a nation of worms. Before the day of the Church's supremacy in the world, men were men and held their heads up, and had a man's pride and spirit and independence; and what of greatness and position a person got, he got mainly by achievement, not by birth. But then the Church came to the front with an ax to grind; and she was wise, subtle, and knew more than one way to skin a cat — or a nation; she invented "divine right of things," and propped it all around, brick by brick, with the Beatitudes — wrenching them from their good purpose to make them fortify an evil one; she preached (to the commoner) meakness under insult; preached (still to the commoner, always to the commoner) patience, meanness of spirit, non-resistance under oppression; and she introduced heritable ranks and aristocracies, and taught all the Christian populations of the earth to bow down to them and worship them.

Was this poison still in the blood of Christendom right down to the days of Mark Twain's own birth, as he said? Was the taint of that reverence for rank and title in the American blood too? — even more in the age of a new and brazen financial "aristocracy" seeking patents of Old World nobility for its primitive and barbarous use of social power. And pawning and manipulating its "innocent young maidens," of the Jamesian fantasy, in order to inveigle and trap and bind securely a decadent and bankrupt European nobility in a kind of international con game whose final victors and victims were difficult to tell apart.

Well, as he added, it just seemed to show "that there isn't

anything you can't stand, if you are only born and bred to it"
— and he continued his discussion of the so-called English
"freeman."

"By a sarcasm of law and phrase they were freemen. Seven-
tenths of the free-population of the country were of just their
class and degree; small 'independent' farmers, artisans, etc.;
which is to say they were the nation, the actual Nation; they
were about all of it that was useful, or worth saving, or really
respectworthy, and to subtract them would have been to subtract the Nation and leave behind some dregs, some refuse, in
the shape of a king, nobility and gentry, idle, unproductive, acquainted mainly with the arts of wasting and destroying . . ."
And then there came the famous passages on the French Revolution, so reviled and misinterpreted in Clemens' day and even
more in our own period. "Why, it was like reading about France
and the French before the ever memorable and blessed Revolution, which swept a thousand years of such villainy away in one
swift tidal wave of blood — one: a settlement of that hoary
debt in the proportion of half a drop of blood for each hogshead
of it that had been pressed by slow tortures out of that people in
the weary stretch of ten centuries of wrong and shame and misery the like of which was not to be mated but in hell. There
were two 'Reigns of Terror,' if we would but remember it and
consider it; the one wrought murder in hot passion, the other
in heartless cold blood; the one lasted mere months, the other
had lasted a thousand years; the one inflicted death upon ten
thousand persons, the other upon a hundred millions; but our
shudders are all for the 'horrors' of the minor Terror, the momentary Terror, so to speak; whereas, what is the horror of
swift death by the ax compared with lifelong death from hunger,
cold, insult, cruelty, and heartbreak? What is swift death by
lightning compared with death by slow fire at the stake? A city

cemetery could contain the coffins filled by that brief Terror which we have all been so diligently taught to shiver at and mourn over; but all France could hardly contain the coffins filled by that older and real Terror — that unspeakable bitter and awful Terror which none of us has been taught to see in its vastness or pity as it deserves."

A cogent indictment of history both past and present in these passages of fiery eloquence on the ever memorable and "blessed Revolution"; passages which enliven and make bearable the tedious plot narrative which Clemens strung out to contain such reflections on history, society, and the sacred institutions of civilization. No wonder that the English nation did not receive the *Yankee* with great plaudits. Or that the United States itself, just then turning away from its own republican heritage of the American Revolution and turning back, as I say, to all the trappings and perquisites of a foundering European nobility — that those privileged and "cultivated" circles of American society also looked with disdain and fear upon such subversive principles and such incendiary talk!

To compound this injury, Clemens insisted upon bringing over his lesson directly to his own period. "You see my kind of loyalty was loyalty to one's country, not to its institutions or its office-holders. The country is the real thing, the substantial thing, the eternal thing; it is the thing to watch over, and care for, and be loyal to; institutions are extraneous, they are its mere clothing, and clothing can wear out, become ragged, cease to be comfortable, cease to protect the body from winter, disease, and death. To be loyal to rags, to shout for rags, to worship rags, to die for rags — that is a loyalty of unreason; it is pure animal; it belongs to monarchy; let monarchy keep it." Were Samuel Clemens' republican impulses still perhaps local, partial, and restricted to an ideal country or democratic nation, a fortunate and cultivated part of humanity as a whole; while the family of man is superior to any particular and usually prejudicial patriotism? He was only midway in his process of artistic self-education; and he shared Whitman's optimistic illusions of America, which were not at base invidious, or partisan in essence; and Clemens was approaching a larger and grander vista of history as a whole. "I was from Connecticut, whose Constitution declares 'that all political power is inherent in the people, and all free governments are founded on their authority and instituted for their benefit; and that they have *at all times* an undeniable and indefeasible right to *alter their form of government* in such a manner as they may think expedient.' "

He was turning Carlyle's doctrine of "clothes" upon its head. What impudence and bad taste to recall these revolutionary origins to an established nation embarked upon a new course of commercialism which had no other concern with democratic principles than to exploit, corrupt, and control them for its own profit and privilege. And already sensing this new condition of affairs, Mark Twain went on to espouse the duty of the rebellious minority *to* rebel. "Under that gospel, the citizen who thinks he sees that the commonwealth's political clothes are worn out, and yet holds his peace and does not agitate for a new suit, is disloyal; he is a traitor. That he may be the only one who thinks he sees this decay, does not excuse him; it is his duty to agitate anyway." Harkening back to the inner voice of the Transcendentalists and their political heirs, the Abolitionists of the earlier nineteenth century, and the revolutionary activists of the pre-Civil War period, thus Mark Twain spoke to the burgeoning epoch of the Robber Barons and the Politicos; thus he spoke to a later age of the Cold War demagoguery and various modes of McCarthyism. Invigorating words! while the Yankee went on to declare that his Sandy was a "daisy," and to describe as "cowboys" such illustrious knights as Sir Launcelot, Sir Pellinore, Sir Carados, and others. These cowboys later became sandwich men to advertise the Yankee's nineteenth-century miracles; and there is another not very entertaining episode about the half sister of King Arthur, Morgan le Fay, who was a medieval sorceress. In the uneven texture of the *Connecticut Yankee* this peculiar plot line contained other brilliant passages on the hypocrisy of man's spirit in those far-off days.

> I will say this for the nobility: that, tyrannical, murderous, rapacious and morally rotten as they were, they were deeply and enthusiastically religious. Nothing could divert them from the regular and faithful performance of the pieties enjoined by the Church. More than once I had seen a noble who had gotten his enemy at a disadvantage, stop to pray before cutting his throat; more than once I had seen a noble, after ambushing and despatching his enemy, retire to the nearest wayside shrine and humbly give thanks, without even waiting to rob the body.

Clemens was not much more helpful on the feudal ladies who all needed a bath, he claimed, who were foul-mouthed, intoxicated, and cruel, and reminded him of nothing so much as a bunch of Comanche squaws. The Twainian panorama of feudal society moved on to the law, as well as religion, to medieval forms of torture and slavery, while the heroic Yankee was developing the toothbrush and stove polish, if, alas, there had been any stoves, and again reflected upon the hopeless passivity of the sixth-century masses. "To wit, that this dreadful matter brought from these downtrodden people no outburst of rage against these oppressors. They had been heritors and subjects of cruelty and outrage so long that nothing could have startled them but a kindness."

Like Clemens, the Yankee abhors cruelty and is bothered by

his conscience, even while he realizes that compassion does not create revolutions. "For it could not help bringing up the un-get-aroundable fact that, all gentle cant and philosophizing to the contrary notwithstanding, no people in the world ever did achieve their freedom by goody-goody talk and moral suasion: it being immutable law that all revolutions that will succeed must *begin* in blood, whatever may answer afterward. If history teaches anything, it teaches that. What this folk needed, then, was a Reign of Terror and a guillotine, and I was the wrong man for them." This was again the objectivity of Clemens, the self-knowledge; in this case the separation of his own temperament from what his mind and heart knew as truth, and the acceptance of that truth — and what more can you really demand from an artist than this open vision of history and his own temperament alike? If Mark Twain still derived from that epoch of an earlier bourgeois society which did not scorn revolution and bloodshed for gaining its purposes — which did not yet fear all social change as a loss of its own power and property — he did not also, in such radical propensities, falsify his own nature, nor overmuch credit his own capacities. "You can't reason with your heart; it has its own laws, and thumps about things which the intellect scorns."

Yet, for an ignorant youth of the southwestern frontier, he had somehow become a self-made Abolitionist.* The middle and later sections of *A Connecticut Yankee* are almost obsessively concerned with a feudal slavery which was certainly not without reference to Twain's own historical period — and the postbellum slavery apologists and newly militant racists who were just then about to reimpose the yoke of white suprem-

---

* Of course Livy's family, the Langdons, were Abolitionists and had been active in the Underground Railway of Civil War days. But even here, Sam Clemens had apparently worked out his own conclusions about slavery very early in his career.

acy upon the "reconstructed South." A far-fetched analogy?
Well, listen to Sam Clemens confirming it. "This was depressing — to a man with the dream of a republic in his head," he
said about the apathy of the feudal slaves.

It reminded me of a time thirteen centuries away when the "poor
whites" of our South who were always despised and frequently
insulted by the slave-lords around them, and who owed their base
conditions simply to the presence of slavery in their midst, were yet
pusillanimously ready to side with the slave-lords in all political
moves for the upholding and perpetuating of slavery, and did also
finally shoulder their muskets and pour out lives in an effort to prevent the destruction of that very institution which degraded them.

Many or most poor-whites, yes; but Clemens had not yet
heard of, and would certainly have applauded the martial virtue of those black slaves — unmasked at last from their Uncle
Tomism — who actually turned the tide of battle in the Civil
War. But now let us note that if *A Connecticut Yankee in King
Arthur's Court* opened in defense of the busy, bustling, scientific,
commercial, and industrialized nineteenth century as the last, best
hope in man's history, there was also a curious kind of underground conflict in both the book and Mark Twain's view of the
book. This was a conflict between the public Twain and the
private Clemens; and the concluding section of this literary satire
on feudal ignorance and superstition is curiously ambiguous,
dark-hued, contradictory and destructive. If the basic vision of
the middle Mark Twain was that of a bold, open, tough, and
radical republicanism, of an older American democracy, as we
have seen, this book marked a turning point not merely in his
personal fortunes and personal temperament, as Mr. Kaplan et al.
would have it, but in something much larger: In Mark Twain's
increasing disenchantment with his own American society — that

society, in short, which was already rejecting all his own agrarian democratic and libertarian beliefs. Intended as a lesson about feudalism and monarchy for the democracy, the *Yankee* ended as a lesson about democracy to Mark Twain himself.

Moreover, even at the start of this mixed chronicle, Sam Clemens was far more sympathetic than he appeared to be with the pagan-plenary mind of the sixth century which he was satirizing — and he was far less sympathetic at base with that nineteenth-century materialistic money society which he was ostensibly defending.

There are, at any rate, very curious episodes and passages in the last sections of *A Connecticut Yankee*. Were such figures as Gutenberg, Watt, Arkwright, Whitney, Morse, Stephenson, Bell the true creators of this world — after God — to the Yankee mechanic? It was a curious listing for Mark Twain, including God. The Yankee himself, this scientific superman with his monomaniacal and paranoidal visions of a "Bossism" based on the magic of nineteenth-century inventions, is a particularly tedious hero for the creator of Tom Sawyer and Huck Finn; or for the central narrator of *Roughing It* and *Life on the Mississippi*. During the disguised king's voyages with the Yankee guide, savage mobs of ignorant peasants become just as distasteful as the slave-masters who burn up women and children for their own warmth and comfort. A young mother and her babe are killed for stealing because of their hunger, while, in a holiday of hellions, a mob of men, women, and children rejoice in the spectacle of her suffering. This whole vista of antique injustice and social barbarism becomes a curious panorama of horrors.

There is civil war in Camelot; the nobility is destroyed; the Church declares a Holy Crusade against the Yankee, who, along with his trusted Clarence and fifty-two loyal boys, is then besieged and imprisoned in a "fortress" which resembles a primitive kind of concentration camp. They have constructed electrical fences which will destroy the feudal knights on their horses at contact. In the fort's inner circle they group a battery of thirteen Gatling guns, protected by the "prettiest garden that was ever planted" — that is, planted with torpedo bombs which explode upon contact.

It was a haunting bit of unconsciousness that made Sam Clemens fall back upon the familiar garden image at the end of a civilization. Nor is Twain's prophetic gift to be altogether scorned in even the poorest flights of his fancy. The last chapters of this lurid chronicle may still remind us today of some harried "preparation" for a nuclear attack. The Yankee orders all factories and homes abandoned, all life removed to "some safe place," since everything is going to be destroyed by his secret bombs. There is a scene in the book where the massed feudal armies attacking the fortress are destroyed. And then as the next step — "I touched a button and shook the bones of England loose from her spine! In that explosion all our noble civilization-factories went up in the air and disappeared from the earth. It was a pity, but it was necessary . . ."

But necessary for whom, or what? This was in fact a horrid ending for Mark Twain's comic satire on feudal civilization. It was a curious conclusion for all the "miracles" of modern civilization: miracles which here, just as they would in later history, culminated in horrifying scenes of mass destruction. The dark fantasy of civilizational collapse was the nightmarish finale to all the nineteenth century's hopes for material achievement, prosperity, and "progress." If *A Connecticut Yankee in King Arthur's Court* is highly uneven, a deeply ambiguous, and often a tedious and haphazard literary production, we must still notice those penetrating and ebullient statements of radical democracy which have been quoted here; and after them, those deeply destructive and pessimistic visions of a purely commercial and material "success" society. The total obliteration of the factories, or the nation's economy, this was a desolate ending for Sam Clemens' mechanical superman. The fantasy of mass killing by scientific machines, of instantaneous destruction had superseded the earlier dream of mass education, physical and material prosperity, intellectual liberation, and spiritual freedom in Arthurian England.

If the *Connecticut Yankee* was partly intended as a juvenile adventure tale with a high moral purpose, in Clemens' uneasy focus on the book, this was hardly an edifying conclusion for eager young minds. The literary establishment of Mark Twain's time which had viewed with distaste the idyllic splendor of *Huck Finn* had here perhaps a better object of protest. At the book's close, the modern hero and his small band of confederates are surrounded by walls upon walls of dead bodies — and by a desolate countryside where the garden of feudal England had flourished.

There is no doubt, of course, that those visions and fantasies of horrible destruction had come partly from Clemens' personal life, as reflected also in the dream life which he used so openly and fully in his work. And indeed the thought of his own destruction translated into the terms of mass destruction and social suicide was only the opposite side of that coin whereby Clemens also identified his own joys and pleasures with nature itself: his primary narcissism in the mythic sense. The state of his personal ego, as a true folk bard, was hardly distinct from the world around him, transmuted into both nature and society. The whole secret of Sam Clemens is right here again in the natural (or "animal") fusion of his own identity with the landscape he occupied; as distinct from a later race of "artists" who deliber-

ately set themselves apart from their society and culture, to become "alienated," "thinking," and "superior" individuals. (But
it is safe to say that American literature as a whole until 1910,
say, was a folk art when compared with the work of the modern
group of expatriated individuals whether at home or abroad.)
If the nineties were a crisis period for Mark Twain, and there
were dry years and bad books, what was remarkable was not the
sorrow and silence but the swiftness of his recovery; and in the
midst of the later domestic tragedies, his refuge, as with all writers, was in the solace of writing itself. What is curious is how
the critics of his collapse — his breakdown, his split career, his
return to childhood, and his escape, above all, from contemporary
American society into the past (!) — all following in each other's footsteps, mouthing the same truisms, have managed to ignore or distort Clemens' mature and later works in order to
follow their fashionable and herdlike theory.

But *The American Claimant,* in 1892, was one of these poorer
or bad works, a novel or novelette which Clemens attempted
to salvage from a poor play he and Howells had written jointly
in another attempt to exploit the popular hero of *The Gilded
Age.* Colonel Sellers is the perennial get-rich-quick entrepreneur of the period, whose fantastical schemes and follies Clemens had originated and then shared. But the play had been a
failure, the novel was tedious, and the character of Sellers himself suffered a comedown from the original projection.

With the death of a certain Simon Lathers in Arkansas, Mulberry Sellers (Beriah in the novel) has established himself as the
American claimant of the Rossmore estate in England. In turn
the young English lord of the story, the son of Earl Rossmore,
relinquishes his hereditary privileges in order to come to the
States and experience a more democratic form of life. These
two central figures in the plot line become involved with each

other through a series of improbable events. The young Vis-
count Berkeley, under his assumed American name of Howard
Tracy, falls in love with Sally Sellers, hailed by her grandilo-
quent father as the "Lady Gwendolyn." There follows a rather
tedious and complicated romance in which the two "branches"
of the Rossmore family are united, while the somewhat heavy
satire in the novel about both the British aristocracy and American democracy finds a sentimental and theatrical resolution.
The play-novel has some interest as another reflection of the prevailing mythology of the Robber Baron period, but Clemens'
(or Howells') parody of this theme was marked by an uncertain
tone of Anglo-American snobbery. (Henry James also wrote an
early and solemn variation on "the American Claimant" idea.)
It almost seemed as though the American landscape was populated by disinherited or unacknowledged British gentry.

Another familiar character from *The Gilded Age,* "Marse
Washington Hawkins," was also exhumed from the literary
grave for this fiasco of Twain's, and the colored couple who are
the loyal domestics of Sellers in *The American Claimant* are
dreadful stereotypes of ex-slaves. Infatuated with the stage
much as Henry James was, and as Howells was, Clemens was
just as crude and careless in preparing his work for this popular
but treacherous medium. If one can guess from the internal
evidence of the book, the account of the young Lord Rossmore
plunged into a lower-class American existence (with slight so-
cialistic overtones, and a barely concealed aversion to working-
class life) was written by Howells; the Sellers-Hawkins narrative
was written by Clemens; but in any case, the net result was unfortunate. In the same year of 1892, *Merry Tales,* a collection
for the most part of mediocre magazine articles and sketches,
contained Clemens' account of his Civil War experiences, "The
Private History of a Campaign That Failed." Now Mr. Kaplan

makes much of this article again as a kind of Freudian expiation of Twain's guilt about his role in the Civil War. Of course
such statements have an element of truth; the real question is
that of actual content and tone, of an *overt,* as well as latent
meaning. The "Campaign That Failed" hardly supports such
charges — in fact, disproves them.

In the summer of 1861 Missouri was invaded by Union
forces, and Sam Clemens joined a group of young men from
Hannibal, Marion County, in forming the Marion Rangers, in
answer to the Governor's call for fifty thousand militia to repel
the invader. Before that, Clemens had wavered between his
Union sympathies and his southern heritage; when the secession
atmosphere thickened on the Lower Mississippi, he became a
rebel. The whole tone of this account is somewhat reminiscent
of Stephen Crane's *The Red Badge of Courage* — of ignorant
young farmers and uncertain battle — except that Clemens projected what Crane lacked: a familiar sense of the common life,
of adolescent ambition and glory, of folk humor. With a Huck
Finn tone, this was an engaging story of old-fashioned, back-
woods kids who all innocently and ignorantly had banded together for the romantic defense of "homeland" and feats of martial prowess. This is a fine narrative of country bumpkins who
had the native good sense to avoid the Union forces whom they
were ostensibly seeking out. "Well, this herd of cattle started
for war," Clemens said, after describing the composition of the
group in vivid terms. "What could you expect of them? They
did as well as they knew how; but, really, what was justly to be
expected of them? Nothing, I should say. That is what they
did."

But in the process of doing nothing, some extraordinary
things happened to this group of amateur warriors. There is the
windy and patriotic speech by Colonel Rolls, veteran of the

Mexican War, which opens their martial career. This little
sketch, indeed in its curiously innocent and gambolsome way, is
one of the best early antiwar documents that Mark Twain wrote:
By making war into such a pleasant and hilarious game, it
suggests all the horror and absurdity of war. Note the lyrical
background, as in the great river-tale itself. The shady and
pleasant piece of woods near the flowery prairie was "an enchanting region for war — our kind of war." Always brilliant
about animals, as far back as *The Innocents Abroad,* the young
Sam Clemens discovered his first mortal enemy in the Civil War
combat was a very small mule which threw him off whenever he
sat on it; and there is a comical description of the various horses
which constituted the mobile equipment of the youthful cavalry
unit. "Sergeant Bowers' horse was very large and tall, with slim,
long legs, and looked like a railroad bridge. His size enabled
him to reach all about, and as far as he wanted to with his head;
so he was always biting Bowers' legs. On the march, in the sun,
Bowers slept a good deal; and as soon as the horse recognized
that he was asleep he would reach around and bite him on the
leg."

There was a crisis of command among the Marion Rangers.
Nobody would cook, there was no dinner, nobody wished to be
an orderly, and they all knew each other too well in civilian life
to take orders from anybody. "The commander of an ignorant
crew like that," said Sam Clemens in straight face, "has many
troubles and vexations which probably do not occur in the regular army at all." Still, they got along in their frontier democracy manner which was not unlike Huck's raft; and they slept
well, guarded by their horses. Again the plenary note is sounded
in this idyll of the Civil War frontier. "For a time life was idly
delicious, it was perfect, there was nothing to mar it" — until,
one day, some farmers brought them alarming news, and there

was the problem of "retreating." (That was their main problem, strategic or tactical — not to retreat *toward* the enemy.) But in their panic they were captured by the dogs of the Mason farm.

> And then before we could open our mouths to give the countersign, several dogs came bounding over the fence, with great riot and noise, and each of them took a soldier by the slack of his trousers and began to back away with him. We could not shoot the dogs without endangering the persons they were attached to; so we had to look on helpless at what was perhaps the most mortifying spectacle of the Civil War.

Humor, yes. Guilt, no! But that is not to say, toward the end of Mark Twain's parody of the Civil War, that darker shades are not present in this amoral and youthful chronicle of the frontier "soldiery." There is a crucial episode when Sam Clemens is persuaded that he has shot an innocent stranger. "The thought of him got to preying upon me every night; I could not get rid of it. I could not drive it away, the taking of that unoffending life seemed such a wanton thing. And it seemed an epitome of war; that all war must be just that — the killing of strangers against whom you feel no personal animosity; strangers whom, in other circumstances, you would help if you found them in trouble, and who would help you if you needed it. My campaign was spoiled. It seemed to me that I was not rightly equipped for this awful business; that war was intended for men, and I for a child's nurse. I resolved to retire from this avocation of sham soldiership while I could save some remnant of my self-respect."

But wasn't this a Huck Finn statement of the true human feeling about all war and all killing — before that sentiment has been perverted and distorted by social institutions, or by the pressures of adult "maturity." The shadow of the *real* Civil War fell upon the whole company of Marion Rangers, and they decided to disband. "Our boys went apart and consulted; then we went back and told the other companies present that the war was a disappointment to us, and we were going to disband." About half of the group, including Clemens, decided to leave; half stayed through the war; and it was years later that Mark Twain discovered (or concluded) that the Union colonel whom they had been avoiding was Ulysses S. Grant. Now if "A Campaign That Failed" still appears in any degree to be Freudian exorcism, even in part, one can only wish that literature had more of such subterfuges. In art as in life, the question of cause is always interesting; but what counts is the *effect,* as merely psychological critics do not always realize. "A Campaign That Failed" is in fact one of Mark Twain's most interesting bits of early fiction in its lyrical evocation of a boys' war in a frontier society.

The rest of the volume called *Merry Tales* included another satirical antiwar story, "Luck," about an incredibly stupid English general who rose to great fame. (Later, during an English visit, Clemens met the real-life prototype of this character and found himself slowly falling backwards.) "A Curious Experience" was an odd tale about a fake spy in a New England fortress during the Civil War. There were other journalistic sketches, and another memorable "set piece" (probably used in lecturing) in which Clemens relates his experiences while acting as his own courier — to save expense — on a trip from Aix-les-Bains to Geneva which I only wish I had some reason to include here. "The £1,000,000 Bank-Note," published in 1893 and also inserted in a later edition of *Merry Tales,* was a trick tale of a young American who was given a fabulous sum of money as part of a betting proposition between two British financiers. It is another ironic parable of unexpected (and undeserved) wealth; and it is interesting to notice how many other stories by Mark Twain in the early nineties dealt with various aspects of this theme. The get-rich-quick mania was the central folk myth of the period; and wasn't Samuel Clemens himself an example of this historical American dream — or nightmare? This was the period of boom and depression in steady succession; of financial wizardry and fiscal legerdemain; of the great Wall Street battles for control, power and manipulation of the new corporations, combines, and monopolies. It was the period of our "interior colonization," so to speak — the development of the internal American empire which, having devoured the enormous wealth of one continent, would soon stretch out its claws for tempting foreign treats. The dominance of this new tribe of cunning, ruthless, unscrupulous, and amoral financial titans and tycoons would change the whole nature of American life as Sam Clemens had known it. In another sense his work may be interpreted as half a lyrical recall of the past, and half an angry, bitter, savage attack on contemporary American society and what he called the future "monarchy" or dictatorship.

But meanwhile he too had shared all the comforts and luxury and material conveniences of sudden wealth on his part, inherited wealth on Livy's part, and now he was suddenly about to taste all the ignoble, sordid, and harrowing consequences of the reverse side — the sudden bankruptcies in this gaudy epoch of primitive finance capitalism — of this negative proposition of the late nineteenth-century American historical scene. At the peak of his own private Gilded Age, Clemens had filled the Hartford mansion with illustrious guests from all over the world. Deserting the Republican party on principle, as a Mugwump, he was intimate with President Cleveland. He associated with such celebrities as Augustin Daly, Edwin Booth, John Drew, the dramatic critic Brander Matthews, and the architect Stanford White. He knew Andrew Carnegie, Jay Gould, Thomas Edison, Whitelaw Reid of the New York *Tribune,* and the Com-

stock millionaire John Mackay who was just then trying to
break the Goulds' monopoly in Western Union. Most of these
figures would be described in Clemens' later essays on the American ruling class, or in his *Autobiography*; these reflections form
a remarkable chapter in American literature.

He had helped to form the New York City Players Club,
among a score of other dazzling projects of the time. But now,
toward the mid-nineties, everything collapsed on Clemens.

Since 1880 he had been intrigued and entranced by the fabulous commercial possibilities of the Paige typesetting machine
which was being developed at the Colt Arms Factory in Connecticut. The machine was spectacular, always on the edge of
being perfect, and finally doomed both in itself and because of
the superior Mergenthaler linotyper being perfected at the same
time. The inventor, James W. Paige of Rochester, New York,
was a near-genius — either a notorious idealist or a consum-
mate rogue about the commercial exploitation of his machine —
and Clemens, composing lyrical paeans of praise for the divine
monster, was being sucked in for huge amounts of cash. By
1886 he was a half-partner with Paige in the machine's parent
company and had spent over thirteen thousand dollars; a year
later, in 1887, it had cost him over fifty thousand dollars —
which was a mere bagatelle when compared with things to come.
The cost of developing the machine was averaging three thousand dollars a month by December, 1887, and Clemens was using both his money and Livy's inherited fortune. He was drain-
ing his own publishing house of cash, and destroying the health
and nerves of the already sick and neurotic Charles Webster, his
nephew-in-law publisher. (The descriptions of Paige and Webster in the *Autobiography* are hilarious; like every artist Clemens
had the last word on life.) The much heralded Webster and
Company's *Life of Leo XIII* did not do well, in both Paine's and

Kaplan's accounts of this period; Henry Ward Beecher's autobiography was never finished. The other memoirs by the
Civil War generals surrounding Grant began to clutter up the
list. It really is a question if Webster was so arrogant, stupid,
and pretentious as Clemens believed him to be; he probably was.
At any rate he resigned, and while the new manager, Fred Hall,
continued to send Clemens optimistic reports, by 1888 the publishing house, too, was in financial straits.

In 1889 Clemens became the sole owner of the Paige typesetter, in return for paying the glossy inventor $160,000, and
$25,000 a year for seventeen years; and he had already paid
out $150,000 for the machine since 1885 — sheer phobic ob-
session and insanity. He was caught; he was hooked in that steel
cage which he later envisioned Paige as dying in, while he
watched. By 1890, Clemens was borrowing money from Livy's
mother, and other members of the family, as Kaplan tells us.
He was trying desperately — and sometimes almost on the brink
of succeeding, when the machine went wrong again — to raise
money from such old friends and acquaintances as another mining millionaire, Senator John P. Jones of Nevada; he invoked
visions of Andrew Carnegie and the Standard Oil trust coming
in on the world exploitation of the fabulous and diseased machine. In 1891, nearing the end, the Hartford mansion was
closed up, the furniture sold, and the servants, after seventeen
years, dismissed.* The Clemens family went on a European
visit of eight years in order to economize; both Sam's and Livy's

---

* Clemens had originally built the Hartford house (for over one hundred
thousand dollars) in the "Nook Farm" community of artists and intellectuals
with an Abolitionist heritage, a bristling women's rights movement, and a
radical hue — until the community was gradually taken over by more respectable and mediocre figures like Charles Dudley Warner . . . Toward the end,
Harriet Beecher Stowe, symbol of the original colony along with her free-
thinking sister, Isabella Beecher Hooker, could be seen wandering among the
handsome houses like a mad ghost.

health began to break down. They were facing the claims of creditors and threats of bankruptcy. Clemens was making a series of hasty and harried Atlantic crossings between Europe and the United States in order to avoid this — when the stock-market crash, and a succession of railroad and business failures, brought about the great depression of 1893–94.

By the time of the final blow, Sam Clemens had lost almost two hundred thousand dollars on the never-to-be-finished Paige typesetter, and he had sunk over one hundred thousand dollars in the publishing firm, which owed Livy $60,000, and other investors over $80,000. This harrowing speculative and financial experience of the nineties, so highly personal with Clemens and so typical of his age, was part of the emotional ambiguity in *A Connecticut Yankee,* yes, but even more so in *The Tragedy of Pudd'nhead Wilson,* in 1894.

This was the first of those dark parables of the later Mark Twain which included some of his best work; and which, though not only because of financial and family reasons, marked a dividing line in Mark Twain's career. (Though not in half, say, but in thirds.) And at first sight, the drowsing river town of Dawson's Landing, in 1830, was simply another Hannibal of Huck Finn's enchanted youth. The opening descriptions project an idyllic image of comfort, grace, and cultivation — the outward signs of "an inward grace," according to the eminent English critic, Professor F. R. Leavis. "Provincial as Dawson's Landing may be, it represents a society that has kept its full heritage of civilisation," we are told. And, not unaware of its provinciality, it is far from having lost the desire to keep in touch "with the remoter centres of its civilisation and with its past" — and as evidence of this, Professor Leavis cites the piano-playing of the Italian twins in the story. In its whole attitude toward distinction, we are told, Dawson's Landing appeals "to standards other than the 'democratic,'" and "repre-

sents a subtler civilisation than accounts of 'the pioneer community' might suggest," and now Professor Leavis cites Judge
Driscoll (York Leicester Driscoll, that is) as a Virginia gentleman without peer. As being fine and just and generous and respected, esteemed and beloved by the community. "It is quite
unequivocal," adds the British arbiter, just because "he is a
'gentleman' — representing an ideal above that of material success and beyond the reach of the ordinary members of the
community . . ."

Enough, I am tempted to add, of this nonsense, which forms
the critical introduction to a standard textbook edition of a
Mark Twain book which is compounded of equivocality; or
which is devoted precisely to showing up *both* the aristocratic
and the democratic codes of behavior in a slave-owning Missouri town. Professor Leavis is solemnly applying the standard
(and procrustean) procedures of the "aristocratic" sensibility
to a writer who had no use for such subtleties, other than upon
occasion to deride them with hilarious parody. But Professor
Leavis insists upon compounding his series of manifest absurdities. His Introduction — besides providing a startling example
of the nature of contemporary "esthetic" criticism when it
strays off its narrow and prim boundaries — is useful to us as
describing precisely what Mark Twain was *not* doing in *Pud-
d'nhead Wilson.* The central point in the Leavis analysis of
Pudd'nhead Wilson is an almost euphoric exaltation of that
code of the Southern Christian Gentleman which Mark Twain
consistently and continually satirized from the start to the finish of his career; and which, in this particular novel of slavery, he was subjecting to its most arduous and ironical moral
judgment.

What could be more obtuse or perverse in the theory and
practice of Formalist criticism? And who but Mark Twain
could better illuminate the limits and failures of such a critical

methodology, not only in relation to Twain's work, where its results are fatal, and laughable; but even in its own area, where
its results can only be sterile and mediocre. What a bad day it
was for the esteemed F. R. Leavis, whose critical opinions colored a whole sector of academic criticism around the mid-twentieth century, when he came to grips (as he thought) with the
primary American genius of the late nineteenth century. "Mark
Twain unmistakably admires Judge Driscoll and Pembroke
Howard," Leavis adds — "they are the two most sympathetic
characters in the drama"(!) and "they give the 'code' itself their
active endorsement" — as though this 'code' was not precisely
what Sam Clemens was crucifying in his somber allegory. Thus
too, Pudd'nhead Wilson himself, who finally succumbs to the
call of race, blood, and prejudice in the story, becomes "the
poised pre-eminently civilised moral centre of the drama." And
this kind of critical dogma ends by debasing even its own language
in such a repetitive and incantative use of words like "moral
centre" and "civilisation."

The real center of *Pudd'nhead Wilson* is not as easy to reach
as Professor Leavis' peculiar analysis might suggest. For after
all both Judge Driscoll and Pembroke Howard, who are the
sympathetic, noble aristocratic heroes of the gentlemanly code
in this culturally aspiring frontier village — according to our
British cousin's view, that is — are the central slave owners of
the story, and therefore responsible for all the social misery,
suffering, and hatred of the novel. And one of the story's mysteries is precisely why "Pudd'nhead" himself, an ostensible outcast hero, surrenders his own humanity and dignity in order
to support Twain's acerbic version of southern chivalry and
honor.*

---

* To anybody who is acquainted with the body of Mark Twain's work, the
Leavis analysis of *Pudd'nhead Wilson* is so aberrant as to illustrate the folly

But all this hardly explains Professor Leavis' propensity for crying "nigger" — "nigger, nigger, nigger!" — in the preface to *Pudd'nhead Wilson,* with a kind of perverse delight in using a word which, as we have noticed, Sam Clemens was extraordinarily punctilious about for his period, and hardly ever used in his own auctorial voice. And finally — "The attitude of *Pudd'nhead Wilson* is remote from cynicism or pessimism," and here Mark Twain "has achieved a mature, balanced and impersonal view of humanity" — while in fact, if this book reveals anything, it is the depths of anger, sorrow, and despair from which Clemens wrote this curious fable of southern slavery and miscegenation.

It is refreshing after all this high-toned, morally righteous, noble Christian esthetic cant, to come upon the salty tang of the book's first aphorism selected from Pudd'nhead Wilson's Calendar. "There is no character, howsoever good and fine, but it can be destroyed by ridicule . . . Observe the ass, for instance; his character is about perfect, he is the choicest spirit among all the humbler animals, and yet see what ridicule has brought him to. Instead of feeling complimented when we are called an ass, we are left in doubt." The first whiff of Clemens' acrid heresy disperses all the sanctimonious spiritual nobility of Dr. Leavis' academe; though we can never quite see any real connection between the Calendar's aphorisms and the novel's action, beyond the fact that Pudd'nhead's "Calendar" was probably taken from Clemens' own notebook.

---

of a whole school of conservative academic literary criticism, which, rising to power during the moral and psychological decline of western European democracy, found an esthetic refuge, a supposedly esthetic haven, in devising the peculiar mode of "Christian" tradition and culture which has been described above. Denying the plain meaning of their own epoch of revolutionary history, these critics have deprived *all* history of any valid meaning; while their notions of Christianity, Culture, and Tradition, when applied to a writer like Mark Twain, are suddenly revealed in all their absurdity.

There is no doubt that this curiously gifted failure as a lawyer, and this superior social outcast in the town, Pudd'nhead Wilson himself — ruined by his humor, and represented as the tale's "observer" — is a projection of Clemens' own derogatory self-vision of the period. For the opening of *Pudd'nhead Wilson* presents almost a deliberately, even artificially, contrived effect of the familiar beauty and bliss of Huck Finn's youth — only here it is the *appearance* of paradise in the Mississippi River setting of Dawson's Landing which Clemens is deliberately invoking. It is a conspicuously false paradise.

It is obvious, similarly, that the glowing phrases of admiration for Judge York Leicester Driscoll, as the highest type of old-fashioned southern grandee, an FFV incarnate, is as ironical, ambiguous, and deceptive as is the whole "happy opening" of this Mississippi River anti-idyll. For the first time in his work, in a major sense, Clemens was deliberately adopting the sardonic and tragic mask which, say, Melville — another innocent native spirit who had felt himself similarly wounded and betrayed by life — used in the *Piazza Tales*. It is the Judge's brother, Percy Northumberland Driscoll (the ornate and aristocratic names are significant) who is Roxy's owner and who threatens to sell his slaves "down the river" — a nightmare vision for any Missouri Negro, as Clemens says — because of petty thievery in his house. It is this threat which forces Roxy to replace the "white" Driscoll baby with her own "black" Driscoll baby. The opening pages of the novel contain a remarkable discourse on "negritude" (and by implication on miscegenation) which immediately casts an ambiguous shadow over the high-flown admiration for the old southern slave-owning gentry. This is also a kind of super stage-setting, a deliberately conceived fictional illusion; or, to anybody but a Professor Leavis, it is pure hogwash.

Percy Driscoll gets all his Negro slaves to confess their guilt (true or not); does not carry through his threat to sell them to the cotton plantations; and makes a notation in his diary about his own magnanimity and humanity before his night's sleep; while the terrified Roxy carries through her fatal deed of duplicity — or revenge, or justice? What could be clearer than this in the novel's opening if one has but eyes to read? "To all intents and purposes Roxy was as white as anybody, but the one sixteenth of her which was black out-voted the other fifteen parts and made her a Negro. She was a slave and saleable as such. Her child was thirty-one parts white, and he, too, was a slave and, by a fiction of law and custom, a Negro." * It is this fiction of law and custom, which Clemens had suggested in *Huckleberry Finn,* that, much more savagely and ironically, *Pudd'nhead Wilson* would deal with. It is also interesting to recall that almost fifty years later, another southern writer, Ellen Glasgow, would state the same theme in almost the same words, in the novel called *In This Our Life,* in 1941.

In the basic structure of *Pudd'nhead Wilson,* too, let us note that when the white Driscoll baby is substituted for the "black" Driscoll baby by Roxy (we are not yet told the real father of Roxy's child), we are to all effects and purposes dealing with another set of twins in Mark Twain's work — and to complicate things further there will be a "real" set of twins later on in the narrative. And the names of the two interchanged infants — "Thomas à Becket" Driscoll and "Valet de Chambre" (Driscoll, though not yet said) carry their own mocking irony, since Roxy's ignorant pretense of grandeur in naming her child also reflected on the false pretenses of the heroic English

---

* This of course became Nazi doctrine about any taint of Jewish blood in any remote ancestor. As we shall notice again in Mark Twain's work, the white man's treatment of the black man became a historical precedent and source for the white man's treatment of the white man.

names in this southwestern frontier society. A "classical" English name that Clemens deliberately exaggerated in his text, for after all which given name was more pretentious or more ridiculous?

Dawson's Landing is halfway between the idyllic Hannibal of Huck Finn and the corrupted town of Hadleyburg in Mark Twain's fiction; and every soul in *Pudd'nhead Wilson,* including the noble slave Roxy herself, is subjected, if not to a cynical reduction of moral stature, at least to curious levels of behavior in Sam Clemens' darkening vision of experience. Irony and tragedy have taken over the center stage in Clemens' comic proscenium of life. What depths of ambiguity are expressed in the history of the transposed Tom — the falsely "Negro" Tom, who is also a later and darker cousin of Tom Sawyer in Mark Twain's genealogy of childhood — the falsely "Negro" Tom who then becomes a false white aristocrat. It is his undoing. He becomes spoiled, arrogant, deceitful, vicious-tempered, nasty (though verbally "clever" in the mode of Tom Sawyer); even while the history of the transposed white "aristocrat" now turned into the black Chambers reveals how easily a slave is made. The transposed "black child" takes on the worst aspects of the white master race, while Chambers Driscoll becomes so versed in human servility, obedience, docility that even when he regains his true personality and social position, he cannot unlearn the slave idiom — the slave ideology — of his youth. If Mark Twain is making a case here for human malleability, as was his wont, this time it is an ironic and rather horrifying case for mobility downward — in both the "highest" and the lowest levels of southwestern frontier society.

After a few severe canings by his father, the generous, humane, and aristocratic Percy Driscoll, Chambers becomes Tom's protector, guardian, and servant; the relationship is ruinous for both of them. So, too, Roxy surrenders all her human pleasures for the sake of her child's security.

Tom had long ago taught Roxy "her place." It had been many a day now since she had ventured a caress or a fondling epithet in his quarter. Such things, from a "nigger," were repulsive to him, and she had been warned to keep her distance and remember who she was. She saw her darling gradually cease from being her son, she saw *that* detail perish utterly; all that was left was master — master, pure and simple, and it was not a gentle mastership either. She saw herself sink from the sublime height of motherhood to somber deeps of unmodified slavery. The abyss of separation between her and her boy was complete. She was merely his chattel, now, his convenience, his dog, his cringing and helpless slave, the humble and unresisting victim of his capricious temper and vicious nature.

Was Roxy's sublime sacrifice really worth it in the end — in the confines of a social system which by its nature corrupted both master and slave, or perhaps even in the larger confines of human nature itself? Clemens' answer is corrosive. Roxy is not only ruined — she is sold down the river — by the son she has protected and elevated in the world. In the process of deception her own character is ruined, rather than elevated, by her suffering; and in the end, when the true nature of her relationship with Tom is revealed, there is no hint, but rather the opposite, of any kind of mother-son affectional bond.

But right here is the flaw of Twain's enigmatic fable. If the *concept* of Roxy as a handsome, brilliant, passionate, and highly emotional mulatto slave heroine is admirable, the literary execution of this idea is uneven and sometimes quite false. Emancipated as Sam Clemens was for his period and place, there is still a kind of southern white paternalism in this portrait of the Negro woman. Her development in *Pudd'nhead*

Wilson is not always consistent and sometimes quite erratic, and her character is often manipulated for the purposes of Clemens' plot line.* Similarly with Tom, the hero-villain of the story; while his white "twin," Chambers, becomes a kind of typical shuffling darkie, and the Italian twins of the story are little more than romantic images of European culture, never fully realized as people. The best that can be said for all the characters of *Pudd'nhead Wilson* as characters is that they are social or literary types whom Clemens is manipulating for the sake of his moral. What we really have here, as in the whole series of these later dark parables of Mark Twain, is a kind of literary surrealism, where the meaning of the artist's message is more important to him than the depiction of human character for the sake of human character.

But still that ambiguous moral or "message" continues to haunt us in the pages of *Pudd'nhead*, and these curious characters, acting out a kind of modern morality play, do have their moments of eloquence or verisimilitude when they emerge as more than fictional props. We are caught by the power of Mark Twain's meaning here even when we are annoyed or uneasy at

* Compare Leslie Fiedler's commendation of Roxy as "a creature of passion and despair rare among the wooden images of virtue or bitchery that pass for females in American literature." But the plain fact is that Mark Twain, who loved women deeply (despite Mr. Fiedler's alternate charge of homosexuality in *Huck Finn*), did not create an effective heroine in the whole body of his work — except perhaps Livy, his Eve, and Mary Baker Eddy, his female Satan. Mr. Fiedler's study of love and death in the American novel is replete with similar misjudgments and shows a curious kind of ignorance and bad taste. For one thing, some admirable heroines — in Fiedler's depiction of women — are ignored; while the effective feminine portraits of Willa Cather, Ellen Glasgow, and Edith Wharton are misinterpreted. These are no wooden images of virtue or bitchery that pass for females in American literature — only Mr. Fiedler doesn't seem to know it. One reaches the conclusion that this critic, while he has picked up some obvious shortcomings in our culture and art, has not himself a perfect understanding of love or women, or of American literature. Dreiser, whose portraits of women are perhaps the best in American literature, is negated or ignored because Mr. Fiedler accepted the Cold War Culture platform that Dreiser was to be negated or ignored.

his use of his literary material. For all that, Roxy is often an angry, bitter, and brilliant mulatto woman, at her core both radical and rebellious. She is a big step forward in Clemens' own conceptualizing of American Negro slave types, and her perfectly natural wariness of the fingerprinting system (which eventually leads to Tom's ruin) even deceives Wilson himself into reflecting upon her black ignorance and "superstitiousness." And what shall we say of this "Pudd'nhead," the brightest man in the town who is yet condemned to a kind of provincial limbo through one careless and ironical remark — who spends all his spare time tinkering with new scientific and mechanical "miracles" like the fingerprinting system itself, and who yet does reach the central truth in the complex plot structure of the novel?

"Pudd'nhead" is of course another obvious projection of Sam Clemens' wounded and increasingly bitter self-image during the period of his mechanical and financial experiments with the printing press and the publishing house. Mark Twain, in his moment of desperation and dark despair, threw out a series of ambiguous and ironical and fractured literary projections of his own wounded and betrayed consciousness. Which character in *Pudd'nhead Wilson* is *not*, indeed, part of this process of psychic projection and catharsis — but a projection and catharsis, in turn, which created great literature?

The twin fantasy is again dominant, and here the true son and heir, the "white" Tom Driscoll, is condemned to a lifelong existence of black servitude from which he cannot free himself even after his actual liberation. (It is interesting to remember that Melville also used the ironical masks of black "slaves" and white "masters" in "Benito Cereno," where again the "black furies" have reduced the ship's master to a complete nervous breakdown and physical collapse.) And similarly,

Tom Driscoll, the "black imposter," when raised to a position of white power, becomes heartless, cruel, vicious — his fall from grace when Roxy tells him that he is her son only increases the depth of his depravity. There is no doubt of Clemens' identification with Roxy's role also: the powerful spirit, rebellious and raging at a hard fate, which goes through life in a false state of servitude, and is destroyed, as it were, by its own act of generosity.

Pudd'nhead Wilson is full of these reverberations and reflections of Clemens' psychic state at the time, and if he hardly bothered to embody his characters in their human complexity, the power of the narrative comes from his own direct emotional involvement with the literary projection. The maxims of Pudd'nhead at the start of each chapter, in most cases having no apparent connection with the literary action, are even more directly Clemens' own mordant reflections about the bitterness of life, the folly, the tragedy here, much more than any sense of comedy. What is curiously absent from the description of Dawson's Landing in the years just before the Civil War is any theoretical or ideological discussion of the slavery issue itself. But the total picture of frontier life is really so negative and destructive in this reversed idyll of a southwestern river town that the social institution of slavery might appear to be only a minor sin, after all, in the sorry conditions of man's total existence. Since Pudd'nhead Wilson is the ostensible hero of the book, the bright and thinking man, the social outcast, it comes as a surprise and disappointment to us that he, too, subscribes without reflection to the southern code of honor in the book.

The subplot of the Italian twins, intended originally as a comic tale, was reworked into Roxy's story to demonstrate the same sense of tragedy and cruel irony pervading the novel. Their treatment as "foreigners" similarly reflects the inner flaw of that aristocratic southern "code" which in these pages condemned Roxy and the son she had sacrificed her life to save to such a hateful and treacherous bond of self-protection against all the destroying artifices of the white man's culture. "It was wonderful to find America," we are told in Pudd'nhead Wilson's Calendar, "but it would have been more wonderful to miss it."

But twins again; two sets of twins in this enigmatic fable that yet provides a key insight into Mark Twain's life and art: his Twinish nature. The irrelevant Italian twins (who do suggest, despite Mr. Leavis, how swiftly frontier society turned upon "foreign" royalty or European culture) lead us back to the original set of "white" and "black" twins who are interchanged — and hence interchangeable, despite all rigid racial taboos — and who constitute one of Mark Twain's most profound intuitions about not merely "the race problem" and the nature of slavery — but the nature of man himself. This shifting, enigmatic relationship of master and slave where the black child becomes the white child, and the white the black; where the seed of the "master race" becomes a perfect serf — and the scion of the submerged black race becomes a noxious, evil and degraded white "master": what a brilliantly disturbing central concept was *Pudd'nhead Wilson* based on! What contradictions, incongruities, contrarieties, hidden affinities, and polar oppositions does this mysterious fable suggest.

We have already noticed and will elaborate further the cultural concept of the double soul which Mark Twain embodied so purely; his embodiment of the pagan-plenary and primitive man conjoined with the moral-historical-social vision which is so clearly the result of civilizational repression. But just consider how accurately Sam Clemens' early identification with the black slave (versus the white masters) supports this thesis, while it echoes and reverberates through his art. The black slave who educates the white "master" in *Huck Finn*; the vagabond king and the king turned vagabond in *The Prince and the Pauper*; the central relationship of master-pilot and impudent cub in *Life on the Mississippi* — these are three obvious variations on this theme. It is quite true that these early meditations on black and white, master and slave, royalty and serfdom — and Twain's natural affinity with the black slave — were at the base of his later thinking, his mature role as America's conscience before the face of the world. This was the true emotional source of that whole later period of penetrating and prophetic social commentary; of that remarkable repudiation of a white Anglo-Saxon culture which was based on colonial conquest and oppression; and of that final identification with the darker-skinned races of the world which has made Mark Twain such a revered figure, not merely in revolutionary Russia, but in India, China, Asia, and South America today.

But the issue is still deeper. We also remember how those American writers of an earlier period, like Hawthorne and Melville, were disturbed by darkness as the symbol of sex, sin, and evil, despite their uneasy animadversions on the duplicity of "whiteness" in such novels as *Moby Dick* and *The Marble Faun*. Later on there was Sherwood Anderson's *Dark Laughter* as the mark of human pleasure and joy — but do you begin to see the matter now? For blackness was pagan freedom and splendor to the early Sam Clemens and the later Mark Twain alike. And whiteness was the "master race" of social repression, imperial power, and the exploitation of human innocence. Law and Order indeed. That fascination with darkness running through all American literature reflects our major writers' unconscious or half-conscious awareness of this problem;

but Sam Clemens was the first and only writer, among all the earlier ones, to rush into the "ambush" of blackness and dusky nature, to embrace it with all his soul, and hence to enrich his whole life and art. That is the real fascination of *Pudd'nhead Wilson,* its true meaning which was perhaps even unknown to the artist who wrote it, and which will be verified by — even while it helps to focus and explain — his later career and his last, best enigmatic fable, *The Mysterious Stranger* itself.

Lurid, sentimental, melodramatic, highly uneven as the central scenes in *Pudd'nhead Wilson* are, they are yet rough gold in a literary sense. And here Clemens anticipated many of the racial insights of Richard Wright, for example, just as the heavily detailed trial scene which concludes the book pointed toward the literary form of both Dreiser's *An American Tragedy* and Wright's *Native Son.* If *Pudd'nhead* was a psychic projection of Clemens' growing sense of despair in the mid-nineties, both a literary configuration of his changing state of mind and a partial catharsis for it, what is always relevant is how completely he was able to project an almost purely personal sense of failure and defeat into the social and historical issue of slavery and miscegenation in a frontier river town. How he merged and fused the personal and the communal again; and after all, it is not with the human sources and origins of *Pudd'nhead* we are finally concerned, but with the literary and artistic result. What matters is not the fact that *Pudd'nhead,* the first of a series of such dark fables by Mark Twain, was the literary projection of a personal mood — but the *kind* of psychological catharsis and literary achievement it was. And just as *Pudd'nhead* was one of the most interesting precursors of the best later work of Mark Twain in this uneasy, uneven, obsessed, and irregular literary career which still remains one of the major achievements of the national letters — so *Per-*

sonal Recollections of Joan of Arc, in 1896, was Sam Clemens' worst book.

This was perhaps the single exception to the Mark Twain rule that there is always something of value in even his worst work. It is difficult to find *anything* of interest in *Joan of Arc* — except its badness.

During the years of its composition, of course, Sam Clemens was still undergoing pangs and throes and horrid nightmare fantasies of the financial bankruptcy which threatened to leave him a broken and disgraced man. His finances had been in a critical condition since 1891. Begging and borrowing not only from Livy and her family, but from his friends and literary and artistic acquaintances, selling off his own securities, Sam Clemens was in an anguished state of mind.*

"I am terribly tired of business," he wrote to Fred Hall, the new manager of the Webster publishing house during those years. "I am by nature and disposition unfit for it, and I want to get out of it . . . Get me out of business!" A realization, rather like that of the Hemingway hero in *To Have and Have Not,* which had taken him all his life to reach — and which would never be quite fulfilled. "Great Scott, but it's a long year — for you & for me!" he wrote Hall again during those hectic days. "I never knew the almanac to drag so." And: "I am very glad indeed if you and Mr. Langdon (Livy's brother)

---

* Although Justin Kaplan's study of Mark Twain has corrected the facts and figures in Albert Bigelow Paine's standard three-volume earlier biography and added much new material, it is still Paine's work that we go to in order to find out the intimate, day-by-day account of the Clemens family and Clemens himself. I am drawing upon this earlier work here for the account of Clemens' alternating and conflicting emotions in his statements at that time. In some respects, indeed, despite Paine's obvious Victorianism (far easier to spot than our imbedded contemporary prejudices), despite his sentimentality, hero-worship, and generally bad literary judgments — all of which are overcorrected, so to speak, by Kaplan's astringent and reductive Freudism — Paine is perhaps closer to the essential truth about Sam Clemens' life, not to mention the complete and intimate documentation which he offers, and which can be evaluated from a modern point of view.

are able to see any daylight ahead. To me none is visible . . ."
But in the curious alternation of the American dream and
nightmare which Sam Clemens personified to the hilt — those
dramatic sequences of pleasure and despair; of fame and success and abysmal, heartsick failure; of gaiety and laughter, and
of utter, tragic depths — it would be the laughter that would
still prevail; and already in September, 1893, he had met his
Fairy Prince. Henry Huttleston Rogers, one of the most ruthless and arrogant and cunning directors of the Standard Oil
complex, and yet one of the most charming, cultivated and
generous of all the Robber Baron tribe, had become Clemens'
close friend, his patron and business manager. In the grand
manner of American finance capitalism at its peak, not unlike
the medieval Medicis who fascinated Theodore Dreiser, Rogers
simply liquidated all of Clemens' failing business enterprises
and took over the control of his finances. The publishing house
went first, although both Sam and Livy, and perhaps Livy
more, could hardly bear the disgrace of bankruptcy, and they
set themselves the hard task of repaying their creditors in full.

Yes, there is no doubt, as Clemens' Freudian detractors have
stated about this great American moralist, that he participated
in some of the dubious manipulations which accompany any
bankruptcy settlement — it must have been particularly hard
for him, and some of its grim irony would show up in his
later work. But Livy was owed $60,000 from the publishing
company; and through Rogers' protective guile she kept the
Hartford house and, what was most important, the Mark Twain
copyrights which at first they had been prepared to surrender.
Clemens still owed some $70,000 to his other creditors, and
what is not stressed by his critics is the fact that he paid it all
back: a remarkable feat for a bankrupt and broken man in his
fifties.

There was no doubt too that their deep affectional bond had

suffered from all the strains and stresses of this crisis; they often expressed to others what they would not express to each other. To Sam, Livy was always the picture of confidence, hope, and love, even while she expressed her despair to her sister, Susan Crane. Daughter that she was of a solid mercantile family in the older tradition of the democracy, Livy had "a perfect *horror* and heart-sickness about the bankruptcy of Webster and Company."

> I cannot get away from the feeling that business failure means disgrace . . . Sue, if you were to see me you would see that I have grown old very fast during this last year. I have wrinkled . . . Most of the time I want to lie down and cry. Everything seems to me so impossible. I do not make things go very well, and I feel that my life is an absolute and irretrievable failure. Perhaps I am thankless, but I so often feel that I should like to give it up and die.

Touching and painful words; and in the depths of his own spirit, in his despair at having brought down upon her head the whole charming, gay, and loving idyll of their domestic life, Sam Clemens felt the same way. What is remarkable is how, in their recorded utterances at least, they kept up such a gallant and hopeful appearance with each other; his guilt, her shame, were kept in abeyance with each other, and to the very end, and moving through even worse human tragedies — despite all the changes and blows and restrictions which life brings to bear upon the deepest human affections — their love and devotion for each other would still remain constant. We shall see that.

And meanwhile, stricken as he was by remorse and apprehension, Sam Clemens himself went into a sensational whirl of social gaiety in New York and Boston during these years —

sensational, perhaps at base also hysterical, and seeking an opiate for his pain. With the publishing house gone he also felt the manic ecstasy of unexpected liberation. "Farewell — a long farewell — to business! I will *never* touch it again!" he wrote to Livy from New York. "I will live in literature, I will wallow in it, revel in it; I will swim in ink!" And this from a man who had recently declared his intention to "resign" from writing, and who has often been accused of not thinking of himself as a writer and not caring enough about his craft. What evidence beyond this "swimming in ink" do we need as to Sam Clemens' depth and seriousness of literary purpose despite whatever mask he was tempted to put upon his true intentions.

And despite all the temptations of the worldly position which preyed upon his weakness, of that materialistic and even corrupt world of social entertainment that he delighted to revel in! Clemens loved to dance, and he stayed up dancing until the parties ended at 4:00 A.M. During one social season he was dubbed "the Belle of New York." He went with Rogers and a group from the Players Club to watch James Corbett box; Stanford White took Clemens in to talk with "the most perfectly and beautifully constructed human animal in the world" — high praise from the artist who always had a secret affinity with the animals and often an overt disdain for humans. At these parties of fashionable wealth and cosmopolitan culture, Clemens used to list the celebrities who were present. At the painter Robert Reid's studio, he wrote to Livy, there were Richard Harding Davis, John Drew, the painters Birge Harrison and William Chase, Bettini, the "inventor of the new phonograph," Nikola Tesla, "the world-wide illustrious electrician," Ancona, the head tenor at the opera, and the French actor Coquelin. Through it all Clemens kept writing his French romance, *Personal Recollections of Joan of Arc,* which his biographer

Paine, reflecting the genteel taste of the time, admired so immensely. "Considered from every point of view, *Joan of Arc* is Mark Twain's supreme literary expression, the loftiest, the most delicate, the most luminous example of his work." This famous heroine was a saint — "she is rare, she is exquisite, she is all that is lovely, and she is a human being besides." Written for, and to a certain degree based on Susy, the novel was dedicated to Livy on their twenty-fifth wedding anniversary "in grateful recognition of her twenty-five years of valued service as my literary adviser and editor." And to his death Clemens insisted that not only did he like *Joan* the best of all his books, but that it *was* the best.

Now the conventional taste of the period, the harried circumstances of his existence, perhaps the sense of guilt about his business disasters and Livy's money, perhaps the even deeper guilt that Clemens felt in the bosom of his family for being only a "funny man," a popular entertainer, instead of the great artist they all wanted him to be — all these obvious reasons still do not explain *Joan of Arc*'s peculiar quality of being the most un-Twainish of Mark Twain's books. (Even more so, much more so than *The Prince and the Pauper*.) It is the polar opposite of everything that Twain was; it embodied every idea, every value, every emotion, every social institution that he despised.

God, King, Patriotism, Nationalism, Purity, Self-sacrifice, Religious Devotion, the Supernatural, Sentimentality, Chastity — Saint Joan embodied every trait that Sam Clemens, in his right mind, could not bear. What was there in this sexless and non-nubile Maid of Orléans which so attracted Clemens, definitely beyond all need for even a best seller which was completely "edifying" for respectable young Americans? One remembers his fervid and frank descriptions of the pagan ladies of the Sandwich Isles; probably his admiration and affection for the women of the darker races (though he equally admired the physical grace of the men) had certain sexual undertones. How could the Twainian narrator of the tale, the Sieur Louis de Conte, remembering in his old age "the dear little figure, with breast bent to the flying horse's neck" — the marvelous child's meteoric flight across the firmament of France — describe her as "the most noble life that was ever born into this world save only One"? One also remembers Sam Clemens' notions about Jesus, God, and the Church — which last still however remains as the official villain in *Joan of Arc,* obstructing the Maid's natural converse with her heavenly Voices.

There is the whimsical opening about Joan's struggle to save the Fairies of the Druidic Tree from the Church's persecution, where first we meet her superior understanding, her moral courage, her unselfishness, her calm confidence, her casual prophecies, her powers of logical and emotional persuasion. But here even Twain's village priest, yielding to Joan's charm and vision alike, is a sympathetic character. There is the early section on the epic "Song of Roland" which Joan (and Sam, apparently) cherished as the symbol of French patriotic fervor. Very early Joan accomplishes her first miracle when she calmly conquers the crazy Benoist, escaped from his cage, carrying his murderous ax, and is quite forgetful of her own danger in her concern for the lunatic's well-being. At sixteen Joan was "shapely and graceful" and of an extraordinary beauty. "There was in her face a sweetness and serenity and purity that justly reflected her spiritual nature." Twain's narrator asserts he might allow himself any extravagance of language to describe this heroine; and in fact he does.

There is the scene where Joan reforms the old military hellion, La Hire, and prescribes no more drinking for her army, no more women, and attendance at divine service twice a day.

It sounds like Clemens pretending to yield to Susy's importunate cries about his own personal vices; but it is simply absurd in the historical context of the Hundred Years' War. La Hire is indeed a kind of rough, bawdy, foul-speaking, obscene frontier fighter before his moral transformation, about which Clemens does remark that "Satan was converted." And what we suddenly realize about *Joan of Arc* is precisely that the familiar Satan-Twain has also been "converted," or exorcised from the book so completely as to leave only the falsely "angelic," the sentimental, the romantic, the devout, pious, conventional, and trite Twain in these peculiar pages. It is an astounding transformation; it is an illuminating vision of Clemens that we'll return to — and perhaps one might add that only Satan would be capable of such an obvious and transparent disguise; such guile, hypocrisy, and cant! And yet Clemens apparently believed it, or was able to make himself believe in it while in the process of composing this narrative. "For there had come a day between, when God's good gift of laughter had gone out from me to come again no more in this life," says the ancient Sieur de Conte about his past, and it almost appears that Mark Twain himself had, for the purpose of writing *Joan of Arc,* destroyed his own gift of laughter.

After the lifting of the siege of Orléans, Joan's military genius is portrayed in the great campaign of the Loire. She fulfills the ancient prophecy of Merlin, which the Connecticut Yankee would have laughed out of court. The "Paladin" of the narrative, comic braggart that he is, reminds us briefly of Twain's true vein; yet even the Paladin is converted again, by Joan's nobility. What a falling-off, what a self-betrayal, what a loss is here! Or conversely, in this interplay of God and Satan, of the Twainian Twins, who also keep changing roles, what depths of duplicity existed in this artist as to allow such an inverted and hypocritical projection — or distortion — of himself! What utter rot was this sanctimonious worship of the "Virgin of Vaucouleurs" which Clemens apparently so deeply and completely believed in — did he not?

There is not the slightest hint here of those intuitive and penetrating social-historical insights which mark the most irregular of Clemens' other writings. This is all romance melodrama in a vein of "historical" fantasy worthy of Henry James — and here indeed these two polar opposites of the late nineteenth-century American literary scene meet in a common cultural hypocrisy and sentimentality. But what still remains curious in *Joan of Arc* is the force of Clemens' narrative power — or the force of his illusionary sense — in that, realizing all these fatal flaws in the story, we still can't quite drop the book; we still continue to read it, and even in a sense to enjoy it. Is this some curious vestige of infantile fantasy which the mature, satiric, radical Mark Twain still shared with the feudal romantic royalist Henry James — and which a supposedly mature reader still feels in such literary works? There *is* a pleasure left in reading *Joan of Arc,* not unlike that when we enjoy a bad movie. The narrative still manages to keep our interest; it is only the quality, tone, content of the narrative which is so appalling. This is the most unlikely Mark Twain to be still Mark Twain.

No wonder, as Clemens claimed, that *Joan of Arc* wrote itself, and all he had to do was to take pen in hand. It was the essence of juvenile romance literature (and of much adult fiction) which he distilled here so fluently, so flawlessly; so falsely.

The brief complicity of Mark Twain and his society in the matter of *Joan of Arc,* however, comes out badly in the second and third books of the novel, when the narrative pace of the military action falls off. Again, as in *Pudd'nhead Wilson,*

Clemens closed his story with an elaborate "trial" which showed, this time, the cunning corruption of fifteenth-century church and state in the punishment and destruction of the Maid of Orléans.

But this trial which could have been used, as trials were used later in the course of classic American literature, to analyze and illuminate the action story which led up to it — which could have been used to add depth, levels of meaning, new facets of insight to the narrative — only illustrates Clemens' temporary lack of historical perspective in this book, and his simple-minded reconstruction of fact, legend, and myth. The historical trial of Jeanne d'Arc *is* a fascinating episode in its revelations of the emergent feudal countries and a divided Church; of a dawning age of nationalism; of new social entities and ruling classes; and a new social power structure, emerging as the historical product of the Hundred Years' War. But all this, which Shaw, for example, embodied in his Joan of Arc, and which Clemens was not unaware of in his own concern with both feudal history and the French Revolution, was now rigorously excluded from his romance for the sake of romance.

If *Joan of Arc* has a curious interest after all this, it is probably that of seeing a great artist at his worst, and in turn his being able to evoke our own maudlin inclinations. *Following the Equator,* in 1897, still reflecting the stress on Clemens in the mid-nineties, and now even the beginnings of a more severe emotional strain, was not among his best travel books either. But there are some fascinating things in it; it marks the start of a new epoch in Mark Twain's literary career; and it is remarkable that the book is as good as it is.*

* *Tom Sawyer Abroad* and *Tom Sawyer Detective,* published in 1896, are very poor juveniles which cause one only to wonder how Clemens could

For the fabulous Paige typesetter, which Rogers had been trying vainly to salvage, and on which the bankrupt Sam Clemens still pinned his hopes of financial recovery, of still becoming a real millionaire, had finally subsided into dust, and had to be consigned to that immense graveyard of scientific failures. During the autumn and winter of 1894, the "marvelous machine," which, as Rogers said, was simply too much of a human being and not enough of a machine — which was the most expensive machine of its size ever built — simply would not function commercially. And hearing the news in Paris, Clemens could still not quite believe it. "I *seemed* to be entirely expecting your letter, and also prepared and resigned," he wrote Rogers,

but Lord, it shows how little we know ourselves and how easily we can deceive ourselves. It hit me like a thunderclap. It knocked every rag of sense out of my head, and I went flying here and there and yonder, not knowing what I was doing, and only one clearly defined thought standing up visible and substantial out of the crazy storm-drift — that my dream of ten years was in desperate peril and out of the 60,000 or 70,000 projects for its rescue that came flocking through my skull not one would hold still long enough for me to examine it and size it up. Have you ever been like that? Not so much, I reckon.

He went around like a madman, debating whether he should rush over to America again. "I must be there and see it die. That is, if it must die; and maybe if I were there we might hatch

---

so openly exploit his famous earlier book while debasing the original characters and concepts. But he did in fact write other sequels to both *Tom Sawyer* and *Huck Finn* which he never published. It took *Life* magazine to reprint one of these in 1969 as a literary "discovery" which in fact did harm to Mark Twain's reputation . . . *How to Tell a Story and Other Essays,* in 1897, was a collection of journalistic articles.

up some next-to-impossible way to make it take up its bed and take a walk." He made plans to return by French steamer the next day; he wired Rogers; only by bedtime had Livy calmed him down — and he spent the sleepless night thinking desperate thoughts and smoking continuously.

Taking over the role of the Yankee mechanic, he sent Rogers a detailed plan for reconstructing the destroyed machine. "Don't say I'm wild. For really I'm sane again this morning." He still pressed Rogers to let him return to New York, and Rogers begged him to stay in Europe, and to allow him (Rogers) to handle all the depressing details of liquidating the typesetter company. Clemens planned to rent the Hartford house, since it was so expensive to maintain. "We can never live in it again; though it would break the family's hearts if they could believe it." He sent a Happy New Year greeting to his benefactor. He also wrote that the financial disaster had reversed his horoscope: this lifelong assumption of the good luck which would always rescue him from any trouble — which still persisted, however, in the fortunate and magical figure of Henry Rogers himself.

"Nothing daunts Mrs. Clemens or makes the world look black to her," he wrote, not knowing her secret thoughts and her private letters, "which is the reason I haven't drowned myself." For they were now, it appeared, hopelessly in debt for the rest of their lives . . . Until, until — and just then Sam Clemens had the inspiration of making a worldwide lecture tour to raise the money to pay off his debts! At his age, and in poor health and low in spirit, it was a formidable undertaking — a form of expiation and atonement even — which turned out to be a spectacular triumph for him and for that old-fashioned American democratic society of the late nineteenth century which Mark Twain, along with Ulysses S. Grant, represented most fully in the world's consciousness.

Following the Equator was the record of that tour and that hard-won victory. Lecturing to huge audiences, Clemens made as much as or more than one thousand dollars a week, all of which was put in a special account for his creditors. In New Zealand both Livy and Sam had birthdays; he was sixty, she fifty, which she did not enjoy, though their love for each other persisted. Livy comforted Sam in his low moods. "Poor old darling, he has been pursued with colds and inabilities of various sorts," she wrote. "He does not believe that any good thing will come, but that we must all our lives live in poverty. He says he never wants to go back to America . . . The platform he likes for the two hours that he is on it, but all the rest of the time it grinds him, and he says he is ashamed of what he is doing."

The book itself is uneven; but its best sections open up an altogether new vein in Clemens' writing — the later vein of criticism and satire which made Clemens famous through the whole world as an American prophet in the tradition of Thoreau, Melville, and Whitman. Here it was that Mark Twain, uniquely among American writers at the turn of the century, had discovered the true nature of modern imperialism, at first abroad and then in his own country. (Most Mark Twain scholars seem hardly to recognize the importance of this element in his work, and of this question in modern history.) *Following the Equator* is a key book in the literary development of Mark Twain, a transitional book, a crucial book setting off the two great periods of work in a writer who is conventionally supposed to have ended his career at the midway point. And it is still today the least recognized and least popular book in the Mark Twain revival.

In the Sandwich Islands, rehearsing the history of primitive Hawaiian history and religion, the advent of the missionaries, and the story of the native kings, Kamehameha and Liholiho, who "modernized" their society, Clemens struck the opening note of the book's theme:

> In Captain Cook's time (1778), the native population of the islands was estimated at 400,000; in 1836 at something short of 200,000; in 1866 at 50,000; it is today, per census, 25,000. All intelligent people praise Kamehameha I and Liholiho for conferring upon the people the great boon of civilization. I would do it myself, but my intelligence is out of repair, now, from overwork.

In this respect it is interesting to remember that Melville, from *Typee* to *Billy Budd,* was enchanted by the same South Sea Islands; that James Jones' epic novel of the American army and destructive modern warfare, *From Here to Eternity,* was based in paradisal Hawaii — and that James Michener's popular historical novel of Hawaii, alas, ended on the patriotic note of statehood over all. Yes, and that Jack London toward the end of his life, for all his superman and superrace leanings, was also enchanted with the tropical fragrance of pagan Hawaii; as was Eugene O'Neill among other American writers. This is a deep theme in the national letters; a deep and buried and haunting countertheme to the national stress on industrial "progress" and "modern" civilization.

But the lyrical opening of the Equator book was only the prelude to Twain's account of slave-trading in Australia, New Caledonia, and the other islands of the South Pacific ocean. (He used Captain Wawn's book on "slave-catching" as one of his literary sources, and again he immortalized this provincial "authority.") On how Queensland exterminated the Kanakas, Sam Clemens is magnificent in *Following the Equator*; and this was his first great thrust at modern colonialism and imperialism — the white man's conquest of the "inferior" (darker) races — which was to be such a central issue in the later phase of his writing, and of his period. Thus in describing the "recruiting" or in fact the slave-catching then active in Australia, as it is in effect in the South Africa of today, Clemens wrote in scathing prose: "It is easy to understand why the Queensland sugar-planter should want the Kanaka recruit; he is cheap. Very cheap, in fact. These are the figures paid by the planter: £20 to the recruiter for getting the Kanaka — or 'catching' him as the missionary phrase goes; £5 to the Queensland government for 'superintending' the importation; £5 deposited with the government for the Kanaka's passage home when his three years are up, in case he shall live that long; about £25 to the Kanaka himself for three years' wages and clothing . . . All this is clear enough; but the thing that is not clear is, what there is about it all to persuade the recruit. He is young and brisk; life at home in his beautiful island is one lazy, long holiday to him; or if he wants to work he can turn out a couple of bags of copra per week and sell it for four or five shillings a bag. In Queensland he must get up at dawn and work from eight to twelve hours a day in the canefields — in a much hotter climate than he is used to — and get less than four shillings a week for it. I cannot understand his willingness to go to Queensland. It is a deep puzzle to me."

And deadpan, Clemens pointed to the series of fatal encounters between the natives and the English and French "recruiting crews" as evidence for the fact that "recruiting was not thoroughly popular among the islanders; else why this bristling string of attacks and blood-curdling slaughter?" (Some of Jack London's later short stories tell just why — though approvingly from the white man's view and the master race's superior armaments — the native resistance to this form of slave-trading was not greater; and what happened to them when it was.) Captain Wawn, whose book Clemens was still happily dramatizing in these pages blamed the native resistance upon the "Exeter Hall influence" — the Australian reformers and liberals. "But for the meddling philanthropists," wrote Twain, "the native fathers and mothers would be fond of seeing their children carted into exile and now and then the grave, instead of weeping about it and trying to kill the kind recruiters." The Australian missionaries, or some of them, were also against the slave-trading, and he quoted their description of the typical Queensland planter's point of view. "When he comes from his home he is a savage, pure and simple. He feels no shame at his nakedness and want of adornment. When he returns home he does so well dressed, sporting a Waterbury watch, collars, cuffs, boots and jewelry . . ."

This planter viewpoint was just like waving a red rag before an already enraged bull. "For just one moment," Clemens said, "we have a seeming flash of comprehension of the Kanaka's reason for exiling himself: he goes away to acquire *civilization.*"

> Yes, he was naked and not ashamed; now he is clothed and knows how to be ashamed; he was unenlightened, now he has a Waterbury watch; he was unrefined, now he has jewelry and something to make him smell good; he was a nobody, a provincial, now he has been to far countries and can show off. It all looks plausible — for a moment . . . However, if the most a Kanaka advantages himself by a three-year course in civilization in Queensland is a necklace and an umbrella and a showy imperfection in the art of swearing, it must be that *all* the profit of the traffic goes to the white man. This could be twisted into a plausible argument that the traffic ought to be squarely abolished.

And he went on to describe, as he had done with the Polynesians of the Sandwich Islands, the terrible rise in the native mortality rate induced by the white man's civilization.

"Queensland is a very healthy place for white people — death-rate 12 in 1,000 of the population — but the Kanaka death-rate is away above that. The vital statistics for 1893 place it at 52; for 1894 (Mackay district), 68. The first six months of the Kanaka's exile are peculiarly perilous for him because of the rigors of the new climate. The death-rate among the new men has reached as high as 180 in the 1,000. In the Kanaka's native home his death-rate is 12 in time of peace, and 15 in time of war. Thus exile to Queensland — with the opportunity to acquire civilization, an umbrella, and a pretty poor quality of profanity — is twelve times as deadly as war."

> Common Christian charity, common humanity, does seem to require, not only that these people be returned to their homes, but that war, pestilence, and famine be introduced among them for their preservation.

And another Australian missionary was quoted on the benefits not merely of the "Recruiting System" (Slave Trade) but of bringing civilization as a whole to these backward pagans. To Thomas Campbell's ode,

> Come, bright Improvement! on the car of Time,
> And rule the spacious world from clime to clime.

Clemens added: "Very well, Bright Improvement has arrived, you see, with her civilization, and her Waterbury, and her umbrella, and her third-quality profanity, and her humanizing-not-destroying machinery, and her hundred-and-eighty death-rate, and everything is going along just as handsome!"

These were handsome pages in the early sections of *Following the Equator,* and there were other variations on the same theme. In these chapters indeed we first meet the hard satiric brilliance, the irony and wit, the moral indignation, the inspired strokes of broad comedy and farce, the savage anger: all the rhetorical, literary, and spiritual weapons which Mark Twain developed and unleashed in the brilliant social criticism of his mature writing. That dazzling social critique of his own period, I should add, and those acute and prophetic visions of the future, which have been denigrated and misunderstood from the very beginning to the present day: from Paine's early qualms about provoking Mark Twain's popular audience, to DeVoto's curiously grudging and backward acceptance of this whole area of Twain's work; to Justin Kaplan's Freudian negation, and to Charles Neider's repudiation of this material.

Was it the series of financial disasters which led Clemens into this vein of observation and expression? Or his guilt about wasting Livy's inherited fortune? Was it the death of Susy, in the shadow of which *Following the Equator* was written — and Sam Clemens' attribution of her death, too, to his own mistakes? It may be interesting to speculate about such things; but it hardly matters, it doesn't matter at all.

For what counts in evaluating the whole area of Mark Twain's social commentary is not the personal origins of his "bitterness," real, fancied, neurotic, or otherwise — but the result. What counts is the *use* to which Sam Clemens put his personal despair and frustration, and the meeting of his own mature temperament with the world of the twentieth century just then developing around him. What counts is the trajectory of these personal and temperamental factors which met and were fused, as always in great art, with the time spirit. What counts is the *way* he used his tragic experience, the *method* of his expression and fulfillment, so that the pain of his life was converted into the catharsis of his work. And a catharsis not for the sake of cure but for the sake of art: a "catharsis" which illuminated crucial factors in contemporary

society, and which got at the meaning of American civilization.

That is what the Freudian ideology cannot ever understand,
and has no real concern with — ignoring for the moment the
fact that the Freudian schema does not suffice to describe or
contain Clemens' original temperament. This is what Justin
Kaplan's *Mr. Clemens and Mark Twain* always misses or distorts, since it views Twain's radical social commentary as some
sort of deviant behavior when it is not the expression of personal neurosis.

Following the Equator, moreover, was the first book of Mark
Twain's to define the essential underlying conflict of all his
work as being that between primary nature and civilization
itself. (We have been tracing this theme; now it comes into
focus.) Freud knew this issue of course, and resolved it in
favor of "civilization" — in favor of "adjustment." Not so,
however, with Otto Rank as a cultural psychologist; and not
so with Mark Twain; nor with Melville, Whitman, Dreiser,
among the other American writers who could not resolve this
conflict so easily and who continued to be haunted and obsessed by it. For the point is that art is the carrier, the vessel,
of *both* the primary life forces and the civilizational morality.

No writer in the national letters reflected both these opposing strains in the human temperament more clearly, more
fully, more beautifully than Mark Twain did. That is his special meaning, and that is the only way to understand the full
weight of his writing and his career. He was the most directly
open and revealing of all these primitive and profound writers, the
closest to childhood feeling and expression — that is the secret of his vision. And simultaneously he was the most social,
historical, and moral artist in the best and highest (noncon-
forming) sense of morality. This factor explains his involve-

ment with the books about his own childhood and childhood in general — rather than any "evasion" of mature conflicts as some critics suggest with typical Freudian condescension. And that is precisely the reason why Sam Clemens in his late fifties, his sixties, his seventies, became one of the most perceptive critics of a changing American civilization — a sharply changing American culture which these critics seem to be unaware of.

But the pagan-plenary side of Twain's temperament still remained, whenever it could, basic — right down to the huge bed where, robed in white or still in his sleeping clothes, he would spend so much of his later life, and always invited his visitors to join him. (One remembers Dreiser's fondness for his rocking chair where, folding and unfolding his handkerchief, he ruminated over man's fate.) We have already noticed Sam Clemens' undying hatred of "work," his great pleasure in the simple processes of living, his continual yearning to "loaf" like Walt Whitman, and to "pass the time" like Huck.

In Fiji he was entranced by the "wrinkled old women, with their flat mammals flung over their shoulders, or hanging down in front like the cold-weather drip from the molasses faucet." He liked also the "plump and smily young girls, blithe and content, easy and graceful" — along with the men:

> Young matrons, tall, straight, comely, nobly built, sweeping by with chin up, and a gait incomparable for unconscious stateliness and dignity; majestic young men — athletes for build and muscle — clothed in a loose arrangement of dazzling white, with bronze breast and bronze legs naked, and the head a swab of solid color combed straight out from the skull and dyed a rich brick-red . . .

Shades of Walt Whitman in the authentic if Black American grain: and one notices how the mature Sam Clemens is remarkably open about the physical details of the dark-hued and pagan island peoples. After all the long years of "censorship" on the part of Howells, on Livy's part and Susy's part, and all the rest of the public and private restraints which were exercised so strongly upon this fresh, rich, and open talent, what had changed in part perhaps was Mark Twain's public utterances in several sensitive areas — but never the inner core of his private sensibility and personal vision of life. Furthermore, he was to grow increasingly frank about *both* sexual and sociopolitical matters in his sixties and seventies, rather than the reverse. As the worldly compulsions and the worldly restraints dropped away from this still-developing talent, he flourished even more grandly.

Just as, in the book, he grew even more lyrical about the Fiji islanders. (Only sixty years ago, they were sunk in darkness, he commented wryly, and now they have the bicycle.) "These men carried no overplus of clothing, and this was wise, for the weather was hot. Handsome, great dusky men they were, muscular, clean-limbed, and with faces full of character and intelligence." As in the earliest travel book, *The Innocents Abroad,* we are reminded, almost thirty years later, of Sam Clemens' sharp and accurate reporting; what a literary eye and ear he did have; how much he took in of the strange scenes and sights and people around him. "It is a fine race, the Fijians, with brains in their heads and an inquiring turn of mind," so Clemens summarized them.

In Fiji, as in the Sandwich Islands, as in the racing, swaying western cradle-coaches of *Roughing It,* or as on Huck Finn's raft drifting down the great flowing river, the aging Samuel Clemens still invoked this deep "womb feeling" — but now perhaps even more deeply. The island wilderness was the very home of romance and dreams and mystery.

The loneliness, the solemnity, the beauty, and the deep repose of this wilderness have a charm which is all their own for the bruised spirit of men who have fought and failed in the struggle for life in the great world; and for men who have been hunted out of the great world for crime; and for other men who love an easy and indolent existence; and for others who love a roving free life, and stir and change and adventure; and for yet others who love an easy and comfortable career of trading and money-getting, mixed with plenty of loose matrimony by purchase, divorce without trial or expense, and limitless spreeing thrown in to make life ideally perfect . . .

"We sailed again, refreshed," Clemens concluded crisply. And to stress his growing conviction that the world was made for man — the white man — and that this was not necessarily good, he quoted another of Pudd'nhead's maxims about America. "It is by the goodness of God that in our country we have those three unspeakably precious things: freedom of speech, freedom of conscience, and the prudence never to practise either of them."

This was from what Clemens called Pudd'nhead's New Calendar, and this calendar marked a break with the past which Clemens stressed again in his account of the white man's conquest of the Australian continent — the opening of another "frontier."

"There must have been a large distribution of acuteness among those naked, skinny aboriginals," said Clemens, "or they couldn't have been such unapproachable trackers and boomerangers and weet-weeters. It must have been race-aversion that put upon them a good deal of the low-rate intellectual reputation which they bear and have borne this long time in the world's estimate of them." But while the Australian native had kept down his own population diligently and deliberately mainly by infancticide, until the whites arrived — "He did not need to practise these artificialities after the white man came. The white man knew ways of keeping down population which were worth several of his. The white man knew ways of reducing a native population eighty per cent in twenty years. The native had never seen anything as fine as that before."

What Clemens had discovered in these pages of *Following the Equator* was the genocide of the native peoples upon which the white man's "civilization" had always been established. That American "Frontier" of Frederick Turner's dubious historical thesis did not exist in a vacuum — but was established on the blood-stained soil of the dark-skinned "savages" who were counted as nonhuman and nonexistent. Quoting an Australian source book which described the case of a squatter who distributed a poisoned pudding to the blacks at Christmas time, Clemens decried this "technical departure" from custom.

> Its unusual nature makes it stand out and attract an amount of attention which it is not entitled to. It takes hold upon morbid imaginations and they work it up into a sort of exhibition of cruelty, and this smirches the good name of our civilization, whereas one of the old harsher methods would have had no such effect because usage has made these methods familiar to us and innocent.
>
> In many countries we have chained the savage and starved him to death; and this we do not care about, because custom has inured us to it; yet a quick death by poison is loving-kindness to it. In many countries we have burned the savage at the stake . . . In more than one country we have hunted the savage and his little children and their mother with dogs and guns through the woods and swamps for an afternoon's sport, and filled the region with happy laughter over their sprawling and stumbling flight, and their wild supplications for mercy; but this method we do not mind because custom has inured us to it; yet a quick death by poison is loving-kindness to it. In many countries we have taken the savage's

land from him, and made him our slave, and lashed him every day, and broken his pride, and made death his only friend, and over-worked him till he dropped in his tracks . . . In the Matabele-land today — why, there we are confining ourselves to sanctified custom, we Rhodes-Beit millionaires in South Africa and Dukes in London; and nobody cares, because we are used to the old holy customs, and all we ask is that no notice-inviting new ones shall be intruded upon the attention of our comfortable con-sciences. Mrs. Praed says of the poisoner, "That squatter deserves to have his name handed down to the contempt of posterity." I am sorry to hear her say that. I myself blame him for one thing, and severely, but I stop there. I blame him for the indiscretion of introducing a novelty which was calculated to attract attention to our civilization.

Devastating irony, lucid phrases, burning sentiments: this was Sam Clemens at his best in *Following the Equator*; and describ-ing the tactics of the French in spreading the blessings of civili-zation in New Caledonia, he added: "You observe the combina-tion? It is robbery, humiliation, and slow, slow murder, through poverty and the white man's whiskey. The savage's gentle friend, the savage's noble friend, the only magnanimous and un-selfish friend the savage has ever had, was not there with the merciful swift release of his poisoned pudding . . . There are many humorous things in the world; among them the white man's notion that he is less savage than the other savages."

Clemens was already preparing himself for that famous es-say, *To the Person Sitting in Darkness* and here he was comic about the contradictions in the Australian literature on the ab-origines. "He is a coward — there are a thousand facts to prove it. He is brave — there are a thousand facts to prove it. He is treacherous — oh, beyond imagination! He is faithful, loyal, true — the white man's records supply you with a harvest of instances of it that are noble, worshipful, and pathetically beau-

tiful. He kills the starving stranger who comes begging for food
and shelter — there is proof of it. He succors, and feeds, and
guides to safety, today, the lost stranger who fired on him only
yesterday — there is proof of it. He takes the reluctant bride
by force, he courts her with a club, then loves her faithfully
through a long life — it is of record." This Australian primitive
beat his wife to death, Clemens added, and laid down his own
life to protect her; he would face "a hundred hostiles" to protect
his child, and he killed his children without qualms; he could
not bear the white man's food, but ate his own uncle with relish;
he was a sociable animal, "yet he turns aside and hides behind
his shield when his mother-in-law goes by."

It is interesting that Clemens noted, if only ironically, the
Freudian taboo on mother surrogates in these primitive tribes,
and he went on at length in these pages to describe their temperaments, character, and foibles. "So much for the Aboriginals.
It is difficult for me to let them alone. They are marvelously interesting creatures" — and so they were for the aboriginal Mark
Twain himself.*

Now he stressed the revolutionary aspects of Australian history
in a period when revolutionary violence was part of the democratic credo and heritage alike, before the darkening shadows
of the Cold War epoch in our own society marked all revolutionary feeling as suspect or subversive. Now he was fascinated
by the Tasmanian savages (in the recurrent underlying theme
of *Following the Equator*); and in the ironical parable of
George Augustus Robinson, called "The Conciliator" for his
heroic feat of persuading the remnant of wild blacks to surren-

---

* In Australia also, as early as 1895, Clemens, noticing the colonial usage of
the mother tongue, anticipated H. L. Mencken's view of the American language. "There is no such thing as 'the Queen's English.' The property has
gone into the hands of a joint stock company and we own the bulk of the
shares."

der their arms in Australasia. "These were indeed wonderful people, the natives," Clemens noted in his Diary. "They ought not to have been wasted. They should have been crossed with the Whites. It would have improved the Whites and done the Natives no harm . . ." And this was heretical thinking for his time, as it is still for ours, when the only conceivable solution for the American race problem is what is called "miscegenation." "But the Natives *were* wasted, poor heroic wild creatures," Clemens added, because they were confined to the white man's reservations to wither away to death and extinction:

> The Whites always mean well when they take human fish out of the ocean and try to make them dry and warm and happy and comfortable in a chicken-coop; but the kindest-hearted white man can always be depended on to prove himself inadequate when he deals with the savages. He cannot turn the situation around and imagine how he would like it to have a well-meaning savage transfer him from his house and his church and his clothes and his books and his choice food to a hideous wilderness of sand and rocks and snow, and ice and sleet and storm and blistering sun, with no shelter, no bed, no covering for his and his family's naked bodies, and nothing to eat but snakes and grubs and offal. This would be a hell to him; and if he had any wisdom he would know that his own civilization is a hell to the savage — but he hasn't any, and has never had any; and for lack of it he shut up those poor natives in the unimaginable perdition of his civilization, committing his crime with the very best intentions, and saw those poor creatures waste away under his tortures; and gazed at it, vaguely troubled and sorrowful, and wondered what could be the matter with them. One is almost betrayed into respecting those criminals, they were so sincerely kind, and tender, and humane, and well meaning.

"*They* didn't know why those exiled savages faded away," so Clemens added, "and they did their honest best to reason it out. And one man, in a like case, in New South Wales, *did* reason it out and arrive at a solution: *'It is from the wrath of God, which is revealed from heaven against all ungodliness and unrighteousness of men.'* That settles it."

And it did, in these inspired pages. For if Sam Clemens was almost "betrayed" into accepting the white man's criminality in regard to the subjugation of the black races during this period, he was never quite able to complete this ironic show of respect. He became indeed the white man's most remorseless historian and chronicler and reporter-on-the-spot during this whole sordid and ignoble phase of modern imperialism whose tragic results have dominated the twentieth century's history.

And just here, at the midway point of the Equator book, one realizes that this volume, uneven or tedious as many parts of it are, is a key document in the record of Mark Twain's thought and intellectual development.

Written in spiritual harassment, after a decade of financial and domestic crisis, written also at the peak of Mark Twain's triumphal worldwide tour — and in the depths of still another personal tragedy: well, perhaps it was just this peculiar set of circumstances around Mark Twain's travels abroad, and this alternation and fusion of defeat and victory, triumph and tragedy, that drew Twain's attention to those "underdeveloped" and "colonized" portions of the earth which he described so vividly in these pages. Which suddenly alerted all his senses to the meaning of history and society in his own time; which brought into such a brilliant and eloquent focus his own primary tensions of nature and civilization. *This* was Mark Twain's import as an artist; not to be described in any scheme of personal neurosis; and as usual it was directed *outward,* and found its great resolution in his art. It throws a new and different light on that "controversial" last portion — or indeed on the whole meaning — of his life and work.

And talking about the animal world, the second volume of

Following the Equator (taken from Twain's Notebook of 1896, in Adelaide) opened with the description of a vulture in the public menagerie in that city. "Bald, red, queer-shaped head, featherless red places here and there on his body, intense great black eyes set in featherless rims of inflamed flesh; dissipated look; a businesslike style, a selfish, conscienceless, murderous aspect — the very look of a professional assassin, and yet a bird which does no murder. What was the use of getting him up in that tragic style for so innocent a trade as his?" The beginning of the second volume introduced, in fact, a whole series of brilliant Twainian animal portraits. There was what Clemens called the Bird of Birds, the Indian Crow. "I came to know him well by and by, and be infatuated with him. I suppose he is the hardest lot that wears feathers. Yes, and the cheerfulest, and the best satisfied with himself. He never arrived at what he is by any careless process, or any sudden one; he is a work of art, and 'art is long'; he is the product of immemorial ages and of deep calculation; one can't make a bird like that in a day. He has been reincarnated more times than Shiva; and he has kept a sample of each incarnation, and fused it into his constitution. In the course of his evolutionary promotions, his sublime march toward ultimate perfection, he has been a gambler, a low comedian, a dissolute priest, a fussy woman, a blackguard, a scoffer, a liar, a thief, a spy, an informer, a trading politician, a swindler, a professional hypocrite, a patriot for cash, a reformer, a lecturer, a conspirator, a rebel, a royalist, a democrat, a practicer and propagator of irreverence, a meddler, an intruder, a busybody, an infidel, and a wallower in sin for the mere love of it. The strange result, the incredible result, of this patient accumulation of all damnable traits is, that he does not know what care is, he does not know what sorrow is, he does not know what remorse is; his life is one long thundering ecstasy of happiness, and he will go to his grave untroubled, knowing that he will turn up again as an author or something, and be even more intolerably capable and comfortable than ever he was before.

"In his straddling wide forward-step, and his springy sidewise series of hops, and his imprudent air, and his cunning way of canting his head to one side upon occasion," Clemens added, he reminded one of the American blackbird, although "the blackbird is a perfect gentleman, in deportment and attire, and is not noisy, I believe, except when holding religious services and political conventions in a tree — "

> but this Indian sham Quaker is just a rowdy, and is always noisy when awake — always chaffing, scolding, scoffing, laughing, ripping, and cursing, and carrying on about something or other. I never saw such a bird for delivering opinions. Nothing escapes him; he notices everything that happens, and brings out his opinion about it, particularly if it is a matter that is none of his business. And it is never a mild opinion, but always violent — violent and profane — the presence of ladies does not affect him. His opinions are not the outcome of reflection, for he never thinks about anything, but heaves out the opinion that is on top in his mind, and which is often an opinion about some quite different thing and does not fit the case. But that is his way; his main idea is to get out an opinion, and if he stopped to think he would lose chances.

This Indian Crow had no enemies among men; and but for this he might have been a reincarnation of Sam Clemens, or vice versa. Perhaps Sam Clemens was just recognizing himself in the Indian Crow; or at least there was some natural affinity here. Birds! Just birds, but what ornithologist has written like this about birds? Like his Crow, Clemens wasn't missing much on his Indian tour; was noticing everything, and bringing out his own opinion, and usually not so mildly either.

Shifting from topic to topic in his impressions of the Indian

scene which utterly fascinated him, Clemens produced a series of
marvelous fireworks in his prose, each phrase igniting the next
one — against a chorus of rippling laughter. There was another
lurid description of an Indian dog where the tone verged on
Dada:

> It was a long, low dog, with very short, strange legs — legs that
> curved inboard, something like parentheses turned the wrong way
> ")(". Indeed, it was made on the plan of a bench for length and
> lowness. It seemed to be satisfied, but I thought the plan poor, and
> structurally weak, on account of the distance between the forward
> supports and those abaft. With age the dog's back was likely to
> sag; and it seemed to me that it would have been a stronger and
> more practicable dog if it had some more legs.

In this Indian scene, where the dividing line between animal
and human was not yet so marked as in late nineteenth-century
industrial United States, Clemens was in his element. Here indeed, he took almost the same pleasure in human as he did
in animal life.

In Ceylon he wrote marvelous pages on the dark-skinned people, their flowing, loose, colorful clothes, the glowing nakedness
of their flesh: this splendid Oriental conflagration of life and
color which swarmed around him, and made him reflect again
on the absurdity of European clothing. Bombay was a bewitching place, a bewildering place, an enchanting place, the Arabian
Nights come again. The whole shining, shifting mysterious spectacle of Asiatic life overwhelmed Clemens and incited his pen to
new bursts of rhapsody. Noticing the working class men and
women, he was Whitmanesque again. "Usually the man is a
nobly built great athlete, with not a rag on but his loin-handker-
chief; his color a deep dark brown, his skin satin, his rounded
muscles knobbing it as if it had eggs under it. Usually the

woman is a slender and shapely creature, as erect as a lightning-
rod, and she has but one thing on — a bright-colored piece of
stuff which is wound about her head and her body down nearly
half-way to her knees, and which clings like her own skin. Her
legs and feet are bare, and so are her arms, except for the fanci-
ful bunches of loose silver rings on her ankles and on her arms.
She has jewelry bunched on the side of her nose also, and showy
cluster-rings on her toes. When she undresses for bed she takes
off her jewelry, I suppose. If she took off anything more she
would catch cold."

It was all color, bewitching color, enchanting color — including the famous dark color which Clemens adored. Color,
and noise. "Why, in the matter of noise it amounted to a riot, an
insurrection, a revolution. And then there were other noises
mixed up with these and at intervals tremendously accenting
them — roofs falling in, I judged, windows smashing, persons
being murdered, crows squawking and deriding and cursing,
canaries screeching, monkeys jabbering, macaws blaspheming,
and every now and then fiendish bursts of laughter and explosions of dynamite." And "even now, after a lapse of a year, the
delirum of those days in Bombay has not left me," Clemens said,
"and I hope never will."

Nor did Clemens miss the poverty and misery, the degrading
social system of starvation, misery, famine, and disease which
lay under this glorious social spectacle, and upon which the
great and noble fortunes of India had been built, and which
English rule perpetuated. Yet he remained, in this phase of his
development, curiously pro-English, and almost Anglophiliac in
sentiment.

He could not quite attack either the Indian ruling classes or
their English masters. Here, strangely, was no mention of the
white man's imperialism and exploitation which Clemens was so

sensitive to everywhere else in the South Pacific islands and Asiatic continent. He even admired and flattered the Indian princes
who in turn feted and courted him during the tour. Comment-
ing only that English rule had been better for India than native
Indian rule (which, if true, was hardly a great achievement),
discussing the fantastic fortunes and evil behavior of such famous Nabobs as Clive and Hastings, Clemens defended all on
the premise of making India safe for the East India Company.
"He was a capable kind of person was Warren Hastings. Some
of his acts have left stains upon his name which can never be
washed away, but he saved to England the Indian Empire, and
that was the best service that was ever done to the Indians themselves, those wretched heirs of a hundred centuries of pitiless
oppression and abuse." In this instance history did not confirm
Mark Twain's judgment, although a liberated India, by 1970,
had not altogether altered the main burden of his charge.

Clemens in fact became almost sentimental in his Anglophiliac rationalizations. Perhaps his admiration for Rudyard Kipling was one source of his error; the obvious English admiration
for his own talent was surely another. The ruins of the Lucknow
Residency were sacred, he said, "and will suffer no neglect nor
be profaned by any sordid or commercial use while the British
remain masters of India." Yet he could not quite explain why
these benevolent and tasteful masters of India had incurred such
a violent insurrection as the Great Mutiny itself. He was on
safer ground again when he described the history of the notorious
Thuggee cult which was another obvious product of social ignorance, misery, and vice.

This clan and cult, almost a religion, specializing in murder
and robbery as a way of life, these Thugs fascinated Clemens
all over again, and *Following the Equator* is full of their lore.
Quoting Thuggee,

How many of your English are passionately devoted to sporting! Your days and months are passed in its excitement. A tiger, a panther, a buffalo, or a hog rouses your utmost energies for its destruction — you even risk your lives in its pursuit. How much higher game is a Thug's!

Clemens went on to develop the theme. "That must really be the secret of the rise and development of Thuggee. The joy of killing! the joy of seeing killing done — these are traits of the human race at large. We white people are merely modified Thugs; Thugs fretting under the restraints of a not very thick skin of civilization; Thugs who long ago enjoyed the slaughter of the Roman arena, and later the burning of doubtful Christians by authentic Christians in the public squares, and who now, with the Thugs of Spain and Nimes, flock to enjoy the blood and misery of the bull-ring. We have no tourists of either sex or any religion who are able to resist the delights of the bull-ring when opportunity offers; and we are gentle Thugs in the hunting season and love to chase a tame rabbit and kill it."

Clemens quoted the more outrageous examples of the Indian Thugs' pleasure in killing their unwary victims — the sadistic games which were enjoyed before the killings:

A gang of forty-two Thugs came across two Brahmans and a shop-keeper on the road, beguiled them into a grove and got up a *concert* for their entertainment. While these poor fellows were listening to the music the stranglers were standing behind them; and at the proper moment for dramatic effect they applied the nooses.

And then, "When the lust in the hunter's heart is for the noblest of all quarries, man, how different is the case? and how watery and poor is the zeal and how childish the endurance of those other hunters by comparison. Then, neither hunger, nor thirst, nor fatigue, nor deferred hope, nor monotonous disappointment, nor leaden-footed lapse of time can conquer the hunter's patience or weaken the joy of his quest or cool the splendid rage of his desire. Of all the hunting-passions that burn in the breast of man, there is none that can lift him superior to discouragements like these but the one — the royal sport, the supreme sport, whose quarry is his brother."

Now these sentiments, even the tone, the expression, the vocabulary, were to become familiar in the historical record of American literature. The later Jack London would approve of this, particularly with regard to the lower or darker races. And Ernest Hemingway carried this theme to a kind of final modern perfection. This was Social Darwinism in its native American form of dog eat dog. But with this difference: that Mark Twain, fascinated as he was with violence from the days of *Roughing It,* and no pacifist ever in his social thinking, was bitterly ironical in the descriptions of Thuggee; just as he became lyrical, after all the decades of "censorship" exerted upon his spirit, about the universal Hindu worship of the lingam in their theology. "It is even a justifiable economy to leave Brahma, the chiefest god of all, out of your studies, for he seems to cut no great figure in India."

> The vast bulk of the national worship is lavished upon Shiva and Vishnu and their families. Shiva's symbol — the "lingam" with which Vishnu began the Creation — is worshipped by everybody, apparently. It is the commonest object in Benares. It is on view everywhere, it is garlanded with flowers, offerings are made to it, it suffers no neglect. Commonly it is an upright stone, shaped like a thimble — sometimes like an elongated thimble. This priapus-worship, then, is older than history. Mr. Parker says that the lingams in Benares *"outnumber the inhabitants."*

In Calcutta, there was a cloud-kissing monument to one Ochterlony. "It is a fluted candlestick two hundred and fifty feet high. This lingam is the only large monument in Calcutta, I believe. It is a fine ornament, and will keep Ochterlony in mind." Clemens began dreaming about lingams, just as he was fascinated by all the Indian religious cults, temples, and idols. "It is a curious people. With them, all life seems to be sacred, except human life." But down in the Indian Ocean, again, near Madagascar and Mauritius, Clemens indulged in some more intuitive and homebred Marxian analysis of the colonial process. "To such as believe that the quaint product called French civilization would be an improvement upon the civilization of New Guinea and the like, the snatching of Madagascar and the laying on of French civilization there will be fully justified. But why did the English allow the French to have Madagascar? Did she respect a theft of a couple of centuries ago? Dear me, robbery by European nations of each other's territories has never been a sin, is not a sin today.

"All the territorial possessions of all the political establishments in the earth — including America, of course — consist of pilferings from other people's wash. No tribe, howsoever insignificant, and no nation, howsoever mighty, occupies a foot of land that was not stolen. When the English, the French, and the Spaniards reached America, the Indian tribes had been raiding each other's territorial clotheslines for ages, and every acre of ground in the continent had been stolen and restolen five hundred times. The English, the French, and the Spaniards went to work and stole it all over again; and when that was satisfactorily accomplished they went diligently to work and stole it from each other. In Europe and Asia and Africa every acre of ground has been stolen several millions of times. A crime persevered in a thousand centuries ceases to be a crime, and becomes a virtue. This is the law of custom, and custom supersedes all other forms of law.

"In fact, in our day, land-robbery, claim-jumping, is become a European governmental frenzy. Some have been hard at it in the borders of China, in Burma, in Siam, and the islands of the sea; and *all* have been at it in Africa. Africa has been as cooly divided up and portioned out among the gang as if they had bought it and paid for it. And now straightway they are beginning the old game again — to steal each other's grabbings . . . There is a tremendous point there. It can be put into the form of a maxim: Get your formalities right — never mind about the moralities."

The last sections of *Following the Equator* also carried Clemens' firsthand reporting on South Africa and the Boer War. There are descriptions of the Boers' use of those guerrilla tactics which, half a century later, would be used again to emancipate Asia, Africa, South America from what Mark Twain then believed would be the perpetual and universal rule of the white race. Despite all his acute and prophetic doubts about the Boer personality and society, he was still on the side of the native revolutionaries — as long as he could be.

For, of course, the Boers were worse to the native Kafirs than the English were to the Boers. Mark Twain praised those Boers who had forced fifteen hundred Kafirs into a cave, and smoked them to death. "The great bulk of the savages must go," he explained. "The white man wants their lands, and all must go excepting such percentage of them as he will need to do his work for him upon terms to be determined by himself. Since history has removed the element of guesswork from this matter and made it certainty, the humanest way of diminishing the black population should be adopted, not the old cruel ways of the past."

Mr. Rhodes and his gang have been following the old ways. They are chartered to rob and slay, and they lawfully do it, but not in a compassionate and Christian spirit. They rob the Mashonas and the Matabeles of a portion of their territories in the hallowed old style of "purchase" for a song, and then they force a quarrel and take the rest by the strong hand. They rob the natives of their cattle under the pretext that all the cattle in the country belong to the king whom they have tricked and assassinated. They issue "regulations" requiring the incensed and harassed natives to work for the white settlers, and neglect their own affairs to do it. This is slavery, and is several times worse than was the American slavery which used to pain England so much; for when this Rhodesian slave is sick, superannuated, or otherwise disabled, he must support himself or starve — his master is under no obligation to support him.

The reduction of the native population by the Rhodesian methods, Clemens claimed, was a return to the "old-time slow-misery and lingering-death system of a discredited time and a crude 'civilization' ":

> We humanely reduce an overplus of dogs by swift chloroform; the Boer humanely reduced an overplus of blacks by swift suffocation; the nameless but right-hearted Australian pioneer humanely reduced his overplus of aboriginal neighbors by a sweetened swift death concealed in a poisoned pudding. All these are admirable and worthy of praise . . .

And you and I, he concluded, "would rather suffer either of these deaths thirty times over in thirty successive days than linger out one of the Rhodesian twenty-year deaths, with its daily burden of insult, humiliation, and forced labor for a man whose entire race the victim hates. Rhodesia is a happy name for that land of piracy and pillage, and puts the right stain upon it."

What had started out, in Mark Twain's mind, as savage irony ended almost as literal fact; and perhaps one mark of true irony is simply the sudden disclosure of such hidden, un-

known truths . . . And then there was the final portrait of
Cecil Rhodes himself, as the archetype of all those exploiting
and colonizing tycoons of finance-capital whom a Theodore
Dreiser too would study with the same mixture of awe, anger,
and tragic despair. "I know quite well that whether Mr. Rhodes
is the lofty and worshipful patriot and statesman that multitudes believe him to be, or Satan come again, as the rest of the
world account him, he is still the most imposing figure in the
British Empire outside of England. When he stands on the
Cape of Good Hope, his shadow falls to the Zambesi . . .
The whole South African world seemed to stand in a kind of
shuddering awe of him, friend and enemy alike . . . He
weeps over the harshly taxed Johannesburgers and makes them
his friends; at the same he taxes his Charter settler fifty per
cent . . . He raids and robs and slays and enslaves the
Matabeles and gets worlds of Charter-Christian applause for
it. He has beguiled England into buying Charter waste-
paper for Bank of England notes, ton for ton, and the ravished
still burn incense to him as the Eventual God of Plenty. He has
done everything he could think of to pull himself down to the
ground . . . yet there he stands, to this day, upon his dizzy
summit under the dome of the sky, an apparent permanency,
the marvel of the time, the mystery of the age, an Archangel
with wings to half the world, Satan with a tail to the other half.

"I admire him, I frankly confess it; and when his time comes
I shall buy a piece of the rope for a keepsake."

If Sam Clemens was still illusioned about English imperial
rule in India, he saw the blunt facts clearly in the southern isles,
in Australia, in South Africa; just as he witnessed so brilliantly
the Boer treatment of the Kafirs, just as he saw everywhere so
clearly the white man's treatment of the darker-skinned people
in the terrible and degrading process of imperialism. There

was to be more of this in Mark Twain's writing — much more
— because in *Following the Equator* he had unearthed a key
factor of contemporary history.

Not only was imperialism — and that is to say the later
struggle against it, the liberation movements all over Asia,
Africa, South America — the key issue of the twentieth century and almost a struggle against the white race by all the
darker races of the earth. And not only would Mark Twain
now describe this issue everywhere he traveled or read about,
and then see it appear in his own country, too. But more.

For what he had witnessed in the colonial territories of the
world was simply the preliminary stages of what was almost
the final holocaust of Western European civilization itself.
What was later viewed as the "Nazi Terror," the Hitlerite reversion to barbarism, all the Fascist horrors — wasn't this simply the culmination of the so-called Christian European nations' process of empire building in the nineteenth century? At
least the same tactics of dehumanizing terror, of mass liquida-
tion, of cultural extermination which were used against the
darker peoples of the world were to be more efficiently, more
scientifically, and more abstractly turned against the "inferior" white people of European civilization itself.

In *Following the Equator* (and henceforth in all his writings),
Mark Twain had prophetically glimpsed and anticipated the
whole dark future of his society and culture. And just as the
so-called Christian nations of Western Europe had participated
in the plundering, looting, and ravishing of all the dark-skinned
primitive cultures everywhere in Asia, Africa, and the South
Pacific islands; just as they insisted on stealing these rich,
black trophies of pagan wealth from each other, so when it became the turn of the European Jews, the Russians, the Poles,
and the Eastern European peoples to undergo the same proc-

ess of human debasement, economic exploitation, and mass
extermination — the Christian nations of the Western world
turned their gaze away; refused succor; remained "ignorant"
as long as it was possible for them to ignore the bestiality in
their midst.

Clemens, at this point of his career, was wrong only about
two things. That the darker-skinned peoples of the world
would accept their own extermination; and that the same process of genocide would not be used by the white man against
the white man.

But how could he have glimpsed such a swift and dramatic
culmination of the imperialist process he was describing?
which would be, on the one hand, violent, revolutionary, ultimately and hopefully curative and creative; on the other hand,
far more savage, obscene, degrading than anything he ever
wrote in his worst moods of "pessimism" or "nihilism."

The historical process outstripped Mark Twain as much
as it outdistanced the complacent critics who accused him of
such "cynical" despair. But he did just about as well as any
artist could with the historical materials which were given to
him. And extremely well, indeed, for an American artist evolving from a cultural and a personal matrix which was apparently so remote from the historical crisis whose origins he had
discovered here. These sections in *Following the Equator* are
brilliantly written — whenever Sam Clemens met with the
darker races and their greedy, cunning, exploiting, sadistic
white masters — and are of clear interest today. In the process
of writing the book, Sam Clemens revived his own flagging
spirits: the writing created the writing, as so often happens
with a major figure. Starting out in such a tired, halting, and
uneven vein of prose, the Equator book is obviously a crucial
document in Clemens' development — what his earlier biog-

rapher, Albert Bigelow Paine, in this case more acutely than the modern biographer Justin Kaplan, called the revival and renascence of Mark Twain's later period.

It was just that, despite all the odds against it. For at the very climax of this triumphal world tour, which rescued him from the horrible bankruptcy, which emblazoned his name in the capitals of the world and re-established his own faith in himself, he had found in the darker-skinned, primitive, and pagan peoples of the world both the historical key to his own epoch and, as we've seen, an embodiment of his own deepest temperamental strains. And all this despite the fact that, at this very point of outward material victory and triumph, and of an inward self-realization and spiritual renewal, Sam Clemens was struck down again by another tragic blow, in a career that was always to be marked, it seemed, by such polar extremes of feeling.

FIVE

THE ENRAGED RADICAL

THOUGH THERE WERE MOMENTS in Mark Twain's life when you wonder if this amiable genius, all embedded in his rocking cradles, his floating rafts, his majestic sleeping couch, meandering and laughing his way through man's brief and essentially comic existence, was nevertheless — quite apart from and beyond the matter of civilizational discontents — pursued by some deeper, eternally vengeful and avenging furies, such as those imagined by man from the dawn of existence, and just as Clemens himself described Nature's perverted malice.

Directly after the return of Sam, Livy, and Clara to England, at the end of the worldwide lecture tour, they heard that Susy, who had been left in America with Jean under Kate Leary's charge, was ill. This was August 15, 1896, and Livy and Clara took passage back home. Three days later, when they were about halfway across the ocean, Clemens received the news that Susy had died of meningitis. Nothing was spared the Clemenses in the terrible end of their favorite child. Three days before her death, Susy had become blind; before that she had wandered through the rooms of the Hartford mansion in delirium and pain, calling for her mother.

After her death nothing was ever quite the same between Sam and Livy and the children, or with the whole domestic scene of affection and gaiety which had made the Clemenses' marriage and homelife so unique in literary history. Despite all the stress and strain, their Hartford house had been "not unsentient matter," as Clemens wrote to Twichell. "It had a heart & a soul & eyes to see us with, & approvals & solicitudes & deep sympathies; it was of us, & we were in its confidence, & lived in its grace & in the peace of its benediction. We never came home from an absence that its face did not light up & speak out its eloquent welcome — & we could not enter it unmoved." But now they knew they were not welcome in the Hartford house, and their temporary home in Chelsea (England) became a dismal place.

Clemens' notes and letters were full of anguished references to Susy, according to Paine's account; he accepted Livy's black despair on top of his own. They saw nobody and wished to see nobody; they concealed their address except for their closest friends. They refused to celebrate Thanksgiving and Christmas that year, and sat alone, nursing their sorrow. Clemens became superstitious about their bad luck and said that it was risky for people to have anything to do with them. He wrote desperate letters to Howells. "Will healing ever come, or life have value again? And shall we see Susy? Without doubt. Without a *shadow* of doubt if it can furnish opportunity to break our hearts again." He took, moreover, the full blame for Susy's death upon himself, as he had, so many years ago, for his brother's. The guilt for his own financial manipulations, for driving his family into the shame of bankruptcy, the ordeal of poverty and of scrimping afterwards — all this was blended with and exacerbated by the final agony of believing that Susy might not have died if they had not been away from her.

If Sam Clemens had a curious identification with Satan at the core of his psychic being, this was a sorrowing and sinful Satan now who took responsibility for all of God's doings, for the moral universe which indeed he had willfully defied. "To Mrs. Clemens," Paine writes, "he poured himself out in a letter in which he charged himself categorically as being wholly and solely responsible for the tragedy, detailing step by step with fearful reality his mistakes and weaknesses which had led to their downfall, the separation from Susy, and this final incredible disaster. Only a human being, he said, could have done these things." Very similarly, later on, in Mark Twain's *Autobiography*, we learn that Clemens blamed himself completely for the death of their first child, their baby son; a guilty "secret" he had contained within himself for almost his entire life. Did Livy also believe this in her secret heart; or did she allow Sam to believe it without relieving his burden? There is no doubt, at least, that after Susy's death the domestic life of the Clemenses turned upon itself. From this point started Livy's psychic and physical decline which also affected Clara's uneasy temperament, while Jean's health had already been failing.

After a long and full career of such extraordinary fame and wealth and pleasure and affection, surviving even the worst blows of harsh adversity with remarkable fortitude, tenacity, and courage; for almost a full decade of their later life facing a penurious and disgraceful old age, as it seemed, and suddenly liberated only to meet with a last deep blow, a fatal domestic tragedy, the once blessed and exceptionally fortunate and graceful spiritual union of the Clemenses finally cracked.

Yet Sam Clemens himself remained forever faithful and loving to his Livy, and incredibly brought his own writing powers back to another triumphant peak, and was even on the point of once again re-establishing some modicum of personal fulfillment and content when (this was almost an accursed house like that, later on, of Eugene O'Neill) the final blow fell — not yet visible to Sam Clemens, though already hinted at. Meanwhile at sixty, with Livy at fifty, the demonism also at the core of Mark Twain's spirit (not unlike the ragings of a Theodore Dreiser, later on, at a God of Justice and Mercy who yet allowed such senseless deeds of suffering and cruelty) was transfused into his art and his social vision. "I wish the Lord would disguise Himself in citizen's clothing & make a personal examination of the sufferings of the poor in London," Clemens jotted in his notebook, at this time. "He would be moved & would do something for them Himself."

This was the same London scene, of course, whose "lowest depths" Henry James found in the ignoble, mean-spirited middle classes of *The Wings of the Dove,* or even worse, the perfidious and unholy storybook "anarchists" of *The Princess Casamassima.* But Clemens was among the first of a whole series of more observant American writers who bore witness to the social misery in England.

Like all great writers he found his opiate and his salvation and his resurrection in the creative act itself. "I don't mean that I am miserable; no — worse than that — indifferent," he wrote to Howells. "Indifferent to nearly everything but work. I like that; I enjoy it, & stick to it. I do it without purpose & without ambition; merely for the love of it. Indeed, I am a mud-image; & it puzzles me to know what it is in me that writes & has comedy fancies & finds pleasure in phrasing them . . ." What it was in him, of course, was his genius — and not being able to sleep, he took pleasure in setting to work, sometimes, at four o'clock in the morning. It was during this period of darkness, too, that Clemens issued that celebrated statement to a newspaper reporter. (The press accounts of the time pictured him as abandoned by his family, deserted by all, drunk, sick, poor, and dying.) "Just say the report of my death has been grossly exaggerated." And when Livy kept on objecting to words like breech-clout, stench, offal, or to "a shady-principled cat" which had a family in every port, Clemens was mild. "You are steadily weakening the English tongue, Livy."

During this period, too, Clemens began developing his interest in dreams and in the dream life (or in illusion and reality) which almost every great writer has had, but which the Freudians find so portentously and ominously significant. Which was the dream, which was the reality, he asked himself, and sometimes he wondered if even his wife and family and his domestic life had been just a dream — a dreamlike fantasy which indeed he felt had now vanished. On the first anniversary of Susy's death, when the Clemenses were spending the summer in Switzerland, Livy took a small bag, went off for the day on a steamer to read over Susy's poetry, while Sam spent the day writing the beautiful ode "In Memoriam." The tension in the house was very great, Paine says. "A gloom settled on the household, a shadow of restraint" which was marked.

Clemens often worked in bed, and when a reporter came to see him, he refused to get up but made another concession to Livy's embarrassment. "Why, Livy, if you think so, we might have the other bed made up for him." And after all his debts had been paid off, his royalties were bringing in an income, and Rogers was investing his money for him, Clemens could hardly resist the old temptation of fascinating mechanical inventions which would yield him immense quick fortunes. He negotiated with the Austrian inventor Szezepanik for the rights to a carpet-pattern machine. He planned to obtain an option at five hundred thousand dollars and to organize a monopoly at a much larger amount to control the carpet-weaving of the world, if Rogers approved. Rogers did not approve; and Clemens did not always ask for Rogers' approval. He bought an interest, according to Paine, in a skimmed-milk invalid food called Plasmon, which would cure the human race of its ills; and meanwhile, in 1900, he published *The Man That Corrupted Hadleyburg and Other Stories and Essays*.

The volume as a whole included stories and articles, mainly in a popular vein and written for cash in the late nineties, but some as early as "The £1,000,000 Bank-Note" in 1893. Uneven in craft, rough in detail, "Hadleyburg" is a remarkable story, a fascinating sequel to *Pudd'nhead Wilson*, an important precursor to *The Mysterious Stranger* in the dark vein of Mark Twain's later fables. This western village was really a Hegelian reversal, or contradiction, of Hannibal, Missouri. Its fame was for its "commercial integrity," the moral virtue, the upright honesty and sobriety of its citizens. But who was the "mysterious stranger" himself who, having been wounded by the town, deliberately set out to corrupt it, to prove that all its pretenses of impeccable respectability were a fraud? This was again a dream-nightmare tale with a satanic figure as the mysterious activating presence; this was the dream turned inside out. Its satire followed that of the Virginia aristocrats in *Pudd'nhead*, those FFV's (First Families of Virginia) who were so honorable about everything except their subhuman slaves; and at base "Hadleyburg" was an eloquent example of the corruption of the old American republic by the great booming nineteenth century's notion of "progress."

The tone of the story was not realistic but symbolical, or closer, like *Pudd'nhead*, to a kind of native surrealism which Clemens invented for his own purposes. And "Hadleyburg" was also a brilliant study, psychological and social, of the influence of money upon the human spirit, or of the prevalence of greed in the human temperament when confronted by temptation. Clemens was projecting his own torment over a decade of financial ruin, surely, but he was projecting it into a specific historical context: the corruption of the town's earlier, more natural and less materialistic human types and social relationships. When the mysterious stranger leaves the sack of gold, poor Mrs. Richards immediately locks the house doors and bars the windows which had previously been open; her first thought is of thieves. The full, open, and easy quality of western frontier existence — the earlier democracy of small means and social equality in the older epochs of the national development — has been lost forever.

"It is dreadful to be poor," says Mr. Richards; but it is much more dreadful for them to be rich. His first thought was to destroy the stranger's written bequest and keep the sack of gold; the virtue of the frontier crumbled under the first temptation. Hadleyburg was indeed an "honest, narrow, self-righteous and stingy" town, as the village rebel, Barclay Goodson, had declared. In these symbolic or surrealist tales, Twain often used rather obvious names for his central figures.

And this is also a story of a terrible moral conformity, a fear of generous or bold human action, a show of public virtue as a mask for private gain, an overwhelming social hypocrisy which covers the contortions of small, if not evil souls.

The Richardses are really a terrible couple whom Clemens described with absolute accuracy; we flinch when we read about them because we understand them so well. The central logic, the developments in the early part of the story, the twists of human temperament and social circumstance alike, are invented by a diabolical intelligence. The greedy cunning of the Richardses is only equaled by their tormented anxiety — not an anxiety about their scheming fancies but as to the possible appearance of their deeds. There is no question of morality in the whole town of Hadleyburg; there is only a question of practical consequences. "God forgive me — it's awful to think such things," says Mary Richards, "but . . . Lord, how we are made — how strangely we are made!" — and her guilt does not prevent her from further manifestations of greed. During the period of his own financial manipulations, Sam Clemens had learned much about the desperate possibilities of the human temperament. "Hadleyburg" is a Balzacian tale of frontier life.

But his financial experiences had added a depth and a bite to Clemens' writing. The foolish artist, as the psychoanalytic critics don't seem to understand, can enrich his art by his folly. And one notices how often the central figures of these stories — the "gambler," the "outcast," the "schemers," the respectable hypocrites — are obvious projections of aspects of Twain's own temperament, now used as his literary pawns.

Mary Richards again admits her guilt. "It is a mean town, a hard, stingy town," and it is her belief that the town's honesty is as rotten as hers is — and still she goes on scheming with her anxiety-ridden husband to get the golden fortune. And the "moral" struggles of the Richardses are repeated by the Coxes and by "Pinkerton," the town banker. And Jack Halliday, who is the loafing, good-natured, no-account, irreverent fisherman, hunter, boys' friend, and bum of the town, Jack Halliday, or Holiday, the pagan Huck Finn character of the story, becomes a kind of a frontier Greek chorus which records the alternation of joy (greed) and depression (fear of financial loss) in the leading townspeople. It develops that the reward will go to the person who knows what the social outcast Goodson told the ruined gambler (the satanic stranger, or doubtless the mask of Sam Clemens himself) which changed his whole life.

Everybody is trying to remember — or invent — that remark in order to get the money, in the malicious development of the story.

Each of the "Nineteen," the leading citizens of the town, gets a similar letter; each thinks he is the only recipient of the prize, each concludes he must have some special virtue to deserve this fortune — their only problem is *what* virtue? When Richards gets his clue to the fortune, his wife is ecstatic. "Oh, Edward, the money is ours, and I am so grateful, *oh,* so grateful — kiss me dear, it's forever since we kissed — and we needed it so — the money," she cries. Clemens is explicit about the repression of sexual pleasure in the face of financial anxiety.

For if Hadleyburg's had been a false virtue, untested by temptation, it is nevertheless true that the "deadly money" has now destroyed the town's whole social fabric and all its personal relations. Poor Richards — "Poor Richard," and one remembers the deadly animus of Twain's earliest attacks on Benjamin Franklin's hypocritical and pleasure-destroying materialism — poor Richards can't sleep for fear that he won't remember the good deed he has done to Goodson (he has done none) which has put him in such a favorable light with the mysterious stranger. "His imagination-mill was hard at work," Clemens remarks, and there is a brilliant section of the story on the endless processes of human rationalization. And then Richards suddenly realizes what the good deed was! Goodson had been engaged to a very sweet and pretty girl named Nancy Hewitt; the match had been broken off, and the girl had died:

Soon after the girl's death the village found out, or thought it had found out, that she carried a spoonful of negro blood in her veins. Richards worked at these details a good while . . .

[and] he seemed to dimly remember that it was *he* that found out about the negro blood; that it was he that told the village; that the village told Goodson where they got it; that he thus saved Goodson from marrying the tainted girl; that he had done him this great service without knowing that he *was* doing it; but that Goodson knew the value of it, and what a narrow escape he had had, and so went to his grave grateful to his benefactor and wishing he had a fortune to leave him.

What a remarkable "inversion" of truth has Mark Twain wrought here — or perhaps what a horrifying statement of truth as it appears to poor Richards. What a nice intuition it was to bring the race question into this parable of financial corruption in the new American Empire — as the small towns of the western frontier also fell under the spell of the great American fortunes in the vast sea change of the Old Republic toward the end of the nineteenth century.*

Just as the literary techniques of "Hadleyburg Corrupted" move from the psychological core of the story — the brilliant rationalizing of highly discreditable behavior — to a social scene of general corruption, so Clemens himself was now projecting the psychological tensions of his own financial crisis into the social and historical scene around him. So all art moves from the specific to the universal; and what is important to note, of course, is not only the foolish behavior of Clemens him-

---

* Yet it was this American artist, who, as we've seen, caught on to the evils and horror of world colonialism in *Following the Equator,* just as he had of racism and the Negro question in the United States, and of the whole political, financial, and moral corruption of his period in *The Gilded Age* — that the contemporary biographer, Justin Kaplan, could describe as turning away from the modern American scene after the *Connecticut Yankee,* and as actually becoming an "expatriate" after *Pudd'nhead Wilson.* Perhaps Mr. Kaplan doesn't appreciate the importance of Mark Twain's social criticism because he does not really understand it, or does not wish to. Perhaps it is Mr. Kaplan himself who is some kind of contemporary expatriate in a never-never land of psychic anxiety without any social context.

self during the whole period of his financial speculations, but
the rich rewards which he reaped in his writing. His bankruptcy was not his undoing, as might have happened with a
lesser talent, and as some Mark Twain critics have maintained
about him — it was instead a kind of spiritual death and re-
birth. What mattered in the end, as I say, was not so much his
own suffering during this whole period as the new artistic purpose formed by his suffering; and he was to endure and, yes,
use, in the highest artistic sense, even to the last ordeal of his
domestic tragedy.

One notices also, in the central figures of "The Man That
Corrupted Hadleyburg," not only the constant attempt to deceive others, but far worse, the continuous and unconscious
process of *self-deception.* When Richards has finally reached the
"solution" of the service he has done Goodson — the matter of
the Negro blood in the "tainted girl" — his spirit is completely
at peace. "It was all clear and simple now, and the more he
went over it the more luminous and certain it grew; and at last,
when he nestled to sleep satisfied and happy, he remembered
the whole thing just as if it had been yesterday. In fact, he
dimly remembered Goodson's *telling* him his gratitude once.
Meantime Mary had spent six thousand dollars on a new house
for herself and a pair of slippers for her pastor, and then had
fallen peacefully to rest."

The whole community indulges in a spree of imaginary
spending. The new architect in "this unpromising town" finds
himself deluged by secret plans for palatial new houses. "The
days drifted along, and the bill of future squanderings rose
higher and higher, wilder and wilder, more and more foolish
and reckless. It began to look as if every member of the 'Nineteen' would not only spend his whole forty thousand dollars before receiving-day, but be actually in debt by the time he got

the money. In some cases lightheaded people did not stop with planning to spend, they really spent — on credit." And while Sam Clemens knew this from deep personal experience, he was also anticipating a whole new epoch of credit-financing and installment-buying on which a later American economy would come to rest — perhaps to thrive.

Hadleyburg was another early example of Thorstein Veblen's conspicuous consumption. What we see here is the disintegration of the whole town's structure, social and personal relationships alike, under the lure and pressure of an "imaginary fortune." While those great fortunes of Clemens' own period which were real did even more harm to the social patterns and moral values of the Old Republic than the symbolic one in Mark Twain's story. Clemens was also describing, in the chronicle of a disintegrating Hannibal — which became Hadleyburg, which became hell — the cultural impact of the titans and the trusts; of the new social-economic regime of monopoly capitalism in the United States. The rest of the mysterious message, which was *not* given to any of the aspiring "Nineteeners" in the town, read: "Go, and reform — or, mark my words — some day, for your sins, you will die and go to hell or Hadleyburg — *try and make it the former.*"

Among the other stories and tales in the *Hadleyburg* volume, "The Esquimau Maiden's Romance," though poor fiction, is a parody of the impact of wealth upon a primitive society (a variation of the Hadleyburg Corrupted theme); just as we have already noticed how so many of Twain's stories, parables, fables of this period are almost obsessively concerned with the meaning of money as romance, fairy tale, delusion, disease, and nightmare. But listen to the Esquimau princess lamenting the moral decline of her father: "He has lowered the tone of all our tribe. Once they were a frank and manly race, now they are measly hypocrites and sodden with servility. In my heart of hearts I hate all the ways of millionaires. Our tribe was once plain, simple folk, contented with the bone fish-hooks of their fathers; now they are eaten up with avarice and would sacrifice every sentiment of honor and honesty to possess themselves of the debasing iron fish-hooks of the foreigner."

Even the Arctic Circle had its Hadleyburgs. During this period Clemens was writing sections of the *Autobiography* and revising certain parts of it for immediate publication, and "My First Lie and How I Got Out of It" may fall into this classification. He was now sixty-four, as he says, and his memory is not as good as it was. "If you had asked about my first truth it would have been easier for me and kinder of you, for I remember that fairly well; I remember it as if it were last week. The family think it was week before, but that is flattery and probably has a selfish project back of it." This is an entertaining familiar essay on the paucity of truth in the human spirit, with an unexpected conclusion. For Clemens' argument is, what does one individual liar amount to when compared to the gigantic conspiracy of lies upon which civilization rests?

The fact is, as Clemens stated, that "all lies are acts, and speech has no part in them" — a nice perception. And then "they" — by which he meant the students of lying in human development — "Then, if they examined a little further they recognized that all people are liars from the cradle onward, without exception, and that they begin to lie as soon as they wake in the morning, and keep it up, without rest or refreshment, until they go to sleep at night. If they arrived at that truth it probably grieved them — did, if they had been heedlessly and ignorantly educated by their books and teachers; for why should a person grieve over a thing which by the eternal law of his make he cannot help? He didn't invent the law; it is

merely his business to obey it and keep still; join the universal
conspiracy and keep so still that he shall deceive his fellow-
conspirators into imagining that he doesn't know that the law
exists."

History would absolve Sam Clemens of being cynical in
these prophetic lines of prose; history would prove he was un-
derstating his case; but then, of course, he was working from
history. "It is what we all do — we that know," he continued.

> I am speaking of the lie of silent assertion; we can tell it without
> saying a word, and we all do it — we that know. In the magnitude
> of its territorial spread it is one of the most majestic lies that the
> civilizations make it their sacred and anxious care to guard and
> watch and propagate.

The epoch of the Third Reich was in the distant future, the
imperialistic horrors of the Belgian Congo, it may be, were resting
in Clemens' prescient spirit, but meanwhile he gave a few other
historical examples.

"For instance: It would not be possible for a humane and
intelligent person to invent a rational excuse for slavery; yet
you will remember that in the early days of the emancipation
agitation in the North, the agitators got but small help or countenance from any one. Argue and plead and pray as they
might, they could not break the universal stillness that reigned,
from pulpit and press all the way down to the bottom of society
— the clammy stillness created and maintained by the lie of
silent assertion — the silent assertion that there wasn't anything
going on in which humane and intelligent people were interested."

There would be those humane and intelligent German citizens who maintained the same silent assertion while the stench
of the concentration camp filled their nostrils; those American

citizens who maintained the same silent-assertion lie while Vietnamese villages and peasants were being bombed and massacred. But Asia and Africa were far away, and the Clemens who had written *Following the Equator* gave some closer examples. "From the beginning of the Dreyfus case to the end of it, all France, except a couple of dozen moral paladins, lay under the smother of the silent-assertion lie that no wrong was being done to a persecuted and unoffending man." During Mr. Chamberlain's South African war, Clemens continued, England lay under the like smother of silence, and "Now there we have instances of three prominent ostensible civilizations working the silent-assertion lie. Could one find other instances in the three countries? I think so. Not so very many, perhaps, but say a billion — just so as to keep within bounds." And this was polemical writing, of course, of high order. The familiar essay "On Lying" had turned into a brilliant social indictment.

"Are those countries working that kind of lie, day in and day out, in thousands and thousands of varieties, without ever resting? Yes, we know that to be true. The universal conspiracy of the silent-assertion lie is hard at work always and everywhere, and always in the interest of a stupidity or a sham, never in the interest of a thing fine or respectable."

This was a prose style of such distinction, a gravamen of such solidity and acuteness and consequence that one almost wants to quote every one of the sentences flowing so fully, so sweetly, from the brimming cup of Mark Twain's wrath. This universal conspiracy of silence upon which all civilization rested, was it the most timid and shabby of all lies? "It seems to have the look of it. For ages and ages it has mutely labored in the interest of the despotisms and aristocracies and chattel slaveries, and military slaveries, and religious slaveries, and has kept them alive; keeps them alive yet, here and there and yonder, all about the globe; and will go on keeping them alive until the silent-assertion lie retires from business — the silent assertion that nothing is going on which fair and intelligent men are aware of and are engaged by their duty to try to stop."

And then he reached his point, as though he had not made it yet. "What I am arriving at is this: When whole races and peoples conspire to propagate gigantic mute lies in the interest of tyrannies and shams, why should we care anything about the trifling lies told by individuals? Why should we try to make it appear that abstention from lying is a virtue? Why should we want to beguile ourselves in that way? Why should we without shame help the nation lie, and then be ashamed to do a little lying on our own account? Why shouldn't we be honest and honorable, and lie every time we get a chance?" Was there an echo of Huck Finn in this plaintive query? It was again a confrontation of primitive innocence and the ambiguities of civilization; but this was a sturdy, even impudent and ravishing innocence which did not flinch at whatever odd inversions of "reason" it reached. That is to say, Clemens concluded, "why shouldn't we be consistent, and either lie all the time or not at all? Why should we help the nation lie the whole day long and then object to telling one little individual private lie in our own interest, to go to bed on? Just for the refreshment of it, I mean, and to take the rancid taste out of our mouth." *

This was the high point, no doubt, of the other tales, sketches, and essays which were collected in the *Hadleyburg* volume, which constantly stressed, as Twain's treatise on lying did, the polar swing of the individual soul and the community. Among the other pieces, "The Belated Russian Passport" was an en-

* The "silent assertion" has just lately been paraphrased in the political rhetoric of the Nixon Administration as the "silent majority."

tertaining bit of popular fiction, as was the sketch about François Millet. "My Boyhood Dreams" was a takeoff on another
Victorian sanctity, and if Mark Twain had outraged the New
England sages at the notorious Whittier dinner, and had
sorely felt the subsequent disgrace and dishonor, now he could
spoof such illustrious figures of the period as Howells, John
Hay, Brander Matthews, Frank Stockton, Cable, and Aldrich
with equanimity. And he did. For all his heavy load of shame
or guilt or spiritual disgrace, the truth is that Sam Clemens was
incorrigible at heart, and kept on being himself.

Speaking about his own old age, he went Dada in a positively
proto-Lardnerian vein.

> From Cradle unto Grave I keep a House
> Of Entertainment where may drowse
>   Bacilli and kindred Germs — or feed — or breed
> Their festering Species in a deep Carouse.
>
> Think — in this battered Caravanserai,
> Whose Portals open stand all Night and Day,
> How Microbe after Microbe with his Pomp
> Arrives unasked and comes to stay.
>
> Our ivory Teeth, confessing to the Lust
> Of masticating, once, now own Disgust
>   Of Clay-plug'd Cavities — full soon our Snags
> Are emptied, and our Mouths are filled with Dust.*

But one must add that the rest of the stories and articles in
the *Hadleyburg* volume were an undistinguished lot, and the

---

* It is entertaining to compare Lardner's version of Cole Porter's "Night and
Day," including, "Night and day under the bark of me/ There's an Oh, such a
mob of microbes making a park of me."

But I do *not* think that Lardner was influenced by Mark Twain's verse; only
that in such instances Sam Clemens was peculiarly sophisticated for a nineteenth-century mind.

novelette *A Double-Barreled Detective Story,* in 1902, was a heavy-footed parody of the popular romance-detective story of the period.*

Perhaps this parody, which included a brief and calamitous appearance of Sherlock Holmes — only to be outwitted by a hero with a bloodhound's nose, because his mother had been attacked by dogs when she was pregnant — was intended as a kind of sequel to "The Stolen White Elephant," which the Russian critics enjoy so much as an attack on the "American police," which it was, though not a very good one. "A Dog's Tale," reprinted from *Harper's* magazine, Christmas Number, 1903, for the National Anti-Vivisection Society of London, is a rather horrifying little item contrasting animal virtue with scientific progress. And with *King Leopold's Soliloquy,* which created almost as much of a national sensation in 1905 as had *To the Person Sitting in Darkness* in 1901, we reach a new, bolder, even more outspoken period of Mark Twain's writings.

Perhaps the best account of Twain's radical social criticism is contained in Janet Smith's *Mark Twain on the Damned Human Race,* which opens with a quote by Clemens from John Macy's book about Twain:

> I am the only man living who understands human nature; God has put me in charge of this branch office; when I retire there will be no one to take my place. I shall keep on doing my duty, for when I get over on the other side, I shall use my influence to have the human race drowned again, and this time drowned good, no omissions, no Ark.

* Both this story and "My Debut as a Literary Person" (1903) are included in *The Man That Corrupted Hadleyburg and Other Stories* in the standard edition of Mark Twain's work. That is to say, in *my* standard edition of Mark Twain's work, Harper & Brothers, Authorized Edition, *The Complete Works of Mark Twain.* But there are several other editions of Twain's complete work, some more complete than others, and all having different groupings of his stories and essays.

To Mrs. Smith, *To the Person Sitting in Darkness* is Twain's masterpiece of this kind of polemics, and still the most timely of his short satires. (Though most modern critics disdain this whole vein of Clemens' writing as crude and vulgar "propaganda," or for a variety of personal and social reasons that I have suggested previously.) "When *To the Person Sitting in Darkness* appeared," she writes, "it produced a cyclone; the sections on the missionaries in China produced savage public warfare between Mark Twain and the American Board of Foreign Missions — a warfare which continued until the Board fell silent."

"The reparations extracted by the missionaries, which Mark Twain discusses, followed upon the victory of an international army, including two thousand Americans, which, in August, 1900, took the city of Peking from Chinese armies led by the Boxers . . . Supposedly, the international army was to punish antiforeign rioting by the Chinese, but, after China's defeat, the reparations extracted by the Great Powers, except the United States, were at least as rapacious as those extracted by the missionaries; the great difference was that they were not the work of professed men of God — and it was this work which Mark Twain ensured should live in infamy."

Meanwhile Clemens had prefaced his sermon to the Person in Darkness with a New Year's Greeting in the New York *Herald* of December 30, 1900.*

A GREETING FROM THE NINETEENTH TO THE
TWENTIETH CENTURY:

I bring you the stately nation named Christendom, returning bedraggled, besmirched, and dishonored from pirate raids in Kiao-Chou, Manchuria, South Africa and the Philippines, with her soul

* The present study of Mark Twain is also indebted to Philip S. Foner's pioneering book, *Mark Twain: Social Critic*, in 1958.

full of meanness, her pocket full of boodle, and her mouth full of hypocrisies. Give her soap and towel, but hide the looking glass.

And let us note incidentally that at the opening of the "American Century," the American press, despite the criticisms of Twain and Howells among others, still felt free enough to feature such indictments, and to accompany them with cartoons.

The pamphlet itself, *To the Person Sitting in Darkness,* reprinted from the *North American Review* by the Anti-Imperialist League in New York, was a loose documentary consisting of statements from newspapers, of quotations from members of the American Board of Foreign Missions, and Clemens' running commentary. Clemens opened with a smug and sanctimonious Christmas Eve editorial from the New York *Tribune* about a nation and a people "full of hope and aspiration and good cheer" who should ignore any carping grumblers. He continued with a vivid description of poverty and crime and corrupt politics in New York's lower East Side taken from the New York *Sun.* He quoted another news article from the same paper about the Reverend Mr. Ament's trip to collect indemnities for damages done by Boxers.

"Everywhere he went he compelled the Chinese to pay. He says that all his native Christians are now provided for. He had 700 of them under his charge, and 300 were killed. He has collected 300 taels for each of these murders and has compelled full payment for all the property belonging to Christians that was destroyed. He also assessed fines amounting to *thirteen times* the amount of the indemnity. *This money will be used for the propagation of the Gospel.* Mr. Ament declares that the compensation he has collected is *moderate* when compared with the amount secured by the Catholics, who demand,

in addition to money, *head for head*. They collect 500 taels
for each murder of a Catholic. In the Wenchu country 680
Catholics were killed, and for this the European Catholics
here demand 750,000 strings of cash and 680 heads."

Mr. Ament denied that the missionaries were vindictive or
that they generally looted or that they did anything after the
siege that circumstances did not demand. "I criticize the Americans. *The soft hand of the Americans is not as good as the
mailed fist of the Germans.* If you deal with the Chinese with
a soft hand they will take advantage of it."

Now you can imagine what Sam Clemens did with such material as this; you should read his entire essay as a coruscation
of polemical writing — since here I have only room for a little
summary. The Reverend Ament, said Clemens, was surely the
right man in the right place. "What we want of our missionaries out there is not that they shall merely represent in their
acts and persons the grace and gentleness and charity and
loving-kindness of our religion, but that they shall also represent the American spirit. The oldest Americans are the Paw-
nees." And he went on to describe examples of Pawnee Indian
"justice" which were equivalent to that of the white American
missionaries. He went on to console the Reverend Mr. Ament
for the larger profits the Catholic missionaries had made from
these murders; he proposed a monument for Mr. Ament composed of the indemnity payments and skulls of murdered Chinese peasants. "Mr. Ament's financial feat of squeezing a thirteenfold indemnity out of the pauper peasants to square other
people's offenses, thus condemning them and their women and
innocent little children to inevitable starvation and lingering
death, in order that the blood money so acquired might be
'used for the propagation of the Gospel,' does not flutter my
serenity; although the act and the words, taken together, con-

crete a blasphemy so hideous and so colossal that, without
doubt, its mate is not findable in the history of this, or of any
other age.* Yet, if a layman had done that thing and justified
it with those words, I should have shuddered, I know. Or, if
I had done the thing and said the words myself — however,
the thought is unthinkable, irreverent as some imperfectly informed people think me. Sometimes an ordained minister sets
out to be blasphemous. When this happens, the layman is out
of the running; he stands no chance."

So much for the Reverend Mr. Ament. Clemens went on to
quote "barbaric" Japanese opinion to the effect that the missionary organizations constituted a constant menace to peaceful international relations, and then posed the crucial question.

Shall we? That is, shall we go on conferring our civilization upon
the peoples that sit in darkness, or shall we give those poor things
a rest? Shall we bang right ahead in our old-time, loud, pious
way, and commit the new century to the game; or shall we sober
up and sit down and think it over first? Would it not be prudent
to get our civilizational tools together, and see how much stock is
left on hand in the way of glass beads and theology, and maxim
guns and hymn books, and trade gin and torches of progress and
enlightenment (patent adjustable ones, good to fire villages with,
upon occasion), and balance the books, and arrive at the profit and
loss, so that we may intelligently decide whether to continue the
business or sell out the property and start a new civilizational
scheme on the proceeds?

* Clemens' descriptions of American missionary behavior in China during the
Boxer crisis are confirmed and indeed surpassed by similar accounts, which are
more detailed, intimate, and illuminating, contained in the first three volumes
of Han Suyin's memoirs. These books. *The Crippled Tree, A Mortal Flower,*
and *Birdless Summer,* though little recognized in the United States, have already proved to be one of the few literary epics of the contemporary period in
the English language; and they come as a revelation to even "informed" western
opinion.

And indeed, if only the avaricious colonial powers of the early 1900s had listened to the advice of this "idealistic" and moral literary genius of the time, the new century might have been spared fifty years — and surely another fifty more to come — of what was essentially race war under the guise of such ambiguous and shifting concepts as socialism, communism, nationalism, capitalism, and imperialism. Nor would the profits of individuals, corporations, and nations, however large, however tempting and momentarily rewarding, ever compensate for the national losses, the sufferings of the entire human community, the universal sacrifice and destruction which were already implicit to Mark Twain in the colonizing process. Much more likely, the twentieth century's wars of liberation, in Asia, Africa, and South America — in the United States itself, divided and torn as it was by racial warfare and ghetto insurrections — would threaten the whole base and future of western European democratic institutions.

And furthermore, in *To the Person Sitting in Darkness* (who became the twentieth century's person striving to discover life and light), Clemens went on to prophesy exactly that.

"Extending the blessings of civilization to our brother who sits in darkness has been a good trade and has paid well, on the whole; and there is money in it yet, if carefully worked — but not enough, in my judgment, to make any considerable risk advisable. The people that sit in darkness are getting to be too scarce — too scarce and too shy. And such darkness as is now left is really of but an indifferent quality, and not dark enough for the game. The most of those people that sit in darkness have been furnished with more light than was good for them or profitable for us. We have been injudicious."

"The blessings-of-civilization trust, wisely and cautiously administered, is a daisy," Clemens continued. "There is more money in it, more territory, more sovereignty, and other kinds of emolument than there is in any other game that is played. But Christendom has been playing it badly of late years, and must certainly suffer by it, in my opinion. She has been so eager to get every stake that appeared on the green cloth, that the people who sit in darkness have noticed it — they have noticed it, and have begun to show alarm. They have become suspicious of the blessings of civilization. More — they have begun to examine them. This is not well. The blessings of civilization are all right, and a good commercial property; there could not be a better, in a dim light. In the right kind of light, and at a proper distance, with the goods a little out of focus, they furnish this desirable exhibit to the gentlemen who sit in darkness."

He listed such virtues of civilization as Love, Justice, Gentleness, Temperance, Liberty, Equality, Mercy, and so on. But, he said, this was merely an outside cover, gay and pretty and attractive, while *inside* the bale "is the actual thing that the customer sitting in darkness buys with his blood and tears and land and liberty." And the civilization-export business was being ruined.

To the Person Sitting in Darkness went on to describe some of the more obvious examples of imperialism's careless mistakes. It explained the manufacture of the Boer War by the English Prime Minister Chamberlain in order to acquire the vast wealth of the diamond mines and black slave labor. It related the history of the German Kaiser as an energetic new partner in dividing up the spoils of China. "He lost a couple of missionaries in a riot in Shantung, and in his account he made an overcharge for them. China had to pay a hundred thousand dollars apiece for them in money; twelve miles of territory containing several millions of inhabitants and worth twenty million dollars; and to build a monument, and also a

Christian church; whereas the people of China could have been depended on to remember the missionaries without the help of these expensive memorials." * The person in outer darkness knew this was an overcharge, and Clemens went on to evaluate the cash value of a missionary with that of an intelligent country editor. "It is no proper figure for an editor or a missionary; one can get shopworn kings for less . . . It got this property, true; but it *produced the Chinese revolt,* the indignant uprising of China's traduced patriots, the Boxers. The results have been expensive to Germany, and to the other disseminators of progress and the blessings of civilization."

Clemens believed that the Chinese were not unreflective. They would muse upon the event, and be likely to say: "Civilization is gracious and beautiful, for such is its reputation; but can we afford it? There are rich Chinamen, perhaps they can afford it; but this tax is not laid upon them, it is laid upon the peasants of Shantung; it is they who must pay this mighty sum, and their wages are but four cents a day. Is this a better civilization than ours, and holier, and higher and nobler? Is not this rapacity? Is not this extortion?" He asked if Germany would have treated America in the same way if the missionaries had been slaughtered in the United States. "And later would Germany say to her soldiers: 'March through America and slay, *giving no quarter;* make the German face there, as has been our Hun-face here, a terror for a thousand years; march through the great republic and slay, slay, slay, carving a road for our offended religion through its heart and bowels'? Would Germany do this to America, to England, to France, to Russia? Or only to China, the helpless . . ."

---

* Incredible to read today, unbelievable and impossible? Much worse follows in Twain's account, all confirmed and elaborated in detail in the Han Suyin memoirs.

He reported the final reflection of the Chinese person. "Can we afford civilization?" These were eloquent passages of immense prophetic weight in *To the Person Sitting in Darkness,* which twentieth-century history would vindicate in full, even while the western mind would be terrified by the "obscure" Chinese revolution.

And next Russia was playing the imperialist game by robbing Japan of its hard-earned spoil: Port Arthur "all swimming in Chinese blood." With the person in darkness again observing and noting, Russia then

> seizes Manchuria, raids its villages, and chokes its great river with the swollen corpses of countless massacred peasants — that astonished person still observing and noting. And perhaps he is saying to himself: "It is yet *another* civilized power, with its banner of the Prince of Peace in one hand and its loot basket and its butcher knife in the other. Is there no salvation for us but to adopt civilization and lift ourselves down to its level?"

And then it was America itself which began playing the imperialist game.

Clemens still felt the American purpose in Cuba, in the Spanish-American War, had been honest and in the tradition of the Old Republic. (During the course of the article, nevertheless, he began to have his doubts about this, too.) But the conquest of the Philippines was horrifying to him, and he said so in some detail.

In particular Clemens was enraged by the treacherous cunning through which the American army had destroyed the small, ill-armed native Filipino army under the guise of assisting its struggle against the Spanish oppressor. This campaign to secure the Philippines for the United States, rather than to allow them the freedom they had fought for, was particularly brutal, like all colonial wars against the colored peoples. And finally the American government announced that it was adopting General Kitchener's methods against the Boers: massacre, extermination, and denudation of the land. Clemens also described the relative casualty rates of Filipino and American soldiers:

> We must stand ready to grab the person sitting in darkness, for he will swoon away at this confession saying "Good God! those 'niggers' spare their wounded, and the Americans massacre theirs!"*

What Kitchener's and General MacArthur's methods meant in detail was illustrated by the words of an American soldier in the Philippines. "We never left one alive. If one was wounded, we would run our bayonets through him." And now, said Clemens, having laid all the historical facts before the person in outer darkness, we should bring him to again, and explain them to him. We should say to him:

"They look doubtful, but in reality they are not. There have been lies; yes, but they were told in a good cause. We have been treacherous; but that was only in order that real good might come out of apparent evil. True, we have crushed a deceived and confiding people; we have turned against the weak and friendless who trusted us; we have stamped out a just and intelligent and well-ordered republic; we have stabbed an ally in the back and slapped the face of a guest; we have bought a shadow from an enemy that hadn't it to sell; we have robbed a trusting friend of his land and his liberty; we have invited

---

* By now Clemens was using quotes around the word "nigger," when he used it ironically, or as part of folk speech, or on the tongue of those people who despised the colored races whom Clemens himself admired and defended. Surely those contemporary critics, like Fiedler and Leavis, who espouse the word "nigger" with such delight, and seemingly with Mark Twain's precedent and authority, can be said to be wholly unaware of this writer's craft.

our clean young men to shoulder a discredited musket and do bandits' work under a flag which bandits have been accustomed to fear, not to follow; we have debauched America's honor and blackened her face before the world; but each detail was for the best. We know this. The head of every state and sovereignty in Christendom and 90 per cent of every legislative body in Christendom, including our Congress and our fifty [sic] state legislatures, are members not only of the church but also of the blessings-of-civilization trust. This world-girdling accumulation of trained morals, high principles, and justice cannot do an unright thing, an unfair thing, an ungenerous thing, an unclean thing. It knows what it is about. Give yourself no uneasiness; it is all right."

And he went on to propose a new American flag with the white stripes painted black and the stars replaced by the skull and crossbones — and to suggest that the U.S. could slip out of its congressional contract with Cuba and give her something better in place of it. "It is a rich country, and many of us are already beginning to see that the contract was a sentimental mistake."

Great history, great writing, and great art, yes, in the polemical tradition of art! Perhaps in this sense *To the Person Sitting in Darkness* is the classic work of all the social tracts written in the fury of Mark Twain's outraged sensibilities during the opening years of the new century. Some of these essays, like "Corn-Pone Opinions," "As Regards Patriotism," "Bible Teaching and Religious Practice," "The War Prayer," we shall discuss later on.* But meanwhile we have noted that this hatred of colonialism, of racism, of slavery in any guise, of cruelty,

* All collected recently, with other articles in the same vein, in Janet Smith's book, but some of them published previously in a volume of Twain's posthumous essays edited by Paine, *Europe and Elsewhere*, in 1923; and in Paine's — but not Charles Neider's — edition of *Mark Twain's Autobiography*.

exploitation, suffering, and misery, was not of course a "new vein" in Clemens' work, nor was it the sick product of his financial ruin and domestic tragedy. What marks all these essays of social protest and personal outrage, instead, is the vein of hilarious humor which Clemens invoked in the midst of his brilliant irony and scathing moral indignation. As early as 1873, writing in the New York *Tribune* about the proposed annexation of the Hawaiian Islands, Clemens had invoked almost the same themes and tone.

> We *must* annex those people. We can afflict them with our wise and beneficent government. We can introduce the novelty of thieves, all the way up from streetcar pick-pockets to municipal robbers and Government defaulters and show them how amusing it is to arrest them and try them and turn them loose — some for cash, and some for "political influence." We can make them ashamed of their simple and primitive justice . . . We can give them juries composed of the most simple and charming leather-heads. We can give them railway corporations who will buy their Legislatures like old clothes, and run over their best citizens. We can furnish them some Jay Goulds who will do away their old-time notions that stealing is not respectable . . . We can give them lecturers! I will go myself.
>
> We can make that bunch of sleepy islands the hottest corner on earth, and array it in the moral splendor of our high and holy civilization. Annexation is what the poor islanders need. "Shall we to men benighted the lamp of life deny?"

The difference was not so much in Mark Twain, indeed, as in his subject matter. As we said, his world had changed more swiftly and brutally and savagely than Sam Clemens had. His series of personal tragedies may have sorrowed and embittered him — but they had not defiled and debauched him, nor made him brutal, savage, ruthless, and avaricious. What we are witnessing in these eloquent, bold, and radical social satires of Twain is not at all the rantings of an embittered old man — how could any serious Mark Twain scholar ever think so? — but the eventful and fateful meeting of the man and the time which creates art. Or of a unique personality, hardened and deepened, as it may be, by life, and of a historical period gone bad, vicious, grasping, and barbaric.

We may only be grateful that the proper chronicler was there, the recording angel indeed of art, civilization, and life.

There are other essays which Clemens wrote at this time about a changing America — moving from the moral simplicity and grandeur of the Old Republic at its best to the imperial dynasty of an industrial-military complex which was to cast its shadow over the land masses of Europe, Asia, and Africa. "A Defence of General Funston," in 1902, was a kind of appendix to *The Person Sitting in Darkness*. This was the specific account of the capture of the Filipino General Emilio Aguinaldo as accomplished by General Funston, and widely acclaimed as a heroic exploit of American military prowess. Mark Twain did not agree. Funston had also characterized all Americans who opposed the conquest of the Philippines as "traitors," a term that would be used recurrently thereafter in American politics — and which Clemens made a point of accepting with pleasure, when compared, say, with the official American "patriots" of the period. Writing his essay on Washington's Birthday, Clemens made a comparison of the two military figures; and he was fearful that General Funston, with all his duplicity, cruelty, and sadism, would become the model of the new American military hero. Describing how the helpless and starving Funston, disguised as a Filipino guerrilla fighter, and accompanied by the treacherous Macabebe tribe of natives, was rescued and refreshed by the Filipino President

Aguinaldo — only to shoot down Aguinaldo's guard and then to wantonly sport with the remnants of Aguinaldo's military staff through shootings and beatings, Clemens commented: "It was left to a Brigadier General of Volunteers in the American army to put shame upon a custom which even the degraded Spanish friars had respected. *We promoted him for it.*"

But just here Clemens reverted to his notorious notion of a kind of dark determinism in human life,* and using it for passages of savage irony, Clemens confessed that he could not really condemn Funston for his savage behavior but only Funston's *It.*

"These being the facts, we come now to the question: Is Funston to blame? I think not. And for that reason I think too much is being made of this matter. He did not make his own disposition, It was born with him. It chose his ideals for him, he did not choose them. It chose the kind of society It liked, the kind of comrades It preferred . . . It, and It only, was to blame, not Funston . . . It had a native predilection for unsavory conduct, but it would be in the last degree unfair to hold Funston to blame for the outcome of his infirmity; as clearly

---

* We shall discuss this later on; but meanwhile what is curious to note in our literary history of the 1950s is the degree of distaste, or even anger, with which the leading critics of the Cold War epoch attacked the concept of "determinism" in a whole line of American writers from Mark Twain to Theodore Dreiser. During this epoch there was apparently presumed to be some underground and devious link between philosophic determinism and radical social criticism, or even Marxism and Communism . . . It is worth remembering that almost every great writer has adhered to some form or another of a deterministic philosophy which has held his own talent as "accidental" and of lesser consequence than the environmental aspects which happened to cause the flowering of the talent — just as Dreiser held a Clyde Griffiths to be the victim of a corrupted American society, and as Mark Twain here views, though ironically, General Funston.

But this is the disclaimer of genius. It is only the small souls of the world who flaunt their own "individualism," or "will power," or "spiritual strength" as superior to the conditioning forces of society, culture, and history. Or even of events, or chance, or accident!

unfair as it would be to blame him because his conscience
leaked out through one of his pores when he was little — a
thing which he could not have helped, and he couldn't have
raised it anyway; It was able to say to an enemy, 'Have pity on
me, I am starving; I am too weak to move, give me food; I am
your friend, I am your fellow patriot, your fellow Filipino, and
am fighting for our dear country's liberties, like you — have
pity, give me food, save my life, there is no other help!' and It
was able to refresh and restore Its marionette with the food,
and then shoot down the giver of it while his hand was stretched
out in welcome . . . It has the noble gift of humor, and can
make a banquet almost die with laughter when It has a funny
incident to tell about; this one will bear reading again — and
over and over again, in fact." And Clemens repeated the sadistic episode of the slaughter of Aguinaldo's bodyguard and
military staff with which Funston had entertained his American
audiences as an example of American military cunning and
power.

They had fished the wounded Filipino officer Villia out of
the river and kicked him up the bank with coarse jokes. This
was a wounded man, said Clemens. "But it is only It that is
speaking, not Funston. With youthful glee It can see sink
down in death the simple creatures who had answered Its fainting prayer for food, and without remorse It can note the re-
proachful look in their dimming eyes, but in fairness we must
remember that this is only It, not Funston . . . And It —
not Funston — comes home now to teach us children what
patriotism is! Surely It ought to know."

Burning words, etched by the acid of Clemens' contempt at
such military behavior in the Philippines, where his America,
too, had joined in the racist conquest and social degradation
which he had already witnessed on the part of the "corrupted"

Old World's imperialism in Asia and Africa. The essay called "Comments on the Killing of 600 Moros," in 1906, was in effect a sequel to Mark Twain's "Defence of General Funston" — a "defence" which only Satan could have devised to cope with human nature.*

A tribe of these "dark-skinned savages," as Clemens called them, had entrenched themselves in the bowl of an extinct crater near Jolo. Since they were "hostiles, and bitter at us because we have been trying for eight years to take their liberties away from them, their presence in that position was a menace." The American commander, General Leonard Wood, discovered that the Moros numbered six hundred including women and children; and that their crater bowl was on a mountain peak 2200 feet above sea level, "and very difficult of access for Christian troops and artillery." There were finally the six hundred savages in the mountain bowl, and about the same number of American troops and allies on the mountain summit overlooking the bowl, with artillery, when General Wood issued his order to attack.

The depth of the crater bowl was about fifty feet, as Mark Twain noted. "The battle began — it is officially called by that name — our forces firing down into the crater with their artillery and their deadly small arms of precision; the savages furiously returning the fire, probably with brickbats — though this is merely a surmise of mine. Heretofore the Moros have used knives and clubs mainly; also ineffectual trade-muskets when they had any. The official report stated that the battle was fought with prodigious energy on both sides during a day and a half, and that it ended with a complete victory for the

---

* The Moro essay was written as part of Mark Twain's *Autobiography*, and first published in 1924, in Albert Bigelow Paine's edition of this book. It is omitted from Charles Neider's "new" version of the *Autobiography*, in 1959, for reasons of "personal taste" and "esthetic values" which the present writer finds both mysterious and meretricious.

American arms. The completeness of the victory is established by this fact: that of the six hundred Moros not one was left alive. The brilliancy of the victory is established by this other fact, to wit: that of our six hundred heroes only fifteen lost their lives.

"General Wood was present and looking on. His order had been, 'Kill *or* capture those savages.' Apparently our little army considered that the "or" left them authorized to kill *or* capture according to taste, and that their taste had remained what it has been for eight years, in our army out there — the taste of Christian butchers."

Clemens pointed out that, then as now, the American newspaper dispatches on the battle extolled and magnified the "heroism" and "gallantry" of the American troops, lamented the loss of a few white men, elaborated the wounds of a few others — and ignored the six hundred dead Moros. He mentioned the casualty rates on both sides in the Civil War, at Waterloo, and in the "pathetic comedy" called the Cuban War. "Contrast these things with the great statistics which have arrived from that Moro crater! There, with six hundred engaged on each side, we lost fifteen men killed outright, and we had thirty-two wounded . . . The enemy numbered six hundred — including women and children — and we abolished them utterly, leaving not even a baby alive to cry for its dead mother. *This is incomparably the greatest victory that was ever achieved by the Christian soldiers of the United States.*"

Then, as public revulsion mounted in the United States when the true nature of the bloody massacre began to emerge, and as General Wood's tone changed from enthusiastic admiration for the American military "triumph" to an uneasy rationalization of the slaughter, Clemens added his final comments to the "Killing of 600 Moros": "Doctor Wood will find that explaining things is not in his line. He will find that where a man has a proper spirit in him and the proper force at his command, it is easier to massacre nine hundred [as it turned out to be] unarmed animals than it is to explain why he made it so remorselessly complete . . . The inference seems plain. We cleaned up our four days' work and made it complete by butchering these helpless people."

But among the polemical writings of this period we can hardly omit what was in its time the most popular pamphlet of all, *King Leopold's Soliloquy*. We have already noticed how the Belgian reign in the Congo can be interpreted historically as the dark rehearsal for the Nazi Terror in Europe. (And to some degree, though in a quite different historical context, the Stalin purges in Russia.) Once this could happen in "savage" Africa, it was made possible in "civilized" Europe; and once mass extermination had been practiced for profit on the black races, it could be used in the name of the highest of patriotic reasons upon the "inferior" white races. No end to this game once started; and whatever the validity of this comparison, it is certain that there were ten million murders in the Belgian Congo between 1885 and 1905; no mean comparison in an earlier age, without the "scientific" and prefabricated death factories that the Nazis developed.

In Jacob Blanck's *Biography of American Literature,* one notes also that *King Leopold's Soliloquy,* described as another "Defence" of the Congo rule, had four reprintings of the first edition in 1905, and a second edition in the next year (Twain refused any royalties for this pamphlet written for the Congo Reform Association) and still two more American editions before the London-Unwin edition in 1907.* The essay itself, as with all Mark Twain's polemical writings, was "crude" and rough in

* In Janet Smith's background material for this essay she quotes another voice from an older world, Vachel Lindsay's *The Congo*: "Listen to the yell of Leopold's ghost/ Burning in Hell for his hand-mained host./ Hear how the demons chuckle and yell,/ Cutting his hands off, down in Hell."

form, even apparently formless to those esthetic and conformist critics who, particularly in the 1950s, used such criteria to rule out this whole phase of Mark Twain's work. The point is, of course, that Clemens had devised his own native form for this whole genre of writing which, rough and careless and "mixed," or even mixed-up, as it appeared to be, was still an extraordinary eloquent, forceful, and historically valuable kind of writing.

In *King Leopold,* as in the previous essays we have discussed, he threw together newspaper headlines, firsthand journalistic accounts of the Congo, photographs of mutilated savages taken by the invaluable new witness of the period, the Kodak, missionary reports, official documents of Congolese administrators, plus his own imaginative reconstructions, and passages of raging moral anger and satire. Clemens has Leopold speaking in person, surrounded by the documents and records of his infamous doings, swearing violently, kissing his crucifix, apologizing, admitting certain errors, rationalizing, defending himself full force without a trace of guilt or conscience for the immeasurable evil he had perpetrated upon an innocent and helpless people. "I have spent millions to keep the press of the two hemispheres quiet . . . I have spent other millions on religion and art, and what do I get?" Leopold asks. "In print I get nothing but slanders — and slanders again . . . Miscreants — they are telling *everything!*" And Clemens then told the story of how Leopold obtained the territory of the Congo from the Great Powers, including America, in order to root out slavery and stop the slave raids, "and to lift up those twenty-five millions of gentle and harmless blacks out of darkness into light, the light of our blessed Redeemer." But the documents surrounding Leopold, which have at last brought *him* to light, record that for twenty years he had ruled the Congo State as the absolute sovereign of a fruitful domain four times as large as the German Empire, claiming millions of inhabitants as his private property, his serfs, his slaves. "Yes, they go on telling everything, these chatterers! They tell how I levy incredibly burdensome taxes upon the natives — taxes which are a pure theft; taxes which they must satisfy by gathering rubber under hard and constantly harder conditions, and by raising and furnishing food supplies gratis — and it all comes out that, when they fall short of their task through hunger, sickness, despair, and ceaseless and exhausting labor without rest, and forsake their homes and flee to the woods to escape punishment, my black soldiers, drawn from unfriendly tribes, and instigated and directed by my Belgians" — those "unspeakable Belgians" as Clemens declared — "hunt them down and butcher them and burn their villages — reserving some of the girls."

Leopold then begins to rage at the diary of a Belgian official in the Congo which was published by the British consul. "Here he leaves it to be recognized that a thousand killings and mutilations a month is a large output for so small a region as the Mambogo River concession, silently indicating the dimensions of it by accompanying his report with a map of the prodigious Congo State in which there is not room for so small an object as that river" . . . And Leopold reads:

> Two hundred and forty persons, *men, women and children,* compelled to supply government with *one ton* of carefully prepared foodstuffs *per week,* receiving in remuneration, all told the princely sum of 15s. 10d!

"Very well, it was liberal! It was not much short of a penny a week for each nigger.* It suits this consul to belittle it, yet he knows very well that I could have had both the food and the

* See previous footnotes on the use of this word by Mark Twain. By now, indeed, it is clear that he placed this word only on the lips of white men whom he utterly despised; which could have been a long list, however.

labor for nothing. I can prove it by a thousand instances . . .
Mm — here is some more of the consul's delicacy! He reports a
conversation he had with some natives." And Clemens put
down some further direct testimony of Belgian barbarism in dealing with the Congo blacks. He quoted the testimony of the
Reverend W. H. Sheppard, talking with a black raider of Leopold's who collected all the chiefs, subchiefs, men and women of
one of these native tribes within a compound, demanded slaves
and other gifts from them, and massacred the whole lot remorselessly when his demands were refused. Some of the eighty or
ninety corpses were still lying in the fields with the flesh carved
away from the skeletons.

"*Another* detail, as we see! — cannibalism. The report cites
it with a most offensive frequency," cries Leopold in despair.
"My traducers do not forget to remark that inasmuch as I am
absolute and with a word can prevent in the Congo anything I
choose to prevent, then whatsoever is done there . . . is my
act, my *personal* act . . . that the hand of my agent is as truly
my hand as if it were attached to my own arm; and so they picture me in my robes of state, with my crown on my head, munch-
ing human flesh, saying grace, mumbling thanks to Him from
whom all good things come . . . They speak out profanely
and reproach Heaven for allowing such a fiend to live. Meaning
me. They think it irregular. They go shuddering around,
brooding over the reduction of that Congo population from
25,000,000 to 15,000,000 in the twenty years of my administration; then they burst out and call me 'the King with Ten Million Murders on his Soul." They call me a record."

What is remarkable, of course, is the mixture of complacency,
rationalizing, indignation, and high moral dudgeon on the part
of Mark Twain's King Leopold. And the usual self-deception
or hypocrisy about black lives.

Clemens compared Leopold's work with the Great Famine in

India, and with such previous tyrants as Attila, Torquemada, Genghis Khan, Ivan the Terrible, and concluded that the only match in history for Leopold was the Flood. He went on to report that "another madman" wanted to construct a memorial for the perpetuation of Leopold's name out of the fifteen million skulls and skeletons killed by Leopold's order. He, Clemens, got carried away by this idea and went into elaborate detail for such an elegant memorial which would serve as a permanent museum to convey the enormity of human destruction in the Congo. (The world does not care for such museums, and they are poorly attended in general, like those of the Nazi holocaust.)

Leopold reads more of the missionary and journalistic reports of the day detailing the individual horrors which occurred daily under a regime designed to make a norm out of human atrocities. Leopold becomes specially irritated at noting that a widow had been forced to sell her little girl. And he is profoundly disturbed by the crucifixion of sixty women. This is profanation of the sacred emblem of Christianity, he cries, and the wrong way to do it. He studies some photographs of mutilated Negroes (which were printed in the pamphlet editions of *King Leopold*) and declaims against the "incorruptible Kodak," when for years the pulpit and press had denied all such rumors. He reads a final journalist summary (written presumably by Clemens):

But enough of trying to tally off his crimes! His list is interminable, we should never get to the end of it. His awful shadow lies across his Congo Free State . . . It is a land of graves; it is *The* Land of Graves; it is the Congo Free Graveyard. It is a majestic thought: that is, this ghastliest episode in all human history is the work of *one man alone;* one solitary man; just a single individual — Leopold, King of the Belgians . . . Lust of conquest is royal; kings have always exercised that stately vice; but lust of money

— lust of shillings — lust of nickels — lust of dirty coin, not for the nation's enrichment but for *the king's alone* — this is new . . . we shrink from hearing the particulars of how it happened. *We shudder and turn away* when we come up to them in print.

And that, says Mark Twain's Leopold, concluding his reverie, "Why, certainly — *that* is my protection. And you will continue to do it. I know the human race."

And surely his prediction of the weakness of the human race in not wishing to acknowledge deeds of cruelty and suffering — of turning its head away, of pretending to be unaware of what lies in front of its eyes; and then of a swift "forgetting," a repression of all unpleasant memories or associations: surely this prediction is justified by history. But perhaps without this trait of callous indifference, of suppression and evasion, humanity itself, facing such recurrent crises of human evil and suffering, could hardly continue its struggle.

"The Czar's Soliloquy", in 1905, was in a sense a sequel to *King Leopold*; it was not so well understood or so popular, but in literary terms it was more compact, direct, and impressive writing. Clemens was one of the few Americans who did not regard Theodore Roosevelt's mediation of the Russo-Japanese war with approval. The Portsmouth, New Hampshire, peace treaty won the Nobel Prize for "the windy and flamboyant President," as Clemens wrote in his *Autobiography,* but it destroyed all of Mark Twain's hopes that a defeated Russia might find a revolutionary release from "an insane and intolerable slavery." "I was hoping that there would be no peace until Russian liberty was safe," he said to the Associated Press at the time. "I think there can be no doubt that that mission is now defeated and Russia's chains riveted; this time to stay. I think the Czar will now withdraw the small humanities that have been forced from him, and resume his medieval barbarisms with a relieved spirit and an immeasurable joy . . . I think nothing has been gained by the peace that is remotely comparable to what has been sacrificed by it."

"The Czar's Soliloquy" was, among other things, a plea for immediate and bloody action, as Janet Smith says: "But what Mark Twain had in mind was not revolution, but a program of assassination. This program various Russian groups — mainly Anarchists and Nihilists, and mainly young people — had been enthusiastically pursuing since before 1881, when they assassinated Alexander II, one of the most liberal of the Russian Czars. But Alexander III, who succeeded his father, was of the same stripe as Nicholas II, who came to the throne in 1894" — and was the Czar Clemens described. As early as 1890, too, he had stated his views about Russia in an unmailed letter to the editor of the American magazine *Free Russia*. "Of course I know that the properest way to demolish the Russian throne would be by revolution. But it is not possible to get up a revolution there; so the only thing left to do, apparently, is to keep the throne vacant by dynamite until a day when candidates shall decline with thanks . . ." In the same letter he made it clear that his vision of history was hardly pacifist. "My privilege to write these sanguinary sentences in soft security was bought for me by rivers of blood poured upon many fields, in many lands, but I possess not one single little paltry right or privilege that came to me as a result of petition, persuasion, agitation for reform, or any kindred method of procedure. When we consider that not even the most responsible English monarch ever yielded back a stolen public right until it was wrenched from him by bloody violence, is it rational to suppose that gentler methods can win privileges in Russia?" *

For these reasons, and others to come, it is easy to see why

---

* Compare the writings of the contemporary theoretician of the Third World, and of the Revolution there, Frantz Fanon, who in far different context repeats Mark Twain's prophetic words.

Mark Twain is regarded with such reverence by modern Russian scholars; why they are so well informed about his work — and why they objected when this whole area of Twain's writing was omitted by American scholars, during the epoch of the fifties on such grounds (as we know) as that it was "too controversial," "too roughly written," "too violent," or "in bad taste." Charles Neider's "reply" to the Russian critics — who pointed out that his version of the *Autobiography* omitted all the episodes of radical social criticism which Clemens had particularly delighted in writing for it — was a particularly blatant example of such Cold War "scholarship," as is Justin Kaplan's *Mr. Clemens and Mark Twain*. The Russians were right, in this case, and the Americans were wrong. As any reader of the polemical essays can testify, this whole area of Mark Twain's social criticism is one of the adornments of his art, as it should be of his country's culture.

In the *Soliloquy* itself, Clemens seized upon a London newspaper item which declared that the Russian Czar, after his morning bath, meditated an hour before getting dressed. Clemens expatiated upon Carlyle's thesis of "clothes" marking human rank and power, and then, "A curious invention, an unaccountable invention — the human race!" continues this blood brother of King Leopold. "The swarming Russian millions have for centuries meekly allowed our family to rob them, insult them, trample them under foot, while they lived and suffered and died with no purpose and no function but to make that family comfortable! These people are horses — just that — horses with clothes and a religion. A horse with the strength of a hundred men will let one man beat him, starve him, drive him; the Russian millions allow a mere handful of soldiers to hold them in slavery — and these very soldiers are their own sons and brothers!"

There was another strange thing, continued Mark Twain's

Russian Czar, "to wit, the world applies to Czar and system the
same moral axioms that have vogue and acceptance in civilized
countries! Because, in civilized countries, it is wrong to remove
oppressors otherwise than by process of law, it is held that the
same rule applies in Russia, where there is no such thing as law
— except for our family. Laws are merely restraints — they
have no other function. In civilized countries they restrain all
persons and restrain them all alike, which is fair and righteous,
but in Russia such laws as exist make an exception — our family. We do as we please; we have done as we pleased for centuries. Our common trade has been crime, our common pastime murder, our common beverage blood — the blood of the
nation. Upon our heads lie millions of murders. Yet the pious
moralist says it is a crime to assassinate us. We and our uncles
are a family of cobras set over a hundred and forty million rab-
bits, whom we torture and murder and feed upon all our days;
yet the moralist urges that to kill us is a crime, not a duty."

Inspired writing, again, from an outraged soul! The central
debate in the radical sector of American thinking in the mid-
1960s was that between the advocates of passive resistance and
of revolutionary violence in both the civil-rights movement and
the shameful war in Vietnam. How was it that Mark Twain had
reached such conclusions of revolutionary violence as the essential lever in history, so easily, so naturally, so forcefully —
while a half century later it was officially declared, also, that
such revolutionary violence was repugnant to the American
notion of justice and progress, of evolutionary history and the
democratic process itself? Well, that is to say, violence was
condemned *within* the United States; while outside its borders,
in every portion of the still under-developed world, the American military felt free to obliterate a whole countryside, a whole
nation's population if necessary, all the cities, towns, villages,

fields, crops of any small country, in a policy of instant armed resistance to social upheavals it did not approve of. Which had changed most, the American nation or its artistic consciousness as exemplified in Sam Clemens?

And which was the obvious historical truth in this argument, and which the transparent historical fabrication for the plain purpose of imperial power, control, exploitation, and plunder in the name of a senseless (but cunningly contrived) "national security"? What a shameful, wicked, devastating kind of lie was perpetrated in the national consciousness during the Cold War epoch; and what can one say of the nation's intellectuals who either accepted this lie, or went along with it because of cowardly or selfish reasons? (I am not speaking here of the truly revolutionary pacifist movements.) And meanwhile Sam Clemens was continuing, with his ruthless and lacerating logic, to expose the pious fraud that the Russian monarchy — like the slave-holding Southern plantation owners of the Civil War period — would willingly abdicate all its power and profits peacefully, under the duress of civilized or religious morality.

"It is not for me to say it aloud," continued Mark Twain's ruminating Czar to himself, unaware that he was giving out his secrets to the whole world of the mid-1900s, unaware that the diabolical Sam Clemens had caught him without his clothes on, and that the Emperor was indeed naked in the full sight of this "childlike" and incorruptible artist: "But to one on the inside — like me — this is naively funny; on its face illogical. Our family is above all law, there is no law that can reach us, restrain us, protect the people from us. Therefore, we are outlaws. Outlaws are a proper mark for anyone's bullet. Ah! what could our family do without the moralist? He has been our stay, our support, our friend; today, he is our only friend. Whenever there has been dark talk of assassination, he has come forward and saved us with his impressive maxim, 'Forbear: nothing politically valuable was ever yet achieved by violence.' He probably believes it. It is because he has by him no child's book of world history to teach him that his maxim lacks the backing of statistics. All thrones have been established by violence; no regal tyranny has ever been overthrown except by violence; by violence my fathers set up our throne; by murder, treachery, perjury, torture, banishment, and the prison they have held it for four centuries, and by these same arts I hold it today. There is no Romanoff of learning and experience but would reverse the maxim and say: 'Nothing politically valuable was ever yet achieved *except* by violence.' "

Thus Mark Twain combined his early rejection of conventional religion and morality, his scornful attacks on the missionaries under the subterfuge and cover of Christianity, with the true workings of history. Here he saw clearly that conventional morality and conventional Christianity were being used as the main prop and "moral support" of the implacable tyranny perpetuated by the Russian emperors. In "The Czar's Soliloquy", he continued with a recital of the Czar's most recent crimes, after the conclusion of the Russo-Japanese War and of the Russian nation's stirrings of revolt. The Czar reads two parallel newspaper clippings: one of the Cossacks' brutalities against the Polish people; the other of the religious awe and servile adulation with which the Russian masses still regarded the presence and "the hallowed features of *the Lord's Anointed*." The Czar is moved: "And it was I that got that grovelling and awe-smitten worship! I — this thing in the mirror — this carrot! With one hand I flogged unoffending women to death and tortured prisoners to unconsciousness; and with the other I held up the fetish toward my fellow deity in heaven and called down His blessing upon my adoring animals whom and whose forebears, with His holy approval, I and mine have been instructing in the pains of hell for four lagging centuries. It is a picture! To think that this thing in the mirror — this vegetable — is an accepted deity to a mighty nation, an innumerable host, and nobody laughs; and at the same time is a diligent and practical professional devil, and nobody marvels, nobody murmurs about incongruities and inconsistencies! Is the human race a joke? Was it devised and patched together in a dull time when there was nothing important to do? Has it no respect for itself?"

Let us remember these words in relation to Twain's celebrated and ambiguous novelette, *The Mysterious Stranger*. And surely Sam Clemens' respect for the human race was drooping, sinking, as he concluded the Czar's Soliloquy — though his writing was strangely exalted. This essay too has been subjected by leading critics to the usual objections I have listed — yes, this "rude and vulgar" and tasteless, formless Mark Twain, who precisely for this sector of his writing even above the rest is reverenced in Russia, Asia, Africa, and South America as America's great literary genius! In this case, to paraphrase Robert Burns, if only *indeed* we could see ourselves as others see us! It should be clear now there is no true note of purely personal frustration in these essays; they are the sentiments of a master artist who was enraged by blatant and callous social injustice — that is to say, human injustice on a mass scale. They are Twain's testimony to his time; and the time's testimony to Mark Twain.

In "The United States of Lyncherdom" (1901), moreover, Twain took a look at his own country in this period of raw colonialism, savage imperialism, and racial genocide. This was indeed such an indignant and heartbroken article that Clemens put it away, and decided not to publish it; while even Paine, using it some twenty years later in the collection of posthumous essays, *Europe and Elsewhere,* was still concerned about its effect.*

"And so Missouri has fallen, that great state!" so Clemens opened his piece. "Certain of her children have joined the lynchers, and the smirch is upon the rest of us. That handful of her children have given us a character and labeled us with a name, and to the dwellers in the four quarters of the earth we are 'lynchers,' now and ever shall be." The world would not stop and think, said Clemens with a familiar irony, that the bulk of Missourians building an honorable name for themselves did not endorse the action; that the hundred Missourians who were lynchers were in fact renegades. "No, that truth will not enter its mind; it will generalize from the one or two misleading samples and say, 'The Missourians are lynchers.' It has no reflection, no logic, no sense of proportion. With it figures go for nothing; to it, figures reveal nothing, it cannot reason upon them rationally . . . It would say, 'There are a hundred lynchers there, therefore the Missourians are lynchers'; the considerable fact that there are two and a half million Missourians who are *not* lynchers would not affect their verdict . . . Oh, Missouri!"

A young white woman had been found murdered, and perhaps raped — the "usual crime" of that period, or the common pretext for lynching Negroes. "Although it was a region of churches and schools," Clemens continued, "the people rose, lynched three Negroes — two of them very aged ones — burned out five Negro households, and drove thirty Negro families into

---

* In a letter to Clemens quoted by Kaplan, Bernard Shaw remarked that he believed Mark Twain was one of the greatest masters of the English language — as indeed almost all of the leading English writers did, with the notable exception of the uncomprehending Matthew Arnold — and that "I am persuaded that the future historian of America will find your works as indispensable to him as a French historian finds the political tracts of Voltaire."

the woods." Churches indeed; one could ask, as Clemens did, what kind of Christianity was practiced in the southern Churches, and what part the ministry played in opposing such mobs. (The ministers looked the other way; or not approving the lynching of Negroes for "rape," deplored the "necessity" for it.) Clemens, moreover, went on to point out that every time a Negro was lynched on the supposition of rape, it encouraged more Negroes to consider the possibility of raping, and more white men to perform the act of lynching. In 1900 there had been eight more cases of lynching than in 1899, and in 1901 he thought there would be more cases than in 1900, mainly in the four southern states of Alabama, Georgia, Louisiana, and Mississippi. The other reason Clemens attributed to the rising rate of lynching during these terrible years in the south was simply the moral cowardice of man:

> It has been supposed — and said — that the people at a lynching enjoy the spectacle and are glad of a chance to see it. It cannot be true; all experience is against it. The people in the South are made like the people in the North — the vast majority of whom are right-hearted and compassionate, and would be cruelly pained by such a spectacle — and *would attend it,* and let on to be pleased with it, if the public approval seemed to require it. We are made like that and we cannot help it. The other animals are not so, but we cannot help that, either. They lack the moral sense; we have no way of trading ours off, for a nickel or some other thing above its value. The moral sense teaches us what is right, and how to avoid it — when unpopular.

Thus Mark Twain on the "moral sense" in man, a favorite source of ironical commentary in his later period of work. Now against the mass drive and mob instinct of man, he asked, why were there not a few bolder spirits to oppose this, like those sheriffs of the period who did hold back the lynchers, or the perhaps more courageous outlaws who could terrorize such mobs? But no, he concluded, his scheme would not work. "There are not enough morally brave men in stock. We are out of moral-courage material; we are in a condition of profound poverty." In the meantime, there was another plan. "Let us import American missionaries from China, and send them into the lynching field. With 1,511 of them out there converting two Chinamen apiece per annum against an uphill birth rate of 33,000 pagans per day, it will take upward of a million years to make the conversions balance the output and bring the Christianizing of the country in sight to the naked eye; therefore, if we can offer our missionaries as rich a field at home, at lighter expense and quite satisfactory in the matter of danger, why shouldn't they find it fair and right to come back and give us a trial?"

The Chinese were universally conceded to be excellent people, honorable, industrious, trustworthy, and all that, Clemens continued. "Leave them alone, they are plenty good enough just as they are; and besides, almost every convert runs a risk of catching our civilization. We ought to be careful. We ought to think twice before we encourage a risk like that; for, *once civilized, China can never be uncivilized again.* We have not been thinking about that. Very well, we ought to think of it now. Our missionaries will find that we have a field for them — and not only for the 1,511 but for 15,011 . . . We must implore them to come back and help us in our need," added Clemens after citing a particularly nasty account of the white man's cruelty in these lynchings. "Patriotism imposes this duty on them. Our country is worse off than China; they are our countrymen, their motherland supplicates their aid in this, her hour of deep distress. They are competent; our people are not. They are used to scoffs, sneers, revilings, danger; our people are not. They have the martyr spirit; nothing but the martyr spirit can brave a lynching mob, and cow it and scatter it. They can save the country, we beseech them to come home and do it."

He referred again to the description of the lynching of one Negro which he multiplied by 115 (the estimated figure for lynchings in 1900), and added 88 (the figures already recorded for lynchings in 1901), and said: "Place the 203 in a row, allowing 600 feet of space for each human torch, so that there may be viewing room around it for 5,000 Christian American men, women, and children, youths and maidens; make it night for grim effect, have the show in a gradually rising plain, and let the course of the stakes be uphill; the eye can then take in the whole line of twenty-four miles of blood-and-flesh bonfires unbroken, whereas if it occupied ground level the ends of the line would bend down and be hidden from view by the curvature of the earth. All being ready, now, and the darkness opaque, the stillness impressive — for there should be no sound but the soft moaning of the night wind and the muffled sobbing of the sacrifices — let all the far stretch of kerosened pyres be touched off simultaneously and the glare and the shrieks and the agonies burst heavenward to the Throne . . . There are more than a million persons present; the light from the fires flushes into vague outline against the night the spires of five thousand churches. O kind missionary, O compassionate missionary, leave China! Come home and convert these Christians!"

Thus the flaming conclusion of "The United States of Lyncherdom" which was indeed "dramatic" and "visual" and "scenic" and "rendered" enough to satisfy all the deepest yearnings of a Henry James. Although this celebrated American expatriate, James I mean, in his own book called *The American Scene,* written during the same years, and in his wanderings southward, would expatiate only on the rude, barbaric, lazy

African tribal types he found there, and on the terrible economic and domestic exigencies forced upon the former southern
aristocrats whose cause and whose sentiments James found himself comprehending more and more clearly and intimately, as it
were.*

And so, as Mark Twain recalled to their mother country
those American missionaries whom he had ridiculed and attacked in the first of the later polemical essays mentioned here
— To the Person Sitting in Darkness — he had come full
circle from what he had first felt to be the Old World's evil imperialism, and then discovered right at hand, before his nose,
in the New World's own burgeoning colonialism and racism.
The cycle was complete.

But that is not to say that he had by any means finished writing in this altogether imperial and majestic vein of radical
social criticism which the Mark Twain scholarship of the Cold
War period would find so regrettable, offensive, and unbecoming. No, Sam Clemens himself knew that he had discovered an
altogether new mood of inspiration in his later and last periods of
writing; a rich and golden realm in these areas of colonialism,
imperialism, and racism as the salient features of his society.

* In what should be a classic literary history of this period but is instead a misleading document, Edmund Wilson's *Patriotic Gore,* this leading American
critic is completely taken in by James' romantic (and at base pathological)
rhetoric about both the Civil War and the post-Civil War scene, in both the
grotesque travelogue, *The American Scene,* and in the baroque *Memoirs.* Somewhat like his alma mater, Princeton, Wilson can now be described as the
northernmost-situated of all the southern critics. Similarly, he has little use
for (or apparent knowledge of) Twain's brilliant social criticism of the scene
of James' snobbish romance, and Wilson himself seems infatuated by Twain's
wealth, social position, and acquaintanceship with the financial tycoons . . .
Wilson's work has been described earlier as that of a genius without any
"center"; in his late period it is obvious that his brilliant esthetic superstructure
lacks any solid social ground. And Irving Howe's "Introduction" to the most
recent edition of *The American Scene* reads as though it were composed some
fifteen years ago. Perhaps the Jamesian cultists cannot *afford* to keep up with
the times.

Returning to such themes would renew his failing fancy and restore his faltering pen, and carry it to new and higher flights of brilliant, ironical, comic, and often quite marvelous passages of polemical prose, both of its time and timeless. With a sounder sense of art and life than his future critics, those who were becoming ever more intimidated by the increasingly repressive nature of their own culture, he would return to this aspect of his art until the end of his life, taking a diabolical pleasure in it, purging his turbulent spirit, refreshing his genius.

SIX

TRAGEDY AND COMEDY

But it is quite true, as to the human and domestic and affectional sources of art, that after Susy's death Livy languished and mourned; the house was in darkness and sorrow for too many years; both Clara and Jean were affected by the decline of the Clemenses' happiness, which had been so delightful, touching, entertaining.

I have spoken of the "domestic abyss" which was the obverse of the domestic idyll, just as Clemens himself during these years was haunted by dream and reality, or dream and nightmare. The years from 1896 onward were marked by even greater personal sorrows.

After Susy's death, after the years of mourning, throwing a dark burden, unnecessarily so to modern thought, on every member of the household, nothing was ever the same in the Clemenses' domestic life. At York Harbor, Maine, in August, 1902, Livy, whose health had been precarious, was taken violently ill. "She could not breathe — was likely to stifle. Also she had severe palpitation. She believed she was dying. I also believed it." So Clemens wrote in his notebook; and for some twenty-two months after that until her death, Livy was bedridden, suffering, isolated from her family and from the world, alternating between little shows of recovery and an ever-deepening decline of health and spirits. Clara Clemens took charge of the household and matters generally, and the patient was secluded and guarded from every disturbing influence, Paine recorded in his *Biography*. In October they returned to Riverdale, and it was many months before Livy left her bedroom at all. "Our dear prisoner is where she is through overwork — day & night devotion to the children & me," Clemens noted. "We did not know how to value it. We know now." He wrote Twichell in October: "Livy drags along drearily. It must be hard times for that turbulent spirit. It will be a long time before she is on her feet again. It is a most pathetic case. I wish I could transfer it to myself."

He was still hopeful; and in his private speculations he alternated in his anxiety about her asthmatic heart and her "neurasthenia." It was during this period that Clemens renewed his interest in Christian Science which led ultimately to his remarkable book on Mary Baker Eddy's new church. The fable called "Was It Heaven? Or Hell?" written during this period, and concerned with the necessity of lies and illusions in order to preserve life and to prevent useless human suffering, was based directly on Livy's precarious position in the family. During the winter of 1902 Jean was down with pneumonia, while Livy became frailer, and Clara was forced to fabricate a daily account of Jean's domestic and social activities. It was a Siege and Season of Unveracity, as Clemens said: "Clara stood a daily watch of three or four hours and hers was a hard office indeed. Daily she sealed up in her heart a dozen dangerous truths, and thus saved her mother's life and hope and happiness with holy lies. She had never told her mother lies in her life before, and I may almost say that she never told her a truth afterward."

"All that winter and spring Mrs. Clemens kept but a frail hold on life," Paine stated. "Clemens wrote little and refused invitations everywhere he could." The second winter in Riverdale marked their thirty-third wedding anniversary, and Clemens noted: "She makes but little progress toward recovery, still there is certainly some, we are sure," while March 19, 1903, marked Susy's birthday. "She would be thirty-one now." Clemens himself took sick for a month, and read and subsequently asked Brander Matthews some questions about the novels of Sir Walter Scott:

1. Are there in Sir Walter's novels passages done in good English — English which is neither slovenly nor involved?

2. Are there passages whose English is not poor & thin & commonplace, but is of a quality above that?

3. Are there passages which burn with real fire — not punk, fox-fire, make-believe?

4. Has he heroes & heroines who are not cads and cadesses?

5. Has he personages whose acts & talk correspond with their characters as described by him?

6. Has he heroes & heroines whom the reader admires — admires and knows *why?*

7. Has he funny characters that are funny, and humorous passages that are humorous?

8. Does he ever chain the reader's interest & make him reluctant to lay the book down?

9. Are there pages where he ceases from posing, ceases from admiring the placid flood & flow of his own dilution, ceases from being artificial, & is for a time, long or short, recognizably sincere & in earnest?

10. Does he know how to write English, & didn't do it because he didn't want to?

11. Did he use the right word only when he couldn't think of another one, or did he run so much to wrong words because he didn't know the right one when he saw it?

12. Can you read him and keep your respect for him?

"Brander," so Clemens concluded, "I lie here dying, slowly dying, under the blight of Sir Walter" — and then coming upon *Quentin Durwood,* which, by comparison with the other novels at least, he enjoyed, he added a final question: "I wonder who wrote *Quentin Durwood?*" But now the Clemenses were preparing to live in Italy, in the final effort to help Livy regain her health (a popular American idea of this period, which really meant that all good Americans went to Europe to die). There was a last summer in Quarry Farm at Elmira; they sailed for Europe that October, and rented the Villa Quarto in Florence. In January, 1904, Clemens wrote "The $30,000 Bequest," and there was another momentary and illusionary revival of Livy's health. The new house and its landlady, the Countess Massiglia, were not satisfactory; Clemens began to search for another place. But "even if we find it," Clemens wrote Howells, "I am afraid it will be months before we can move Mrs. Clemens. Of course it will. But it comforts us to let on that we think otherwise, and these pretensions help to keep hope alive in her."

She collapsed again in February, and her pulse went to 192. She improved again, for a while, and was absorbed by the news of Clara's concert in Florence. And she collapsed again a few days later.

In May Clemens wrote to R. W. Gilder: "For two days now we have not been anxious about Mrs. Clemens (*unberufen*). After 20 months of bedridden solitude and bodily misery she all of a sudden ceases to be a pallid, shrunken shadow, & looks bright & young & pretty. She remains what she always was, the most wonderful creature of fortitude, patience, endurance, and recuperative power that ever was. But ah, dear! it won't last; this fiendish malady will play new treacheries upon her, and I shall go back to my prayers again — unutterable from any pulpit!" And on the next day he found what he had feared and learned to expect: regression. On Sunday, June 5, just when Clemens and Jean had found a new villa for the family, Clara declared her mother seemed better than she had been for three months. Mrs. Clemens was, according to Paine, bright and cheerful, and her husband remained with her for an hour. Returning to say good night, he discovered that Livy was dead, and wrote in his notebook:

> At a quarter past 9 this evening she that was the life of my life passed to the relief & the peace of death after 22 months of unjust and unearned suffering. I first saw her near 37 years ago & now I have looked upon her face for the last time. Oh, so unexpected! . . . I was full of remorse for things done & said in these 34 years of married life that hurt Livy's heart.

To Twichell he wrote:

> How sweet she was in death, how young, how beautiful, how like her dear girlish self of thirty years ago, not a gray hair showing! This rejuvenescence was noticeable within two hours after her death; & when I went down again (2:30) it was complete. In all that night & all that day she never noticed my caressing hand — it seemed strange.

And to Howells, about the death scene:

> I bent over & looked in her face & I think I spoke — I was surprised and troubled that she did not notice me. Then we understood & our hearts broke. How poor we are today! But how thankful I am that her persecutions are ended! I would not call her back if I could . . . Today, treasured in her worn, Old Tes-

tament, I found a dear & gentle letter from you dated Far Rock-away, September 13, 1896, about our poor Susy's death. I am tired & old; I wish I were with Livy.

Yet in his summary of Livy's terminal illness and death, Justin Kaplan, in *Mr. Clemens and Mark Twain,* surrounds this whole tragic and touching episode with an aura of psychological suspicion and malice by stressing only the very brief visits which Clemens was allowed to pay to his Livy, and the fact that Clara Clemens had a nervous breakdown after her mother's death, during which she refused to let her father visit her . . . Now it is quite true that Livy might have carried resentment for Clemens' having deprived her of her religion; for his squandering of her inheritance in the period of his financial gambling; and perhaps even for Susy's death while they were absent on their world tour. It is possible that Clara was identified with Livy's illness; that she resented her father just because of the spiritual and physical intimacy of her parents. But there is no *evidence* of Livy's final feeling other than affection for Sam; there is abundant evidence, of which I will quote much more, of Clemens' utter, touching devotion to Livy, and his desolation at her death. By stressing the enigmatic aspects of this episode at the expense of all the obvious signs of love and devotion, Mr. Kaplan distorts the whole central relationship of the Clemens family. (The Clemens children were perhaps another matter, which we will discuss in due time.)

The later, more detailed description of Livy's death which Charles Neider was allowed to publish in his edition of Twain's *Autobiography* was even more touching about the central relationship of the Clemenses, and Livy's love and Sam's utter devotion. Meanwhile, all three of the books which Clemens published in 1906 testified again to his singular love for Livy; his sense of loss, loneliness, and despair after her death. *Eve's Diary* was a specific tribute to her, and perhaps its companion piece, *Extracts from Adam's Diary,* published in 1904, although written over a decade earlier, and revised in 1901, was even more eloquent in its praise. One notices again, in the years of Livy's illness and death, Clemens' backward-looking yearning for that Eden of man's childhood and goodness and pleasure. This artist was equally identified with Adam and Eve and with Satan; with the angel in man and with the fallen angel — with the opposite poles of good and evil; and in this case they recalled to him the idyllic years of his own early marriage, love, and domestic plenitude, now all gone, ravaged, ruined and destitute. Mark Twain's Adam is first of all disturbed and annoyed by the odd creature who appears before him and changes the whole aspect of the Garden. A Keep-Off-the-Grass sign marks the first inhibition in Eden; and the primitive hero declares that "my life is not as happy as it was." He also notes "the new creature eats too much fruit. We are going to run short, most likely." The first Sunday that Eve also introduces into the Creation, Adam finds most trying. "It was selected and set apart last November as a day of rest. I had already six of them per week before." This naturalistic Adam of Mark Twain's is a very factual man who values the peace of mind and the freedom from which he is now being gradually deposed. The whole fable of the Creation is retold here in miniature with great charm and a deadpan humor, a poker-faced irony which shields a tenderness and affection of spirit. There is no better rebuttal than this in all Sam Clemens' work as to Livy's "censorship" of his temperament and work. "She has taken up with a snake now," adds this native hero. "The other animals are glad . . . and I am glad because the snake talks, and this enables me to get a rest . . . She says the snake advises her to try the fruit of that tree, and says the result will be a great and fine and noble education. I told her there would be another result, too — it would introduce death into the world . . . I foresee trouble. Will emigrate."

This benevolent Adam may be taken in by Eve's scheming, but not quite, when she brings the forbidden apples, and he eats. "It was against my principles but I find that principles have no real force except when one is well-fed. She came curtained in boughs and bunches of leaves, and when I asked her what she meant by such nonsense, and snatched them away and threw them down, she tittered and blushed. I had never seen a person titter and blush before, and to me it seemed unbecoming and idiotic. She said I would soon know how it was myself. That was correct." And ten days later, noted this Adam: "She accuses *me* of being the cause of our disaster!" He finds their new clothes uncomfortable but stylish, and the real point is

I find she is a good deal of companion. I see I should be lonesome and depressed without her, now that I have lost my property. Another thing, she says it is ordered that we work for our living hereafter. She will be useful. I will superintend.

This is a bright little comedy of innocence on the part of the benevolent Adam, who takes all the blame from Eve's shoulders since he considers himself responsible for what goes on, despite his own blunders — a parable of original sin which is touching and wistful. There is much ado about the creature named Cain which Eve has caught, and whose species Adam does not understand, along with some tender reflections on the Clemenses' younger domestic life. "The coming of the creature seems to have changed her whole nature and made her unreasonable about experiments. She thinks more of it than she does of any of the other animals, but is not able to understand why. Her mind is disordered — everything shows it. Sometimes she carries the fish in her arms half the night when it complains and wants to get to the water . . . She doesn't work Sundays, but lies around all tired out, and likes to have the fish wallow over her; and she makes fool noises to amuse it, and pretends to chew its paws, and that makes it laugh. I have not seen a fish before that could laugh. This makes me doubt."

"I have come to like Sunday," Adam adds. "Superintending all the week tires a body so. There ought to be more Sundays . . ." And these were indeed scarcely veiled reminiscenses of the Clemenses' idyll from the very depths of the domestic abyss. There is further discussion about Abel whom Eve also has caught while Adam was away; and the First Father of Creation suddenly discovers they are *boys*. "We found it out long ago . . . Abel is a good boy, but if Cain had stayed a bear it would have improved him." And there is Mark Twain's final tribute to his Livy:

> After all these years, I see that I was mistaken about Eve in the beginning; it is better to live outside the Garden with her than inside without her. At first I thought she talked too much; but now I should be sorry to have that voice fall silent and pass out of my life. Blessed be the chestnut that brought us near together and taught me to know the goodness of her heart and the sweetness of her spirit!

Written near the beginning of Livy's illness, published near the end, *Adam's Diary* was an eloquent testament of Sam Clemens' lifelong affection for her. If she had in any way restricted the freedom of his own primary Eden — and we see this view of her attempts — he freely forgave her now that her voice had indeed fallen silent and passed out of his life. If, moreover,

Mark Twain's Eve is not as convincing as Adam, and somewhat whimsical and coy in her own *Diary,* there is echoed the same refrain of a mutual love, admiration, and affection. She has indeed carried the sweet fragrance of the Garden within her, and forty years later, at Eve's grave, Adam repeats: "Wheresoever she was, *there* was Eden."

The $30,000 Bequest and Other Stories (1906) was in an altogether different vein; the volume itself carried too many trivial and minor tales and sketches for padding; yet the tributes to Livy were not missing here, too. The title story of the book was a kind of sequel to "The Man That Corrupted Hadleyburg," as another example of what money and greed can do to the human psyche; another fable of the cultural damage wrought by the epoch of the great fortunes upon the agrarian-mercantile simplicity of the Old Republic. Saladin Foster is a bookkeeper in the Far West town of Lakeside; his wife Electra is a capable helpmate who has done some minor speculations in real estate from their frugal life and modest savings. (Saladin is called Sally, Electra Aleck, in a curious sexual transposition of Clemens' in this dream and nightmare tale.) Their two daughters are Clytemnestra and Gwendolen; they are a loving, affectionate, virtuous family — until the fraudulent promise of wealth ruins them all.

From a distant relative, Tilbury Foster, they learn they are to receive some thirty thousand dollars cash "not for love, but because money had given him most of his troubles and exasperations, and he wished to place it where there was good hope that it would continue its malignant work." And provided that the Fosters could prove to the executors of the estate that they had never taken any notice of this gift, had made no inquiries about "the moribund's progress toward the everlasting tropics," and had not attended the funeral, etc. Now the story's scene is set,

and once again Clemens was projecting his own gambling fever
and financial follies into his art and his society alike.

The ordeal of the Fosters begins; their whole obscure, commonplace, decent, and affectionate small-town life is corrupted
and devalued. But just as Clemens had reversed symbolically
the sexual roles of these domestic partners, so he reversed their
financial roles. It is Aleck who spends her days absorbed in
investing this imaginary fortune; while Sally is planning how to
spend it. One might say, Freudianly, that Clemens was now
shifting his own financial guilt to the dead Livy in part. But it
makes more sense to say that the two central characters in the
story represent the double personality of Clemens himself: the
romantic and naive financial "promoter"; the idle and happy
pleasure-lover. Meanwhile the children slip away from these distraught parents who make their first imaginary gamble in can-
nel-coal mining stocks; the whole tissue of their domestic life
together is eroded by their mutual obsession of making and
spending their new fortune. (Based on the inheritance which
they have not yet received, which we surmise does not exist.)
Here indeed Mark Twain was showing how easily our ordinary
material life can be controlled by, and made completely and
obsessively part of, our dream and fantasy life . . . if indeed
our daily material existence *does* exist apart from our psychic
existence, in the curious interchange of illusion and reality.

But this tale was part of the whole literary process, as we
know the psychologists don't seem to understand, by which Clemens himself was expressing an artistic catharsis of his own earlier panic and frustration in the business world. If he had not
suffered through the bankruptcy ordeal, he would not have
understood, much less created such literature — in which a
deeply personal experience was fused with a very pertinent kind
of social criticism. Without the personal experience, the cul-

tural force of these stories would not have been so valid; without the cultural framework of the material change in the older American Republic which Mark Twain both witnessed and described, the personal experience would have been trivial and meaningless. The Fosters soon raise their imaginary capital to imaginary heights; they make a hundred thousand dollars by speculating on margin; they are completely absorbed by their obsession at the expense of children, friends, and homelife, even while they decide to invest (in their fancy) in a luxurious new home, and give a party to celebrate (since they are unable to confide their secret dream of wealth to anybody) the "Discovery of America." Then, of course, no ordinary village suitors are up to the financial-social position of the children whom in fact they have almost rejected as human beings. Starting with a dreamlike fantasy indeed, Clemens makes "The $30,000 Bequest" into a brilliant parody (anticipating a favorite theme of Ring Lardner's) of small American souls on the make; or of the ambitious new financial-social aristocracy which Veblen was describing in similar terms during the same years.

We realize too, while "Hadleyburg" was a savage and ironical parable of the hypocrisy of human virtue, and the ease of human temptation, that "The $30,000 Bequest" is primarily a comedy on the same theme. The relations between the Fosters are good-humored and affectionate in the depths of their mutual obsession. This is even a tender comedy about poor, weak human nature on the part of the "bitter," the "thwarted," the "frustrated" and "defeated" Mark Twain. There are the imaginary gas bills that Aleck frets about and Sally enjoys. And if there are curious elements of Freudian displacement in this story, one realizes that Clemens was describing one of the worst periods of the domestic abyss with all the grace, affection, humor of the domestic idyll. This is a remarkable re-creation of experience in literary terms whereby the artist was purging himself through the divine release of humor and self-humor. Now indeed the Foster daughters are no longer available in matrimony to the mechanics and shopkeepers of the Old Republic; their wealthy, successful, respectable parents are surveying the lists of lawyers, doctors, and successful financiers.

The Fosters themselves take on a new dignity and gravity of deportment as befitting superior souls who have become persons of property — substantial property. They have now accumulated half a million dollars — a million — and they exhibit, said Clemens, "the pride of riches." Mansion succeeds mansion in their dream life; they finally select Newport, Rhode Island, "Holy Land of High Society, ineffable Domain of the American aristocracy" . . . As a rule they spent a part of every Sabbath — after morning service — in this sumptuous home, the rest of it they spent in Europe, or in dawdling around in their private yacht.* And then: "Aleck, in her dream life, went over to the Episcopal camp, on account of its large official titles; next she became High-church on account of the candles and shows; and next she naturally changed to Rome, where there were cardinals and more candles."

Veblenian accents indeed of conspicuous consumption and ostentatious display, and the whole modern drift of American society. And then comes the passage of Sally-Sam's burlesque "confession" after he has accused Aleck of shipping off her missionaries "to persuade unreflecting Chinamen to trade off twenty-four carat Confucianism for counterfeit Christianity."

---

* Those critics of Mark Twain who have maintained that he was corrupted and his career foreshortened and blighted both by his own wealth and then by Rogers' munificent hospitality towards the Clemenses, including of course such things as private railway cars and the use of the Rogers yacht, seem not to realize how Clemens saw through and literally *used* all the material comforts that indeed he enjoyed so much, and so frankly.

Aleck bursts into tears at his teasing and the spectacle breaks Sally's heart and leads him to tremendous self-accusation. "His cheeks burned and his soul was steeped in humiliation. Look at her life — how fair it was, and tending ever upward; and look at his own — how frivolous, how charged with mean vanities, how selfish, how empty, how ignoble! And its trend — never upward, but downward, ever downward!"

> He instituted comparisons between her record and his own. He had found fault with her — so he mused — *he!* And what could he say for himself? When she built her first church, what was he doing? Gathering other blasé millionaires into a Poker Club; defiling his own palace with it; losing hundreds of thousands to it at every sitting, and sillily vain of the admiring notoriety it made for him. When she was building her first university, what was he doing? Polluting himself with a gay and dissipated secret life in the company of other fast bloods, multi-millionaires in money and paupers in character. When she was building her first foundling asylum, what was he doing? Alas! When she was projecting her noble Society for the Purifying of the Sex, what was he doing? Ah, what, indeed! When she and the W.C.T.U. and the Woman with the Hatchet, moving with resistless march, were sweeping the fatal bottle from the land, what was he doing? Getting drunk three times a day. When she, builder of a hundred cathedrals, was being gratefully welcomed and blest in papal Rome and decorated with the Golden Rose which she had so honorably earned, what was he doing? Breaking the bank at Monte Carlo.

And so much, you might say, for those Mark Twain critics, and perhaps primarily Messrs. Kaplan and Fiedler and their Freudian cohorts who continually stress the burden of Samuel Clemens' "guilt" in his relations with Livy and the children. For Clemens himself in his best moments completely dissipated the whole psychological syndrome of "guilt-anxiety-shame-and-self-punishment" which might apply to ordinary mortals. At

the worst moment of his defeat and despair — the moment
of Livy's final fatal illness — he could yet seize upon the liberation of art which was based upon self-insight, affection, and humor. How Clemens, in "The $30,000 Bequest," satirized both
himself and Livy while projecting their private torment outward into a comic fable of human greed. How the incorrigible
and finally *unrepentant* spirit that was Mark Twain, this demonic and diabolical angel of our literature — this mad scoundrel, if you like, of whose compulsions and contradictions great
art was made — always pushed things one step *more!* And thus
to redeem and reclaim and indeed to end up celebrating all his
human failings under the light of his literary grace. In the
same story, moreover, Clemens concluded by a sweet and touching parody of his lifelong "confessions" of sin to Livy. The
"guilty" hero decides he must tell all to his wife and financial
mate:

> He stopped. He could go no farther; he could not bear the
> rest. He rose up, with a great resolution upon his lips: this secret
> life should be revealed, and confessed; no longer could he live it
> clandestinely; he would go and tell her All.
> And that is what he did. He told her All; and wept upon her
> bosom; wept and moaned, and begged for her forgiveness. It was
> a profound shock, and she staggered under the blow, but he was
> her own, the core of her heart, the blessing of her eyes, her all in
> all, she could deny him nothing, and she forgave him. She felt
> that he could never again be quite to her what he had been before;
> she knew that he could only repent and not reform; yet all morally
> defaced and decayed as he was, was he not her own, her very
> own, the idol of her deathless worship? She said she was his serf,
> his slave, and she opened her yearning heart and took him in.

Touching lines indeed; but was Sam taking liberties with
Livy's true feeling about him, her true vision of their bond?

Maybe so, but this theme is repeated so steadily in the writings both during and after Livy's death, and with such confidence, affection, and beneficent humor, that we must really assume that Samuel Clemens knew more about his own private life than some of the later, and more skeptical critics. And the final record, in any case, is always in a writer's art rather than in his "other" — that is to say his private, personal, and much less important — life.

The ending of "The $30,000 Bequest," like so many of Mark Twain's endings, was lurid and heavy, as the Fosters receive the news that they have been tricked by a malicious relative who had no fortune to bequeath; and like the "honest" couple in "The Man That Corrupted Hadleyburg," they lose their sanity. (The symbolic moral of the story, however, is quite accurate; and Sally does finally reflect, at the peak of his insanity, that the whole trouble was that Tilbury Foster should have left them *more* money.) The volume itself for which this was the title story also contained reprints of Adam's and Eve's diaries; and another collection of Twain's earlier stories and sketches of which I can mention only a few.

"The Californian's Tale" was concerned with an aging gold miner in a western ghost town who was kept alive by the illusion of his dead wife's yearly return — just as so many of the stories both in this collection and in this period of Mark Twain's life, as we know, deal with the conflict, or perhaps the mutual necessity, of illusion and reality. Along with every other great artist in American letters, Mark Twain knew that it was *illusion* which sustained life and perhaps even created "reality." But illusions, too, must be judged, finally, by their connection with, or their interpenetration by, an outside reality which exists quite independently of man's consciousness.

"The Five Boons of Life" was another dark fable wherein

Fame, Love, Riches, and Pleasure were contrasted with life's only real boon: death. (A theme which Clemens was to render with variations in the rest of his writings.) But there were little farces and satires here, too, from early days to the present. "A Telephone Conversation" was a pre-Robert Benchley conceit of Clemens listening to one half of a telephone conversation (Livy's) and inferring the remainder with some exaggeration. A piece called "A Burlesque Biography," dating from 1871, has provided another field day for the Freudians because Clemens linked himself only to criminals, thieves, murderers, and other ancestors of like repute. This was obviously, of course, an early example of Clemens' western satire on the Gilded Age's frenetic search for a cultural "past," as was dutifully and all-admiringly approved of in the work of Henry James. A cultural "background" and ancestors and husbands, even if fraudulent and bankrupt and corrupt, as Clemens recorded here and elsewhere. But this little sketch also recorded the true affinity of the artist with the outcast and the wretched of the earth — as with Charlie Chaplin — rather than with nobility, respectability, social position, and wealth. And here Twain's persistent distaste for missionaries found early expression. "Charles Henry Twain" lived during the latter part of the seventeenth century and was a zealous and distinguished missionary:

> He converted sixteen thousand South Sea islanders, and taught them that a dog-tooth necklace and a pair of spectacles was not enough clothing to come to divine service in. His poor flock loved him very, very dearly; and when his funeral was over, they got up in a body (and came out of the restaurant) with tears in their eyes, and saying, one to another, that he was a good tender missionary, and they wished they had some more of him.

Believe me, this early Sam Clemens, this crude, coarse, vulgar,

and illiterate western journalist, was one of the most sophisticated talents to appear in a literature all unprepared for him,
to preside over it for more than forty years, and to remain
one of its most distinguished ornaments for another fifty
years as of this date. Early and late, too, the theme of the
drunkard, and of intoxicated, rebellious pagan laughter echoed
in Mark Twain's work, just as here another "ancestor" was the
Mighty-Hunter-with-a-Hog-Eye Twain who assisted General
Braddock to resist the oppressor Washington, until he could not
stand up any longer.

In this "Biography," Mark Twain was also related to certain ancestors better known in history for their aliases, among
them Richard Brinsley Twain, Guy Fawkes Twain, Baron
Munchausen Twain, Captain Kidd Twain, and Nebuchad-
nezzar and Baalam's Ass Twain. As for himself, "I was born
without teeth." And "My parents were neither very poor nor
conspicuously honest." And his own history was so tame when
contrasted with that of his ancestors, he had decided to leave
it unwritten until he was hanged. "If some other biographies
I have read had stopped with the ancestry until a like event
occurred, it would have been a felicitous thing for the reading
public. How does it strike you?"

What strikes us truly is the freshness and vivacity of this kind
of "journalistic sketch" written in the 1870s when the American language was in one of its worst phases of inflated, genteel
Anglican rhetoric. It is really astonishing to read this writing
from such an antique epoch of American culture, when even
Melville, Whitman, and Howells subscribed to many of the conventions.

Clemens also had his say on the southern rhetoric of that
period (and our own, in such writers as William Faulkner who
continued to bear the burden of this literary heritage), and

there are two hilarious sketches on the Italian language, and another essay on a Portuguese "Guide" to conversation. There are also some poorer things in *The $30,000 Bequest* volume, trick tales and literary conceits like "George Washington's Negro Body-Servant," whose death was reported periodically by the American press from 1809 to 1864, when he was, by Twain's count, 151 years old. Finally there were a couple of his social satires, "A Humane Word from Satan" and "Does the Race of Man Love a Lord?" Nor did Livy's illness and the poor health of the two daughters prevent Sam Clemens from reprinting in this volume two essays on "Amended Obituaries" and "Post-Mortem Poetry." In the first of these pieces he suggested that, as he was nearing seventy, the press should publish its obituaries of Mark Twain while he was alive, so that he could revise and correct "not the Facts, but the Verdicts — striking out such clauses as could have a deleterious influence on the Other Side." And he would collect these "Amended Obituaries" to leave behind him "as a perennial consolation and entertainment to my family, and as an heirloom which shall have a mournful but definite commercial value for my remote posterity."

Yes, from the depths of tragedy and despair, Sam Clemens would still reiterate his heretical views of such revered institutions as death, religion, publicity, the press, and commerce. And in the second of these articles, written as early as 1870, Clemens, quoting extensively from the typical examples of postmortem poetry in his period about departed children, noted that "A child thus mourned could not die wholly discontented." Very different in stress and tone, however, from these gay sketches and from the title story of *The $30,000 Bequest* volume, was Twain's next and perhaps most notorious work, *What Is Man?*, published anonymously in 1906. The form of this little book, only published under Mark Twain's name in 1917, was that of a Socratic dialogue between the Old Man (Clemens) and the Young Man, who may have represented, but probably did not, Clemen's earlier and "idealistic" self. No, the dialogue was really not so much Socratic as deliberately contrived and one-sided; and the young man was surely not ever the younger Clemens, but some pathetic dupe of the Victorian idealistic conventions. Called by some one of Mark Twain's "darkest" and most despairing documents, *What Is Man?* is actually not so much dark and desperate as it is a kind of deliberately cynical refutation of the genteel Victorian taboos about life.

The essay is indeed not only tangential in many aspects, but self-contradictory; in some senses it is not pessimistic at all but hopeful and "scientific" about man's training, his habits, his environment, or his "circumstances," as Zola called them in the movement of French Naturalism to which Twain's philosophy here was obviously related. If man was a poor weak thing, motivated only by his own self-interest, as Clemens said over and over again in this essay; if human nature was never idealistic but always self-serving; if man never had a fresh thought or a fresh contribution to his existence but depended purely on "outside" stimulation — then the simple answer was to change the outside environment. But of course the central propositions were only half true; this was a deliberately low, false, and narrow view of the creative spirit in humanity which does indeed depend upon and reflect its social environment — and those worldly circumstances which in turn it can alter, change, or recreate. In the complex syndrome of the human spirit and social circumstances (or culture), each element influences the other; each cannot exist without the other; each must be viewed in terms of the other, or in terms of union rather than singularity. In stressing only the man-machine reacting to "outside" stimulus, Clemens was ignoring almost completely the biological and psychological elements of human nature, or the biopsychic forces in man which have created his culture.

Moreover, for almost the only time in his career, after *Joan of Arc,* Sam Clemens, not daring to publish this essay under his own name in 1906, wrote mostly as though he were not Sam Clemens. *What Is Man?* is not so much pessimistic as it is contradictory and confused; and it is finally not so much contradictory and confused as it is tedious. It is not so black a book as it is a boring one, and in this book of Mark Twain's there is almost — that "almost" of Twain's — not a redeeming passage.

For, toward the last half of *What Is Man?* Clemens was forced to break through the narrow trap of mechanistic materialism which he had fashioned for himself, and restore just those elements of biology and psychology, or of the biopsychic, and thus of man's creative spirit working *with* and through man's external and conditioning circumstances, which gives us a more complete account of what culture and human nature really are.

Still describing the mind as "purely a machine," an independent machine within man, Clemens began talking about the unconscious, uncontrollable aspects of the human psyche, and when he came to dreams — just as earlier in his personal life he had been interested in Doctor Charcot's hypnosis — he was on the Freudian brink. What fascinated Clemens in his own free associations and dream life was the compression of time and space. From childhood memories of a yellow cat, the Young Man said here, a cat struggling to free itself from a large sheet of sticky flypaper, he saw the silent congregation quivering like jelly, and the tears running down their faces. "I saw it all. The sight of the tears whisked my mind to a far distant and a sadder scene — in Terra del Fuego — and with Darwin's eyes I saw a naked great savage hurl his little boy against rocks for a trifling fault; saw the poor mother gather up her dying child and hug it to her breast and weep, uttering no word. Did my mind stop to mourn with that nude black sister of mine? No — it was far away from that scene in an instant and it was busying itself with an ever-recurring and disagreeable dream of mine. In this dream I always find myself, stripped to my shirt, cringing and dodging about in the midst of a great drawing-room throng of finely dressed ladies and gentlemen, and wondering how I got there . . ."

In this case the Young Man of the dialogue was in fact the Old Man, and the Old Man was clearly Sam Clemens; and Sam Clemens, either with complete innocence or with complete confidence, was revealing sides of his nature that most men would prefer to keep hidden. (Some of his most fascinating dreams were concerned with the black women of his youth or of his fancy, and Clemens, if he did not seem to understand these dreams, also did not bother to conceal them.) In this case also, *What Is Man?* — if it had earlier broken the "iron law" of Mark Twain's own writing: that *nothing* he ever wrote was entirely without interest — now confirmed it. Despite all of Twain's sterile and repetitious stress on mechanistic human nature, we come upon his interest in instinct as a kind of "petrified thought." This was hardly mechanistic; it was close to Samuel Butler's version of creative evolution which led so directly into the Freudian insights; and in that case it was Darwin who was more materialistic and mechanistic in his theoretical speculations.

With Clemens also, instinct was "inherited thought" which wasn't always quite so "petrified," and which originally had been relegated to the unconscious psyche from the conscious. And in this essay, for the most part on the man-machine whom Clemens was stressing for his own purposes, and against the whole burden and testimony of his own temperament and art, the few sections of familiar Twainian warmth, affection, and humor came — as suddenly we realize was to be expected — in the closing sections on animal rather than human temperament. The Old Man of the dialogue insists upon abolishing the "intellectual frontier" which separates man and beast; or rather as he says, "I beg your pardon. One cannot abolish what does not exist." There is no such frontier in Clemens' mind and he also refuses the honor of "elevating" the dumb beasts. "Let us drop that lying phrase and call them the Unrevealed Creatures; so far as we can know, there is no such thing as a dumb beast."

In the animal kingdom there is only "the great army of the Unrevealed." And Clemens went on to describe the various modes of animal life and existence with the kind of emotional affinity that we are by now so familiar with. Despite all his contempt for the man-machine, he was still in love with the animal (or primitive) psyche. "It is just like man's vanity and impertinence to call an animal dumb because it is dumb to his dull perceptions." He spoke glowingly of "Sir John Lubbock's ants" (despite an earlier parody of the ant) in a day and age when it was still possible to marvel at the social engineering of nature without references to any "atheistic, godless, communistic slave society."

It is interesting to note how temporal and fashionable ideologies of one period can distort all the basic values of another, and it does prove one of Clemens' central themes in *What Is Man?* In the essay's summary, the Young Man of the dialogue complains that this philosophy is a desolating doctrine:

It is not inspiring, enthusing, uplifting. It takes the glory out of man, it takes the pride out of him, it takes the heroism out of him, it denies him all personal credit, all applause; it not only degrades him to a machine, but allows him no control over the machine; makes a mere coffee-mill of him, and neither permits him to supply the coffee nor turn the crank, his sole and piteously humble function being to grind coarse or fine, according to his make, outside impulses doing all the rest.

To which the Old Man says only: "Correctly stated; but *I* have not made man a machine. God made him a machine. I am merely calling attention to the fact, nothing more. Is it wrong to call attention to the fact? Is it a crime?" And he adds that ideas are not really important compared to the temperaments of man (another unwitting concession to biopsychic influences in man's spirit), and that culture itself can condition and adapt the human temperament to any form of existence.

"Nations do not *think,* they only *feel.* They get their feelings at second hand through their temperaments, not their brains. A nation can be brought — by force of circumstances, not argument — to reconcile itself to *any kind of government or religion that can be devised;* in time it will fit itself to the required conditions; later, it will prefer them, and will fiercely fight for them." As proof, he cited all of history from the Greeks to the Hindus and Turks:

a thousand wild and tame religions, every kind of government that can be thought of, from tiger to house-cat, each nation *knowing* it has the only true religion and the only sane system of government, each despising all the others, each an ass and not suspecting it, each proud of its fancied supremacy, each perfectly sure it is the pet of God, each with undoubted confidence summoning Him to take command in time of war, each surprised when He goes over to the enemy, but by habit able to excuse it and resume compliments — in a word, the whole human race content, always content, persistently content, indestructibly content, happy, thankful, proud, *no matter what its religion is, nor whether its master be tiger or house-cat.* Am I stating facts? You know I am. Is the human race cheerful? You know it is. Considering what it can stand, and be happy, you do me too much honor when you think that *I* can place before it a system of plain cold facts that can take the cheerfulness out of it. Nothing can do it. Everything has been tried. Without success. I beg you not to be troubled.

Now with this concluding passage, Clemens in effect denied the whole validity of his own thesis, and just perversely enough stressed his own underlying sardonic pleasure in the lurid spectacle of life. But despite a few such passages of the familiar Mark Twain, and a few sections of genuine insight in *What Is Man?*, the essay itself remains a curious hodgepodge of Victorian sentiment and the "modern" mechanism of the time; an expression of personal and temporal despair during a period of intense crisis. It is among Twain's poorest works both in content and tone. And just as it is always a mistake to evaluate a writer by his formal "philosophy" rather than by the shifting currents of feeling and the emotional undertones of the creative work itself, so it is usually a mistake for a writer to attempt, as Clemens did here, to formulate his own beliefs and vision of life in philosophical rather than creative terms. But a mistake that most writers continue to make, and often a revealing one in terms other than those which are stated.

Christian Science, in 1907, was much different and, irregular as the form also was and uneven in terms of literary effect, a much more interesting, even a fascinating work. It is perhaps one of the singular "curiosities" of a career which is composed of curiosities. In his personal life Clemens had been drawn to the art of spiritual healing both by the vicissitudes of family illness and his own concern with psychic phenomena. As early as 1899 in Vienna, and thereafter, he had written the chapters which form the first half of the book; his tone became more extravagantly satirical as he learned more about the organizational set-up of the new religion and about the personality of its founder. During the 1900s, he set to work in earnest; he warmed to his task with vigor.

The full title of the book when issued was *Christian Science with Notes Containing Corrections Today,* and in the first half of the book, Clemens went over his earlier articles and revised certain statements. Yet there are some entertaining inventions in the early pages of his chronicle, and there is his first description of reading Mrs. Eddy's *Science and Health.*

> I took up the Christian Science book and read half of it, then took a dipperful of drench and read the other half. The resulting experiences were full of interest and adventure . . . For of all the strange and frantic and incomprehensible and uninterpretable books which the imagination of man has created, surely this one is the prize sample. It is written with a limitless confidence and complacency, and with a dash and stir and earnestness which often compel the effects of eloquence, even when the words do not seem to have any traceable meaning. There are plenty of people who imagine they understand the book; I know this, for I have talked with them; but in all cases they were people who also imagined that there were no such things as pain, sickness, and death, and no realities in the world, nothing actually existing but Mind. It seems to me to modify the value of their testimony.

But that this argument was directed at certain aspects of Christian Science, and not toward the religion itself or its effects, Clemens also made clear:

> Remember its principal great offer: *to rid the Race of pain and disease.* Can it do so? In large measure, yes. How much of the

pain and disease in the world is created by the imaginations of the
sufferers, and then kept alive by those same imaginations? Four-
fifths? Not anything short of that, I should think. Can Christian
Science banish that four-fifths? I think so. Can any other organized force do it? None that I know of . . . In the mean
time, would the Scientist kill off a good many patients? I think so.
More than get killed off now, by the legalized methods? I will take
up that question presently.

He was not, however, completely convinced by the testimo-
nies of various persons saved and healed by Christian Science,
which he examined in some detail in these pages; and particularly by those of the child converts. "A little Far-Western girl of
nine, equipped with an adult vocabulary, states her age and
says, 'I thought I would write a demonstration to you.' She
had a claim derived from getting flung over a pony's head and
landing on a rock-pile. She saved herself from disaster by remembering to say 'God is All' while she was in the air. I
couldn't have done it. I shouldn't even have thought of it. I
should have been too excited. Nothing but Christian Science
could have enabled that child to do that calm and thoughtful
and judicious thing in those circumstances. She came down on
her head, and by all the rules she should have broken it."

There was the account of a small boy who got broken all up
into small bits by an accident, but said over the Scientific
Statement of Being, and some of the other incantations, and
got well and sound "without having suffered any real pain and
without the intrusion of a surgeon." There was an account of
a Christian Science *horse* — but here Mark Twain rebelled as
he usually did when the animal rather than the human kingdom was intruded upon. "I can stand a great deal, but I recognize that the ice is getting thin here. That horse had as many
as fifty claims; how could *he* demonstrate over them? . . .

Let us draw the line at horses. Horses and furniture." After
this section on testaments in *Christian Science,* Clemens went
on to consider the financial arrangements which had been set
up by Mrs. Eddy, and the lucrative trade that she had con-
ducted for the Mother Church, and the immensely larger future
membership and profits that he prophesied for the new religion.
"The Christian Scientist has *organized* the business . . . the
Christian Scientist has taken a force which has been lying idle
in every member of the human race since time began, and has
organized it, and backed the business with capital, and concentrated it at Boston headquarters in the hands of a small
and very competent Trust, and there are results. Therein lies
the promise that this monopoly is going to extend its commerce
wide in the earth."

Discussing the fact that each Christian Science family was
an agency for the Cause — "and makes converts among the
neighbors, and starts some more factories" — Clemens had
some sharp passages on typical American middle-class ignorance, snobbery, and complacency; on all the false "knowledge"
and "authority" of purely material circumstance. (Whereas
a Ring Lardner would concentrate his outraged moral sense
on this single aspect of American life, Mark Twain included it
within a wider critique of American society.) And by January, 1903, Clemens had become totally fascinated by the figure
and career of Mary Baker Eddy. "But in the matter of motives
and of a few details of character we agree to disagree upon
Napoleon, Cromwell, and all the rest; and to this list we must
add Mrs. Eddy. I think we can peacefully agree as to two or
three extraordinary features of her makeup, but not upon the
other features of it. We cannot peacefully agree as to her motives, therefore her character must remain crooked to some
of us and straight to the others.

"No matter, she is interesting enough without an amicable agreement. In several ways she is the most interesting woman that ever lived, and the most extraordinary. The same may be said of her career, and the same may be said of its chief result. She started from nothing. Her enemies charge that she surreptitiously took from Quimby* a peculiar system of healing which was mind-cure with a Biblical basis. She and her friends deny that she took anything from him. This is a matter which we can discuss by and by. Whether she took it or invented it, she has turned it into a Klondike; its spiritual dock had next to no custom, if any at all: from it she has launched a world-religion which has now six hundred and sixty-three churches, and she charters a new one every four days.* When we do not know a person — and also when we do — we have to judge his size by the size and nature of his achievements, as compared with the achievements of others in his special line of business — there is no other way. Measured by this standard, it is thirteen hundred years since the world has produced any one who could reach up to Mrs. Eddy's waist-belt.

"Figuratively speaking, Mrs. Eddy is already as tall as the Eiffel tower. She is adding surprisingly to her stature every day. It is quite within the probabilities that a century hence she will be the most imposing figure that has cast its shadow across the globe since the inauguration of our era."

From here Clemens went on to discuss Mrs. Eddy's temperament as revealed in her autobiography, and her poetry. Sample:

* Phineas Parkhurst Quimby (1802-1866) was a clockmaker and mental healer in Portland, Maine, working on a science of mental health when Mary Baker Eddy consulted him in 1862 and 1864 and became his most famous patient, or disciple.

* In 1969, there were 2995 churches of Christ, Scientist, but this new religion had not by any means achieved the world dominion which Mark Twain prophesied.

And laud the land whose talents rock
  The cradle of her power,
And wreaths are twined round Plymouth Rock
  From erudition's bower.

Minerva's silver sandals still
  Are loosed and not effete.

"You note it is not a shade above the thing which all human beings churn out in their youth. You would not think that in a little wee primer — for that is what the *Autobiography* is — a person with a tumultuous career of seventy years behind her could find room for two or three pages of padding of this kind, but such is the case. She evidently puts narrative together with difficulty and is not at home in it, and is glad to have something ready made to fill in with."

Here fame-honored Hickory rears his bold form
And bears[1] a brave breast to the lightning and storm,
While Palm, Bay, and Laurel in classical glee,
Chase Tulip, Magnolia, and fragrant Fringe-tree.

"Vivid? You can fairly see those trees galloping around. That she could still treasure up, and print, and manifestly admire those Poems, indicates that the most daring and masculine and masterful woman that has appeared in the earth in centuries has the same soft, girly-girly places in her that the rest of us have."

Clemens was fascinated, moreover, at Mrs. Eddy's account of her early education:

I gained book-knowledge with far less labor than is usually requisite. At ten years of age I was as familiar with Lindley Murray's Grammar as with the Westminster Catechism; and the latter

---

[1] Meaning *bares?* I think so. — M. T.

I had to repeat every Sunday. My favorite studies were Natural Philosophy, Logic, and Moral Science. From my brother Albert I received lessons in the ancient tongues, Hebrew, Greek, and Latin.

But then, he said, your eye falls upon the next sentence but one with evil satisfaction:

After my discovery of Christian Science, most of the knowledge I had gleaned from school-books vanished like a dream.

And that "disappearance," said Mark Twain, accounted for so much in her miscellaneous writings.

He had more to say on Mrs. Eddy's style, from which he derived his principal ideas about her mind, spirit, and character, apart from the organizational genius that he marveled at. Her Bible, revised and revised, had at last become a compact, grammatical, dignified and workman-like body of literature. But "we are now confronted with one of the most teasing and baffling riddles of Mrs. Eddy's history — a riddle which may be formulated thus: How is it that a primitive literary gun which began as a hundred-yard flintlock smooth-bore muzzle-loader, and in the course of forty years has acquired one notable improvement after another — percussion cap; fixed cartridge; rifled barrel; efficiency at half a mile — how is it that such a gun, sufficiently good on an elephant-hunt (Christian Science) from the beginning, and growing better and better all the time during forty years, has always collapsed back to its original flintlock estate the moment the huntress trained it on any other creature than an elephant?"

If the armament analogy was puzzling to anybody, Clemens made it clear through illustration. "Something more than a generation ago Mrs. Eddy went out with her flintlock on the rabbit-range, and this was a part of the result":

After his decease and a severe casualty deemed fatal by skillful physicians, we discovered that the Principle of all healing and the law that governs it is God, a divine Principle, and a spiritual not material law, and regained health.

Preface to Science and Health,
first revision, 1883.

"N.B. Not from the book *itself;* from the *Preface.*

"You will notice the awkwardness of that English. If you could carry that paragraph up to the Supreme Court of the United States in order to find out for good and all whether the fatal casualty happened to the dead man — as the paragraph almost asserts — or to some person or persons not even hinted at in the paragraph, the Supreme Court would be obliged to say that the evidence established nothing with certainty except that *there had been a casualty* — victim not known.

"The context thinks it explains who the victim was, but it does nothing of the kind. It furnishes some guessing-material of a sort which enables you to infer that it was 'we' that suffered the mentioned injury, but if you should carry the language to a court you would not be able to prove that it necessarily meant that. 'We' are Mrs. Eddy; a funny little affectation." She replaced it later with the more dignified third person, just as the main body of *Science and Health* continued to be improved in clarity and grammar through the edition of 1902.

Yet after twenty years of pen-practice, and fifty years after the poetic verses that Clemens had already cited, Mrs. Eddy was still capable of some further literary passages which Clemens quoted and added some italics to:

1. "What plague spot or bacilli were (sic) gnawing (sic) at the heart of this metropolis . . . and bringing it (the heart) on bended knee? Why, it was an *institute* that had entered its *vitals* — that, among other things, taught" et cetera — *C. S. Journal,* p. 670, article entitled "A Narrative" — by Mary Baker Eddy.

2. "Parks sprang up (sic) . . . electric cars run (sic) merrily through several streets, concrete sidewalks and macadamized roads dotted (sic) the place," et cetera. — *Ibid.*

3. "Shorn (sic) of its suburbs it had indeed little left to admire, save to (sic) such as fancy a skeleton above-ground *breathing* (sic) slowly through a barren (sic) breast." *Ibid.*

"This is not English — I mean, grown-up English. But it is fifteen-year-old English, and has not grown a month since the same mind produced the Poems. The standard of the Poems and of the plague-spot-and-bacilli effort is exactly the same. It is most strange that the same intellect that worded the simple and self-contained and clean-cut paragraph beginning with 'How unreasonable is the belief,' should in the very same lustrum discharge upon the world such a verbal chaos as the utterance concerning that plague-spot or bacilli which were gnawing at the insides of the metropolis and bringing its heart on bended knee, thus exposing to the eye the rest of the skeleton breathing slowly through a barren breast."

Clemens suggested the possibility in Mrs. Eddy's case of *two* guns — the Mauser-magazine which had written *Science and Health,* and the old-fashioned flintlock which had written Mrs. Eddy's other pieces. He went on to quote a bit more from her *Autobiography*:

"I remember reading in my childhood certain manuscripts containing Scriptural Sonnets, besides other verses and enigmas" (etc.). (Page 7.)

(On page 27.) "Many pale cripples went into the Church leaning on crutches who came out carrying them on their shoulders."

It was awkward, Clemens said, because at the first glance "it seems to say that cripples went in leaning on crutches which went out carrying the cripples on their shoulders. It would have cost her no trouble to put her 'who' after her 'cripples.' I blame her a little; I think her proof-reader should have been shot. We may let her Capital C pass, but it is another awkwardness, for she is talking about a building, not about a religious society."

And right here in *Christian Science,* Sam Clemens warmed to his theme again, and his prose took on heat and light, and fire. He talked about Mrs. Eddy's chapter, in her autobiography, on Marriage and Parentage.* "You imagine she is going to begin a talk about her marriage and finish with some account of her father and mother. And so you will be deceived. 'Marriage' was right, but 'Parentage' was not the best word for the rest of the record. It refers to the birth of her own child. After a certain period of time 'my babe was born.' Marriage and Motherhood — Marriage and Maternity — Marriage and Product — Marriage and Dividend — either of these would have fitted the facts and made the matter clear."

"Without my knowledge he was appointed a guardian." (Page 32.)

She is speaking of her child. She means that a guardian *for* her child was appointed, but that isn't what she says.

"If spiritual conclusions are separated from their premises, the nexus is lost, and the argument with its rightful conclusions, becomes correspondingly obscure." (Page 34.)

We shall never know why she put the word "correspondingly" in there. Any fine, large word would have answered just as well: psychosuperintangibly — electrincandescently — oligarcheologi-

---

* Mrs. Eddy's autobiography was called *Retrospection and Introspection,* and published in 1891, though Clemens calls it simply the *Autobiography.* As described in Stefan Zweig's study of Mrs. Eddy in *Mental Healers* (New York, 1932), she had little concern with the upbringing of her babe after he was born.

cally — sanchrosynchrostereoptically — any of these would have answered, any of these would have filled the void.

"His spiritual noumenon and phenomenon silenced portraiture." (Page 34.)

"Yet she says she forgot everything she knew when she discovered Christian Science. I realize that noumenon is a daisy; and I will not deny that I shall use it whenever I am in a company which I think I can embarrass with it; but, at the same time, I think it is out of place among friends in an autobiography. There, I think a person ought not to have anything up his sleeve. It undermines confidence. But my dissatisfaction with the quoted passage is not on account of noumenon; it is on account of the misuse of the word 'silenced.' You cannot silence portraiture with a noumenon; if portraiture could make a noise, a way could be found to silence it, but even then it could not be done with a noumenon. Not even with a brick, some authorities think."

"It may be that the mortal life-battle still wages." (Page 35.)

"This is clumsy. Battles do not wage; battles are waged. Mrs. Eddy has one very curious and interesting peculiarity: whenever she notices that she is chortling along without saying anything, she pulls up with a sudden 'God is over us all,' or some other sounding irrelevancy, and for the moment it seems to light up the whole district; then, before you can recover from the shock, she goes flitting pleasantly and meaninglessly along again, and you hurry hopefully after her, thinking you are going to get something this time; but as soon as she has led you far enough away from her turkeylet she takes to a tree. Whenever she discovers that she is getting pretty disconnected, she couples up with an ostentatious *But* which has nothing to do with anything that went before or is to come after, then she hitches some empties to the train — unrelated verses from the Bible usually — and steams out of sight and leaves you wondering how she did that clever thing."

This was Clemens' description of Mrs. Eddy's overall style, and he devoted many more pages in *Christian Science* to specific examples. He quotes again: " 'Evil is not mastered by evil; it can only be overcome with Good. This brings out the nothingness of evil, and the eternal Somethingness vindicates the Divine Principle and improves the race of Adam.' " This was *too* extraneous for him, said Clemens, and "the minute you think the light is bursting upon you, the candle goes out and your mind begins to wander." He quoted again: " 'No one else can drain the cup which I have drunk to the dregs, as the discoverer and teacher of Christian Science,' " and added "that is saying we cannot empty an empty cup."

> We knew it before; and we know she meant to tell us that that particular cup is going to remain empty. That is, we think that that was the idea, but we cannot be sure. She has a perfectly astonishing talent for putting words together in such a way as to make successful inquiry into their intention impossible. She generally makes us uneasy when she begins to tune up on her finewriting timbrel. It carries me back to her Plague-Spot and Poetry days, and I just dread those.

And then Clemens quoted another of Mrs. Baker's purple passages. " 'Into mortal mind's material obliquity, I gazed and stood abashed. Blanched was the cheek of pride. My heart bent low before the omnipotence of Spirit, and a tint of humility soft as the heart of a moon beam mantled the earth. Bethlehem and Bethany, Gethsemane and Calvary spoke to my chastened sense as by the tearful lips of a babe.' "

The heart of a moonbeam was pretty enough, Clemens said,

and he let it pass. "But humility has no tint, humility has no complexion, and if it had, it could not mantle the earth. A moonbeam might — I do not know — but she did not say it was the moonbeam. But let it go. I cannot decide it. She mixes me up so . . ."

Circling around this subject once more, unable to abandon Mrs. Eddy's prose style, Clemens tried to summarize its salient traits:

Desert vacancy, as regards thought.
Self-complacency.
Puerility.
Sentimentality.
Affectations of scholarly learning.
Lust after eloquent and flowering expression.
Repetition of pet poetic picturesqueness.
Confused and wandering statement.
Metaphor gone insane.
Meaningless words, used because they are pretty, or showy or unusual.
Sorrowful attempts at the epigrammatic.
Destitution of originality.

Clemens went on to quote still another of Mrs. Eddy's passages from the *Miscellaneous Writings* (and it is hard to stop quoting *him*); and then to analyze her unquestioned financial genius, from her first insistence on a "modest payment" of three hundred dollars for a term of twelve half-days for any applicant wishing to become a Christian Science healer. But it was God who had finally arranged the amount of money to be paid by her disciples in the healing art, as Clemens noted: "The price was arranged above. This view is constructively supported by the fact . . . that God afterward approved, 'in multitudinous ways' her wisdom in accepting the mentioned fee. 'Multitudinous ways' — multitudinous encoring — suggests enthusiasm. Business enthusiasm. And it suggests nearness. God's nearness to His 'little one.' Nearness, and a watchful personal interest. A warm, palpitating, Standard-Oil interest, so to speak. All this indicates inspiration. We may assume, then, two inspirations, one for the book, the other for the business."

Since Mrs. Eddy had claimed copyright for *Science and Health,* while attributing the book to the Deity under whose spell she had written it, Clemens thought the royalties should be divided. "That seemed to settle the matter. It seemed to distribute the percentages of credit with precision among the collaborators: ninety-two per cent to Mrs. Eddy who did all the work, and eight per cent to the Deity who furnished the inspiration." But then Mrs. Eddy changed her line again. She was a most trying witness, Clemens added, perhaps "*the* most trying witness that ever kissed the Book, I am sure." She could prove both sides of her case, he said, or "nine sides, if desired." And he described her financial genius in the epoch of financial geniuses.

"She published her book. She copyrighted it. She copyrights everything. If she should say, 'Good morning; how do you do?' she would copyright it; for she is a careful person, and knows the values of small things." He went on to trace her early development, and the astonishing growth of the Church of Christ, Scientist. He studied the internal organization of the Church, where Mrs. Eddy had been careful to guarantee herself every possible form of censorship and control. This was indeed a brilliant study of a womanly despot, and all despite himself Clemens showed, in these pages of *Christian Science,* a kind of unwilling admiration for the commercial acumen, the boldness, the effrontery of Mary Baker Eddy. "Mrs. Eddy's inborn disposition to copyright everything, charter everything, secure the rightful and proper credit to herself for everything she does, and everything she thinks she does, and everything she thinks, and everything she thinks or has thought or intends to think, is illustrated in Sec. 5 of Art. IV, defining the duties of official Readers in church." She borrowed many of her business ideas, Clemens said, but still hers was no ordinary business head. "There has been no other commercial skull in a thousand centuries that was equal to it . . . One must respect the business brain that produced it — the splendid plug and impudence that ventured to promulgate it, anyway."

He was writing some of this in the years after 1903, the period of his darkest domestic tribulations; and perhaps in this fervent, funny, and scorching indictment of Mrs. Eddy's Christian Science Church, Clemens found another literary release for his own tormented spirit — but a release and a catharsis again, not of blind acceptance and conformity, but of irony, parody, and rebelliousness.*

This was certainly a forthright, angry, and entertaining attack upon a sect noted for its sensitivity; this was an unrelenting study of a typical new American religion — but it was the total power-drive of Mrs. Eddy that fascinated Clemens, that fascinated and infuriated him and entertained him, too. And curiously enough it is the figure of Mary Baker Eddy — who emerges as the central feminine portrait in all of Mark Twain's work — which was the central achievement of *Christian Sci-*

* What is interesting to notice, in respect to the satire of Mark Twain's *Christian Science,* is the hesitant and reserved judgment of his two main biographers. It is barely mentioned in Paine as "delightful humor" — which is better at least than the judgment of the contemporary biographer, Justin Kaplan, who cites this book as another example of Clemens' increasing cautiousness, or even of his publishing cowardice! Kaplan does not mention the book otherwise, or quote from it, or venture any critical opinion of it; and one suspects the caution and cowardice in this case belongs more to Twain's biographers than to their subject.

ence, and which made the virtuous Joan of Arc look like the dull puppet she was in Clemens' picture of her.

"The Christian world has *two* infallibles now," Clemens cried. "Of equal power? For the present only. When Leo XIII passes to his rest another Infallible will ascend his throne; others and yet others and still others will follow him, and be as infallible as he decides questions of doctrine as long as they may come up, all down the far future; but Mary Baker Eddy is the *only* Infallible that will ever occupy the Science throne. Many a Science Pope will succeed her, but she has closed their mouths; they will repeat and reverently praise and adore her infallibilities, but venture none themselves. In her grave she will still outrank all other Popes, be they of what Church they may. She will hold the supremest of earthly titles, The Infallible — with a capital I. Many in the world's history have had a hunger for such nuggets and slices of power as they might reasonably hope to grab out of an empire's or a religion's assets, but Mrs. Eddy is the only person alive or dead who has ever struck for the *whole* of them. For small things she has the eye of a microscope, for large ones the eye of the telescope, and whatever she sees, she wants. Wants it all."

These were bolts of thunder and lightning that Sam Clemens was unleashing at perhaps the only American figure of the period who had a historical stature equal to his own: perhaps even, like the jealous Jehovah, he felt the threat to his own godlike presence. And yet he felt the force of Mrs. Eddy's character; in his angry wrath there was still the underlying note of an astounded admiration. The master-passion in Mrs. Eddy's heart, he said, was a hunger for power and glory; and while her hunger for money remained, it was now in the service of extending her present and future power and glory, forever, until world's end. "I wish to enlarge a little upon this matter. I think it is quite clear that the reason why Mrs. Eddy has concentrated in herself all power, all distinctions, all revenues that are within the command of the Christian Science Church Universal is that she desires and intends to devote them to the purpose just suggested — the upbuilding of her personal glory — hers, and no one else's; that, and the continuing of her name's glory after she shall have passed away. *If she has overlooked a single power, however minute, I cannot discover it. If she has found one, large or small, which she has not seized and made her own, there is no record, no trace of it."*

Clemens was pursued and pressured by the Christian Scientists of the time; Mrs. Eddy herself started to answer him, and abruptly held her silence. And meanwhile he went through his familiar ritual of a satanic meekness and humble apologies which insisted upon turning into further attacks — a false humility and a series of devastating "apologies" which became new pitfalls for the unwary.

Again, however, he never disputed Christian Science's value as psychological healing. "But there is a mightier benefaction than the healing of the body, and that is the healing of the spirit — which is Christian Science's other claim. So far as I know, so far as I can find out, it makes it good. Personally, I have never known a Scientist who did not seem serene, contented, unharassed. I have not found an outsider whose observation of Scientists furnished him a view that differed from my own. Buoyant spirits, comfort of mind, freedom from care — these happinesses we all have at intervals; but in the spaces between, dear me, the black hours! They have put a curse upon the life of every human being I have ever known, young or old. I concede not a single exception. Unless it might be those Scientists just referred to."

Beneath the broad comedy, the irony, the polemics of *Chris-*

tian Science, there still lurked Sam Clemens' well-earned familiarity with the darker tragedy of life itself. Beneath the comedy lay the tragedy; below the tragic lay more of the comic; and it was this fortunate amalgam which set off his later and his last writings, up to, and yes, well beyond his death.

An unusual history in the records of American literature, whose promise is so often confined to and burned up in youth; but this kind of spiritual development was typical of our former literary generations in that "Older World" of the democracy before it turned into a military-industrial and colonial empire where art was valued no more than individualism, dissent, or perhaps human life itself. Meanwhile he spent the last part of *Christian Science* vainly endeavoring, over and over again, to summarize his great love-hate portrait of Mrs. Eddy, and his own mixture of feelings from admiration to abomination, from violent rage to wild laughter. This became also a "defense" of Mrs. Eddy, just as there had been Mark Twain's "defense" of General Funston and King Leopold; only here there was genuine awe, affection, amazement. After all among the archetypal figures of the new age of American Empire, Mrs. Eddy alone — this extraordinary person — had, with all her errors and faults, tried to *save,* not to destroy, the fullness of the human spirit.

It was these qualities too which forced another relentless analyst of Mrs. Eddy, Stefan Zweig, in his *Mental Healers,* to place her, along with Mesmer and Freud, among the key figures of the early twentieth century. Clemens, moreover, went on to list those traits of character which he considered most important in constituting Mrs. Eddy's formidable personage: "A clear head for business, and a phenomenally long one . . . Intelligence in planning a business move . . . Firmness in sticking to it after it has been decided upon . . . Extraordinary daring; indestructible persistence; devouring ambition; limitless selfishness . . . a knowledge of the weaknesses and poverties and docilities of human nature and how to turn them to account which has never been surpassed if ever equaled . . . And — necessarily — the foundation stone of Mrs. Eddy's character is a never-wavering confidence in herself . . . It is a granite character."

Quite naturally, said the smitten Sam Clemens, there was a measure of the talc of smallnesses common to human nature mixed up and distributed through that granite character. "When Mrs. Eddy is not dictating servilities through her throne in the clouds to her official domestics in Boston, or to her far-spread subjects round about the planet, but is down on the ground, she is kin to us and one of us: sentimental as a girl, garrulous, ungrammatical, incomprehensible, affected, vain of her little human ancestry, unstable, inconsistent, unreliable in statement, and naively and everlastingly self-contradictory — oh, trivial and common and commonplace as the commonest of us! just a Napoleon as Madame de Rumsat saw him, a brass god with clay legs."

This was nice writing again as Clemens neared the end of his book and rose to the peak of his powers of malice, vindictiveness, laughter, prophetic rage, and grudging admiration. If the beginning, perhaps even the first half, of this book seems to be a series of desultory, scattered essays (as indeed they are) put together as a prologue in Mark Twain's inimitable kind of formlessness, the middle and end of *Christian Science* have great passages and paragraphs and pages in the highest form of Twain's polemical style. Possibly they are some of his best passages precisely because they are formed not out of that pure anger and hatred which were almost strong enough to make Clemens speechless (though never really) in his hatred of money, materialism, bigotry, evil, racism, and colonial exploitation in the decline of the American democracy whose guiding spirit he had been. Here there was a kind of animadvertent splendor of Mrs. Eddy for him to muse upon. The comic mood is present at every point of Clemens' hot rages directed at the remarkable exploits of this "extraordinary creature," this character which was granite indeed, but vain, trivial, and — the worst of all sins for Mark Twain — ungrammatical.

Now there were just three more and lesser books which ended this last decade of Mark Twain's writings — and of his own life.

A Horse's Tale, in 1907, was written at the request of the actress Minnie Maddern Fiske who, after reading Twain's tract, *A Dog's Tale,* in 1904, written for the Anti-Vivisection Society, had been pleading with him to do as much for the aged and crippled beasts used as animal fodder in the bullfights. It was in effect a sentimental novella about a talented and appealing army horse in the days when Buffalo Bill was chief of scouts to the Army of the Frontier. "Soldier Boy" was in fact Buffalo Bill's favorite horse "out of dozens," and he in turn entrusts Soldier Boy to little Cathy, the precocious heroine of the story who is adopted and made a pet of by the bronzed veterans of the frontier. Despite the obvious whimsy of the story, where the animals also talk to each other, and where little Cathy becomes quite obnoxious in her charm and her conquests, still, Clemens, using all the power of his animal empathy, and of the underlying fairy-tale romance so deeply embedded in his nature — and so compelling when used in the right context — manages to make the story interesting and entertaining, at least until the sadistic end. Just as in the sudden seizure of the charming little dog for "scientific purposes," here too Soldier Boy, wounded and crippled, is stolen and ends up in the bullring. Cathy is taken out of her army post and returns to her native Spain. In a horrid trick-ending, which perhaps Clemens prided himself on developing, Cathy sees Soldier Boy disemboweled in the bullring, rushes toward him and is herself gored to death.

Maybe effective propaganda, and maybe necessitated by the dictates of his propaganda theme, but yet a story curiously cruel and hard for Clemens who used all his force to gain the reader's sympathy for Soldier Boy — and whose prototype for little Cathy was his own daughter Susy. Intent on immortalizing Susy, Clemens perhaps did not realize he was in effect subjecting her to *another* cruel, if "imaginary," literary death.

Extract From Captain Stormfield's Visit to Heaven, was less sentimental, less sadistic, more satiric and funny. It was in fact a reworking of an old religious parody, based on a dream of Clemens' sea friend, Captain Ned Wakeman, which Clemens had considered too bold to publish some forty years before, had kept for his *Autobiography,* and then decided to publish in *Harper's* magazine in December–January of 1907–8. This Captain Wakeman had made a great impression on Sam Clemens' youthful mind, and his new house in Redding, Connecticut, was called "Stormfield." What was curious about this fantasy-essay was the opening in a kind of orbital flight, with its endless vista of planets streaming about in limitless space, where the Christian earth was recognized only with some confusion and difficulty.

For this was a parody of heaven and heavenly bliss as conceived by the formal and orthodox Christian churchly vision. In this opening fantasy, of huge heavenly bodies, infinite in number and nameless, rushing about wildly in space there was also some reference to the Mississippi River steamboat races now enthroned in a species of cosmic nightmare. This was the blind rushing universe of Darwinian astronomy, as it were, in which the formal Christian God and Christian Man were obliterated in the multitudinous universe of planets. There is a Huck Finn tone of wistful loneliness when Captain Stormfield finds himself in "the wrong heaven" which does not recognize the earth. "A man's got to be in his own heaven to be happy," Clemens commented, and we feel the vanity of *all* heavens, all religions projected by an anthropomorphic man-child upon an indifferent and perhaps essentially hostile universe. Even when Eli Stormfield does reach his own heaven, his most deeply cherished sentiments of bliss are quickly dissipated. For one thing he meets "Pi Ute Injun" whose funeral pyre he had attended. Here Clemens' earliest, most deeply rooted prejudice against the native western Indians was finally exorcised. But meanwhile, since in heaven you could resume any younger age you wished to, Mark Twain, quite unlike the famous Lost Generation of post World War I, to whom youth, beauty, and virility was all, and both age and wisdom were dubious or nonexistent compensations — Twain, quite in the tradition of the Old Republic, discoursed here on the horrors of maturity and old age trying to be young and "gay" again. Captain Stormfield soon learns also to drop his heavenly wings; rather like a bicycle for an aged novice, they are too difficult to handle. His halo, harp, and other traditional props of the Christian heaven have already been discarded as a useless burden.

The interlocutors through whom Clemens made clear the message of *Captain Stormfield* are Sandy McWilliams who knows the ropes in heaven and Cap'n Stormfield who is the eager apprentice asking the questions which have such depressing answers. It is curious that the tone is reminiscent of another "Sandy" and the Connecticut Yankee who is trying to get around in King Arthur's court. Clemens habitually fell

back, in all these dialogues, upon the wistful queries of the innocent and childlike Huck Finn, and the disappointing re-
sponses of maturity. So, here, as Sandy genially records the experiences, adventures, discoveries he has had and made, the
literal Christian heaven becomes a most ridiculous and horribly
tedious bore; the fit reward as Sam Clemens might say, for respectable American Christian souls. But there are not really
so many of these characters in heaven as you might expect.
"What a man mostly misses, in heaven," says Sandy, pathetically, "is company — company of his own sort and color and
language." Says Captain Stormfield, "Sandy, I notice that I
hardly ever see a white angel; where I run across one white
angel, I strike as many as a hundred million copper-colored
ones — people that can't speak English."

As early as the original edition of *Captain Stormfield's
Visit to Heaven,* and as late as the revised version in 1909,
Clemens had already exported his notions of "race" — and by
implication his indictment of the white man's colonial exploitation of the darker peoples — into the Christian heaven itself,
which, of course, was the responsible moral agent in this business. Here indeed, in the framework of racist thinking, Clemens
penned a total indictment of the American continent. "You
can't expect us to amount to anything in heaven, and we *don't,*"
says Sandy. "Now that is the simple fact and we have got to do
the best we can with it. The learned men from other planets
and other systems come here and hang around a while, when
they are touring around the Kingdom, and then go back to
their own section of heaven and write a book of travels, and
they give America about five lines in it. And what do they say
about us? They say this wilderness is populated with a scattering few hundred thousand billions of red angels, with now
and then a curiously complected *diseased* one. You see they

think we whites and the occasional nigger are Injuns that have been bleached out or blackened by some leprous disease or other — for some peculiarly rascally *sin,* mind you. It is a mighty sour pill for us all, my friend — even the modestest of us, let alone the other kind, that think they are going to be received like a long-lost government bond, and hug Abraham into the bargain."

Mark Twain had, in fact, come so far along from his original ingrained prejudices about the Indians of his youth that he was now in effect returning the whole Northern continent to them. Conversely, he was expressing his disenchantment with all of white American civilization. His concept of the colored races as the basic stock of life, moreover, extended even to the presumably purest Nordic or Anglo-Saxon races. "As long as you run across Englishmen born this side of three hundred years ago, you are all right; but the minute you get back of Elizabeth's time the language begins to fog up, and the further back you go the foggier it gets. I had some talk with one Langland and a man by the name of Chaucer — old-time poets — but it was no use. I couldn't quite understand them and they couldn't quite understand me. I have heard from them since, but it is such broken English I can't make it out. Back of those men's time the English are just simply foreigners, nothing more, nothing less; they talk Danish, German, Norman, French, and sometimes a mixture of all three; back of *them,* they talk Latin, and ancient British, Irish, and Gaelic; and then back of these come billions and billions of pure savages that talk a gibberish that Satan himself couldn't understand. The fact is, where you strike one man in the English settlements that you can understand, you wade through awful swarms that talk something you can't make head nor tail of. You see, every country on earth has been overlaid so often in the course of a billion years, with different kinds of people and different sorts of languages, that this sort of mongrel business was bound to be the result in heaven."

Yes, certainly, it is all very clear today, but in Mark Twain's historical epoch it took his special kind of genius to view the white Christian heaven as populated by such masses of "mongrels."

But this hardly made heaven more attractive or companionable to Captain Stormfield, and the fable ends with a rather broad burlesque of the arrival up there of a converted bartender who also gets short shrift from the powers that be. *Is Shakespeare Dead?*, published as another short book in 1909, and originally intended for the *Autobiography,* was a half-serious and half-hilarious treatise in support of the Baconian theory — that is to say, disbelief in Shakespeare's existence as a writer. The opening sections of this article dealt with the great "Claimants" in history — Satan, the Golden Calf, Louis XVII, Shakespeare, Arthur Orton, and Mary Baker Eddy among them: that whole affinity, even in sound, between "Clemens" and "Claimants" which the Freudian critics have stressed to establish Mark Twain's own feelings of insecurity and falsehood as to his own nature and career. But the point is, of course, that Clemens was absolutely intrigued and delighted by these "Claimants" — foremost of whom was perhaps the Satan with whom he identified so closely. The real relationship between Sam Clemens and his celebrated Claimants was one of delight and pleasure, rather than pain or guilt. (Oh, those prurient, sour-minded, humorless, unperceptive, and rigid Freudian critics, who, just like the orthodox Marxists, are bound down by their own dogmas!)

Eminent Claimants, successful Claimants, defeated Claimants, royal Claimants, pleb Claimants [so Clemens said here] — showy Claimants, shabby Claimants, revered Claimants, despised Claimants, twinkle star-like here and there and yonder through the mists of history and legend and tradition — and, oh, all the darling tribe are clothed in mystery and romance, and we read about them with deep interest and discuss them with loving sympathy or with rancorous resentment, according to which side we hitch ourselves to. It has always been so with the human race.

Did such a paragraph really describe Clemens' own sense of fraud, failure, and frustration? If anything, just the opposite: his own affection and curiosity and admiration — yes, and his own identification — with the false, the fraudulent, the "mysterious" scheming and cunning aspects of life itself. What the Freudians always attribute to Mark Twain's personal neurosis is always better understood by his identification with humanity in general. In him the supposed specific is almost always generic; and no psychology of individualism will really penetrate the secrets of this unique American individualist.

For the great "pretenders" in life and history are often linked in a curious way with the great rebels. The archangel Satan had indeed his pretensions of being the Almighty Being — and Clemens was for him. But there are "true" pretenders and false pretenders. While Sam Clemens was being feted in London society all during the latter half of the nineteenth century just because of his American individuality, Henry James (the artist above all who must be studied on a singular basis rather than a common one, whose links with humanity are very thin indeed, and whose esthetic vision is so strangely personal as to be utterly baroque) was "pretending" also to being part of an inherited English aristocracy, about which in fact he invented so much and knew so little. James was a far greater pretender than Mark Twain, but a false one who did not even recognize his own illusions and who always concealed his true personality even from himself. And James was almost unknown, as I

say, to the same British society that welcomed the blunt, debunking, irreverent Western American genius.

An ironical literary polarization which could lead to further
speculation. But meanwhile Twain's *Is Shakespeare Dead?*
veered from this lyrical opening passage on historical and
tribal pretenders to his first acquaintanceship with the Shake-
speare-Bacon controversy during his early days on the Mississippi under a certain river pilot named George Ealer, who was
a prime chess-player and an idolater of Shakespeare. The
trouble was that Ealer used to read Shakespeare aloud while
giving orders to his cub pilot . . . "What man dare, I dare!
Approach thou *what* are you laying in the leads for? what a
hell of an idea! Like the rugged ease her off a little, ease her
off! rugged Russian bear, the armed rhinoceros or the *there*
she goes! meet her, meet her! didn't you know she'd smell the
reef if you crowded it like that? Hycran tiger; take any shape
but that and my firm nerves she'll be in the *woods* the first you
know! stop the starboard! come ahead strong on the larboard!
back the starboard! . . . *Now* then, you're all right; come
ahead on the starboard; straighten up and go 'long, Never
tremble: or be alive again, and dare me to the desert *damnation* can't you keep away from that greasy water? pull her
down! snatch her! snatch her baldheaded! With thy sword; if
trembling I inhabit then, lay in the leads! — no, only the starboard one, leave the other alone, Protest me the baby of a girl.
Hence horrible shadow! eight bells — that watchman's asleep
again, I reckon, go down and call Brown yourself, Unreal
mockery, hence!"

And Mark Twain was also, I daresay, the only late nineteenth-century American writer who was bold enough to meet
the Elizabethan master on his native grounds.

He went on with the discussions between Ealer and himself
on the Stratford Pretender or the Baconian Pretender: the

scholarly debate is hilariously intertwined in the dialogues of the river pilot and his wily cub. "He was silent awhile, and I knew what was happening," said Clemens about Ealer. "He was losing his temper. And I knew he would presently close the session with the same old argument, the one I couldn't answer, because I dasn't — the argument that I was an ass, and better shut up. He delivered it, and I obeyed . . . Oh dear, how long ago it was — how pathetically long ago! And here am I, old, forsaken, forlorn, and alone, arranging to get that argument out of somebody again."

With these tones, so very similar to those of the aging Whitman saluting the God of life — "old, poor, and paralyzed, I thank Thee!" — Clemens completed his last return — but one, or two — to the Mississippi River days, and went on to his argument, or rather his tirade on Shakespeare and Bacon. Now modern Shakespearean scholarship has all but dismissed the Baconian claim; yet many of the questions that Clemens raised in 1909 still remain unanswered as to the material existence of the great Elizabethan.*

Serious as he was in the Baconian argument, Clemens' *Is Shakespeare Dead?* did not have the single-minded obsessiveness of *Christian Science,* and he indulged in some wayward asides, including some of his other famous "claimants." "When I was a Sunday-school scholar, something more than sixty years ago, I became interested in Satan, and wanted to find out all I could about him. I began to ask questions, but my classteacher, Mr. Barclay, the stone-mason, was reluctant about answering them, it seemed to me." Thus Sam Clemens' youthful rebellion was early symbolized in Satan — psychological

---

* Perhaps the best case to be made for "a" Shakespeare, whoever he was, must be made from the *internal* evidence of the plays themselves, which contain so many areas of knowledge that a noble or aristocratic personage like Bacon would *not* be conversant with. See, for example, J. B. Priestley's excellent *Literature and Western Man.*

and mythical symbol of repressed paganism, or of man's natural drives (sexual desires) gone underground and taboo — within a conventional religious context. And — "I was greatly interested in the incident of Eve and the serpent, and thought Eve's calmness was perfectly noble. I asked Mr. Barclay if he had ever heard of another woman who, being approached by a serpent, would not excuse herself and break for the nearest timber. He did not answer my question, but rebuked me for inquiring into matters above my age and comprehension."

Here indeed Clemens described again, perhaps most openly, his own earliest and deepest affinity with Satan, "the great enemy of man and goodness," the Lucifer of the fallen angels who dared challenge the reign of the Divine (Moral) Being, and the symbol of man's pleasure before the repressions of civilization. He assured his Sunday-school teacher "that he had wholly misconceived my attitude; that I had the highest respect for Satan, and that my reverence for him equaled, and possibly even exceeded, that of any member of any church."

At the tender age of seven when all this occurred, so the aging Clemens confided to his beloved *Autobiography,* he had even started to write a biography of Satan, based on about the same number of facts as was Shakespeare's life. "How curious and interesting is the parallel — as far as poverty of biographical details is concerned — between Satan and Shakespeare. It is wonderful, it is unique, it stands quite alone, there is nothing resembling it in history, nothing resembling it in romance, nothing approaching it even in tradition. How sublime is their position, and how over-topping, how sky-reaching, how supreme — the two Great Unknowns, the two Illustrious Conjecturabilities! They are the best-known unknown persons that have ever drawn breath upon the planet."

He went on to list the paucity of known facts in Shakespeare's life during his apprenticeship, his great period of writing, and his retirement to Stratford. He stressed Shakespeare's will as a thorough-going businessman's will which mentioned not a single book by this author — "not a play, not a poem, not an unfinished literary work, not a scrap of manuscript of any kind." He mentioned the lack of Shakespearean signatures, the fact that Shakespeare's death was completely obscure when compared with the deaths of Ben Jonson, Francis Bacon, Spenser, or Raleigh, not to mention the other notable Elizabethans, and the most curiously trite inscription on Shakespeare's tombstone which is still not properly accounted for by Shakespearean scholarship. He recalled the famous hoax in which the younger Mark Twain and Professor Osborn had built a colossal skeleton brontosaur that stood fifty-seven feet long and sixteen feet high in the Natural History Museum (so Clemens asserted). "We had nine bones, and we built the rest of him out of plaster of Paris. We ran short of plaster of Paris, or we'd have built a brontosaur that could sit down beside the Stratford Shakespeare and none but an expert could tell which was biggest or contained the most plaster."

In this pre-modern argument about Shakespeare's identity, Mark Twain is indeed so convincing as well as so comic that one begins to doubt the validity of all the recent books of scholarship which have filled in the missing facts of the Bard's life — or have they? "Shall I set down the rest of the Conjectures which constitute the giant Biography of William Shakespeare? It would strain the Unabridged Dictionary to hold them. He is a brontosaur: nine bones and six hundred barrels of plaster of Paris."

Since Clemens had originally intended to put his reflections about Shakespeare's identity into the *Autobiography,* the narrative line of *Is Shakespeare Dead?*, in typical Twainish form, alternates between his argument proper and his memories of youth and adolescence. He had no compunction about comparing his own career to the bard's, and pointing out what a sensation his own death would make in the world, contrasted with the silence of Shakespeare's. All the river pilots would testify about *his* life, said Clemens. "They know about me, and can tell. And so do printers, from St. Louis to New York; and so do newspaper reporters from Nevada to San Francisco. And so do the police. If Shakespeare had really been celebrated, like me, Stratford could have told things about him; and if my experience goes for anything, they'd have done it."

Comparing Richard Henry Dana's *Two Years Before the Mast,* with the sea jargon in *The Tempest,* Clemens came forth with this Shakespearean passage:

Master. Boatswain!
Boatswain. Here master; what cheer?
Master. Good, speak to the mariners: fall to 't, yarely, or we run ourselves to ground; bestir, bestir! (*Enter Mariners.*)
Boatswain. Heigh my hearts! cheerly, cheerly, my hearts! yare, yare! Take in the topsail. Tend to the master's whistle . . . Down with the topmast! yare! lower, lower! Bring her to try wi' the main course . . . Lay her a-hold, a-hold! Set her two courses. Off to sea again; lay her off.
    That will do for the present; let us yare a little, now for a change.

"If a man should write a book and in it make one of his characters say, 'Here, devil, empty the quoins into the standing galley and the imposing-stone into the hell-box; assemble the comps around the frisket and let them jeff for takes and be quick about it,' I should recognize a mistake or two in the phrasing, and would know that the writer was only a printer theoretically, not practically."

Twain's tone became more informal and idiomatic in these pages of *Is Shakespeare Dead?* "Am I trying to convince anybody that Shakespeare did not write Shakespeare's Works? Ah, now, what do you take me for?" And he expounded the central thesis of *What Is Man?* with more telling effect. "I haven't any idea that Shakespeare will have to vacate his pedestal this side of the year 2209 . . . It took several thousand years to convince our fine race — including every splendid intellect in it — that there is no such thing as a witch; it has taken several thousand years to convince that same fine race — including every splendid intellect in it — that there is no such person as Satan; it has taken several centuries to remove perdition from the Protestant Church's program of post-mortem entertainments; it has taken a weary time to persuade American Presbyterians to give up infant damnation and try to bear it the best they can; and it looks as if their Scotch brethren will still be burning babies in the everlasting fires when Shakespeare comes down from his perch.

"We are the Reasoning Race, and when we find a vague file of chipmunk-tracks stringing through the dust of Stratford village, we know by our reasoning powers that Hercules has been along there. I feel that our fetish is safe for three centuries yet. The bust, too — there in the Stratford Church. The precious bust, the priceless bust, the calm bust, the serene bust, the emotionless bust, with the dandy mustache and the putty face, unseamed of care — that face which has looked passionlessly down upon the awed pilgrim for a hundred and fifty years and will look down upon the awed pilgrim three hundred more, with the deep, deep, deep, subtle, subtle, subtle expression of a bladder."

Fine writing in this curious tract; and it must be confessed that as late as the most recent *Encyclopaedia Britannica* this calm, serene, emotionless bust with the dandy mustache, the putty face unseamed by care, still gazes out at us in a variety of poses looking like nothing so much as twelve different bladders. Here at least Clemens' shrewd eye had caught something real in the elusive history of the Stratford Bard . . . And now this hard, honest, penetrating, and unequivocating gaze of Mark Twain's which, during such a long lifetime of pleasure, honor, sorrow, disaster, disgrace, regeneration, and achievement, had pierced to the core so many worldly and human hypocrisies, was finally darkened; this voice, so rich and truthful, so eloquent, so entertaining, was stopped. Returning home from a Bermuda vacation on April 14, 1910, about a month after his final illness had started, he died of heart failure at Stormfield a week later.

In his later years, following the series of tragic deaths in his own domestic idyll, Samuel Clemens had devoutly come to feel that death was indeed the final blessing, the only true refuge from life's pain and suffering and tragedy. He welcomed his own death in this spirit. But destiny would not yet abandon to the blindness and darkness he yearned for, this singular personality. The ironical fact was that Mark Twain would continue to produce "new" books for another fifty years after his own death; that his career would develop and grow to even greater heights after he had so willingly abandoned it; that in the 1960s, above all, would appear, as if miraculously, some of his very best work: the most pertinent commentary about our own contemporary scene, made resplendent in prose as light as air, as intense as fire, as fresh as the dew. But now let us describe the manner of his death.

SEVEN

DEATH OF AN EPIC POET

By August of 1908 Samuel Clemens had made his final and astounding comeback to an atmosphere of comfort, pleasure, luxury, of world fame and, odd as it may have seemed, to domestic happiness. Howells' son John, an architect, had designed the Italian-looking mansion. How many gorgeous mansions had the poor western boy, Sam Clemens, dwelt in with glory and munificence; how many had he exited from in bankruptcy and disgrace; and still he came back to another one (in Redding, Connecticut), called Stormfield from Twain's ironical vision of heaven.

There he surrounded himself with his familiar pleasures once more and abandoned himself to the small happinesses of his declining years. The girls were away; even when Jean, apparently restored and buoyant in health, became her father's secretary she appeared only at meals, and the aging Clemens depended more and more on the never-failing amanuensis, diarist, and chronicler, Paine. In this final relationship of the declining master and the worshipful, obsequious apprentice, the sycophantic note of Paine's *Mark Twain: A Biography* intrudes itself to a small (Jamesian) degree. Indeed, "I have dismissed my secretary," Clemens wrote to the Howellses, "and have entered upon a holiday whose other end is the grave."

He had already piled up, during a period of two and a half years, about half a million words for the *Autobiography*. At Stormfield he spent the morning in bed reading and answering letters; in the afternoons there were two regular games for himself and guests: cards and billiards, still his great domestic pastime. In the evening, as Paine tells us, there was the music, the stately measures of the orchestrelle which he had brought along from his 21 Fifth Avenue house.

Even then, without experience of fascism, Clemens believed the American republic was already doomed to become a monarchy, because in the nature of man there was a deep desire to reverence a king, and because, secondly, while little republics have lasted long, protected by their poverty and insignificance, great ones have not. "And the condition is, vast power and wealth, which breed commercial and political corruptions, and incite public favorites to dangerous ambitions."

It was clear to Clemens, and should be pointed out to our own sactimonious business community, that it was *commercial* corruption which led to (and actually controlled) political corruption; just as the Christian plans and schemes for "universal peace" during these years were a hypocritical mask for armed imperialism, and for the First World War. "The gospel of peace is always making a deal of noise, always rejoicing in its progress but always neglecting to furnish statistics. There are no peaceful nations now. All Christendom is a soldier-camp. The poor have been taxed in some nations to the starvation point to support the giant armaments which Christian governments have built up, each to protect itself from the rest of the Christian brotherhood, and incidentally to snatch any scrap of real estate left exposed by a weaker owner." Clemens went on to recap the history of King Leopold II of Belgium — "the most intensely Christian monarch since Alexander VI, that has escaped hell thus far, has stolen an entire kingdom in Africa, and in fourteen years of Christian endeavor there has reduced the population from thirty millions to fifteen." And then:

> Within the last generation each Christian power has turned the bulk of its attention to finding out newer and still newer and more and more effective ways of killing Christians, and, incidentally, a pagan now and then; and the surest way to get rich quickly in Christ's earthly kingdom is to invent a gun that can kill more Christians at one shot than any other existing kind. All the Christian nations are at it. The more advanced they are, the bigger and more destructive engines of war they create.

Prophetic words again in which Clemens saw not only the First World War already on his horizon, but perhaps even the Second, and the whole nature of "modern civilization." During the same period he had, rather oddly, and to a certain degree reminiscent of Lewis Carroll's intense interest in young girls (not to mention many other writers of great stature such as Theodore Dreiser, who had the same uneasy yearnings), formed an association of little "Angel-Fish" admirers and companions at home and in Bermuda. In the Mark Twain who is not primarily to be viewed in orthodox psychoanalytic terms at all, there was still a curious strain — or a complex — about youthful innocence and "virginity" (as in his deplorable version of Joan of Arc) which commonly shows up in the later years of intensely sensual artists.

"My child," Clemens wrote to one of his young and adoring companions, "it's as tranquil & contenting as Bermuda. You will be very welcome here, dear"; and there are other curious intimations and associations with Dreiser's erotic baby-talk in *The "Genius"* and *An American Tragedy,* and elsewhere.

At Stormfield he debated the existence of Jesus Christ with Paine, and reading two books on the Baconian viewpoint of Shakespeare, one of which he used and literally, as was his wont, and embellished with his own asides and conclusions, he began to write *Is Shakespeare Dead?* Started as a hobby, it became in familiar fashion almost one of his obsessions, though with less disastrous consequences than most, and with much more comedy attached to it. Harpers' demurring, Clemens had the volume printed on his own, another example, as we've seen, of Mark Twain's publishing "cowardice."

Clara had recovered from her troubles, Jean was still improving in health as her father's secretary. He had a home once more with his children around him; he who had already survived so many tragic epochs and domestic disasters, until one admires Sam Clemens' enduring personal fortitude, in these last years, as well as his still effervescent literary talent. But now too, at this brief moment of personal fulfillment and happiness in Samuel Clemens' long and full life, he was on the edge of a new series of disasters. In May, 1909, he made a final trip to consult Henry Rogers on business only to learn that the valued friend who had rescued him from bankruptcy and ruin had died the night before. Clemens felt that he had been cast adrift, his old friends dissolving all around him. Nevertheless he worked hard and long, with his political friend Champ Clark, for the establishment of a new copyright bill for which he had been working since 1906. He was attacked for plagiarizing George Greenwood's book, *The Shakespeare Problem Restated*, which of course he had, in his own inimitable way. And he suffered the first pains of the heart disease which would kill him.

As usual, he went on with his reading, just now Suetonius and — "When I take up one of Jane Austen's books, such as *Pride and Prejudice,* I feel like a barkeeper entering the kingdom of heaven. I know what his sensations would be and his private comments." But he liked the early verse of Willa Cather; a curious little encounter in our letters. As his heart attacks increased during this year, he began to make preparations, both private and public, for his own departure:

> I came in with Halley's comet in 1835 [he said to Paine]. It is coming again next year, and I expect to go out with it. It will be the greatest disappointment of my life if I don't go out with Halley's comet. The Almighty has said, no doubt: "Now here are these two unaccountable freaks; they came in together, they must go out together.

In these final notes and jottings of Mark Twain, according to Paine's *Autobiography,* he still remained a natural (and unconscious) Marxist in part of his thinking: "Morals are not the important thing — nor enlightenment — nor civilization," he noted. "A man can do absolutely well without them, but he can't do without *something to eat.* The supremest thing is the *needs of the body,* not of the mind & spirit." He still remained pagan. "I am old now and once was a sinner. I often think of it with a kind of soft regret. I trust my days are numbered. I would not have that detail overlooked." And he was still enchanted by Livy. "She was always a girl, she was always young because her heart was young; & I was young because she lived in my heart & preserved its youth from decay."

There was even one more peak of happiness and joy. There was a concert for the Redding library, planned by Clemens around the musical careers of the talented pianist Ossip Gabrilowitsch, and Clara Clemens whom he was courting. The library concert was an immense success; the subsequent marriage of Clara and Ossip brought felicitations from Mark Twain's friends and admirers the world over. Ossip was handsome, gay, and already famous; Clara was stately, rather heavy-bodied and of a brooding disposition, even at the moment of their wedding.*

When the aging Mark Twain was asked whether he was pleased with the marriage, his answer reflected his life's anguish. He was pleased, he said, as fully as any marriage could please him. "There are two or three solemn things in life, and a happy marriage is one of them, for the terrors of life are to come. I am glad of this marriage, and Mrs. Clemens would be glad, for she always had a warm affection for Gabrilowitsch."

His health was running down seriously during this time, and he should perhaps have been happier than he was at Clara's marriage; and, as usual, he would not follow his doctor's orders about smoking and exercise. To Miss Wallace, part of the Bermuda "Angel-fish" group of Mark Twain's little girls, he wrote: "I can't walk. I can't drive. I'm not down-stairs much, and I don't see company, but I drink barrels of water to keep the pain quiet; I read, and read, and read, and smoke and smoke all the time (as formerly) and it's a contented and comfortable life." (It even appears that the medical advice incited Sam Clemens to smoking.) He revised his will.† And he began writing another

---

* She had had an uneasy childhood and adolescence, both physically and psychologically. Perhaps her early life was burdened by the extravagant affection which the Clemenses had extended to her sister Susy, and the extended and exorbitant period of mourning over Susy's death. At any rate Clara's daughter, and Ossip's, was institutionalized and died at an early age, and there are no living descendants of Mark Twain. There was indeed a certain curse which afflicted all of the Clemens children — the baby son who died early, the three daughters who led such inbred, domestic and tragic lives. Some biographers attribute their fates to Clemens' own devoted but jealous and overbearing fatherly arrogance; but we should not forget Livy's delicate health and temperament which had also presided over the domestic menage. The combination of events which doomed the Clemens daughters was physical as well as psychological; in the blood stream as well as in the mind. But then too, how obviously and how extravagantly these parents, Sam and Livy, loved each other to the very end; and perhaps all unconsciously the children were paying for *that*.

† According to Paine (whose *Mark Twain, a Biography* I am following in this account), Twain's estate was valued at over $600,000, which was not a bad recovery for an artist bankrupt in his prime of life.

book, *Letters from the Earth,* which Clemens said would never be published, but which was published, as he must have known it would be.

Letters from the Earth was in fact to contain some of Mark Twain's best writing, polemical and otherwise, just as into all these late books "never intended for publication" and written, as he said, purely for his own pleasure (but what major artist does not write for posterity?), he poured forth all the hidden depths of his nature and all its prophetic peaks in that "last style" which was infinitely his best style. A style which he had taken a lifetime to fashion in all its deceptive simplicity and brilliant lucidity.

Clemens was considering the idea of the new American empire following the way of Rome. Reading always, he was attracted to memoirs and history: Saint-Simon, Casanova, Pepys, Carlyle's *French Revolution* still at hand, Francis Parkman — and Clemens could hardly refrain from remarking about *The Jesuits in North America*:

> That men would be willing to leave their happy homes and endure what the missionaries endured in order to teach these Indians the road to hell would be rational, understandable, but why they should want to teach them a way to heaven is a thing which the mind somehow cannot grasp.

After Parkman, there was Greville's *Memoirs,* Plutarch, P. T. Barnum, the *Letters of Madame De Sévigné,* Dana's *Two Years Before the Mast,* and the great Darwin's *Descent of Man.* And Clemens still kept his admiration for Kipling's poems, even while his own thinking had advanced far ahead of the illustrious bard of imperialism and the white man's burden, which meant, in effect, the black man's destruction.

In mid-November, 1909, Clemens and Paine went together for another vacation in Bermuda, the blessed isles; on Clemens' seventy-fourth birthday he appeared to Paine as looking "wonderfully well." Upon their return to Stormfield for the Christmas holidays, Jean was busy with her holiday preparations on December 23, and on that night she was struck by an epileptic fit (or heart failure) and died in the bathtub. It was the "final disaster," as Clemens said. It marked the failure of his last attempt at rebuilding his domestic life; it marked the end of his writing (as it was the final section of the *Autobiography*) and it hastened his impending death. Although Paine believes that Clemens was hardened and inured to the deaths of his friends and his family, anybody who reads the last section of the *Autobiography* may feel differently. Despite all of Clemens' irony and factualism as to death being the only true gift of life, his description of Jean's death is one of his most touching, affectionate, lyrical, bitter-sweet paeans to life, his daughter's life, and, ever again, her mother's life. Here again, as often with Mark Twain, this great comedian brings tears to our eyes.

He spent the next two days after Jean's death writing the full account of it. "I am setting it down — everything. It is a relief for me to write it. It furnishes me an excuse for thinking." On Christmas Day, 1909, he watched Jean's baby nurse, Katie Leary, accompany Jean's body as it set out on its last pilgrimage to the Elmira cemetery.

> From my windows I saw the hearse and the carriages wind along the road and gradually grow vague and spectral in the falling snow, and presently disappear. Jean was gone out of my life, and would not come back any more. Jervis, the cousin she had played with when they were babies together — he and her beloved old Katie — were conducting her to her distant childhood home, where she will lie by her mother's side once more, in the company of Susy and Langdon.

He was too weary and too disheartened to make the journey, but later that day, according to Paine's account, he felt a cold current of air around him in the bathroom which he associated with Jean's burial.

Reading the many letters of condolence, to the ones which offered the orthodox Christian view that God does not willingly punish us, Mark Twain replied: "Well, why does he do it then? We don't invite. Why does He give Himself the trouble?" And to Mrs. Gabrilowitsch, he poured out his anguished heart. "You can't imagine what a darling she was that last two or three days; & how *fine,* & good, & sweet, & noble — & *joyful,* thank Heaven! — & how intellectually brilliant. I had never been acquainted with Jean before. I recognized that . . . But I mustn't try to write about her — I *can't.* I have already poured my heart out with the pen, recording that last day or two. I will send you that — & you must let no one but Ossip read it. Good-by. I love you so! And Ossip." *

According to Paine, also, Clemens really attempted no further writing after Jean's death; it was the last disaster of his life, and the rest was a brief epilogue. There was another "gorgeous letter" from Howells on an essay which Twain published in *Harper's Bazar*; there was a final meeting with this old friend and literary adviser. Clemens went back to Bermuda briefly, but in April, 1910, he was suffering severe pains around his heart and was living on hypodermic injections and opiates. Paine went to Bermuda to fetch him back home; as we know, Sam Clemens did not want either to die in a foreign place or to return as a corpse. It was a question for a while whether he could make the trip back; he recovered enough to

* Clemens, like most geniuses, was undoubtedly a difficult father. The Clemens children, as we've noted, had a strong vein, hereditary or environmental, of neurosis and physical illness; in the later years we've seen how the household was darkened by financial worries, grief, and sickness. But letters such as this from Clemens to Clara, do much to recall the essential harmony, grace, and sweetness of their domestic life at its best, and to refute studies (Freudian for the most part, but including to a degree Edith Colgate Salsbury's *Susy and Mark Twain*) of Twain's oppressive effect upon his daughters, and their covert hostility or enmity.

reach his home, dying, in a horrible trip. "I am sorry for you, Paine," he is reported as saying, "but I can't help it — I can't hurry this dying business. Can't you give me enough of the hypnotic injunction [as he called the needle] to put an end to me?" And then: "After forty years of public effort I have become just a target for medicines." And, only half awake, or half alive: "Isn't there something I can resign and be out of all this . . . I am like a bird in a cage: always expecting to get out, and always beaten back by the wires . . . Oh, it is such a mystery, and it takes so long."

Great men, it is said, die great deaths, and the last days of Samuel Clemens have this mark upon them. At the end of the first day he asked Paine how many days and nights were left for his trip home: "We'll never make it. It's an eternity . . . It's a losing race; no ship can outsail death" — but nevertheless he arrived in New York, and was driven back to Stormfield.

"There was never anybody like him; there never will be," William Dean Howells said after their final meeting in New York, and after a loving relationship of over forty years between two men so strangely assorted, and despite such differences of opinion as theirs on the Haymarket Riots, when Howells spoke out publicly in favor of the "anarchist criminals" falsely condemned for the crime, and Mark Twain did not. Howells suffered from public persecution and literary boycott for his great act of moral courage. Twain, for whatever reasons, made no public statement. Yet there is no discussion of this matter in their public papers so far available; and their deep friendship apparently remained undisturbed.

On a still, sweet April night, Thursday the fourteenth, 1910, according to Paine, Clemens returned home to Stormfield, and by Sunday, when Clara arrived, he was still articulate. "This is a peculiar kind of disease," he said. "It does not invite you to read; it does not invite you to be read to; it does not invite you to talk, nor to enjoy any of the usual sick-room methods of treatment. What kind of a disease is *that?*" On Tuesday the nineteenth, he asked Clara to sing for him some of the Scotch songs he loved; when she left, he said goodbye, he might never see her again. On April 20, Halley's Comet, which had accompanied his birth, appeared in the heavens again, as Clemens had predicted; and on Thursday, the twenty-first, in the peaceful spring evening, he died in his seventy-fifth year.

EIGHT

POSTMORTEM EBULLIENCE

HE HAD ARRIVED as he said in the only happy state, which he had envied so long. He had arrived "at the dignity of death — the only earthly dignity that is not artificial — the only safe one." The others were traps that merely beguiled one into humiliation. "Death — the only immortal who treats us all alike, whose pity and whose peace and whose refuge are for all — the soiled and the pure — the rich and the poor — the loved and the unloved."

Yet this extraordinary soul who hungered so for death, whose life and death alike testified to the vitality and nobility of his talent, had, as we know, finished only the first half of a career which was to extend another fifty years or more. Between 1910 and the present, almost every year witnessed the publication of some new Mark Twain volume or study; and perhaps the years from 1950 to 1970, when so much new Mark Twain material, and some of it among his best work, was released, were the real climax of his writing. He had saved up almost as many letters — essays, parables, chronicles — from the earth, from his grave, as he had published during his lifetime. This Diabolical Prince of Darkness intended to shed his light over his world for some time to come.

The first posthumous book, *Mark Twain's Speeches,* was published in 1910, the year of his death.

From very early in his career Clemens had perfected the art of lecturing; much of his creative energy had been wasted in this medium for the sake of money-raising; and later on he had come to lecture only for pleasure. His series of after-dinner talks was a minor variation of all this; at first he prepared them with care; later on he relied on his impromptu associations, sometimes good, sometimes poor, and sometimes indeed very funny as a stream of the Clemens consciousness, if also very irregular in form. All of this is reflected in *Mark Twain's Speeches.*

There is the talk on "The Sandwich Islands," given by Clemens in San Francisco, October 2, 1866, after his first visit to those isles — a talk many times repeated in this country and England — which was an eloquent mixture of social observation, satiric reflections on civilization, and Clemens' own delight in his aboriginal paradise. Here, too, in his first period, Clemens used the word "nigger" in his talk, which he never did in his fiction, speaking for himself, and he soon stopped using it in his lectures and talks also. And here he first showed his own fascination and pleasure in these darker-skinned, "uncivilized," and uninhibited island folk. The lecture is still very interesting reading.

Clemens described all the beauty, the freedom, the tenderness and cruelty of primitive man; and in turn he used this to cast some light upon western "civilization." Down there in the islands, he said, they have exploded one of our most ancient and trusted maxims: *Be virtuous and you will be happy.* "The Kanakas are not virtuous — neither men, women, nor children —

and yet they are the happiest creatures the sun shines on. They are as happy as the day is long. They wail and carry on grievously when a friend or relative dies, but it is all a pretense; they do precisely the same thing when a friend returns from a month's absence. In both instances the tears are manufactured to order and the joy and sorrow counterfeited. A woman returns from a distance and a lot of her female friends will huddle around her on the ground and twine their arms about her and weep and whine and blubber and howl for an hour — and they would cheerfully repeat the same thing the next day if she died, and dance the hula-hula into the bargain. It is rarely that they show any genuine tribulation. Theirs is a state of placid happiness. All they want is unfettered liberty to eat, drink, sing, dance, swindle, lie, and pray, and then, whether school keeps or not is a matter of no interest to *them*."

As early as this (1866) Sam Clemens was an acute observer of pagan man and pagan culture — and in turn this caught his fancy and corresponded with deep strains of his own temperament. He went into a long history of the Sandwich Islands which he had studied with the same fascination. The descriptions of the islands' landscape are lyrical; and by comparison the following lecture on "The American Vandal," after his excursion to the Holy Land on the steamship *Quaker City* in 1867, was a derisive picture of Christian morality in foreign circumstances. (This talk was an early takeoff of Babbittry abroad.) He was at home again, puncturing the Victorian sanctities in an early tribute to "Women" at the Washington Correspondents Club. He was delighted to talk about this theme, Clemens said, because he loved the sex, he loved all women, irrespective of age or color:

"Human intellect cannot estimate what we owe to women . . . She sews on our buttons; she mends our clothes; she ropes us in at the church fairs; she confides in us; she tells us whatever she can find out about the little private affairs of the neighbors; she gives us good advice, and plenty of it; she soothes our aching brows; she bears our children — ours as a general thing. In all relations of life, it is but a just and graceful tribute to women to say of her that she is a brick. Wheresoever you place women . . . she is an ornament to the place she occupies, and a treasure to the world . . . Look at Cleopatra! — look at Desdemona! — look at Florence Nightingale! — look at Joan of Arc! — look at Lucretia Borgia! — Well, suppose we let Lucretia slide. Look at Joyce Heth! — look at Mother Eve! You need not look at her unless you want to, but Eve was ornamental — particularly before the fashions changed."

Clemens was displaying that irreverent fancy and wild comedy which was his natural heritage: which was suppressed or subdued in some part, perhaps, by New England and Eastern culture; which sometimes went underground, yet remained unchanged in his deepest soul, and surfaced again so brilliantly in his later and last works, and particularly in his postmortem literary career. Women, in an epoch dominated by the vision of the "lady" and that ineffable "young American girl" of both Howells and Henry James — in a literature that was determined and controlled by an almost purely feminine audience — became one of Mark Twain's favorite subjects of parody. In 1872, at the anniversary festival of the Scottish Corporation of London, Clemens explained why he really preferred to use the term woman. "I have noticed that the Bible, with that plain, blunt honesty which is such a conspicuous characteristic of the Scriptures, is always particular to never refer to even the illustrious mother of all humanity as a 'lady,' but speaks of her as a woman." About women, Clemens continued, he always recalled the verses of the most noble, the most gracious, the purest, and sweetest of all poets:

> Woman! O Woman! — er —
> Wom —

Well, they all knew what he meant, said the early Clemens still in pursuit of the Victorian taboos and the highly tabooed Victorian lady, whom he went on to describe in terms of the most profoundly sentimental delicacy: the ideal of a true and perfect woman — with such sorrowful, tragic ending to her pathetic story, described in poetic lines "so wild, so regretful, so full of mournful retrospection":

> Alas! — alas! —— a — alas!
> —— Alas! —— alas!

"And so on," said Clemens, "I do not remember the rest, in this poet's matchless lines, but "the phases of the womanly nature are infinite in their variety. Take any type of woman, and you shall find in it something to respect, something to admire, something to love.

"Who does not sorrow for the loss of Sappho, the sweet singer of Israel?" he added. "Who among us does not miss the gentle ministrations, the softening influences, the humble piety of Lucretia Borgia?" And against this model of female virtue, he presented the iniquities of the "free" or the yellow press of that period. "That awful power, the public opinion of a nation, is created in America by a horde of ignorant, self-complacent simpletons who failed at ditching and shoemaking and fetched up in journalism on their way to the poorhouse."

Among these early lectures was the description of New England's weather. There was the apostrophe to babies at the Chi-

cago banquet given by the Army of the Tennessee to their commander, General Grant — where Twain opened thus: "If you
will stop and think a minute — if you will go back fifty or one
hundred years to your early married life and recontemplate
your first baby . . ." There was the notorious (or so it was
felt at the time by Howells and others) parody of Holmes, Emerson, and Longfellow which Twain delivered at the *Atlantic*
dinner in honor of John Greenleaf Whittier in 1877. The
parody was rather rough and flat; it was perhaps an early example of Clemens' underlying rejection of all the New England
proprieties which he felt he had to court in his early career.
But certainly Howells' horror and despair about this talk was
exaggerated, as we know, while Clemens alternated between
shame and apologies, and a false pride in the talk.

The whole episode has been made too much of, particularly
by the Freudian critics who have made it a field day for speculations about Mark Twain's divided self; it was at worst a boner,
a gaffe, over which Howells should not have been so horrified,
nor Twain so humiliated. And even this early disaster was grist
to the later Mark Twain who in 1906 described the whole episode again:

> I wondered what the trouble was. I didn't know. I went on, but
> with difficulty — I struggled along and entered upon that miner's
> fearful description of the bogus Emerson, the bogus Holmes, the
> bogus Longfellow, always hoping — but with a gradually perishing
> hope — that somebody would laugh, or that somebody would at
> least smile, but nobody did. I didn't know enough to give it up
> and sit down . . . When I sat down it was with a heart which
> had long ceased to beat. I shall never be as dead again as I was
> then. I shall never be as miserable again as I was then. I speak
> now as one who doesn't know what the conditions of things may
> be in the next world, but in this one I shall never be as wretched

again as I was then. Howells, who was near me, tried to say a comforting word, but couldn't get beyond a gasp. There was no use — he understood the whole size of the disaster. He had good intentions but the words froze before they could get out. It was an atmosphere that would freeze anything. If Benvenuto Cellini's salamander had been in that place he would not have survived to be put into Cellini's autobiography.

Thus, as ever to the very close of Sam Clemens' life, the comic spirit could revisit the scene of the original "catastrophe" (not the true tragedies) and project it anew, not to rationalize away, but to use it as another commentary on man's tragi-comic existence. To make laughable, that is, what had been so falsely sorry.

In this collection of speeches there are some absolute gems of the informal essay, such as the talk about accident insurance, when he became a director of the Hartford Accident Insurance Company, in which not an extra word is used, and where that "genius of perfection," so foreign to Twain's work as to be irrelevant, presided over him. I cannot, much as I'd like to, quote the whole talk — since *Mark Twain's Speeches,* appearing so shortly after his death, is one of his essential volumes, both an introduction to his career, and an outline summary of it.

But it is hard not to quote a few paragraphs from "Accident Insurance — Etc." "Certainly there is no nobler field for human effort than the insurance line of business," said Clemens. "Ever since I have been a director in an accident-insurance company I have felt that I am a better man. Life has seemed more precious. Accidents have assumed a kindlier aspect. Distressing special providences have lost half their horror. I look upon a cripple now with affectionate interest — as an advertisement. I do not seem to care for poetry any more. I do not care for politics — even agriculture does not excite me. But to me now

there is a charm about a railway collision that is unspeakable
. . . There is nothing more beneficent than accident insurance.
I have seen an entire family lifted out of poverty and into afflu-
ence by the simple boon of a broken leg. I have had people
come to me on crutches, with tears in their eyes, to bless the
beneficent institution. In all my experience of life, I have seen
nothing so seraphic as the look that comes into a freshly mutilated man's face when he feels in his vest pocket with his remaining hand and finds his accident ticket all right . . . I will
say, in conclusion, that my share of the welcome to our guest
is none the less hearty because I talk so much nonsense, and I
know that I can say the same for the rest of the speakers."

In the same volume is Mark Twain's talk on "Plymouth Rock
and the Pilgrims," containing some insights about our ancestors which were later confirmed by "serious" historians. "Celebrating their landing!" Clemens cried, at the First Annual Dinner of the New England Society to Honor the Pilgrims. "What
was there remarkable about it, I would like to know? What can
you be thinking of? Why, those Pilgrims had been at sea three
or four months. It was the very middle of winter: it was cold as
death off Cape Cod there. Why shouldn't they come ashore?
If they *hadn't* landed there would be some reason for celebrating the fact." He went on to detail some of the Pilgrims' most
salient shortcomings. "They were a mighty hard lot — you
know it . . . They took good care of themselves, but they
abolished everybody else's ancestors." He went on, remarkable
early as 1881, to state that *his* ancestors were a different lot from
the Puritans. "My first American ancestor, gentlemen, was
an Indian — an early Indian. Your ancestors skinned him
alive, and I am an orphan." This from the Sam Clemens who
in the 1870s had the deep prejudice of the frontiersman against
the native American Indian. Twain's other ancestors, he

claimed, were the Quakers, whom the Pilgrim Fathers had condemned to exile, torture, and death. The Pilgrims had not come to a new cradle of freedom, either of worship or of politics — in order to allow anybody else but themselves to exercise those rights. Clemens mentioned "the Quaker woman Elizabeth Hooten" as another ancestress of his, who was treated pretty severely but who changed her beliefs just before she died; or had her beliefs changed for her; along with Roger Williams, and yes — "All those Salem witches were ancestors of mine! Your people made it tropical for them."

> Yes, they did; by pressure and the gallows they made such a clean deal with them there hasn't been a witch and hardly a halter in our family from that day to this, and that is one hundred and eighty-nine years. The first slave brought into New England out of Africa by your progenitors was an ancestor of mine — for I am of a mixed breed, infinitely shaded and exquisite Mongrel. I'm not one of your sham meerschaums that you can color in a week. No, my complexion is the patient art of eight generations. Well, in my own time, I had acquired a lot of my kin — by purchase, and swapping around, and one way or another — and was getting along very well. Then, with the inborn perversity of your lineage, you got up a war and took them all away from me. And so, again am I bereft, again am I forlorn; no drop of my blood flows in the veins of any living being who is marketable . . .

Now wasn't this an interesting sequel to the John Greenleaf Whittier dinner embroglio which had left Clemens covered with shame and humiliation just four years earlier? There he had mocked the New England notables, and here he completely, if still under the cloak of comedy, disassociated himself from the Puritan lineage and culture. More, he identified his ancestry — himself — not merely with the American Indians who were obliterated in America, but even more directly with the darker

races in the world, and quite specifically with the line of American slaves and American blacks. What a remarkable opening-
up of the ignorant frontier mind was revealed in Samuel Clemens; or what an open disclosure of some thoughts perhaps privately held in the 1870s, and publicly aired only a few years
later. If indeed, we have already placed the beginning of Mark
Twain's radical criticism in the *Following the Equator* of 1897,
we can see that some of these variant — and perverse and inspired — ideas were stirring around in his mind by the early
eighties.

Between 1880 and 1885 he gave another salute to his favorite ancestor, Adam, and again his fancy roamed in the Garden
of pre-civilizational man. Adam had been neglected too long, he
said.

> You always place Women at the bottom of the toast list; it is but
> simple justice to place Adam at the top of it — for if it had not
> been for the help of these two, where would you and your ban-
> quets be? Answer me that. You must excuse me for losing my
> temper and carrying on in this way; and in truth I would not do
> it if it were almost anybody but Adam; but I am of narrow and
> clannish disposition, and I can never see a relative of mine mis-
> used without going into a passion. It is no trick for people with
> plenty of celebrated kin to keep cool when their folk are misused;
> but Adam is the only solitary celebrity in our family, and that
> man that misuses him has got to walk over my dead body, or go
> around, that is all there is to that. That is the way I feel about
> Adam.

And here Samuel Clemens was tracing back all the various and
hostile clans and colors and "races" of man to a single source —
though he neglected to mention that Adam, too, was probably of
darker skin.

As early as this, he had also polarized Life and Death as of equal value, if later Death would take the upper hand in life. To Adam, he declared, we owe the two things which are most precious —

> Life, which the young, the hopeful, the undefeated hold above all wealth and honors; and Death, the refuge, the solace, the best and kindliest and most prized friend and benefactor of the erring, the forsaken, the old, and weary, and broken of heart, whose burdens be heavy upon them, and who would lie down and be at rest.

About this time also, Clemens delivered another one of his parodies on war to the Thirteenth Annual Reunion of the Army of the Potomac. In those earlier days of the Republic, it seemed that all the veterans of the Civil War yearned most to listen to the man who ridiculed war — and who hated it. Clemens claimed he had gone to West Point for a briefing on the martial arts which, in his hands, became another example of pure Dada. "Never fetch on your reserves at the start," Clemens advised the veterans. "This was Napoleon's first mistake at Waterloo; next he assaulted with his bomb proofs and embrasures and ambulances, when he ought to have used a heavier artillery; thirdly, he retired his right by ricochet — which uncovered his pickets — when his only possibility of success lay in doubling up his center flank by throwing out his chevaux-de-frise by the left oblique to relieve the skirmish line and confuse the enemy — and at West Point they said it would. It was about this time that the emperor had two horses shot under him . . ."

And Clemens went on to say it was better to shoot a horse *over* a general, in hopes of hitting something farther away, than to waste a missile of that size, if you could not shoot a horse to hit the general himself. There followed another famous talk by Mark Twain, his "Advice to Youth," including such gems as "Always obey your parents, when they are present. This is the best policy in the long run, because if you don't they will make you." He advised his audience of Huck Finns to avoid violence and simply hit any offending person with a brick. He advised them to go to bed early and get up with the lark — "and if you get the right kind of a lark, and work at him right, you can easily train him to get up at half past nine." He delivered a discourse on lying, and the necessary training for it which might have been the words of Samuel Butler. "I believe I am right, that the young ought to be temperate in the use of this great art until practice and experience shall give them that confidence, elegance, and precision which alone can make the accomplishment graceful and profitable. Patience, diligence, painstaking attention to detail . . ."

In the early eighties, he was at once taking off the high moral tone of their educational precepts, and the precepts themselves. He was at his best on the subject of young boys handling firearms in the presence of their parents or other relatives. He quoted the example of a sweet old grandmother whose grandson fired a rusty, unused rifle at her — which was empty. "He had supposed it was not loaded. And he was right — it wasn't. So there wasn't any harm done. It is the only case of that kind I ever heard of. Therefore, just the same, don't you meddle with old unloaded firearms; they are the most deadly and unerring things that have ever been created by man. You don't have to take any pains at all with them; you don't have to have a rest, you don't have to have any sights on the gun, you don't have to take aim, even. No, you just pick out a relative and bang away, and you are sure to get him."

A youth who can't hit a cathedral at thirty yards with a Gatling gun in three-quarters of an hour can take up an old empty musket and bag his grandmother every time at a hundred. Think what

Waterloo would have been if one of the armies had been boys
armed with old muskets supposed not to be loaded, and the other
army had been composed of their female relations. The very
thought of it makes one shudder.

Once again the hedonistic, sensuous, and a-civilized artist
was rollicking away at the expense of the Victorian virtues and
sanctities. The middle period of Twain's public speeches (when
he had vowed never to enter upon a lecture platform again except
for his own pleasure) started out, however, with some highly
moral talks about the Republican Party's nomination of James
G. Blaine in 1884, and Clemens' subsequent desertion to the
Mugwumps who brought Grover Cleveland to the White House.
Yet here Clemens became too serious, perhaps, about democratic politics, patriotism, and party loyalty within the framework of his lingering belief in the Old Republic. Or perhaps, as
with many writers, it was harder for him, *on a personal level,*
to part with old friends, ties, bonds of a satisfying and comfortable nature; even while his mind and spirit had wandered far
afield and far ahead of this provincial area of partisan politics
in the U.S.A. Who is to say that Blaine might not have been a
better President than Cleveland? and the difference was one of
appearances and technicalities in the Robber Baron epoch. At
least this public action, for whatever reasons, seemed to bother
Mark Twain far more than many of his more radical and more
important utterances before this point. It was disturbing what
a writer needs most to keep intact: his inner peace within his
own domestic and social sphere.

And worst of all, he was stung by those accusations of being
a political turncoat, even a traitor, which later on, in the nineties, he would be more indifferent to, more inured to; which he
would come even to accept and rejoice in, and to cast back

with relish into the enemy's face. So this little episode, too, was a step in Mark Twain's emancipation, rather than his "Ordeal."

But here indeed, the volatile and perverse side of Samuel Clemens got into one of its obsessive sieges which, for a while, he could hardly rid himself of; and even his defense of "General Grant's Grammar" against Matthew Arnold's obtuse mediocrity in judging Grant's masterpiece, lacked Twain's customary flair. He was better, and nicely nostalgic in his reminiscences of the old-fashioned American printers whom he had grown up with; he was back to his own version of native Dada in the Yale College speech in which he abolished the college's curriculum and fired the professors. He had his usual fun about the Sandwich Islands in 1889, those islands where "the cats haven't any tails, and the snakes haven't any teeth; and what is still more irregular, the man that loses a game gets the pot. And as to dress; the native women all wear a single garment — but the men don't. No, the men don't wear anything at all; they hate display. When they even wear a smile they think they are overdressed . . ." Those happy pagan islands, said Clemens again, which still represented man's highest dream of bliss. "No alien land in all the world has any deep, strong charm for me but that one, no other land could so longingly and so beseechingly haunt me, sleeping and waking, as that one has done. Other things leave me, but it abides; other things change, but it remains the same."

And almost directly after this unaltering remembrance of those paradisal islands which have figured continually in North American writing from Melville's time to Eugene O'Neill's, but whose meaning Mark Twain, more than anyone, knew and felt and described so well — directly after this familiar pagan apostrophe, came the last famous speech on the German language, written in German as "Die Schrecken der Deutschen Sprache," and translated into Mark Twain's "English" quite as literally as was the "Jumping Frog."

THE HORRORS OF THE GERMAN LANGUAGE

Address to the Vienna Press Club, November 21, 1897

(A Literal Translation)

It has me deeply touched, my gentlemen, here so hospitably received to be. From colleagues out of my own profession, in this from my own home so far distant land. My heart is full of gratitude, but my poverty of German words forces me to greater economy of expression. Excuse you, my gentlemen, that I read off, what I you say will. [But he didn't read.]

The German language speak I not good, but have numerous connoisseurs me assured that I her write like an angel. Maybe — maybe — I know not. Have till now no acquaintance with the angels had. That comes later — when it the dear God please — it has no hurry.

Since long, my gentlemen, have I the passionate longing nursed a speech on German to hold, but one has me not permitted. Men, who no feeling for the art had, laid me ever hindrance in the way and made naught my desire — sometimes by excuses, often by force. Always said these men to me: "Keep you still, your Highness! Silence! For God's sake seek another way and means yourself obnoxious to make."

In the present case, as usual it is me difficult become, for me the permission to obtain. The committee sorrowed deeply, but could me the permission not grant on account of a law which from the Concordia demands she shall the German language protect. *Du liebe Zeit!* How so had one to me this say could — might — dared — should. I am indeed the truest friend of the German language — and not only now, but from long since — yes, before twenty years already. And never have I the desire had the noble language to hurt; to the contrary, only wished she to improve — I would her only reform. It is the dream of my life been. I have already visits by the various German governments paid and for contracts prayed. I am now to Austria in the same task come. I would only some changes effect. I would only the language method — the luxurious, elaborate construction compress, the eternal parenthesis suppress, do away with, annihilate; the introduction of more than thirteen subjects in one sentence forbid; the verb so far to the front pull that one it without a telescope discover can. With one word, my gentlemen, I would your beloved language simplify so that, my gentlemen, when you her for prayer need, One her yonder-up understands.

I beseech you, from me yourself counsel to let, execute these mentioned reforms. Then will you an elegant language possess, and afterward, when you some thing say will, will you at least yourself understand what you said had. But often nowadays, when you a mile-long sentence from you given and you yourself somewhat have rested, then must you have a touching inquisitiveness have yourself to determine what you actually spoken have. Before several days has the correspondent of a local paper a sentence constructed which hundred and twelve words contain, and therein were seven parentheses smuggled in, and the subject seven times changed. Think you only, my gentlemen, in the course of the voyage of a single sentence must the poor, persecuted, fatigued subject seven times change position!

Now, when we the mentioned reforms execute, will it no longer so bad be. *Doch noch eins.* I might gladly the separable verb also a little bit reform. I might none do let what Schiller did: he has the whole history of the Thirty Years' War between the two members of a separate verb in-pushed. That has even Germany itself aroused, and one has Schiller the permission refused the History of the Hundred Years' War to compose — God be it thanked! After all these reforms established be will, will the German language the noblest and the prettiest on the world be.

Since to you now, my gentlemen, the character of my mission known is, beseech I you so friendly to be and to me your valuable help grant. Mr. Potzl has the public believed make would that I to Vienna come am in order the bridges to clog up and the traffic to hinder, while I observations gather and note. Allow you yourselves but not from him deceived. My frequent presence on the bridges has an entirely innocent ground. Yonder gives it the necessary space, yonder can one a noble long German sentence elaborate, the bridge-railing along, and his whole contents with one glance overlook. On the one end of the railing pasted I the first member of a separable verb and the final member cleave I to the other end — then spread the body of the sentences between it out! Usually are for my purposes the bridges of the city long enough; when I but Potzl's writings study will I ride out and use the glorious endless imperial bridge. But this is a calumny; Potzl writes the prettiest German. Perhaps not so pliable as the mine, but in many details much better. Excuse you these flatteries. These are well deserved.

Now I my speech execute — no, I would say I bring her to the close. I am a foreigner — but here, under you, have I it entirely forgotten. And so again and yet again proffer I you my heartiest thanks.

After this celebrated tour de force, there were Clemens' talks to the Whitefriars Club, the Authors' Club and the American Society Club, the New Vagabonds Club, the Dramatic and Literary Society, all in London. The five-year worldwide lecture tour was devised by Clemens' pangs of conscience and despite his physical ailments in his late fifties in order to pay off the creditors of his publishing company. From now on his speeches became briefer, mostly impromptu, usually in return for some further public honor, and they are less interesting as literature.

What we get mainly in the second half of *Mark Twain's Speeches* are his brief little talks to various and sundry clubs, committees, organizations of public welfare and charities. There are his addresses, for example, to the Public Education Association, the St. Nicholas Society; to the New York City Club, the Temple Emmanuel's Hebrew Technical School for Girls, the University Settlement Society of New York City, the Eastman College Alumni, the dinner in honor of Hamilton W. Mabie as editor of the *Outlook* magazine, the dinner for Am-

bassador Joseph H. Choate at the Lotus Club, including such
other notables as Andrew Carnegie, Senator Chauncey Depew,
William Allen White, and Speaker Thomas Reed: those ruling luminaries of American society with whom Mark Twain was
on such intimate terms, or whose literary pet he was. But all
these talks in 1900 and 1901 have little interest today beyond
that of local color.

On his sixty-seventh birthday, at a dinner at the New York
Metropolitan Club given by Colonel Harvey, of Harper &
Brothers, Clemens drew even more financiers, industrialists,
and other tycoons of the period. "I see around me captains of
all the illustrious industries, most distinguished men; there are
more than fifty here, and I believe I know thirty-nine of them
well. I could probably borrow money from — from the others,
anyway." The list included Thomas Reed again, Secretary of
State John Hay, the Reverend Joseph Twichell, Howells, Rogers, Chauncey Depew, St. Clair McKelway, among Clemens'
closer friends — and it was to this group that Twain said:
"And now, my wife and I, out of our single heart, return you
our deepest and most grateful thanks, and — yesterday was
her birthday." Clemens also stated to Livy's friends in the audience that while she was going to be confined to her bed for many
months to come from "that nervous prostration," there was not
any real danger, and she was coming along finely.

In the *Speeches* there is just one more burst of life and joy
and laughter, and of his wild Dadaism, in the valedictory which
was given at his seventieth birthday, at Delmonico's in New
York on December 5, 1905. Clemens talked about his first
birthday where everything was so crude, unesthetic, primeval —

Nothing like this at all. No proper imaginative preparation made;
nothing really ready. Now, for a person born with high and delicate
instincts — why even the cradle wasn't whitewashed — nothing

ready at all. I hadn't any hair, I hadn't any teeth, I hadn't any clothes, I had to go to my first banquet just like that.

It was a long stretch between his first birthday speech and this one, he said. "That was my cradle song, and this is my swan song, I suppose. I am used to swan songs; I have sung them several times."

He expatiated upon the new freedom conferred by a seventieth birthday in which you could throw aside "the decent reserves which have oppressed you for a generation," and describe honestly the course of your life "with senile rapture." We have, he said, "no permanent habits until we are forty. Then they begin to harden, presently they petrify, then business begins." A nice observation, and how well it described the hardening psychological process of life itself, in most cases a barely post-adolescent intellectual petrification upon which all of the rest of experience is lost. And how few "open souls," — which Mark Twain personified to the hilt in the area of the arts — are there who are able to break through and conquer this original biopsychic bondage.

Just *how* Sam Clemens had escaped this destined foreshortening of all life he proceeded to illustrate by describing some of his personal habits. Since forty he had been regular about going to bed and getting up: he went to bed when there was nobody left to talk to, and he made it a rule "to get up when I had to." For thirty years he had taken coffee and bread at eight in the morning and nothing else until seven-thirty in the evening; but this routine could be suicidal for other people. "And I wish to urge upon you this — which I think is wisdom — that if you find you can't make seventy by any but an uncomfortable road, don't you go. When they take off the Pullman and retire you to the rancid smoker, put on your things, count

your checks, and get out at the first way station where there's
a cemetery."

Appealing lines to celebrate the high wisdom of life and
death which are echoed by all the great writers; these are quite
Dreiserian lines about destiny dressed up in Twain's satiric
elegance. And he went on to describe the ruling vice of his life,
the overpowering compulsive habit which no doubt did contrib-
ute to his final illness and death:

> I have made it a rule never to smoke more than one cigar at a
> time. I have no other restriction as regards smoking. I do not
> know just when I began to smoke, I only know that it was in my
> father's lifetime early in 1847, when I was a shade past eleven;
> ever since then I have smoked publicly. As an example to others,
> and not that I care for moderation myself, it has always been my
> rule never to smoke when asleep, and never to refrain when
> awake . . .

"I smoke in bed until I have to go to sleep," he said. "I
wake up in the night, sometimes once, sometimes twice, sometimes three times, and I never waste any of these opportunities
to smoke."

> This habit is so old and dear and precious to me that I would feel
> as you, sir, would feel if you should lose the only moral you've
> got — meaning the chairman — if you've got one: I am making
> no charges. I will grant, here, that I have stopped smoking now
> and then, for a few months at a time, but it was not on principle,
> it was only to show off; it was to pulverize those critics who said
> I was a slave to my habits and couldn't break my bonds.

And where was the mark of Livy's ruthless censorship of
Sam in these lines? As for drinking, Clemens added, "I have
no rule about that. When the others drink I like to help; otherwise I remain dry by habit and preference," although there have

been persistent rumors from Clemens' day on that he was an alcoholic; and especially during and after the period of Livy's collapse, that he often drank himself to sleep — which I think he elsewhere admitted. (There is no doubt he was a jag-drinker at parties from the time of his early life.) "This dry-ness," he added deadpan, "does not hurt me, but it could eas-ily hurt you, because you are different. You let it alone."

Since he was seven, Clemens added, in this seventy-year-old ironical celebration of life and joy and comedy despite all the pain and suffering he knew so well and still had endured and survived, he had seldom taken a dose of medicine. "But up to seven I lived exclusively on allopathic medicines. Not that I needed them, for I don't think I did; it was for economy; my father took a drug store for a debt, and it made cod-liver oil cheaper than the other breakfast foods. We had nine bar-rels of it, and it lasted me seven years. Then I was weaned. The rest of the family had to get along with rhubarb and ipecac and such things, because I was the pet. I was the first Standard Oil Trust. I had it all. By the time the drug store was ex-hausted my health was established and there has never been much the matter with me since."

About exercise, Clemens was very specific also. "I have never taken any exercise, except sleeping and resting, and I never intend to take any. Exercise is loathsome. And it can-not be any benefit when you are tired; and I was always tired."

As about morals: "I have lived a severely moral life. But it would be a mistake for other people to try that, or for me to recommend it. Very few would succeed: you have to have a perfectly colossal stock of morals; and you can't get them on margin; you have to have the whole thing, and put them into your box. Morals are an acquirement — like music, like for-eign language, like piety, poker, paralysis — no man is born with them. I wasn't myself, I started poor. I hadn't a single moral. There is hardly a man in this house that is poorer than I was then. Yes, I started like that — the world before me, not a moral in the slot. Not even an insurance moral. I can remember the first one I ever got. I can remember the landscape, the weather, the — I can remember how everything looked." And then Clemens launched into a typical piece of comedy about his acquiring one secondhand rusty old moral and taking such good care of it and saving it for Chautauquas and World Fairs and using it only on Sundays . . . And concluding:

> Morals are of inestimable value, for every man is born crammed with sin microbes, and the only thing that can extirpate these sin microbes is morals. Now you take a sterilized Christian — I mean, you take *the* sterilized Christian, for there's only one. Dear sir, I wish you wouldn't look at me like that.

Threescore years and ten, he concluded, was the Scriptural statute of limitations. "After that, you owe no active duties; for you the strenuous life is over . . . You are become an honorary member of the republic, you are emancipated, compulsions are not for you, nor any bugle call but 'lights out.' You pay the time-worn duty bills if you choose, or decline if you prefer — and without prejudice — for they are not legally collectible. The previous-engagement plea, which in forty years has cost you so many twinges, you can lay aside forever; on this side of the grave you will never need it again."

This was in effect Mark Twain's last formal public talk, and delivered just five years before his death, it reminds us again of all the charm and affection and humorous sophistication of this deathless spirit. And just as the volume of *Mark Twain's Speeches* summarizes a neglected literary side of this artist — who yet gladly relinquished all the prestige and financial gain

of being America's, or perhaps the world's, greatest lecturer —
so the next posthumous volume, *The Mysterious Stranger,* in
1916, was not only his best short story (or novelette), but must
be included among the best American short stories.

NINE

SATAN AS PRANKSTER

THE MYSTERIOUS STRANGER had a somewhat mysterious history. Was it never published during Clemens' lifetime because, as he believed, he never could find "the right end" for it? That was usually the trouble with his stories, as we know. Or because he was afraid in truth of this dark fable which was the highest and best climax of this vein in his work, from *The Tragedy of Pudd'nhead Wilson* in 1894 to *The Man That Corrupted Hadleyburg* in 1900 and *The $30,000 Bequest* in 1906. At the base of *The Mysterious Stranger* was the nihilistic philosophy of *What Is Man?* too, only here that pounding and persistent pessimism of Clemens' lowest period was transmuted into highly complex, ambiguous art. In its tone *The Mysterious Stranger* is light, satirical, even gay just when its message is most horrid. Talk about Melville! Talk about the *Piazza Tales* such as "Bartleby the Scrivener," "The Encantadas," and perhaps the greatest of them, "Benito Cereno." Mark Twain's vision of life in *The Mysterious Stranger* was just as demonic, nihilistic, and enigmatic.

This is one of the major short stories of evil and emptiness at the core of life; and both Melville and Twain eclipsed in their depth and range of vision the short stories of Ernest Hemingway on the same theme. But just as Melville was to live on and write, in his last fable of *Billy Budd,* of a more mixed universe of both good and evil, or perhaps beyond good and evil, so Twain's somber view of man's life in *The Mysterious Stranger* was curiously balanced by a sense of light and joy, mysterious to behold, in the story itself. The background history of the story still remains obscure. (*I am not here concerned with the academic controversy over the various editions of this book.*) One might speculate it was started in the lowest depths of Clemens' life, the period of Livy's last illness and the family's collapse, and then refined and refined, subtly altered, in his last years. For the story's opening is full of paradoxes, enigma upon enigma, which bewilder and dazzle us — which are resolved slowly in the story's development . . . if they are resolved.

The scene was Austria in 1590. The town was called Eseldorf (or "Jackassville"), as the successor to Hannibal, Hadleyburg, and Dawson's Landing. This little transposed frontier settlement was still "a paradise for us boys," but this time a paradise ringed round with more ominous taboos and evil omens. Of the village's two priests, Father Adolf was held in more respect because "he had absolutely no fear of the Devil." He mocked at him in fact, and had actually met Satan face to face and defied him. "This was known to be so. Father Adolf said it himself." The other priest, Father Peter, believed that God was all goodness and would find a way to save his poor human children; the villagers loved but were sorry for him. The village Astrologer was the third member of this peculiar trinity, the possessor of occult wisdom and ancient magic, pre-religious

in essence, whom the good Father Peter denounced but Father
Adolf and the Bishop respected.

As the story opens, Father Peter is already on the road to
ruin, along with his niece Marget. The village money-lender,
Solomon Isaacs, is about to foreclose the mortgage on their
house. Against the prevailing trinity of religious and superstitious authority Clemens set up a kind of pagan trinity of three
boys who were always together and had been so from the cradle.
Theodor Fischer, son of the church organist, is the story's narrator; his friends are Nikolaus Bauman and Seppi Wohlmeyer. As in *Huck Finn* these three are natural boys. "We
knew the hills and the woods as well as the birds knew them;
for we were always roaming them when we had leisure — at
least, when we were not swimming or boating or fishing, or
playing on the ice or sliding down hill." But here the castle
park is a feudal scene and the castle servingman, Felix Brandt,
provides the aura of primitive mysticism — of ghosts, witches,
enchanters, bats, and incubae — formerly supplied by the Negro slaves . . . Yet the Mysterious Stranger seems far away
from all this.

He is a handsome and well-turned-out young man with a
winning face and a pleasant voice, "and was easy and graceful
and unembarrassed, not slouchy and awkward and diffident
like other boys." He wins over the three youths by his charm
and beguilements, while he makes fire out of air and ice out of
water and fills their pockets with goodies. He makes living
animals out of clay after he has told them he is an angel, and
proceeds to make a toy castle filled with five hundred active
little people as a replica of medieval life. He outfits a cavalry
division and lets the boys make the horses and cannon. It is
then he tells them his name is Satan, named after his uncle who
was blameless before the Fall, and this fills the boys with divine

wonder. "I should not be able to make any one understand how exciting it all was. You know that kind of quiver that trembles around through you when you are seeing something so strange and enchanting and wonderful that it is just a fearful joy to be alive and look at it — "

> and you know how you gaze, and your lips turn dry and your breath comes short, but you wouldn't be anywhere but there, not for the world.

And this theme of satanic enchantment — of a revelatory excitement that thrills the mind and the senses alike — is a persistent one throughout *The Mysterious Stranger* and we must ask ourselves what its true meaning is, both to Samuel Clemens and in the larger realm of psychological feeling.

Satan also answers the unasked questions of the boys. "Have I seen him? Millions of times. From the time that I was a little child a thousand years old I was his second favorite among the nursery angels of our blood and lineage — to use a human phrase — yes, from that time until the Fall, eight thousand years, measured as you count time." But which "Him" is Clemens referring to, even while he is careful not to use the customary capitalization — God or the Devil? In point of fact they are equated in the story; it is actually the Devil — or to minimize man's nature and destiny even more — it is the Devil's nephew who is the Acting God, to all purposes the real God, of the chronicle.

There is another favorite notion of the later Mark Twain, the notion of time being imaginary and man-made, and hence important only to man in his delusionary universe. The youthful Satan is sixteen thousand years old, by human count, and as he says, without sin. "No, the Fall did not affect me nor the rest of the relationship. It was only he that I was named for

who ate of the fruit of the tree and then beguiled the man and
the woman with it. We others are still ignorant of sin; we are
not able to commit it; we are without blemish, and shall abide
in that estate always. We — " And then he squeezes the life
blood out of two of the toy workmen he has created, wipes off
the stain of blood with his handkerchief, and continues. "We
cannot do wrong; neither have we any disposition to do it, for
we do not know what it is."

The boys are horrified by this act of wanton bloodshed on the
part of their dazzling young friend while he is uttering the
strange speech about being without sin. Then, in the toy kingdom, the wives of the dead men start to lament, a priest arrives, masses of people assemble to grieve and weep — and
Satan, annoyed by the tiny tumult, wipes out the whole assem-
blage. "It made us sick to see that awful deed," says Clemens'
young narrator, and these people had not been prepared by
the Church for death, and the boys feel it their duty to bring
their supernatural acquaintance to worldly justice. And yet —

> He went on talking right along, and worked his enchantments
> upon us again with that fatal music of his voice. He made us for-
> get everything; we could only listen to him and love him, and be his
> slaves, to do with us as he would. He made us drunk with the
> joy of being with him, and of looking into the heaven of his eyes,
> and of feeling the ecstasy that thrilled along our veins from the
> touch of his hand.

Accents of enchantment and love indeed, of a fatal charm, a
divine and diabolical and utterly thrilling bondage! Was Clemens' symbolical man-child thus profoundly linked to a cruel
and hostile force, to a personage of super-evil? The Stranger,
moreover, "had seen everything, he had been everywhere, he
knew everything, and he forgot nothing," and he made, for his

enthralled trio of boys, the entire history of creation come alive
to their eyes. "He told of the daily life in heaven; he had seen
the damned writhing in the red waves of hell; and he made us
see all those things, and it was as if we were on the spot and
looking at them with our own eyes. And we felt them, too but
there was no sign that they were anything to him beyond mere
entertainments. Those visions of hell, those poor babes and
women and girls and lads and men shrieking and supplicating
in anguish — why, we could hardly bear it, but he was as
bland about it as if it had been so many imitation rats in artificial fire."

With these lines Clemens was of course achieving a double
purpose. He was presenting his familiar parody of religious
superstition; and at the same time he is pointing out how man's
notion of religion — for which so much has been endured, suffered, and sacrificed during the long course of history — is irrelevant to any cosmic Being, or in any cosmic sense. When
Satan describes men and women, here on earth, even in their
most sublime moments, the boys are ashamed, "for his manner showed that to him they and their doings were of paltry
poor consequence," and Satan's (Clemens'?) comparison of
mankind was with flies. What strikes Theodor Fischer in the
story is that Satan is not even angry; his tone is matter-of-fact.
The truth of this kind of revelation to the eager young eyes of
childhood is so clear as not to be questioned. Meanwhile, when
the boys have finished every detail of the medieval clay castle,
complete with halberdiers and cavalry, the Stranger invokes
storm, earthquake, fire in order for them to witness the sudden and complete destruction of all their work. "Our hearts
were broken; we could not keep from crying. 'Don't cry,' Satan
said, 'they were of no value.' 'But they are gone to hell!' 'Oh,
it is no matter; we can make plenty more.'" The castle and people have disappeared into a common grave.

Satan's consistent answer, in fact, to the boys' horrified plea that he is destroying human lives is that he can make more of them. "It was no use to try to move him; evidently he was wholly without feeling, and could not understand. He was full of bubbling spirits, and as gay as if this were a wedding instead of a fiendish massacre. And he was bent on making us feel as he did, and of course his magic accomplished his desire. It was no trouble to him; he did whatever he pleased with us."

> In a little while we were dancing on that grave, and he was playing to us on a strange, sweet instrument which he took out of his pocket; and the music — but there is no music like that, unless perhaps in heaven, and that was where he brought it from, he said. It made one mad, for pleasure; and we could not take our eyes from him, and the looks that went out of our eyes came from our hearts, and their dumb speech was worship. He brought the dance from heaven, too, and the bliss of paradise was in it.

This is the conclusion of the prelude, introduction, or invocation, to *The Mysterious Stranger*. The Devil leaves the boys on an errand, though they beg and beseech him not to. He announces that while to them he is Satan, he is taking the worldly name of Traum, or "Dream." But what a mysterious, complex, beguiling introduction this is; which is almost a short story in itself. What is the meaning of this divine and diabolical music that Satan brings from "heaven," while the boys rejoice in his presence, bow down to his power, his charm, and dance on the grave of the feudal castle and its inhabitants, so casually created, so casually obliterated. On the premise that more can be made, they are of no consequence. Many of Mark Twain's critics have stressed the utter dark despair and cynicism of this story, which is yet, however, cast in these accents of joy and gaiety, of comedy and boundless pleasure. From where did Mark Twain himself evoke the note of delicious pleasure,

of almost uncontrollable and orgiastic delight, of a complete
sensuous pleasure on the boys' part even while they are witness to these scenes of crime and evil in terms of the little
clay figures of human life? What is the strange and haunting
esthetic medium and message of *The Mysterious Stranger*?

We should notice Clemens' own pleasure and identification
with his Satan, the master magician whose creation and destruction of human life is so casual, sadistic, good-humored, and
ironical. If indeed this strange story was written during Sam
Clemens' own period of deepest human suffering, there are
elements again of a creative projection and catharsis. The artist was in a sense taking his revenge on those forces of life
and death which had so deeply tormented him. If you can't
beat them, join them.

There are other notes here of a return to a religious kind of
debate about life and death on the part of a writer who so
very early had decided to cast aside all religious superstitions
and formalities. And to those critics who have stressed Sam's
guilt at having deprived Livy of her own religious solace in the
later years of sorrow and need, it can be pointed out that Mark
Twain's Satan is a patent justification of Twain's own convictions . . . But on a deeper and wider level of historical or
metaphysical content, we notice that the Clemens who, in his
Carnival of Crime, had rejected social conventions to embark
on a life of pagan "crime" and pleasure, now was deriving a
mysterious sense of joy and exaltation from the spectacle of
social crime itself, and human suffering. And here he was
closer to the speculations of Wilhelm Reich, along with Rank,
that the social repression of our primary nature can lead only
to the corrupted sexuality and social blood baths of Hitler's
Germany, or Fascism's true appeal. Was it not strange that
he was describing the "Satanic enchantment" of the sexually

innocent and pagan boys in almost purely sexual terms? In
the almost classic terms of black magic, the witchcraft cult, the
underground worship of Priapus-Satan from the oldest of ancient days?

In the story itself, meanwhile, Father Peter is helped by Satan,
at the boys' urging, and in Satan's most satanic manner, by
discovering eleven hundred ducats which will rescue him from
his worldly troubles — and lead to his further persecution.
Gold and money, as a symbol of human disaster to Clemens,
are viewed here just as in *The Man That Corrupted Hadleyburg, The $30,000 Bequest,* and *Pudd'nhead Wilson*; just as
it had been at the core of Clemens' own tragedy and the whole
American social tragedy of his period.

With Father Peter's mysterious "redemption" comes the fact
that the whole village is gossiping about the mysterious money;
and the Astrologer emerges in the story as Father Peter's per-
secutor by declaring the money was stolen from him. Father
Peter is put in jail pending the outcome of his trial, while the
boys and their "protector," Satan, now devote their efforts to
saving Father Peter's niece Marget. Her serving maid, the poverty-stricken old peasant, Ursula, "discovers" a mysterious
kitten who produces four silver groschen (and much, much
more) every day. And Clemens described this peasant spirit
as the human matrix. "In her heart she probably believed it
was a witch-cat and an agent of the Devil; but no matter, it was
all the more certain to be able to keep its contract and furnish a
daily good living for the family, for in matters of finance even
the piousest of our peasants would have more confidence in an
arrangement with the Devil than with an archangel."

Satan appears himself at Marget's house, in the person of
Philip Traum, and is so beautiful that Marget can hardly keep
her eyes off him. "That gratified me, and made me proud. I

hoped he would show off some, but he didn't. He seemed only interested in being friendly and telling lies. He said he was an orphan." In fact Satan declares he hardly knows his own parents. "But he had an uncle in business down in the tropics, and he was very well off and had a monopoly, and it was from this uncle that he drew his support."

The Huck Finn "tone" appears steadily in this last tale of enchanted and illusioned (and yes, comic) youth which was set against such a gloomy background. Philip Traum even declares he was studying for the ministry, while a mysterious and abundant meal is produced for all of them, and poor Ursula, corrupted by Satan's compliments, begins on the course of her own downfall. And Marget's also; but the boys still do not understand that anything is preferable, in one sense, to Satan's — or God's? — "sympathy." And meanwhile, on another level of the story's plot, Satan conducts the boys to a medieval torture chamber where a heretic is being "questioned," and to a French village where the peasant-workers are condemned to lives of utmost poverty, shame, and horror. "Have they committed a crime, these mangy things?" Satan asks. "No. What have they done, that they are punished so? Nothing at all, except getting themselves born into your foolish race." It is the "Moral Sense," cries Satan-Twain again, which sets off man from the innocent beasts, and enables him to perform, with clear conscience, all the atrocious acts that no animal would think of.

The story shifts back to the present, and to Seppi Wohlmeyer, who is also intoxicated by Satan's presence.

He had felt his blood leap and his spirits rise in a way that could mean only one thing, and he knew Satan was near, although it was too dark to see him. He came to us, and we walked along

together, and Seppi poured out his gladness like water. It was as
if he were a lover and had found his sweetheart who had been lost.

A lost lover, a lost sweetheart indeed. Some lover, some sweetheart! while Seppi proceeds to say that the village loafer, Hans
Oppert, has disappeared after clubbing his dog and knocking
out one of its eyes. Seppi calls Hans a "heartless brute," and
Satan becomes severe. "There is that misused word again —
that shabby slander. Brutes do not act like that, but only
men." Well, says Seppi, it was inhuman. "No, it wasn't, Seppi;
it was human, quite distinctly human. It is not pleasant to hear
you libel the higher animals by attributing to them dispositions
which they are free from, and which are found nowhere but
in the human heart. None of the higher animals is tainted with
the disease called the Moral Sense. Purify your language,
Seppi; drop those lying phrases out of it."

In these pages perhaps Clemens stressed his old enemy,
man's "moral sense," too heavily; there are passages which
are as if taken directly from the moralistic sermons of *What Is
Man?* — but on the whole *The Mysterious Stranger* is the creative *product,* and filled with creative fancy, of that simplistic
and tedious volume of philosophy. In art, to stress and repeat
an essential concept, one must never take an artist's ideology
literally. It is what develops *artistically* from the artist's "philosophy" which really counts; as for example again, in the difference between Theodore Dreiser's philosophical "determinism"
(or mechanism), so heavily stressed by Dreiser's recent biographers and critics, and Dreiser's truly remarkable creativity,
which seems to be ignored.

Even when Clemens was being most blunt and bitter about
man's destiny — as *The Mysterious Stranger* itself, so entertaining and humorous in its opening texture, begins to assume

a darker and more deadly hue — there are passages of devastating, bitter eloquence. Man is made of dirt, Satan says when the boys question him about mortal and immortal beings: "I saw him made . . . Man is a museum of diseases, a home of impurities; he comes today and is gone to-morrow; he begins as dirt and departs as stench." And the difference between man and the angels is again that man has the Moral Sense which offends everything Satan believes in. There is a dull week or so in the story's action when Satan is absent, while Marget and Ursula are prospering mightily through their wishing-kitten, and have hired Gottfried Narr as an errand boy. A mistake, the boys know, since Gottfried, while personally a dull, good creature, is under a cloud. "And properly so, for it had not been six months since a social blight had mildewed the family — his grandmother had been burned as a witch. When that kind of malady is in the blood it does not always come out with just one burning."

There follows the remarkable section on witches in *The Mysterious Stranger* which Clemens adduced to illustrate still another phase of man's temperament — or was there a still more sinister import to these pages? The witch terror had risen higher than ever before in Eseldorf, befuddling everybody's wits, and yet "This was natural enough because of late years there were more kinds of witches than there used to be."

> In old times it had been only old women, but of late years they were all ages — even children of eight and nine; it was getting so that anybody might turn out to be a familiar of the Devil — age and sex hadn't anything to do with it. In our little region we had tried to extirpate the witches, but the more of them we burned the more of the breed rose up in their places.

This was a variation on a familiar thesis of Mark Twain's about lynchings among other things; and as Twain's Satan might have added: It proved once more the development and "progress" of human society. Just recently there had been a mass burning of little-girl witches, Clemens added in a passage that might remind one of Salem, Massachusetts; and the story moved into the subplot, or parallel plot, of Marget and Ursula's doom as incurred by Satan's kindness. Father Adolf suspects Marget's abundant household of witchcraft and orders the villagers to gather together there and discover the truth. "The bars were down, and we could all go there now, and we did — our parents and all — day after day." The cat began to strain herself, adds Theodor Fischer. The meals and parties became more and more opulent.

The sorry history of Marget's "good fortune" is replete with ambiguous irony: a combination of satanic "kindness" and human frailty . . . and mob hysteria. For Marget, being human, is delighted with her opulence and popularity in the village society; she tries to surpass herself in providing foods and wines for her neighbors, out of her kindness and her vanity. Her "innocence" is terrible to behold; Clemens seems to be saying that the victim deserves his punishment.

One party is so celebrated that even Satan arrives, along with the Astrologer and Father Adolf, and there is much village gossip about the charming stranger. Satan "defends" Marget — temporarily, for his own purposes, and for a worse fate. Theodor (the last or lost Huck) even has the idea of "reforming" his charming and beloved friend:

> We talked together, and I had the idea of trying to reform Satan and persuade him to lead a better life. I told him about all these things he had been doing, and begged him to be more considerate and stop making people unhappy. I said I knew he did not mean any harm, but that he ought to stop and consider the possible consequences of a thing before launching it in that impulsive and random way of his; then he would not make so much trouble.

Alas, for our youthful illusions. In passages such as these Clemens conveyed all the delightful and nostalgic and sweet-sounding and sweet-feeling "innocence" of childhood quite as accurately as he had in *Huck Finn,* though with far deeper and deadlier undertones. A remarkable achievement for such an aging and tragic and weary writer who yet retained the inviolate pagan core of his earliest being. Maybe it is just this series, or sequence, or delicate fusion of such different and almost incompatible emotions which makes *The Mysterious Stranger* so interesting and puzzling to read.

And Satan is indeed a much blacker version of Huck's wisest teacher, "Nigger Jim." He only looks amused at Theodor's statement and declares that none of his acts are random. "I know what the consequences are going to be — always." And he adds: "I have wrought well for the villagers, though it does not look like it on the surface. Your race never knows good fortune from ill. You are always mistaking the one for the other. It is because they cannot see into the future." (A happy thought indeed.) Satan then expands on Twain's earlier theme of determinism in human life — but says that he can change this if they want him to. Then comes the harrowing episode of Lisa and Nikolaus in *The Mysterious Stranger,* when Satan arranges for their early and immediate death — one of Clemens' own boons of life — rather than a prolonged existence of illness and misery and pain. At this time Satan also assures the boys that Father Peter's name will be cleared in the court trial about his magic fortune, and he too will be "happy" — an ominous word in the satanic lexicon.

Theodor is allowed to tell Seppi about Nick's impending death; but in this subplot Clemens invoked too much of the romance-melodrama — the sentiment he was wont to fall back upon when inspiration failed. The action is contrived, but the

theme that Mark Twain stressed was not: in childhood, man
— this vile and lowly being — in childhood even man is good,
and closer to the animal levels of life which Twain also equated
with the angelic. The boy is closer to pure feeling than the
analytic "reasoning powers" bent on manipulation and power,
and using the "moral sense" as the cover for all sorts of hypocrisy. Here Theo learns, both from Satan and from Mark Twain,
not only that death is life's single blessing, but perhaps an early
death is best of all. "Many a time since I have heard people
pray to God to spare the life of sick persons, but I have never
done it." (Twain himself said this elsewhere.)

In despair over her daughter's death, Lisa's mother has sworn
that she will never pray to God again; and the weaver Fischer
has betrayed her to the church authorities to have her burned
at the stake; but Satan reassures the boys that she is going to
heaven and escaping twenty-nine years of misery on earth.
On the other hand Fischer, the informer, will have a long life
full of joy — and go to hell. Satan even disperses the lynch
mob which follows Frau Brandt to the stake, but the boys
have learned their lesson:

> We did not ask if he had brought poor Fischer's luck to any of
> them. We did not wish to know. We fully believed in Satan's
> desire to do us kindnesses, but we were losing confidence in his
> judgment. It was at this time that our growing anxiety to have
> him look over our life-charts and suggest improvements began to
> fade out and give place to other interests.

In this statement, couched in Twain's deadpan irony, Theodor
has learned one of life's great lessons.

Frau Brandt also echoes the pagan-infancy-edenic theme
at the base of *The Mysterious Stranger*. She is tired of village
society, of life itself, and goes willingly to the stake; yet her final

words are "We played together once, in long-gone days when
we were innocent little creatures. For the sake of that, I forgive you." Satan then provides the boys with a kaleidoscopic
view of the race's development from the Garden of Eden to Cain
and Abel and a long series of crimes, murders, and massacres.
Next the Flood and the Ark, and Satan declares, "The progress
of your race was not satisfactory. It is to have another chance
now." And the boys see Noah overcome with wine, Sodom
and Gomorrah, Lot and his daughters, the Hebraic wars, the
Egyptian wars, the Greek wars, the Roman wars, and the birth
of Christianity. "Then those ages of Europe passed in review
before us, and we saw Christianity and Civilization march
hand in hand through those ages, leaving famine and death
and desolation in their wake, and other signs of the progress
of the human race." And always there were wars, as Satan
added, and more wars, "but never a war started by an aggres-
sor for any clean purpose — there is no such war in the history
of the race." While the future contained only "slaughters more
terrible in their destruction of life, more devastating in their
engines of war, than any we had seen."

There is another statement by Theodor in *The Mysterious
Stranger*. "Then he began to laugh in the most unfeeling way,
and make fun of the human race, although he knew what he
had been saying shamed us and wounded us. No one but an
angel could have acted so; but suffering is nothing to them;
they do not know what it is, except by hearsay." For these
children still have the capacity for shame, in a true sense,
which most adults have long repressed except in a vanity, ego
and face-saving sense. And is mental or psychological suffering denied to the angels because human suffering, to the later
Twain, no longer had any meaning? But Christianity, Satan
concluded, had done the most of all for human progress; and

here, in those swift interchanges of both feeling and intellect which mark *The Mysterious Stranger,* Clemens moved imperceptibly from "human" or biopsychic evil and sin to social-historical evil. The ironical and devastating theologian of man's heart was simultaneously the radical social critic. "It is a remarkable progress. In five or six thousand years five or six high civilizations have risen, flourished, commanded the wonder of the world, then faded out and disappeared; and not one of them except the latest ever invented any sweeping and adequate way to kill people. They all did their best — to kill being the chief ambition of the human race and the earliest incident in its history — but only the Christian civilization has scored a triumph to be proud of. Two or three centuries from now it will be recognized that all the competent killers are Christians; then the pagan world will go to school to the Christian — not to acquire his religion but his guns."

And Clemens was not too far off in *this* prophecy. In a later age much different from the still-placid, peaceful, and "established" society at the turn of the century, Asiatic China, minus the missionaries, was busily developing its own atomic weaponry, after the Christian world of Western European society had produced Hitler and the Bomb as its civilizational end products. There is another witch-hunt and stone-throwing in these pages, a denunciation of those human spirits who don't join the celebration, and then again Twain's account of the martial (and the mob) spirit operating on the modern civilizational matrix. There has never been a just war, Satan repeats, never an honorable one on the part of the instigator, but "the loud little handful — as usual — will shout for the war. The pulpit will — warily and cautiously — object — at first; the great, big, dull bulk of the nation will rub its sleepy eyes and try to make out why there should be a war, and will say, earnestly and indignantly, 'It is unjust and dishonorable, and there is no necessity for it.' Then the handful will shout louder. A few fair men on the other side will argue and reason against the war with speech and pen, and at first will have a hearing and be applauded; but it will not last long; those others will out-shout them, and presently the anti-war audiences will thin out and lose popularity. Before long you will see this curious thing: the speakers stoned from the platform, and free speech stran-gled by hordes of furious men who in their secret hearts are still at one with those stoned speakers — as earlier — but do not dare to say so. And now the whole nation — pulpit and all — will take up the war-cry, and shout itself hoarse, and mob any honest man who ventures to open his mouth, and presently such mouths will cease to open. Next the statesmen will invent cheap lies, putting the blame upon the nation that is attacked, and every man will be glad of those conscience-soothing falsities, and will diligently study them, and refuse to examine any refutations of them; and thus he will by and by convince himself that the war is just, and will thank God for the better sleep he enjoys after this process of grotesque self-deception."

In such passages as these in *The Mysterious Stranger,* the logic flows almost imperceptibly from the individual to his social order and back again to the individual, so that the re-sult is a complex interwoven net of human-social deception, which is perhaps the most accurate description of what actu-ally happens. Even though Sam Clemens had seen only "minor" wars, and the simpler imperialistic campaigns of his period, it was just as though he stood at the outbreak of World War I, World War II, of the wars in Korea and Vietnam, and the pos-sible inception of World War III. That is the way it happened. In the narrative, the trial of Father Peter (and by implication of his unfortunate niece Marget) proceeds apace, while the boys worry about Satan's absence. "If Satan would only come! That was my constant thought," says Theodor Fischer. And Satan does come, and in the person of Wilhelm Meidling, Marget's suitor, wins the case for Father Peter handily. (Meidling, alas, soon loses "that luminous look in his eyes" that he had when Satan was in him.) They bring the good news to Father Peter in jail only to discover he has lost his sanity. When the boys rebuke Satan for accomplishing this deed, he reminds them of his promise to restore Father Peter's good name — and to make him happy for the rest of his life.

"There it was, you see," says Theodor. "He didn't seem to know any way to do a person a favor except by killing him or making a lunatic out of him. I apologized, as well as I could; but privately I did not think much of his processes — at that time." In the course of this macabre tale we come to realize that Theodor is indeed learning much for his age; is beginning to understand the satanic logic of life. He is becoming, as it were, the Devil's disciple. Satan pursues the argument with his familiar contention "that our race lived a life of continuous and uninterrupted self-deception. It duped itself from cradle to grave with shams and delusions which it mistook for realities, and this made its entire life a sham." The one great weapon it possessed, added Satan-Twain, was humor, the assault of laughter against which no sham, hypocrisy, or evil could really stand; and this kind of humor, too, the human race hardly ever understood.

There follows the final, complex, and elusive chapter of *The Mysterious Stranger*: the disappearance of Satan.

"For as much as a year Satan continued these visits, but at last he did not come at all. This always made me feel lonely and melancholy. I felt he was losing interest in our tiny world and might at any time abandon his visits entirely." Thus the boys' deepest thrill at the satanic presence is compounded by their sense of loss in his departure. "When one day he finally came to me," says Theodor, "I was overjoyed, but only for a little while. He had come to say good-by, he told me, and for the last time. He had investigations and undertakings in other corners of the universe, he said, that would keep him busy for a longer period than I could wait for his return."

Beneath the surface irony of this statement, that the human race was no longer worthy of Satan's interest, there was a deeper chord, perhaps not entirely known but surely felt by Sam Clemens. If the world was to lose all its satanic thrills of pleasure and excitement, then the pagan yearnings of which Clemens himself was such a deep and devout exponent, were yielding, in the Freudian-Rankian thesis, to all the discontents and repressions of civilization. And a "civilizing" process had indeed happened in the American scene of Mark Twain's own life. Primitive, wild Nature was being devoured and conquered by the scientific-industrial and urban complex. The rebellious Satan would surely lose interest in such a dehumanized area which finally denied him and his works. Such a world would be without interest to Sam Clemens too, since it was simultaneously narrowing and suppressing that area of personal rebellion, human dissent, and social questioning which he, above all, had always typified. This was indeed the United States at the turn of the century, at its "watershed," or that deep, impassable canyon-gulf between the Old Republic and the conquering Empire.

Older human evils disappearing, new and much worse, abstract and dehumanized (industrialized, mass-produced) evils would follow. Vainly Theodor pleads with Satan, who admits it has been a pleasant and comradely experience. "But I must go now, and we shall not see each other any more." "In this life, Satan, but in another? We shall meet in another, surely?" pleads Theodor in a variation of Sam Clemens' contention he would always rather go to hell than to any human heaven. Then, all tranquilly and soberly, Satan made his strange answer. "*There is no other.*" And thus Mark Twain's final parable demolished his own lifelong artistic mythology of heaven and hell — and accomplished even more in Theodor's response to this assertion. "A subtle influence blew upon my spirit from his, bringing with it a vague, dim, but blessed and hopeful feeling that the incredible words might be true — even *must* be true." A blessed and hopeful feeling indeed reflecting the maturer Clemens' deepest intuition that one taste of life was sufficient for any human being. When Theodor asks again if this could be true, outstripping all his own religious beliefs and superstitions in the story, and Satan reaffirms it is true, and that all visions of future life are merely visions without real existence, Theodor can hardly breathe "for the great hope that was struggling in me." *"Life itself is only a vision, a dream,"* Satan repeats, and Clemens, like Shakespeare in *The Tempest,* steps out of his own fiction. "It was electrical. By God! I had had that very thought a thousand times in my musings!" — "*Nothing* exists," Satan adds. "All is a dream. God — man — the world — the sun, the moon, the wilderness of stars — a dream, all a dream; they have no existence. *Nothing exists save empty space — and you!*"

And this "you" was not Theodor but only the *thought* of Theodor, so Twain ended this mysterious story with a thought "alone in shoreless space, to wander its limitless solitudes without friend or comrade forever." And there followed one of the most curious and imperfect ending-passages of *The Mysterious Stranger,* in which Clemens vented all his rage and bitterness at the cruel and savage universe of nature upon the religious God that he and Satan alike had already dismissed as a fiction. (Some of these ending passages were in fact too close to the grim sermonizing of *What Is Man?*, and perhaps that is why Clemens was not satisfied with the story's end and refused to print it in his own lifetime.) Not to mention that they appear to contradict themselves in part; for Clemens seems to be saying there is and is not a God, or a meaning to life. "You perceive *now*, that these things are all impossible except in a dream," Satan concludes. "You perceive that they are pure and puerile insanities, the silly creations of an imagination that is not conscious of its freaks — in a word, that they are a dream, and you the maker of it. The dream-marks are all present; you should have recognized them earlier."

Once more Satan repeats a passage that was compulsive in this late artist despite his own sense of art. "It is true, that which I have revealed to you; there is no God, no universe, no human race, no earthly life, no heaven, no hell. It is all a dream — a grotesque and foolish dream . . ." "He vanished, and left me appalled; for I knew, and realized, that all he had said was true." Thus the famous ending line of *The Mysterious Stranger*, and despite the repetitions and confusions of the story's ending which never satisfied Mark Twain himself, it is still an effective if a perplexing conclusion. There has been much discussion of this conclusion among the Mark Twain critics, too, but what has not been stressed in this case is the psychological rather than the philosophical impact. The philosophic vision here is as simplistic as in *What Is Man?*; and the psychoesthetic meaning is very interesting. There is no doubt that Clemens himself, along with Satan, is bidding farewell to human life, is indeed denigrating human beings to the point of not being worthy of Satan's or God's interest — of indeed having really created a monstrous God, an amiable but disinter-

ested and sadistic Satan. And quite like the Shakespeare of
The Tempest (of which there are other echoes here), Clemens was dismissing not only life itself but the life of his own
artistic kingdom! Even while he and Shakespeare and Satan
still stood apart from their work as the Master Magicians
who created and could just as easily obliterate it.

There was certainly also a form of spiritual confessional as
well as esthetic release in this dark ending to an otherwise
ironical, entertaining, and even gay fiction.

During his later period Clemens, as we know, was constantly
playing on the theme of dream and reality, both in published
and unpublished material. It is a theme that every great writer
has dealt with, like that of innocence and evil. It is such an
integral factor in art that with some writers it becomes almost
a *technique*. Any mature artist, any mature person, looking
back upon his own life experience from the peak, or the mo-
tionless plateau, of his career — in that period when we know
that "we are all defeated," as Willa Cather said, enemies and
friends, successes or failures, healthy and sick, rich and poor —
must wonder at a certain dreamlike texture that the past begins to assume; must wonder if life is life and death is death;
and which is dream, and which reality? And what does it
matter, all the things we fought so hard for, all the victories
which were gained at such cost, all the failures we mourned so
bitterly? Who comes out ahead — except the complacent, the
unseeing, the totally self-immersed, who do not understand the
blind and chance meaning of human life? This is in the complex texture of *The Mysterious Stranger,* as well as in the sermonizing end; this is a central element which makes the story
great and which did not need the explicit statement that Clemens concluded with. (And how many forms of human euphoria
are invoked to conceal and becloud the true moral of life.)

In those dark years of his mature life, Clemens, moreover,

might well have thought the glorious triumphs of his youth were but a dream, illusionary victories, compared with the black nightmare of "reality." In his blackest periods, he must, like Melville, have questioned all the false semblances of success, wealth, love, and happiness which he had previously reveled in so innocently. In terms of personal guilt too, his own tender and smarting conscience, how much more comforting, if also equally illusionary, to see the whole processes of being and existence as a passing dream, and man himself as irrelevant and inconsequential even in the midst of his cruelty, stupidity, and hypocrisy.

Thus if *The Mysterious Stranger* shares, in a curious way, some of the enigmatic obscurity, the ironical twists and turns of plot, of a typical Henry James novella, say, it has at base a much more profound vision — since James, to the very end, was obsessed by all those special privileges and worldly honors, all those "goodies" of life, which Mark Twain had enjoyed so abundantly, and had discarded as so meaningless and empty. And whereas Melville, at the peak of his own literary achievement in *Moby Dick,* and in the chasm of worldly disgrace which attended upon his epic, had seen life, as in the *Piazza Tales,* purely in terms of horrors and evils and crimes, Sam Clemens, much closer to a Theodore Dreiser, saw it as a matter of cosmic indifference, or as the *plaything* of vast cosmic forces who indifferently created and destroyed our world as of no consequence, and indeed of a questionable reality.

In this sense human life, and nature as the creating force of life are not evil, as so many lesser writers and other injured souls have proclaimed, but a matter of cosmic indifference, which is beyond such anthropomorphic terms as good and evil. More profound, this is also a less paranoid view of existence in which man is the puppet (free will or not) of natural forces that can create him, advance him, or maim him and destroy him with Mark Twain's satanic indifference. This was the true end, the esthetic projection and climax of Sam Clemens' own happiness and sorrow: this dream and nightmare of life as felt by an especially gay, pagan, and pleasure-loving spirit.

But despite the black ending of this fable (and Twain's familiar penchant for lurid melodrama in such cases) what is the quality which really sets off *The Mysterious Stranger* from all other stories on the same theme both in American and world literature? Which makes it so priceless and unique? We have noticed its enchantment with crime and evil, couched not merely in sexual but almost orgiastic emotional terms. Was there a difference here between Satan's joy and gaiety even at his worst, and the dull inhumanity of man? If life was evil on all levels, perhaps it was preferable to join with the Evil Life Spirit itself, as only Mark Twain could portray it, in all its delight and charm? Now this is close to the story's underlying, never stated theme. This desperate nihilism turns out to be very entertaining. This black despair is undergoing the purgation of humor — that humor which, as Twain himself declared, was the only possible defense against man's poor little existence on earth. Evil is not quite evil when it becomes a parody, a comedy of evil. (Yes, this does lead back to the plenary-pagan childhood world of comic make-believe in *Tom Sawyer* and *Huckleberry Finn*. Exactly.) And when evil itself can become as charming and beguiling as Satan was at Marget's party! What an extraordinary view this was of Satan himself, this charming young "pretender" spreading his "favors" — his fatal gifts — with such an insouciant style. The beautiful and devastating irony of *The Mysterious Stranger* is touched by Twain's irrepressible comedy; the Twainian man has been down into the black pit of mortal disaster, and has emerged laughing.

Though it is important to stress that Mark Twain, like all

great writers, never attempted to deny the basic tragedy of life. He was only discounting its long history of sordid evil. In this sense, just as Nigger Jim had been Huck's first great counselor in this life, so Mark Twain's Satan was Theodor Fischer's far more sophisticated counselor in the matter of death. And that is to say, paralleling the form of *Life on the Mississippi*, the mature and elderly Twain is now looking back on the more youthful Twain of life and letters. (This double vision is of course an intuitive part of the double soul.) And here Mark Twain was repeating that laughter belongs to man as well as the Gods, in perhaps the only area of existence where man achieves equality with the careless and indifferent, rather than evil or malevolent, life forces. If Satan disposed those ironic "favors" with such equanimity, man could still receive them with equal and knowing composure. Talk about the "frustrated and bitter and old" Mark Twain! *The Mysterious Stranger* is the purest bit of divine sunlight to illuminate all the long, dark, endless abyss of human history. Satan as the Great Prankster, yes; and laughter as the only salvation for the whole muddy mess of man's life — this was Mark Twain's final (or nearly final) verdict. And that is why *The Mysterious Stranger* is so very special among the great stories of the world which deal with the problem of human existence.

TEN

THEY DROVE US
FROM THE GARDEN WITH
THEIR SWORDS OF FLAME

But still, this was not the last word Mark Twain was to utter on human destiny, just as his own life had transcended, if it was still marked by, the years of trauma and tragedy. If in one sense *The Mysterious Stranger* was a kind of final psychological catharsis, what is more important to know is that the story is an esthetic masterpiece, belonging to world literature.

What Is Man? was republished in 1917 (the original London edition of this book had disclosed the author's identity, kept secret at home) along with other essays. Chief among these was the moving description of "The Death of Jean," which Clemens also intended to use as the end of the *Autobiography*. As in fact it ended his public writing career, and shortly thereafter, his life. The same volume included the long essay, or perhaps the novelette, called "Is Shakespeare Dead?" and another familiar essay called "How to Make History Dates Stick," which is memorable for the illustrations that Clemens prepared for it. But apart from this, the book was composed of minor essays perhaps worth publishing but not worth more attention. In the same year appeared another volume, *Mark Twain's Letters,* full of fascinating detail about Clemens' daily life, work, human relations. It is another guidebook to this talent which produced so many guidebooks about itself; this native genius whose whole life and work were a kind of extended "Autobiography" — whose various forms, however, are always different, fresh, and interesting.

I am omitting any description of *Mark Twain's Letters* in this narrative because of space — the book is another rehearsal of Clemens' life, as was the volume of *Mark Twain's Speeches* — and mainly because these two big books were the raw material from which all the other "autobiographies" in Twain's last period were formulated. We shall discuss them under other guises.

In 1918 appeared one of Twain's most curious volumes of *Literary Essays* — in 1918, I say, as Volume XVI of *my* edition of the complete works of Mark Twain, although I can find no mention of this volume at all in the standard bibliographies of Mark Twain.* But the volume is too good to be missed, because of three or four essays.

The title essay of the volume is in itself one of Mark Twain's most strange and perplexing items. Upon his first reading of Dowden's *Life of Shelley,* he was enraged that the Victorian professor tried to "rationalize" Shelley's love life by blaming his series of love affairs upon Harriet Shelley herself. (This was an odd approach typical of the *aficionado* school of biographers such as Mr. Leon Edel today.) Twain was enraged, at times very funny, in this essay which, purporting to defend that Young

* Most likely also Volume XVI in the Authorized Edition of Mark Twain's complete works, but now titled *In Defence of Harriet Shelley,* and subtitled *Literary Essays,* copyright 1918 by the Mark Twain Company, and 1925 by Clara Gabrilowitsch. This is apparently an enlarged and updated version of the volume called *How to Tell a Story and Other Essays,* first published in 1897. This was reprinted, with new material as Volume XXII of the Autograph Edition in 1900, and again (apparently) in 1918, and 1925. The history of the book is confusing, however.

American Maiden of the late nineteenth century from "perverse" matters of this sort, was actually very outspoken about them — and at times he was curiously ambiguous or Victorian himself. Twain first described Professor Dowden's style — one of his favorite and always entertaining devices — as an American Negro "cake-walk" style. "If the book wishes to tell us that Mary Godwin, child of sixteen, had known afflictions, the fact saunters forth in this nobby outfit: 'Mary was herself not unlearned in the lore of pain' — meaning by that that she had not always traveled on asphalt . . . If the book wishes to tell us that Harriet Shelley hired a wet-nurse, that commonplace fact gets turned into a dancing-master, who does his professional bow before us in pumps and knee-breeches, with his fiddle under one arm and his crush-hat under the other, thus: 'The beauty of Harriet's motherly relation to her babe was marred in Shelley's eyes by the introduction into his house of a hireling nurse to whom was delegated the mother's tenderest office.' "

Dowden's *Shelley* was the strangest book that had seen the light since Frankenstein, Clemens added. "Indeed, it is a Frankenstein itself; a Frankenstein with the original infirmity supplemented by a new one, a Frankenstein with the reasoning faculty wanting. Yet it believes it can reason, and is always trying . . . Every time it sets up a premise and starts to reason from it, there is a surprise in store for the reader. It is strangely near-sighted, cross-eyed, and purblind . . . The materials of this biographical fable are facts, rumors, and poetry. They are connected together and harmonized by the help of suggestion, conjecture, innuendo, perversion, and semi-suppression." The biography had one purpose, Clemens continued, that of making Harriet Shelley responsible for Shelley's leaving her for another woman. (Another whole series of women in fact, and sometimes concomitantly rather than serially.)

This was a difficult task for Professor Dowden in Mark Twain's eyes. "Any one will suspect that this task has its difficulties. Any one will divine that nice work is necessary here, cautious work, wily work, and that there is entertainment to be had in watching the magician do it. There is indeed entertainment in watching him. He arranges his facts, his rumors, and his poems on his table in full view of the house, and shows you that everything is there — no deception, everything fair and aboveboard. And this is apparently true, yet there is a defect, for some of his best stock is hid in an appendix-basket behind the door, and you do not come upon it until the exhibition is over and the enchantment of your mind accomplished — as the magician thinks . . . There is an insistent atmosphere of candor and fairness about this book which is engaging at first, then a little burdensome, then a trifle fatiguing, then progressively suspicious, annoying, irritating, and oppressive. It takes some little time to find out that phrases which seem intended to guide the reader aright are there to mislead him; that phrases which seem intended to throw light are there to throw darkness; that phrases which seem intended to interpret a fact are there to misinterpret it; that phrases which seem intended to forestall prejudice are there to create it; that phrases which seem antidotes are poisons in disguise."

And this is a nice description of a whole class of scholarly works in our own period, in particular the texts of the Jamesian Cult — and even more specifically those shifting, spurious, ambiguous, and baroque masterpieces of the later Henry James himself.

Clemens then went on to describe the marriage and married life of Harriet Westbrook and Shelley, who in fact did marry her on the rebound from his passion for his cousin, Harriet Grove, and in the midst of his growing interest in Miss Hitchner, the schoolteacher. "Shelley was nineteen. He was not a youth, but a man. He had never had any youth. He was an erratic and fantastic child during eighteen years, then he stepped into manhood, as one steps over a door-sill." What is evident in the pages of this essay is Mark Twain's deep admiration for Shelley the radical revolutionary who lived out his views in a way that perhaps Mark Twain could not. "He was curiously mature at nineteen in his ability to do independent thinking on the deep questions of life, and to arrive at sharply definite decisions regarding them, and stick to them — stick to them and stand by them at cost of bread, friendship, esteem, respect and approbation . . . For the sake of his opinions he was willing to sacrifice all these valuable things, and did sacrifice them; and went on doing it, too, when he could at any moment have made himself rich and supplied himself with friends and esteem by compromising with his father, at the moderate expense of throwing overboard one or two indifferent details of his cargo of principles."

It was this complete — even "needless," so to speak — integrity that endeared the romantic poet to Mark Twain, who was well aware, as we know, of the need for compromise in his life and yet, despite all, was also keeping that inner core of integrity and personality in the depth of his own being. Describing Hogg, Harriet and Shelley, and the child called Ianthe; and then launching into the story of Shelley's romance with Mrs. Boinville and her daughter, Cornelia Turner — the whole Bracknell entourage in which, among other things, Shelley learned Italian and stopped teaching his wife Latin — even here Clemens directed his scorn mainly at Shelley's apologist-biographer. "For instance, when a man has been hard at work at the Italian poets with a pretty woman, hour after hour, and responding like a tremulous instrument to every breath of passion or of sentiment in the mean time, that man is dog-tired when he gets home, and he *can't* teach his wife Latin; it would be unreasonable to expect it."

Some of these pages of unrelenting satire in the mounting abuse of the good Professor Dowden become hilarious indeed, and remind us of the fiery narrative of *Christian Science*. Fascinating also is Clemens' complete immersion in the Shelley narrative, as though he himself was a member of this literary circle so utterly different in morals and manners. Much as in the obsessive love-hate portrait of Mrs. Eddy, Clemens pursued Mrs. Boinville — the "white-haired Maimuna" of Dowden's phrase, which Twain leaped upon. Where Dowden quoted her self-serving epistles as the words "of a considerate and judicious friend," Clemens rose to another peak. "That is what he thinks. That is, it is what he thinks he thinks. No, that is not quite it: it is what he thinks he can stupefy a particularly and unspeakably dull reader into thinking it is what he thinks."

Poor Professor Dowden may have been sorry that he ever thought of defending his idol (and Twain's) by the simple process of blaming Shelley's defection on Harriet's faults. Clemens produced evidence of another mistress of Shelley accepting far larger gifts for her bankrupt father. "First and last, Shelley emptied into that rapacious mendicant's lap a sum which cost him — for he borrowed it at ruinous rates — from eighty to one hundred thousand dollars." This was Mary Godwin's father, while she rode in the best of private carriages on the Continent — and wasn't there some affinity with Clemens' financial woes? There is a summary of the whole Godwin ménage, also, painted in brilliant colors by the remorseless (and infatuated) Clemens. Mary Wollstonecraft Godwin was another child-bride; but English children in those days were rather precocious. "Yes, Shelley had found this child of sixteen to his liking, and had wooed and won her in the graveyard." But that is nothing, so Clemens said. "It was better than wooing her in her nursery, at any rate, where it might have disturbed the other children."

But she was a child in years only. "From the day that she set her masculine grip on Shelley he was to frisk no more. If she had only occupied the kind and gentle Harriet's place in March it would have been a thrilling spectacle to see her invade the Boinville rookery and read the riot act. That holiday of Shelley's would have been of short duration, and Cornelia's hair would have been as gray as her mother's when the services were over."

Thus, if Twain's "Defence of Harriet Shelley" was such an uneven but inspired piece of writing, it was because there was a curious affinity between these two very different-looking poets, while Clemens was engrossed by that earlier literary scene he was pretending to excoriate — and Professor Dowden was both the scapegoat of the piece and immortalized by it. In the same volume was another better known piece of Mark Twain's literary criticism, "Fenimore Cooper's Literary Offenses."

Quoting Professors Lounsbury and Brander Matthews on Cooper's books, Clemens concluded they could not have read them. "Cooper's art has some defects. In one place in *Deerslayer,* and in the restricted space of two-thirds of a page, Cooper has scored 114 offenses against literary art out of a possible 115. It breaks the record . . . There are nineteen rules governing literary art in the domain of romantic fiction — some say twenty-two. In *Deerslayer* Cooper violated eighteen of them." Clemens went on to list these rules and these faults in elaborate detail of which I can only quote a few examples. Rule number three, he claimed, required "that the personage in a tale shall be alive, except in the case of corpses, and that always the reader shall be able to tell the corpses from the others.

But this detail has often been overlooked in the *Deerslayer* tale."
Rule number four required "that the personages in a tale, both
dead and alive, shall exhibit a sufficient excuse for being there.
But this detail also has been overlooked in the *Deerslayer*
tale." Rule number five required "that when the personages deal
in conversation,"

> the talk shall sound like human talk, and be talk such as human
> beings would be likely to talk in the given circumstances, and have
> a discoverable meaning, also a discoverable purpose, and a show of
> relevancy, and remain in the neighborhood of the subject in hand,
> and be interesting to the reader, and help out the tale, and stop
> when the people cannot think of anything more to say. But this
> requirement has been ignored from the beginning of the *Deerslayer*
> tale to the end of it.

Rule number seven was in effect an amplification of number
five, and required "that when a personage talks like an illustrated, gilt-edged, tree-calf, hand-tooled seven-dollar *Friendship's Offering* in the beginning of a paragraph, he shall not
talk like a Negro minstrel in the end of it. But this rule is flung
down and danced upon in the *Deerslayer* tale." In addition to
these larger rules, Clemens added, there were some little rules
requiring that the author shall:

12. *Say* what he is proposing to say, not merely come near it.
13. Use the right word, not its second cousin.
14. Eschew surplusage.
15. Not omit necessary details.
16. Avoid slovenliness of form.
17. Use good grammar.
18. Employ a simple and straightforward style.

But even these minor rules were coldly and persistently violated in *Deerslayer,* said Clemens, and he went on to write one

of the most entertaining analyses of Fenimore Cooper's literary art that has ever been penned. (It is a wonder that Cooper's books survived this attack, and one is not quite sure that they did.) Clemens talked about Cooper's gift of invention. "In his little box of stage-properties he kept six or eight cunning devices, tricks, artifices for his savages and woodsmen to deceive and circumvent each other with, and he was never so happy as when he was working these innocent things and seeing them go. A favorite one was to make a moccasined person tread in the tracks of a moccasined enemy, and thus hide his own trail. Cooper wore out barrels and barrels of moccasins in working that trick."

There was Cooper's broken twig which Clemens described. "It is a restful chapter in any book of his when somebody doesn't step on a dry twig and alarm all the reds and whites for two hundred yards around. Every time a Cooper person is in peril, and absolute silence is worth four dollars a minute, he is sure to step on a dry twig . . ." Then there was Cooper about the sea, as about the forest; and Cooper as artillery expert in the episode when a cannonball lands directly at the feet of Natty Bumppo and the Cooper "females." "To the females this suggests nothing. The case is very different with the admirable Bumppo. I wish I may never know peace again if he doesn't strike out promptly and *follow the track* of that cannon-ball across the plain through a dense fog and find the fort. Isn't it a daisy? If Cooper had any real knowledge of Nature's ways of doing things, he had a most delicate art in concealing the fact. For instance: one of his acute Indian experts, Chingachgook (pronounced Chicago, I think) has lost the trail of a person he is tracking through the forest . . ."

Clemens went on to detail the exploits of Cooper's "Chicago," and dwelt at some length on a river which changed its proportions from page to page according to Cooper's plot needs — a river, a stream, a lake, all depending on Cooper's "richness of invention." "Cooper's eye was splendidly inaccurate. Cooper seldom saw anything correctly. He saw nearly all things as through a glass eye, darkly." Then there is Cooper as architect of a famous canalboat being attacked by six Indians who all misjudge the distance. Then comes Cooper on Indians: "Other Indians would have noticed these things, but Cooper's Indians never notice anything. Cooper thinks they are marvelous creatures for noticing, but he was almost always in error about his Indians. There was seldom a sane one among them."

There is a discussion of Deerslayer–Hawkeye–Long-Rifle–Leatherstocking–Pathfinder–Bumppo performing their prodigies of marksmanship; and Mark Twain returned to the opening theme of this essay — Cooper's style. "Cooper's word-sense was singularly dull. When a person has a poor ear for music he will flat and sharp right along without knowing it. He keeps near the tune, but it is *not* the tune." After more examples of Cooper's stylistic eccentricities, and some further mention of Professor Lounsbury — "There have been daring people in the world who claimed that Cooper could write English, but they are all dead now — all dead but Lounsbury" — Clemens came to his own conclusion:

"Now I feel sure, deep down in my heart, that Cooper wrote about the poorest English that exists in our language, and that the English of *Deerslayer* is the very worst that even Cooper ever wrote . . . I may be mistaken, but it does seem to me that *Deerslayer* is not a work of art in any sense; it does seem to me that it is destitute of every detail that goes to the making of a work of art; in truth, it seems to me that *Deerslayer* is just simply a literary *delirium tremens*."

What did Mark Twain leave to the credit of North America's

first famous novelist and artist? Not much, it would seem. In the same volume of literary essays there was Mark Twain's description of "Stirring Times in Austria," in 1897, which in turn led him into "Concerning the Jews." Now this essay has had a long history of controversy — as to Twain's anti-semitism — in sectarian circles and also in those groups of liberal purists who would outlaw *Huck Finn* from the libraries because its hero is called Nigger Jim. Unlike Shakespeare's Shylock, Jim *is* a hero, if in what may now seem at times to be a paternalistic view of the heroic slave. (How much of this was a put-on by Clemens for the sake of his story, we have already discussed.) But in the controversial essay Clemens manifested some of the typical prejudices which have existed in American literature and culture about "The Jew." Perhaps at this period of his life, this was his single remaining area of ignorance and prejudice about the "inferior" — or in this case precisely because he felt the Jews were *superior* — races. He was probably wrong in not attributing anti-Semitism to Christian prejudice. Since then it has been demonstrated all too clearly that Hitlerism was the end product of over a thousand years of anti-Semitism in Christian religious thought and teaching. What was at stake in the Nazi holocaust was not merely the lives of the Jews but the fate of Christianity itself, in its extreme moment, and also the destiny of a so-called Christian Europe.

But Clemens was accurate and persuasive when he attributed the fear and hatred of Jews to economic causes where, just as in modern colonialism, financial gain could be linked with moral hypocrisy; though he was perhaps overgenerous in attributing to all Jews the virtues that only some possessed. He did not really understand the meaning of the whole heritage of Jewish culture in the historical epoch of Judeo-Christian civilization — but he was also open to suggestion and quick to correct his own ignorance. Perhaps, all in all, this particular essay should be regarded as a typical example of *American* thinking about the Jews, in an area where Clemens had admittedly not done much thinking for himself; and one should compare Twain's relatively "advanced" views about the Jews with the embedded anti-Semitism of Henry James and Edith Wharton in the same period; and of Willa Cather and Ernest Hemingway — even of Theodore Dreiser and Thomas Wolfe — in a later and supposedly emancipated period.

In any study of the vein of anti-Semitism that has run through the American novel ever since the tides of European immigration began in the 1880s and 1890s — a study which would be of particular interest, and one which hasn't, to my knowledge, yet been done — Mark Twain would come off not too badly. Our only regret should be that this master artist does not come off better; and the protruding edges of Twain's opinions about the Jews show, perhaps, how deeply this strand of prejudice is woven into our whole cultural fabric.*

In some versions of "Concerning the Jews," even Twain's famous quip, "A Jew is also a human being; worse I could say of no man," is watered down for fear of further controversy. In the ending sections of *In Defense of Harriet Shelley,* there are some casual sketches "About All Kinds of Ships" where Clemens returns to his earliest love in passages which recall the glow-

* In the post World War II period of American literature, particularly during the 1950s, in some sort of acknowledgment of and atonement for this fact, there was almost a school of "Jewish writing" in the United States, including such popular authors as Saul Bellow, Bernard Malamud, and Philip Roth. But the Jewish hero of this writing is generally an assimilated white American Jew, who moves uneasily between his lost spiritual heritage and the successful, conformist, and material values of American society. One looks in vain for any novels like Henry Roth's *Call It Sleep,* written during the 1930s. In the whole series of these so-called Jewish novels, one looks in vain, indeed, for the traditional values of social criticism and social justice that are the central content not only of the Judeo-Christian heritage, but of American literature itself.

ing pages of *Life on the Mississippi*. There is a curious and mor-
bid little piece of "science-fiction" almost dreamlike in essence
(Clemens was playing with this genre of tales in his later period and in unpublished works) called "From the 'London
Times' of 1904" which carried a satiric undertheme of the
Dreyfus case and of his own friendship with the Austrian inventor Szezepanik. Shades of the Paige typesetting machine;
Clemens was still toying with magical inventions. Sam Sellers
Clemens had planned, as we've noticed, to organize an international cartel to control the rights of Szezepanik's carpet-pattern
machine.

There is a comic little account here of the Dr. Johnson–Dr.
James *Dictionary of Medicine*. Published as it was during the
Scottish-English rebellion of 1745, Clemens remarked that "If it
had been sent against the Pretender's troops there probably
wouldn't have been a survivor. In 1861 this deadly book was
still working, working the cemeteries — down in Virginia. For
three generations and a half it had been going quietly along,
enriching the earth with its slain. Up to its last free day it was
trusted and believed in, and its devastating advice taken, as was
shown by notes inserted between its leaves. But our troops captured it and brought it home, and it has been out of business
since." And with this casual reference to "our troops" during
the American Civil War, Clemens had also repudiated the prejudices, more than medical, of his own Southern lineage.

The Curious Republic of Gondour, in 1919, was a reprint of
an early essay when both Howells and Twain were endeavoring
to reform the ways of the Democracy — in this case the matter
of the right to vote. In 1922 *The Mysterious Stranger* of 1916
was reprinted as the title story of *The Mysterious Stranger and
Other Stories,* but the other stories were of little consequence.
And in 1923 came *Europe and Elsewhere,* a diversified collec-

tion of essays containing some reprinted, some remarkable new material. Professor Brander Matthews' "An Appreciation" in this volume was originally his "Biographical Criticism" used as the introduction to the Uniform Edition of Mark Twain's Works in 1899. But in either case it was an example of a classical academic critic trying to describe a natural phenomenon. Paine's introduction to *The Mysterious Stranger* also included some uneasy allusions, if not euphemisms, about Twain's radical essays in this volume.

This collection was also a catchall of Twain's occasional essays starting back as early as 1870 with his editorials for the Buffalo *Express*. There was a curiously mixed piece, in the early seventies, about the Temperance Crusade and Woman's Rights in which Clemens half admired and half satirized these militant female reformers — he wanted them to vote but not to censor. There is a long series of letters written for the New York *Herald* on the elaborate English reception for the Shah of Persia, where Clemens was again half impressed, half satiric, but as yet innocent of the true nature of the celebration. Well, not quite: Mark Twain is always full of surprises, and there is a knife-edged final section on the economic concessions which the Shah had given to "the ingenious Baron Reuter." As early as this, Clemens noted that Persia's railways, land, mines, forests, customs, banks, and manufacturing enterprises had all been handed over to the pioneer German newsgatherer and financial wizard.

"It is a good 'concession' in its way," Clemens remarked. "It seems to make the Shah say: 'Run Persia at my expense and give me a fifth of the profits.' One's first impulse is to envy the baron; but, after all, I do not know. Some day, if things do not go to suit the Shah, he may say, 'There is no head I admire as much as this baron's; bring it to me on a plate.' " Only the later Mark Twain would realize that Baron Reuter was not taking on so much of a personal risk as it then appeared.

Following this essay is one of the "Letters to Satan." (Satan becomes not merely Twain's confidante in these later years, but in Jungian terms, say, the earlier-repressed but now reversed and dominant half of Twain's soul; and in Rankian terms, more accurately, the repressed primitive soul which took rightful power over the "rational" social soul.) There were some further references to English imperialism, and in particular to England's great empire builder in Africa. "I will close . . . by saying that I was charmed with England and sorry to leave it. It is easy to do business there. I carried out all of Your Grace's instructions, and did it without difficulty. I doubted if it was needful to grease Mr. Cecil Rhodes' palm any further, for I think he would serve you just for the love of it; still, I obeyed your orders in the matter."

> I made him Permanent General Agent for South Africa, got him and his South African Company whitewashed by the Committee of Inquiry, and promised him a dukedom. I also continued the European Concert in office, without making any change in its material. In my opinion this is the best material for the purpose that exists outside of Your Grace's own personal Cabinet. It coddles the Sultan, it has defiled and degraded Greece, it has massacred a hundred thousand Christians in Armenia and a splendid multitude of them in Turkey, and has covered civilization and the Christian name with imperishable shame. If Your Grace would instruct me to add the Concert to the list of your publicly acknowledged servants, I think it would have a good effect. The Foreign Offices of the whole European world are now under your sovereignty, and little attentions like this would keep them so.

In the following essay, "A Word of Encouragement for Our Blushing Exiles," Clemens admitted his earlier error about the "Liberation of Cuba" in the Spanish-American war. He admitted that the United States had meddled with the private affairs of a sister nation "under a sham humanitarian pretext."

And that the United States was doing this in order to filch Cuba — "the formal and distinct disclaimer in the ultimatum being very, very thin humbug, and easily detectable as such . . ." And finally he told these Blushing Exiles: "You are ashamed of all this because it is new, and base, and brutal, and dishonest . . . We? Land thieves? We? Shedders of innocent blood? We? Traitors to our official word?" Yet he went on to compare modern American imperialism to Europe's, to Russia's, France's and particularly Spain's. "Is she remembering with pride how she sent Columbus home in chains; how she sent half of the harmless West Indians into slavery and the rest into the grave, leaving not one alive; how she robbed and slaughtered the Inca's gentle race, then beguiled the Inca into her power with fair promises and burned him at the stake; how she drenched the New World in blood, and earned and got the name of 'The Nation with the Bloody Footprint'; how she drove all the Jews out of Spain, allowing them to sell their property, but forbidding them to carry any money out of the country; how she roasted heretics by the thousands and thousands in her public squares, generation after generation, her kings and her priests looking on as at a holiday show; how her Holy Inquisition imported hell into the earth . . . how, with a spirit unmodified by time, she still tortures her prisoners to-day; how, with her ancient passion for pain and blood unchanged, she still crowds the arena with ladies and gentlemen and priests to see with delight a bull harried and persecuted and a gored horse dragging his entrails on the ground; and how, with this incredible character surviving all attempts to civilize it, her Duke of Alva rises again in the person of General Weyler — today the most idolized personage in Spain — and we see a hundred thousand women and children shut up in pens and pitilessly starved to death?"

It is curious incidentally that Hemingway, who derived so

much from Mark Twain's prose, learned so little from his spirit. But then Hemingway had nothing of Twain's historical knowledge or social concern, while he had all the attributes of the high individualist in a later and more decadent culture. And the United States was simply a late-comer (though not quite so late as Clemens believed) to the grand consort of imperialistic Christian European nations which had indeed celebrated the discovery of the "New World" in blood and gold. Also in *Europe and Elsewhere* was the first printing of the "United States of Lyncherdom" which we have already discussed, and about which the good Albert Bigelow Paine, printing it at long last, was still somewhat evasive. "The article was not offered for publication, perhaps, because the moment of timeliness had passed. Its general timeliness, however, is perennial and a word from 'America's foremost private citizen' on the subject is worthy of presentation." As indeed this essay was worth publishing; and as perhaps, who knows, if Paine had not published it in 1923, and if, still later, it had fallen into the hands of the Cold War critics of the 1950s, it would still remain unpublished. In this group of essays, was the first book publication of Mark Twain's celebrated "Greetings to the Twentieth Century" and of the famous essay (again discussed earlier in these pages) called *To the Person Sitting in Darkness,* and Mark Twain's subsequent rejoinder to the American Board of Foreign Missions, "To My Missionary Critics."

It was an effective rejoinder which disclosed among other things how the American-Christian missionaries in China, after the Boxer revolt had been quelled, resorted to the looting which was prohibited to the soldiers. For the greater glory of God, as Clemens added, and so that "For a century to come Chinese converts will consider looting and vengeance Christian virtues." Here, moreover, Clemens carried his attack over the head of the

notorious Reverend Dr. Ament to the Secretary of the American
Missionary Board itself, the Reverend Dr. Judson Smith. "I am
not blaming Dr. Smith for these discrepancies — it would not
be right, it would not be fair. I make the proper allowances. He
has not been a journalist, as I have been — a trade wherein a
person is brought to book by the rest of the press so often for
divergencies that, by and by, he gets to be almost morbidly
afraid to indulge in them. It is so with me. I always have the
disposition to tell what is not so; I was born with it; we all have
it. But I try not to do it now, because I have found out that
it is unsafe. But with the Doctor of course it is different."

Indeed he carried his vitriolic satire of the missionaries in
China over the head of the Reverend Dr. Judson Smith to the
American Missionary Board itself.

The only way the Board could justify its own behavior in con-
doning the anti-Christian actions of its foreign agents, in justi-
fying their thefts and extortions from the poverty-stricken
Chinese villages, Clemens asserted, was to revise the Ten Commandments, and bring them down to date for use in pagan
lands. For example: *"Thou shalt not steal* — except when it is
the custom of the country . . ."" "I am not meaning to object
to the substitution of pagan customs for Christian, here and
there and now and then, when the Christian ones are incon-
venient. No; I like it and admire it. I do it myself. And I admire the alertness of the Board in watching out for chances to
trade Board morals for Chinese morals, and get the best of the
swap":

For I cannot endure those people, they are yellow, and I have never
considered yellow becoming. I have always been like the Board —
perfectly well-meaning, but destitute of the Moral Sense. Now,
one of the main reasons why it is so hard to make the Board un-

derstand that there is no moral difference between a big filch and a little filch, but only a legal one, is that vacancy in its make-up. Morally, there are no degrees in stealing. The Commandment merely says, "Thou shalt not *steal*," and stops there. It doesn't recognize any difference between stealing a third and stealing thirteenfold.

In the "recapitulation" of his arguments against the American Missionary Board, Clemens even absolved the Board, and Dr. Smith, and the original villain of his essay, the Reverend Dr. Ament. "But there is no need to sum up. Mr. Ament has acknowledged the 'one third extra' — no other witness is necessary. The Reverend Dr. Smith has carefully considered the act and labeled it with a stern name, and his verdict seems to have no flaw in it. The morals of the act are Chinese, but are approved by the Board, and by some of the clergy and some of the newspapers, as being a valuable improvement upon Christian ones — which leaves me with a closed mouth, though with a pain in my heart."

Of course, Mark Twain was play-acting here, since he had already acknowledged that "pagan Chinese morals" were far superior to Christian ones, or to the rule of the white man's "civilization" in its colonial aspects. In another key essay first published in *Europe and Elsewhere,* he was in a darker and more desperate mood. "As Regards Patriotism" opened with the argument that in absolute monarchies patriotism was furnished from the throne, cut and dried; but in England and America "it is furnished, cut and dried, to the citizen by the politician":

The newspaper-and-politician-manufactured Patriot often gags in private over his dose; but he takes it, and keeps it on his stomach the best he can. Blessed are the meek.

And Clemens concluded that these mass-made patriots in England and America were not really to blame for their training. "For many a year — perhaps always — the training of the two nations has been dead against independence in political thought, persistently inhospitable toward patriotism manufactured on a man's own premises. Patriotism reasoned out in the man's own head and fire-assayed and tested and proved in his own conscience. The resulting Patriotism was a shopworn product procured at second-hand. The Patriot did not know just how or when or where he got his opinions, neither did he care, so long as he was with what seemed the majority — which was the main thing, the safe thing, the comfortable thing." What may strike you here, if you have had the experience of opposing popular opinion, is how acutely Mark Twain described "the main thing, the safe thing, the comfortable thing," on the part of the great majority — and the bitter-sweet emotions of isolation and alienation; the hostile pride which accompanies the possession of unpopular truth.

It was all a matter of social conditioning, he said. "Training does wonderful things." It had led the people of the United States into supporting the Mexican War which they had opposed at first; in the Civil War it had made the North — which was originally "indifferent to slavery and friendly to the slave interests" — commit itself to the destruction of slavery. "There is nothing that training cannot do," so Clemens concluded. "Nothing is above its reach or below it. It can turn bad morals to good, good morals to bad; it can destroy principles, it can recreate them; it can debase angels to men and lift men to angelship. And it can do any one of these miracles in a year — even in six months."

After the contemporary epoch of civilizational reversion, these dark words can hardly be denied; yet oddly enough, this view of man as the product of social conditioning held within it, also, all the hope of revolutionary change. Rather like the dominant thinkers of the late nineteenth century, as for example in Zola's Naturalism, Clemens placed almost too little value on the element of heredity in this formulation. But he did not make the twentieth century's error of contending that environmental "training" led only to evil; an evil which was inherent in man's soul. That is the most fatal and degrading and enervating doctrine of all, implicit in all decadent cultures. For Mark Twain concluded that men *could* be trained to "manufacture their own Patriotism . . . They can be trained to labor it out in their own heads and hearts and in the privacy and independence of their own premises." And in the very next essay, "Dr. Loeb's Incredible Discovery," he mounted another demonstration against mass opinion, against the "consensus" of even scientific authorities.

He pointed out that all of the great discoveries in science, religion, medicine, the arts had been achieved despite the "consensus" of that time — or the "Established opinion" of any historical epoch, the established opinion which was always wrong — and in telling the tale of this, he became vehement: "This is warm work! It puts my temperature up to 106 and raises my pulse to the limit. It always works just so when the red rag of a Consensus jumps my fence and starts across my pasture. I have been a Consensus more than once myself, and I know the business — and its vicissitudes . . . These sorrows have made me suspicious of Consensuses. Do you know, I tremble and the goose flesh rises on my skin every time I encounter one, now. I sheer warily off and get behind something, saying to myself, 'It looks innocent and all right, but no matter, ten to one there's a cyanide process under that thing somewhere.' "

I have said that in these later essays of Mark Twain, one notices his prose has become more and more colloquial, homely, personal, and vivid; he will tell us more about this prose style in the pages of the *Autobiography*. In the present book, there followed another dialogue of Mark Twain's, "The Dervish and the Offensive Stranger," about the nature of illusion and reality, intention and deed, and causes and effects operating in the historical process. It discussed the extermination of the American Indians as the price of "civilization" in the New World; passed through the good and evil of the French Revolution; continued up to the Boers and the Philippines.

But just as in *The Mysterious Stranger,* Mark Twain's "cynicism" here was marked again by a kind of diabolical wit and humor. "In our well-meant effort to lift up the Filipino to our own moral altitude with a musket," says the Offensive Stranger, "we have slipped on the ice and fallen down to his." This, says the Dervish, is a large evil result. But, says the Stranger, as an offset we are a World Power. "Give me time," answers the Dervish, "I must think this one over. Pass on."

"By help of three hundred thousand soldiers and eight hundred million dollars," says the Stranger, "England has succeeded in her good purpose of lifting up unwilling Boers and making them better and purer and happier than they could ever have become by their own devices." Certainly, says the Dervish, that is a good result. "But there are only eleven Boers left now," says the Stranger, and take one more instance: "With the best intentions the missionary has been laboring in China for eighty years." "The evil result is —" asks the Dervish. "That nearly a hundred thousand Chinamen have acquired our Civilization." And the good result is? asks the Dervish: "That by the compassion of God four hundred millions have escaped it," answers the Offensive Stranger, kin to Satan and to Mark Twain.

And then *Europe and Elsewhere* draws to a close with more variations on "That Day in Eden" in both Adam's and Eve's reflections on the Fall. How that primal scene haunted Samuel Clemens in his later years and how often he toyed with it in his fancy. The Fall: the advent of Sin and the shame of the innocent flesh; the start of "morality" and "civilization" through the relinquishment of innocence and pleasure and joy; the establishment of prohibitions and repressions in man's soul, the advent of work, suffering, sorrow, and death in the carefree realm of animal nature! That was the origin, too, of Man's "Moral Sense" which Mark Twain derided as being so hypocritical, so alien to the other animals, and which had corrupted human nature under the guise of elevating it. In this regard, if Henry James was a petty voyeur as to the human condition, we might say that Sam Clemens was a kind of cosmic peeper. Where had man gone wrong? What was the true destiny of man which finally Twain had embodied in the Satan who was the acknowledged agent of revolt against God (morality, society): the symbol of sin, of the underground cult of fertility, of sexual pleasure and emotional release? What was the great hold on the human spirit of all those world religions which had *preceded* the Judeo-Christian ethics; which indeed both Christianity and Judaism had absorbed within them while subtly trying to change the whole nature of primitive man? And notice that "primitive man," so beneficent when free and functioning, so evil and sadistic and cruel when repressed, still forms the emotional matrix of so-called civilized man.

Without quite realizing the nature of the edenic enigma which possessed him, Mark Twain realized that somewhere in this area was the missing key to all that concerned his own temperament and art, his own view of humanity, society, and civilization.

The portraits of Adam and Eve are a study in the primary narcissism which betokens the unconscious pleasure in the functioning of the animal organism. The comfort and joy of the animal world, that is, before the separation of the individual organism from the rest of nature and nature's harmony. How Twain's true ancestors delight in their innocent fleshly grace; while here they receive unknowingly the first blow of civilization: clothes.

In other words, their knowledge of Good, Evil, and Death. "That Day in Eden" is purportedly a passage from Satan's Diary (read: Clemens') in which the Angel tells Eve her fate before she eats the fruit. "But it is just as I said — you would not know any better; you have no idea of duty, command, obedience; they have no meaning for you . . . In your present estate you are in no possible way responsible for anything you do or say or think. It is impossible for you to do wrong, for you have no more notion of right and wrong than the other animals have. You and they can do only right; whatever you and they do is right and innocent. It is a divine estate, the loftiest and purest attainable in heaven and in earth. It is the angel gift. The angels are wholly pure and sinless, for they do not know right from wrong, and all the acts of such are blameless. No one can do wrong without knowing how to distinguish between right and wrong."

The angel state indeed! the lost paradise of man which figures so constantly in the work, the dreams and myths of all our writers — and whose secret Mark Twain was surely the closest of all to approach. And note that it is Satan speaking, and Satan, knowing this crucial distinction, is still an angel; is in fact the crucial dark and mysterious Angel of human history. It was again the moral sense which was the creator of wrong, Clemens declared; for "wrong cannot exist until the Moral Sense brings it into being." And in every profound sense he was right; because the growth and development of civilization itself entailed greater and greater injury to the original, beneficent natural harmony of animal existence. Adam is indifferent to the satanic injunction, he is always rather dumb in Mark Twain's fancy, but Eve eats the apple . . . and suddenly shows her hundred years of age. "All this the fair boy saw: then loyally and bravely he took the apple and tasted it, saying nothing."

Now these fancies of angelic bliss were written at the time of Livy's breakdown and the threat to the Clemens' marriage. There is no doubt that the peculiar aura of innocence, tenderness, delight, and tragedy with which Mark Twain imbued his picture of the edenic Fall, and his Eve in particular, was closely connected with his own sense of past pleasure, and imminent or future disaster in the Clemenses' family life. In most of these sketches Livy was definitely the prototype of Twain's Eve. And thus the native frontier artist had linked himself not merely with Satan but with the beginnings of creation, the great delight and pleasure of pure existence before the tragic exile from the Garden of life.

Here Sam Clemens himself embodied the creative narcissism he described in primitive organisms; he identified himself directly (as in some measure all artists do) with the shape of all nature. As he did with Satan as the prankster-creator of life, and with the Garden of Eden as the earliest sanctuary (the native essence) of creation. Yet Mark Twain's Eve still cannot conceive herself to be wicked! "I am as I am; I did not make myself." And what overtones of lost innocence, lost happiness, there still are in her plea to a remorseless, an uncomprehending "God" of morality, society, and civilization:

They drove us from the Garden with their swords of flame, the fierce cherubim. And what had we done? We meant no harm. We were ignorant, and did as any other children might do . . .

They drove us out. Drove us out into this harsh wilderness, and shut the gates against us. We that had meant no harm. It is three months. We were ignorant then; we are rich in learning, now — ah, how rich! We know hunger, thirst, and cold; we know pain, disease, and grief; we know hate, rebellion, and deceit; we know remorse, the conscience that prosecutes guilt and innocence alike, making no distinction; we know weariness of body and spirit, the unrefreshing sleep, the rest which rests not, the dreams which restore Eden, and banish it again with the waking; we know misery; we know torture and the heartbreak; we know humiliation and insult; we know indecency, immodesty, and the soiled mind; we know the scorn that attaches to the transmitted image of God exposed unclothed to the day; we know fear; we know vanity, folly, envy, hypocrisy, we know irreverence; we know blasphemy; we know right from wrong, and how to avoid the one and do the other; we know all the rich product of the Moral Sense and it is our possession. Would we could sell it for one hour of Eden and white purity; would we could degrade the animals with it! . . . We have it all — that treasure. All but death. Death . . . Death. What may that be?

What a catalogue of man's infirmities! And what a falling-off of man is contained in this lament of Eve's; and how deeply Mark Twain had plumbed both the innocence of the Garden and the sorrows of exile. It is Satan who utters the last word in this beautiful homily of "That Day in Eden," after the incident of Cain and Abel. "Death has entered the world, the creatures are perishing; one of The Family is fallen; the product of the Moral Sense is complete. The Family think ill of death — they will change their minds."

There are a few more casual essays in *Europe and Elsewhere* and another diversionary essay on "Adam's Soliloquy" in which Twain's Ancestor is inspecting the dinosaur at the Museum of Natural History in New York City, and speaks a kind of Cockney English which he calls "heavenly." There is a Twainian aside on babies who have not changed in three hundred thousand years: "The same insufficiency of hair, the same absence of teeth, the same feebleness of body and apparent vacancy of mind, the same general unattractiveness all around." And yet he recalls that Eve's look of adoring motherhood is precisely the same in the present baby's mother. "To think that so subtle and intangible a thing as a *look* could flit and flash from face to face down a procession three hundred thousand years long . . ." It is almost as though Sam Clemens were beguiling us with his soft tenderness, humor, charm, his playful fancy and nostalgic sorrow over the Fall of man — just before the furious tirade entitled "Bible Teaching and Religious Practice." Religion had its share in the changes of civilization and national character, Clemens said here. "What share? The lion's." In the history of the human race, religion had been and would be dominant to the end of time: "or at least until man by the slow processes of evolution shall develop into something really fine and high — some billions of years hence, say."

Clemens went on to state that the Christian's Bible is a drug store, and for eighteen hundred years medical practice had remained almost the same. "The dull and ignorant physician day and night, and all the days and all the nights, drenched his patient with vast and hideous doses of the most repulsive drugs to be found in the store's stock; he bled him, cupped him, purged him, puked him, salivated him, never gave his system a chance to rally, nor nature a chance to help. He kept him religion sick for eighteen centuries, and allowed him not a well day during all that time. The stock in the store was made up of about equal portions of baleful and debilitating poisons, and healing and comforting medicines; but the practice of the time confined the physician to the use of the former; by consequences, he could only damage his patient, and that is what he did."

The Church, Clemens pointed out, had never changed any of its practices until popular opinion forced it to. "The patient fell to doctoring himself, and the physician's practice began to fall off." First it was the daily dose of hell and damnation, then only on Sundays, then the replacement of Christ's love and compassion instead. He went on, this eloquent and outraged atheist — who still held himself responsible for Livy's loss of faith in her final crisis, and nevertheless went on with his own Luciferian indictments of organized religion — to deal with the Church and the slave trade. "In all the ages the Roman Church has owned slaves, bought and sold slaves, authorized and encouraged her children to trade in them. Long after some Christian peoples had freed the slaves, the Church still held on to hers . . . So unassailable was her position that in all the centuries she had no word to say against human slavery."

Clemens presented a brief history of England, along with Rome, on the matter of slavery: of Christian England, clerical and monarchical, until at long last an illegitimate Christian rose against slavery. "It is curious that when a Christian rises against a rooted wrong at all, he is usually an illegitimate Christian, member of some despised and bastard sect." He summarized the American record on the same issue, not much more leniently, and went on to record the history of Christianity and witches.

During many ages there were witches. The Bible said so. The Bible commanded that they should not be allowed to live. Therefore the Church, after doing its duty in but a lazy and indolent way for eight hundred years, gathered up its halters, thumbscrews, and firebrands, and set about its holy work in earnest. She worked hard at it night and day during nine centuries and imprisoned, tortured, hanged, and burned whole hordes and armies of witches, and washed the Christian world clean with their foul blood.

Then it was discovered, Clemens added, that there was no such thing as witches, and never had been. "One does not know whether to laugh or to cry . . ." And he pointed out that in all the Biblical texts used to rationalize and authorize the deep-rooted wrongs in the world, man had never once expunged a *good* and useful one. The result seemed to him dimly encouraging. "It does certainly seem to suggest that if man continues in the direction of enlightenment, his religious practice may, in the end, attain some semblance of human decency."

Following this diatribe, *Europe and Elsewhere* also contained the famous "War Prayer" which Clemens dictated around 1904–05.

The scene of this essay was a time of great and exalting excitement. "The country was up in arms, the war was on, in every breast burned the holy fire of patriotism." It was indeed a glad and gracious time, said Clemens, "and the half dozen rash spirits that ventured to disapprove of the war and cast a doubt upon its righteousness straightway got such a stern and angry warning that for their personal safety's sake they quickly shrank out of sight and offended no more in that way." The Sunday church services were packed with the visionary volunteers — "their young faces alight with marital dreams" — and their adoring sweethearts, proud families and friends, while in the prayer God the Father was beseeched to watch over the army and encourage them to victory. "Bless our arms, grant us this victory, O Lord our God, Father and Protector of our land and flag." Into this scene erupts still another "stranger" of Mark Twain's — one of those strangers, those aliens, exiles, and satanic angels — who ascends the pulpit with the statement that he comes from the Throne and bears a direct message from God as to the consequences of their war prayer in both the spoken and unspoken parts. "Upon the listening spirit of God the Father fell also the unspoken part of the prayer. He commandeth me to put it into words. Listen!"

O Lord our Father, our young patriots, idols of our hearts, go forth to battle — be Thou near them! With them — in spirit — we also go forth from the sweet peace of our beloved firesides to smite the foe. O Lord our God, help us to tear their soldiers to bloody shreds with our shells; help us to cover their smiling fields with the pale forms of their patriot dead; help us to drown the thunder of the guns with the shrieks of the wounded, writhing in pain; help us to lay waste their humble homes with a hurricane of fire; help us to wring the hearts of their unoffending widows with unavailing grief; help us to turn them out roofless with their little children to wander unfriended the wastes of their desolated land in rags and hunger and thirst, sports of the sun flames of the summer and the icy winds of winter, broken in spirit, worn with travail, imploring Thee for the refuge of the grave and denied it — for our sakes who adore Thee, Lord, blast their hopes, blight their lives, protract their bitter pilgrimage, make heavy their steps, water their way with tears, stain the white snow with the blood of their wounded feet! We ask it, in the spirit of love, of Him Who is the Source of Love, and Who is the ever-faithful refuge and friend of all that are sore beset and seek His aid with humble and contrite hearts. Amen.

Desolate and prophetic words indeed that almost seemed to anticipate the precise nature of the war upon a humble nation in Southeast Asia waged by a rich, powerful, arrogant and callous super-power. It was no wonder the "War Prayer" became a favorite sermon among those who protested the Vietnam war in the 1960s as the most shameful war in U.S. history; as the most ruthless, cruel, brutal, and amoral product of the American Empire which Twain himself had foreseen as emerging from the ruins of the Old Republic. During this period of violent anti-war protest among students, liberals and radicals alike, the "War

Prayer" was quoted widely again and again, and reprinted finally as a separate volume.

Here also the "Stranger," the equivalent both of Twain's Satan (exiled man) and of the contemporary "alienated man," asks the Christian congregation if they still want their prayer fulfilled under these repressed, unconscious terms. There was a silence; and — "It was believed afterward that man was a lunatic, because there was no sense in what he said." And the closing essay in *Europe and Elsewhere* is another notable Mark Twain meditation called "Corn-Pone Opinions," written in 1900.

It opened with Clemens' recollection of a childhood friend "whose society was very dear to me because I was forbidden by my mother to partake of it. He was a gay and impudent and satirical and delightful young black man — a slave — who daily preached sermons from the top of his master's woodpile, with me for sole audience. He imitated the pulpit style of the several clergymen of the village and did well, and with fine passion and energy. To me he was a wonder."

Thus Mark Twain's sympathy for, or his affinity with, the black race, almost his deepest affinity, despite some earlier overtones of ignorance, despite a sometimes apparently paternalistic (to us) but actually more esthetic and human view, highly advanced for its own time outside of Abolitionist circles — started in his own as well as Huck Finn's childhood. And this satirical young black preacher had a favorite text: "You tell me whar a man gits his corn pone, en I'll tell what his 'pinions is." This black philosopher's idea was:

> that a man is not independent, and cannot afford views which might interfere with his bread and butter. If he would prosper, he must train with the majority; in matters of large moment, like politics and religion, he must think and feel with the bulk of his

neighbors, or suffer damage in his social standing and in his business prosperities. He must restrict himself to corn-pone opinions — at least on the surface. He must get his opinions from other people; he must reason out none for himself; he must have no first-hand views.

But Clemens also concluded that his boyhood friend Jerry did not go far enough. He went on to do so. He took first the example of women's fashions and man's (women's) instinct for conformity; his and her need for approval, not within oneself, but from other people; or was there any difference? "An empress introduced the hoopskirt, and we know the result. A nobody introduced the bloomer, and we know the result. If Eve should come again, in her ripe renown, and reintroduce her quaint styles — well, we know what would happen. And at first we should be cruelly embarrassed, along at first." He went on to discuss table manners and company manners, fashions in literature, standards of prose writing, morals, religions, politics all embraced by the one law of man's self-approval coming not from himself, but from mass opinion in one form or another. Mohammedans are Mohammedans, he said, because they are born and reared among that sect, not because they have thought it out and can furnish sound reasons for being Mohammedans. "We know why Catholics are Catholics, why Presbyterians are Presbyterians, why Baptists are Baptists, why Mormons are Mormons; why thieves are thieves . . .

"We know it is a matter of association and sympathy, not reasoning and examination; that hardly a man in the world has an opinion upon morals, politics, or religion which he got otherwise than through his associations and sympathies. Broadly speaking there are none but corn-pone opinions. And broadly speaking, corn-pone stands for self-approval. Self-approval is acquired mainly from the approval of other people. The result is con-

formity. Sometimes conformity has a sordid business interest —
the bread-and-butter interest — but not in most cases I think.
I think that in the majority of cases it is unconscious and not calculated; that it is born of the human being's natural yearning to
stand well with his fellows and have their inspiring approval and
praise."

If these ideas were first expressed in the grim and black determinism of *What Is Man?*, we can see the extent to which
the later Mark Twain inflected and declined them, infused them
with an almost sympathetic (mock-ironic) satire and parody,
acute as they also are about the nature of the human animal
. . . But no, Clemens would protest: you should say "the human spirit," set far apart from animal virtue. He went on to
describe how a political emergency involving war and patriotism
brought out corn-pone opinion in its finest form. The first phase
was of that pocketbook variety which had its origin in self-interest — and which Mark Twain rather preferred for its honesty, as
against the sentimental variety of corn-pone which he flayed.
The bigger variety of corn-pone was always sentimental: "the
one which can't bear to be outside the pale; can't bear to be in
disfavor; can't endure the averted face and the cold shoulder;
wants to stand well with his friends, wants to be smiled upon,
wants to be welcome, wants to hear the precious words, '*He's* on
the right track!' Uttered perhaps by an ass, but still an ass of
high degree, an ass whose approval is gold and diamonds to a
smaller ass, and confers glory and honor and happiness, and
membership in the herd. For these gauds many a man will dump
his life-long principles into the street, and his conscience along
with them. We have seen it happen. In some millions of
instances."

Was there an element of personal guilt in these matters, of
self-disgust and self-distrust in these lines? Mark Twain had been

there, yes, of course. But he had been there enough, on *both* sides of the fence, to know what it was like, really, and to infuse these descriptions of human or social behavior with a burning and satiric eloquence. He went on to describe man's affinity for his "party," which in Twain's mind meant also his country, his nationalism, his capitalism, and imperialism.

"Men think they think upon great political questions, and they do; but they think with their party, not independently; they read its literature, but not that of the other side; they arrive at convictions, but they are drawn from a partial view of the matter in hand and are of no particular value. They swarm with their party, they feel with their party, they are happy in their party's approval, and where the party leads they will follow, whether for right and honor, or through blood and dirt and a mush of mutilated morals."

In the context of his time, Twain also mentioned the great silver debate of the nineties in which half the nation believed one view as passionately as the other half believed the other, and not even a tenth part of the people had any reason behind their opinion. "I studied that mighty question to the bottom — came out empty." He included the national conflict over high and low tariffs. "I have deeply studied that question, too — and didn't arrive."

> We all do no end of feeling, and we mistake it for thinking. And out of it we get an aggregation which we consider a boon. Its name is Public Opinion. It is held in reverence. It settles everything. Some think it is the Voice of God.

Thus the bitter-sweet ending of "Corn-Pone Opinions" as the final essay in *Europe and Elsewhere*. But how can you really describe such searching, sardonic essays in a literary genre which Mark Twain developed, perfected, and made his own? The later essays in this remarkable volume are, if you like, great "black" classics — in a vein of depth and despair not merely with society, though surely that, but with the race of man itself. But a depth of despair that is so inextricably woven through with strands of brilliant irony, searing satire, hilarious parody, and even a vein of touching sentiment as to make them unique in our letters; and probably so in world literature. They are written, too, in a kind of "absolute prose," a prose which in its best moments is absolutely right in every word, nuance, and rhythm, and which looks — coming from such a rough, untutored craftsman (they say), such a careless, formless artist — as though Mark Twain had just tossed it off in a fit of divine inspiration.

That is roughly what I mean when I say that *Europe and Elsewhere* represents the second high climax of Mark Twain's radical social criticism. (This whole vein of his work which we know has been rejected by Twain scholars and critics for *their* personal reasons, which were never and could never have been his.) That is the delight he took in writing such essays, which permeates their texture and which affects any reader who cares to read them. Nor was he finished yet; by no means. There was to be a third outpouring of this radical vein emerging as late as the 1950s and 1960s. There was to be another "final period" — with caution we might say "semifinal," since Mark Twain's work is still being unearthed and published as I write — of postmortem publications which would include more of his best work. This unprecedented talent in our culture, just at the moment of its flowering and first signs of social decline, which is usually the moment for such talent to emerge — this demonic angel of an artist made sure, as I've said, to keep the world busy with his presence for a long time. Like Whitman, his brother in native bardic lore, he was the man, he was there. And because of that, he is one of the nineteenth-century writers who is still the most with us today.

ELEVEN

THE STORY OF A LIFE

Most of Mark Twain's work is autobiographical in essence from *Roughing It* and *Life on the Mississippi* to his *Autobiography* in 1924; and the final (semifinal) period of his work was even more directly filled with the personal utterances which are almost always his best statements. Twain was not essentially a novelist or fiction writer; that is why all the criticism concerned with his "formlessness," lack of structure, uneven texture, has little relevance to his work. It takes a bard, a large and various talent, to talk always about himself without tedium, since he is in fact talking about the world with which he is inextricably and pantheistically joined at the very moment he is so separate and original as an individual voice. Clemens had started jotting down notes for the *Autobiography* as early as 1870. In Vienna in the late nineties, solvent again and recognized for the world figure he was, he began jotting down notes of his youth in Missouri: those curious frontier river towns whose color shifts so suddenly from white to black, from innocence to guilt, from Eden to the

Fall, from happy childhood to the unpleasant maturity of both an individual and a nation.

Some years later in Florence, where Livy had gone in a last effort to regain her health, Clemens returned to the *Autobiography,* and again in 1906, linking himself with his amanuensis and future biographer and editor, Albert Bigelow Paine, he set to work in earnest dictating his last work. Paine brought along a secretary, and Clemens talked to a select audience of two, often from his bed. "It was his custom to stay in bed until noon, and he remained there during most of the earlier dictations, clad in a handsome dressing-gown, propped against great snowy pillows . . ." Snowy white pillows, and Mark Twain's famous white suits: symbol of that lost innocence which Clemens still wanted to preserve symbolically; and that "whiteness" which Melville, even more desperate and outraged at the world, inveighed against as the very color of evil, parading as innocence. (Twain, knowing this also, preferred to keep the illusion, which he had also lost.) "He loved this loose luxury and ease," Paine tells us, "and found it conducive to thought," while it was also Clemens' way of avoiding as long as he could the societal straightjacket. It was Bill Nye, Clemens' friend and early associate on the lecture platform, who said he always slept as much as he could, and only regretted he could not carry his bed around with him.

It was in these circumstances that Twain evolved the "formless form" of the *Autobiography,* as an extension of the form he had to a large degree used in all his writing; an early mode of the "stream of consciousness" which became fashionable in the epoch of James Joyce. "Often he did not know until the moment of beginning what was to be his subject for the day," Paine tells us. "Then he was likely to go drifting among his memories in a quite irresponsible fashion, the fashion of table conversation, as he said, the methodless method of the human mind. 'Start at no particular time of your life; wander at your free will all over your life; talk only about the things which interest you for the moment; drop it the moment its interest threatens to pale, and turn your talk upon the new and more interesting thing that has intruded itself into your mind and meantime.' "

But in a certain sense Clemens was conning his confidante Paine in dramatizing this form of the *Autobiography*; in another sense he conned himself into allowing himself too much freedom in using this system of natural thought association. This may be the way that thinking does think itself; this is the source and inspiration of art perhaps, but art is the end product of this source and inspiration when it is formed and disciplined to its own shape, as it is in the best of Mark Twain, too. Clemens was also aware of some of the flaws of pure dictation and free association. "When I was younger I could remember anything, whether it happened or not; but I am getting old and soon I shall remember only the latter."

Paraphrasing Josh Billings, another of the gifted frontier humorists from whom Sam Clemens descended, he added: "It isn't so astonishing the things that I can remember, as the number of things I can remember that aren't so." But he was on safer ground and more profound in the Preface to his final book. "In this Autobiography I shall keep in mind the fact that I am speaking from the grave. I am literally speaking from the grave, because I shall be dead when the book issues from the press . . . I speak from the grave rather than with my living tongue, for a good reason: I can speak thence freely." He declared that all men shrink from expressing their private lives in public, and he argued that "the frankest and freest and privatest product of the human mind and heart is a love letter; the writer gets his limitless freedom of statement and expression from his sense that no stranger is going to see what he is writing. Everybody would hesitate to write such letters if they faced the possibility of publication, Twain added, and such letters indeed were embarrassing when they were published. But yet, "It has seemed to me that I could be as frank and free and unembarrassed as a love letter if I knew that what I was writing would be exposed to no eye until I was dead, and unaware, and indifferent."

These words are as though carved in stone, and it is interesting that Mark Twain concurred with Freud, if unconsciously, when he equated the love letter with death (Eros and "Death Wish") in such a balancing of the life forces.

The earlier sections of the *Autobiography,* titled "Early Fragments, 1870-77," are just that. As in the case of Mark Twain's *Christian Science,* he played and toyed with his subject for around a decade before he got seriously interested and produced, mainly in the second volume of the book, a solid narrative. "What a wee little part of a person's life are his acts and his words!" so Clemens declared in his opening "text" or little sermon. "His real life is led in his head and is known to none but himself. All day long, and every day, the mill of his brain is grinding, and his *thoughts,* not those other things, are his history . . ." He said this to prove that the mass of any man is hidden, that biographies are but the clothing of the true man whose biography cannot be written. But it suggests also that the *work* — the literary production of a writer — rather than his life and actions, is the writer's true biography, his thoughts preserved in his art.

The volume opens with his reflections on "The Tennessee Land," which his father had purchased to make his family wealthy, and which, as the illusion of great sudden, miraculous wealth, pursued Samuel Clemens' life in other guises as well. Written around the later seventies also, the section on Clemens' early life in Florida and Hannibal, Missouri, is beautiful, crisp, nostalgic writing about frontier life in the 1830s. Yet this is broken off shortly by the account of Twain's friendship with General Grant, the days of Grant's power and poverty, the writing of the famous *Memoirs* while the epical hero of the Old Republic was in his terminal illness. This also marked the beginning of Mark Twain's publishing house, the Charles Webster Company whose failure contributed to Twain's bankruptcy in the nineties. Elsewhere Clemens remarked it would have been better if he had been struck dead the moment he decided to publish the *Memoirs*. But the account of Grant himself is touching, warm, affectionate, illuminating, one of the best original sources about this historical figure. The Freudian concept of Grant as a "surrogate father" of Clemens is again nonsensical, since it precludes the notion of mutual friendship between two such different geniuses of the American past. Or even more accurately, Freudism misses the sense of awe, and respect and worship at the base of Clemens' pantheistic temperament; those noble emotions which alone make life worth living, which are also at the core of art; and are viewed always as ignoble "sublimations" to the Freudian orthodoxy — thus making of art and life alike a kind of mean and narrow subterfuge. It is true that Grant was the symbol of that military science which Clemens always derided, ridiculed, and attacked; there was perhaps a touch of vanity and self-justification in the fact that *he,* Mark Twain, was the General's friend and benefactor. But Grant admired *him.*

The memoir of Grant, fascinating as it is, was too close to Clemens' heart in those days, and it takes up too much space in the wrong part of the *Autobiography.* Although, as by some unknown sense of esthetic balance, Clemens followed the long, glowing account of the heroic general by a short biting sketch of the inventor James W. Paige whose typesetting machine cost him a total of $150,000, as Clemens asserted at the time of his writing, and $190,000 in the end, as Paine asserts. This marked the beginning, along with the publishing house, of the financial crisis which was such a critical point in Twain's later life and art. Yet Clemens' account of Paige is still marked by the kind of genial tolerance (amid much malevolent wit) he always accorded to the great frauds and scoundrels of the world with whom he had his secret affinity. Shades of Mary Baker Eddy whom Clemens remorsely pursued with such a love-hate: he still shook his head in puzzled awe over Paige's business behavior. "Paige and I always meet on effusively affectionate terms, and yet he knows perfectly well that if I had him in a steel trap I would shut out all human succor and watch that trap till he died."

The reverse was really true; Paige had Clemens in a trap of steel until the artist, not the inventor, almost died. But here Clemens went back to his childhood once more and to another "false claimant" or "false claim" which had bewitched his family. This was the story of the Clemenses' connection with the American-born English earldom of Fairfax which also figures in Mark Twain's work — and which, along with the Tennessee Land, gave the Clemens family such a false sense of great wealth and hereditary aristocracy. As for Sam, he went back to Noah, so he said, or better yet, to Adam and to Satan. There is an account of Twain's mother's ancestry, including the James Lampton who was the prototype of Colonel Mulberry (or Beriah) Sellers in *The Gilded Age* and elsewhere, and another close relative of Sam Clemens in person and in spirit. There is a glowing account of Uncle John Quarles' farm in Missouri which, whether in fact or in fancy or both, was in effect the true Edenlike home of Clemens' boyhood. A series of American writers, from Edith Wharton to H. L. Mencken and Sinclair Lewis, have condemned and ridiculed the American west; another group including Theodore Dreiser and Sherwood Anderson have looked back upon it with affection and nostalgic sadness. But Mark Twain's description of Missouri life in the *Autobiography* is just about the best thing we have on this scene, western and southwestern, in the national letters. What forces changed his later view of his origins into a blackened and debased literary scene we have already noticed; but here again, toward the close of his life, it shines forth in all its pristine pleasure, joy, and beauty.

Including the Negroes, whom Mark Twain described here with his customary affection and insight. Among the boys, black and white, they were friends and comrades and yet not quite. "Color and condition interposed a subtle line which both parties were conscious of and which rendered complete fusion impossible."

Among the slaves there was the famous "Uncle Dan'l," who was used in several books under his own name and under the better-known name of Jim in *Huck Finn*. And Clemens added frankly: "In my schoolboy days I had no aversion to slavery. I was not aware that there was anything wrong about it. No one arraigned it in my hearing; the local papers said nothing against it; the local pulpit taught us that God approved it, that it was a holy thing, and that the doubter need only look in the Bible if he wished to settle his mind — and then the texts were read aloud to us to make the matter sure; if the slaves themselves had an aversion to slavery, they were wise and said nothing."

Maybe it was in the course of his self-education about slavery that Sam Clemens saw the true nature of the forces of social conformity: the press, the pulpit, the false use of the Bible and Christianity itself. Certainly it was a long way from the slave-owner to the anti-imperialist radical critic of American society; while the issue of human property, of slavery and the darker races, was crucial in the spiritual development of Mark Twain.

And Clemens went on to describe some other details in the texture of frontier life on his uncle's farm, including the caves and
the half-breed "Injun Joe" of *Tom Sawyer*; the snakes, the countryside, the games and sports and accidents of childhood existence there; the practice of medicine and of dentistry in those
days.

In the most nostalgic and pleasing pages of the *Autobiography,* Clemens described "education" in the river towns,
childhood loves (though still either puritanically or curiously
without sexual overtones), and the ritual of childhood smoking.
"As I have said, I spent some part of every year at the farm until
I was twelve or thirteen years old. The life which I led there
with my cousins was full of charm, and so is the memory of it
yet. I can call back the solemn twilight and mystery of the deep
woods, the earthy smells, the faint odors of the wild flowers, the
sheen of rain-washed foliage, the rattling clatter of drops when
the wind shook the trees, the far-off hammering of woodpeckers
and the muffled drumming of wood pheasants in the remoteness
of the forest, the snapshot glimpses of disturbed wild creatures
scurrying through the grass — I can call it all back and make it
as real as it ever was, and as blessed. I can call back the prairie,
and its loneliness and peace, and a vast hawk hanging motion-
less in the sky, with his wings spread wide, and the blue of the
vault showing through the fringe of their end feathers. I can see
the woods in their autumn dress, the oaks purple, the hickories
washed with gold, the maples and the sumachs luminous with
crimson fires, and I can hear the rustle made by the fallen leaves
as we plowed through them. I can see the blue clusters of wild
grapes hanging among the foliage of the saplings, and I remember the taste of them and the smell. I know how the wild blackberries looked, and how they tasted, and the same with the
pawpaws, the hazelnuts, and the persimmons; and I can feel the

thumping rain, upon my head, of hickory nuts and walnuts when we were out in the frosty dawn to scramble for them with the pigs and the gusts of wind loosed them and sent them down. I know the stain of blackberries, and how pretty it is, and I know the stain of walnut hulls, and how little it minds soap and water, also what grudged experience it had of either of them. I know the taste of maple sap, and when to gather it, and how to arrange the troughs and the delivery tubes, and how to boil down the juice, and how to hook the sugar after it is made, also how much better hooked sugar tastes than any that is honestly come by, let bigots say what they will."

These sections of the *Autobiography* are simply lovely to read or to listen to, as the lyrical side of Mark Twain's genius which is often overlooked — and there are many more of them. This essential worship and awe before the beauty of natural life lie back of his great satire, humor, and parody; and are fused with them to establish his unique tone: tender, haunting, touching, affectionate as well as angry, aroused, irascible, ironical, and comic. In a tradition of nature worship which is peculiarly American from Thoreau and Emerson to Whitman, Mark Twain, as I say, is joined with but surpasses the frontier reminiscences of Dreiser and Sherwood Anderson and Willa Cather among the last of our "nature writers" — before a modern generation of urban, even industrial, and now computerized, novelists took over the literary scene.

Probably this was also a key distinction between the writers of the Old Republic — our "older world" — and the generations of American writers who grew up in the modern U.S.A. In the *Autobiography*, meanwhile, Clemens went on to eulogize watermelons and their eating. "I know how a boy looks behind a yard-long slice of that melon, and I know how he feels; for I have been there. I know the taste of the watermelon which has been honestly come by, and I know the taste of the watermelon which has been acquired by art. Both taste good, but the experienced know which tastes best. I know the look of green apples and peaches and pears on the trees, and I know how entertaining they are when they are inside of a person." He went on, in this haunting ode to the western frontier life of his childhood, to discuss frozen apples in barrels, and apples that are roasting on a hearth in wintertime, and hot apples along with sugar and a drench of cream.

He described Uncle Dan'l's kitchen with the white and black children grouped on the hearth, and Uncle Dan'l's tales of black folklore. He remembered the howling of the wind and the quaking of the house on stormy nights, and the dismal hoo-hooing of the owl, and the wailing of a wolf sent mourning by on the night wind. "I remember the raging of the rain on that roof, summer nights, and how pleasant it was to lie and listen to it, and enjoy the white splendor of the lightning and the majestic booming and crashing of the thunder." There was a lightning rod atop his room on that farm, "an adorable and skittish thing to climb up and down, summer nights, when there were duties on hand of a sort to make privacy desirable . . . I remember the 'coon and 'possum hunts, nights, with the negroes, and the long marches through the black gloom of the woods . . . I remember the pigeon seasons, when the birds would come in millions and cover the trees and by their weight break down the branches . . . I remember the squirrel hunts, and prairie-chicken hunts, and wild-turkey hunts, and all that; and how we turned out, mornings, while it was still dark, to go on these expeditions, and how chilly and dismal it was, and how often I regretted that I was well enough to go . . . But presently the gray dawn stole over the world, the birds piped up, then the sun rose and poured light and comfort all around, everything was fresh and dewy and fragrant, and life was a boon again. After three hours of tramping we arrived back wholesomely tired, overladen with game, very hungry, and just in time for breakfast."

Shades of those later American writers, uneasy provincials moving to the eastern culture centers, who decried their western childhood and background as sterile, oppressive, bleak, and colorless. For the older generations, if not for figures like Sinclair Lewis, these western origins gave them a sense of life, of nature — that young dawn when everything was indeed "fresh and dewy and fragrant." There followed in the *Autobiography* the great tribute of Sam Clemens to his mother Jane Lampton Clemens — a field day for psychoanalysts, if you like, but which ended up, as Mark Twain himself did, by being super- or post-Freudian, or by simply going beyond and surpassing the narrow Freudian strictures. Clemens made no secret of his admiration for and adoration of "this first and closest friend" of his whole life. "She had a slender, small body, but a large heart — a heart so large that everybody's grief and everybody's joys found welcome in it, and hospitable accommodation." Like her famous son — and all innocently and happily Clemens described in her many of his own traits of temperament and character — Jane Clemens had a continuous curiosity about the world around her. In all her life, "she never knew such a thing as a half-hearted interest in affairs and people, or an interest which drew a line and left out certain affairs and was indifferent to certain people. The invalid who takes a strenuous and indestructible interest in everything and everybody but himself, and to whom a dull moment is an unknown thing and an impossibility, is a formidable adversary for disease and a hard invalid to vanquish. I am certain that it was this feature of my mother's makeup that carried her so far toward ninety."

And thus we learn of a certain relationship between Sam Clemens' invalid mother and his invalid wife. But what invalids! And it is possible that the deepest emotional rhythms of this remarkable human being were contained in this sequence between his "first and closest friend," Jane Lampton Clemens, and his first, last, and deepest love, Olivia Langdon Clemens. There is a curious phonetic connection between the two names, of course, but rather than expressing any traits of the embedded infantile or autistic personality, such as Henry James par excellence, Mark Twain was describing through his mother, perhaps by inference his wife, all the symptoms of the outgoing and life-embracing soul. His mother's interest "in people and other animals" was warm, personal, friendly. She always found something to excuse and to love in the toughest of characters, said Clemens, "even if she had to put it there herself. She was the natural ally and friend of the friendless." And it comes as no surprise in this maternal profile that "she could be beguiled into saying a soft word for the devil himself." Whether it was Clemens' own arguments in defense of Satan that he put into his mother's words is not important. "Who prays for Satan," asked these two spirits as one. "Who, in eighteen centuries, has had the common humanity to pray for the one sinner that needed it most, our one fellow and brother who most needed a friend yet had not a single one, the one sinner among us all who had the highest and clearest *right* to every Christian's daily and nightly prayers, for the plain and unassailable reason that his was the first and greatest need, he being among sinners the supremest?"

But the tone of these arguments was in fact that of the mother —this "friend of Satan" who was a most gentle spirit and yet was the most eloquent person that Clemens had heard when defending weakness against force or cruelty, or hurt or shame.

Here too was one obvious source of Clemens' identification with that animal race which was in so many ways superior to the reasoning animal called man. "All the race of dumb animals had a friend in her." This profile of Jane Clemens had more detail as it merged, in the *Autobiography,* with another description of the environment, the habits and manners, the social structure of those bygone western towns in which Sam Clemens had lived so fully and so happily. There was the detailed description of the "Boys' Town" in Hannibal in 1849, when Clemens was fourteen years old, which formed the background of *Tom Sawyer* and *Huck Finn.* Howells had also written on the same subject; but his memoirs lacked the spice of Clemens' account, and then the *Autobiography* ventured almost into the forbidden area of childhood sexuality.

But a boy's life is not all comedy; much of the tragic enters into it; and Clemens went into those areas of his youth which were dominated by anxiety, fears, and torments; the whole "underside" of life and art alike, which so often appears to be the only side. He went into the enforced Presbyterian morality of his youth which later on he defied, and was tormented by — and still defied. "But no matter, mine was a trained Presbyterian conscience and knew but the one duty — to hunt and harry its slave upon all pretexts and on all occasions, particularly when there was no sense nor reason in it." There are the familiar episodes of Clemens' early life which became such integral parts of his writing, described here with great precision as examples of the somber side of "innocent" provincial life. And then Clemens proceeded to "analyze" a little further that whole tortured, neurotic, superstitious, moral-religious strain of his temperament which his modern critics have seized upon.

The cases of raw frontier violence and sudden death obsessed the young Clemens, it is true, and furnished many of his night-

mares. "I went home to dream, and was not disappointed."
But he had his own view of them even at an early age. "My
teaching and training enabled me to see deeper into these tragedies than an ignorant person could have done. I knew what
they were for. I tried to disguise it from myself, but down in
the secret depths of my troubled heart I knew — and I *knew*
I knew. They were inventions of Providence to beguile me to a
better life. It sounds curiously innocent and conceited, now,
but to me there was nothing strange about it; it was quite in accordance with the thoughtful and judicious ways of Providence
as I understood them. It would not have surprised me, nor even
overflattered me, if Providence had killed off that whole community in trying to save an asset like me. Educated as I had
been, it would have seemed just the thing and well worth the expense. *Why* Providence should take such an anxious interest
in such a property, that idea never entered my head, and there
was no one in that simple hamlet who would have dreamed of
putting it there. For one thing no one was equipped with it."

Thus Clemens' "explanation" of the singular conscience
which indeed informed his life and work, the early sense of life's
torment and horror which accompanied the very early sense of
his own singular destiny. What is remarkable is that while, in
the *Autobiography,* he was in the throes of these compulsions,
he could examine them so objectively, so eloquently, and with
such a comic sense. Perhaps he was here, at least, as he claimed
for the whole book, speaking from the grave, from beyond the
limited horizons of life. And thus he himself described that
"morbidity" or "blackness" or "pessimism" or "cynicism," or
that "rigid, mechanical determinism" which his critics have
speculated about so much. "It is quite true, I took all the tragedies to myself, and tallied them off in turn as they happened,
saying to myself in each case with a sigh, 'Another one gone —

and on my account; this ought to bring me to repentance; the patience of God will not always endure.' And yet privately I believed it would."

There follows Twain's description of his own daylight and nighttime existence — the polarized daylight and night-dark aspects of his temperament and work — which, despite all the later critical discussion of this theme, still remains as the definitive statement. And why not? Sam Clemens knew himself better than anybody else would ever know him. He remains in literary history as a prime example of the outgoing and life-gathering spirit combined with the most acute sense of self-knowledge and self-vision. That is, he added, he believed in the endurance of God's patience with him in the daytime, but not at night. "With the going down of the sun my faith failed and the clammy fears gathered about my heart. It was then that I repented. Those were awful nights, nights of despair, nights charged with the bitterness of death. After each tragedy I recognized the warning and repented; repented and begged; begged like a coward, begged like a dog; and not in the interest of those poor people who had been extinguished for my sake, but only in my *own* interest. It seems selfish, when I look back on it now."

Selfish indeed! What a description of the human soul: of sin, guilt, atonement — and sin. Of bravado and fear. Of the utterly self-centered sources of religious or superstitious worship. And Clemens went on to describe the meaning of these nights of fear and guilt, despair and death. "My repentances were very real, very earnest; and after each tragedy they happened every night for a long time. But as a rule they could not stand the daylight. They faded out and shredded away and disappeared in the glad splendor of the sun. They were the creatures of fear and darkness, and they could not live out of their own place. The day gave me cheer and peace, and at night I repented again. In all my boyhood life I am not sure that I ever tried to lead a better life in the daytime — or wanted to. In my age I should never think of wishing to do such a thing. But in my age, as in my youth, night brings me many a deep remorse. I realize that from the cradle up I have been like the rest of the race — never quite sane in the night. When 'Injun Joe' died . . . But never mind. Somewhere I have already described what a raging hell of repentance I passed through then. I believe that for months I was as pure as the driven snow. After dark."

It is interesting to note, at the climax of his self-analysis, that Mark Twain described himself in the classical terms, not so much of Freudian individualism, as of the racial consciousness of Jung. And so, despite the experiences of failure, pain, despair, and death, the guilt of the bankruptcy, the series of domestic tragedies; even so, with all these visions of suffering described in the *Autobiography*, and still more to come as in all human experience, so that life without its elements of death is hardly to be called life — even so, Mark Twain's biggest and best and last book emerges as a "daylight book," full of life, love, and laughter. Revealing all his nighttime fears only to smile at them, Mark Twain himself emerges, not as a split, divided, tormented figure. But rather, if he still acknowledged and bowed down to all this in a yet rebellious mood of comedy, as a daylight writer of the highest sort who gives us, so many years later, a chronicle full of sweetness, affection, tenderness, and humor *about* the tragic experience of life.*

* Bernard DeVoto, discussing without much humor some of Twain's excoriating anger in the *Autobiography*, concluded it was a black book written in the framework of Twain's financial troubles and family difficulties. But this is to miss the real point of the *Autobiography* completely — as a book which allows its author to indulge in personal wrath, envy, parody, and satire fully, and yet is itself beyond anger and hatred and fear in its main stress, almost achieving an angelic peace and tenderness in its comic vision of human motives.

The *Autobiography* is in fact the last great spiritual legacy of the Old Republic to the modern American Empire, more truly living out its destiny in a mood of nightmarish fear and darkness. Despite all the critics and editors who had their own reasons for disparaging the original edition of this work (Kaplan describes it as "magnificent talk" — taken from De-Voto's "table talk," which DeVoto took from Twain's own words), it is a gem of a book — even though we have barely begun to discuss it here, and must try to limit the scope of its treatment. In the series of keys it provides for the real meaning of Mark Twain's work, it is the comic rebellion of a Tom Sawyer, and the edenic flight of a Huck Finn which still remains at the center of Mark Twain's earthly vision — but again we must stress that while this writer was centered in childhood, as many critics have observed, he was hardly limited to it. It is a fatal mistake to assume this about Mark Twain, since *all* great artists remain "childlike" in their vision of social and civilizational repressions, and Twain was only the most obviously and brilliantly so. His last great work, the *Autobiography* itself, was a work of the highest and most sophisticated maturity.

It was a maturity which had learned, despite all the risks and gambles and losses and disasters and farces of experience, that the main purpose of life-in-death is to enjoy itself, and to play, and take what soft pleasures it can in its tiny and dubious span of existence. What else do we live for? Then Clemens moved on to the story of "Jim Wolfe and the Cats," which became another bit of legendary comic folklore in the later sixties, at the start of his writing career. He moved from here to reminiscences of his lecturing period, including such figures as George Dolby, the famous theatrical agent of the time, Petroleum Vesuvius Nasby, Josh Billings, and the other frontier humorists who were collected, together with such eastern celebrities as Henry Ward

Beecher, Horace Greeley, and Wendell Phillips, under the auspices of the Redpath lecture bureau. There were famous women on the lecture platform in those days, too; and Clemens described certain "house-emptiers" like Olive Logan and Kate Field. Lecturing was a craft of its own, and some of its tricks are described here by probably the most famous lecturer of all time. There was another example of "The Beauties of the German Language," and Clemens went on to describe Viennese life in the late nineties, including a great parade that he loved, the best parade he had ever seen — while adding: "At the end of this year I shall be sixty-three — if alive — and about the same if dead."

In discussing the background of *Innocents Abroad,* Clemens was, after all this time in the first volume of the *Autobiography,* describing the origins of his first book, the true start of his literary career; no wonder he dwelt upon it with such a multitude of facts, and probably too fully. He went on to some of his earliest literary friends and acquaintances: Robert Louis Stevenson, Thomas Bailey Aldrich, and the unspeakable Bret Harte upon whose memory Clemens summoned all his powers of abuse and invective.

But more on this later on. There was an interesting and touching account of Twain's friendship with Henry Huttleston Rogers: that ruthless, cunning, arrogant, and heartless Standard Oil mogul, who was also a most charming and cultivated personality, and who did indeed befriend Sam Clemens in his hour of need, and in effect made him a new fortune, and presented him, like a Machiavellian patron perhaps, or a Medici, to the whole circle of powerful American financiers. The barons and titans and tycoons almost considered Mark Twain their court jester, the more fools they not to realize what was really happening — as Twain's later portraits of them would show. This was

invaluable experience for a great American writer in the heyday
of finance industrialism, to be close to the very center of the
structure, and, so to speak, the favorite guest in Capitalism's
house.

Mark Twain never missed a chance like this, which we've
already seen, which we are seeing right here, and which we
shall see in the future pages of this book. If I seem to bear down
on this a little heavily, it is because Biographer Kaplan has
stated that the price of Rogers' friendship and aid was that Mark
Twain was henceforth gagged and mute in regard to any free
opinions about his society, or capitalism or the Standard Oil trust
in particular. Well, we already know that just the opposite is
true; it was *after* Twain's bankruptcy that both his fiction and
his social criticism took on all its bite and brilliance; not to mention the allusions he made to the Rockefellers and Standard Oil
particularly. In fact Mark Twain's *personal* ties, with a few
intimate exceptions, never, in the end, prevented him from
speaking as he pleased. The reverse was more likely with this
perverse and satanic spirit, as almost anybody should know.

Perhaps it was Mr. Kaplan, rather than Sam Clemens, who
was incapable of social criticism, as I've said, and was unable
to recognize it when it rose into flaming print right before his
eyes. Meanwhile, dictating the *Autobiography* (and telling
Paine to fashion the final book out of all this raw material), Clemens reminisced about another millionaire friend of
his, John Mackay, from the early days of the great Bonanza in
Nevada in 1871. This was another fine section of history and
reporting about the silver-mine epoch in the west. Men who
were penniless prospectors, living by dint of the worst physical
labor, became fantastically wealthy overnight. The Bonanza
rose in value from $26,000 to $16,000,000 in six years. These
new millionaires became multimillionaires after that, and then,
naturally, United States Senators.

If Sam Clemens did not already have the gambling fever in his bloodstream, he would have been sure to acquire it in his years of apprenticeship. Together the two were too much for him, and the end — for him, though not for some others — could have been foreseen. As a result of the Bonanza strike, all the mines in that area, so he recorded here ironically, rose to a value of $400,000,000 in the stock market — "And six months after that, that value had been reduced by three-quarters; and by 1880, five years later, the stock of the Consolidated Virginia was under $2 a share, and the stock in the California was only $1.75" — for the Bonanza was now exhausted. (This was background material for the epical *Roughing It* of 1872.)

A period of fairy-tale success and of sudden disaster which almost prophesied, and to a certain extent helped to shape, Sam Clemens' future career. From the silver mines his narrative moved to the notorious Morris incident of the period. A respectable matron, trying to see President Roosevelt, was dragged away screaming by the White House police, maltreated physically, and then, overcome by the shock of her experience, languished in bed while the nation was horrified. While noting the affair was hardly of great historical importance, Clemens was possessed by this episode which added fuel to his dislike of the heroic Teddy, whose Cuban military campaign, as Clemens said elsewhere, compared well with Waterloo.

But the Morris case led him into other comments about the state of the nation. "I wonder what the Morris incident will look like in history fifty years from now. Consider these circumstances: that here at our own doors the mighty insurance upheaval has not settled down to a level yet. Even yesterday, and day before, the discredited millionaire insurance magnates had not all been flung out and buried from sight under the maledictions of the nation, but some of the McCurdies, McCalls, Hydes, and Alexanders were still lingering in positions of trust, such as directorships in banks. Also we have to-day the whole nation's attention centered upon the Standard Oil corporation, the most prodigious commercial force existing upon the planet . . . Also we have Congress threatening to overhaul the Panama Canal Commission to see what it has done with the fifty-nine millions, and to find out what it prosposes to do with the recently added eleven millions. Also there are three or four other matters of colossal public interest on the board to-day. And on the other side of the ocean we have Church and State separated in France; we have a threat of war between France and Germany upon the Morocco question; we have a crushed revolution in Russia, with the Czar and his family of thieves — the grand dukes — recovering from their long fright and beginning to butcher the remnants of the revolutionaries in the old confident way that was the Russian way in former days for three centuries; we have China furnishing a solemn and awful mystery. Nobody knows what it is, but we are sending three regiments in a hurry from the Philippines to China, under the generalship of Funston, the man who captured Aguinaldo by methods which would disgrace the lowest blatherskite that is doing time in any penitentiary."

After this, Clemens still pursued the Morris case, not of course for its own sake, as he realized, but for the light it threw upon President Roosevelt. "Roosevelt's biographer will light up the President's career step by step, mile after mile, through his life's course with illuminating episodes and incidents. He should set one of the lamps by the Morris incident, for it indicates character. It is a thing which probably could not have happened in the White House under any other President who has ever occupied those premises. Washington wouldn't call the police and throw a lady out over the fence!" And there followed an acerbic attack upon the blustering, warmongering, and imperialistic President whom Mark Twain hated both on principle and in person. Well, he conceded that he enjoyed Roosevelt's qualities when he was acting in the capacity of a private citizen. "But when he is acting under their impulse as President, they make of him a sufficiently queer President. He flies from one thing to another with incredible dispatch — throws a somersault and is straightway back again where he was last week. He will then throw some more somersaults and nobody can foretell where he is finally going to land after the series. Each act of his, and each opinion expressed, is likely to abolish or controvert some previous act or expressed opinion. This is what is happening to him all the time as President. But every opinion that he expresses is certainly his sincere opinion at that moment, and it is as certainly not the opinion which he was carrying around in his system three or four weeks earlier, and which was just as sincere and honest as the latest one. No, he can't be accused of insincerity — that is not the trouble. His trouble is that his newest interest is the one that absorbs him; absorbs the whole of him from his head to his feet, and for the time being it annihilates all previous opinions and feelings and convictions. He is the most popular human being that has ever existed in the United States, and that popularity springs from just these enthusiasms of his — these joyous ebullitions of excited sincerity. It makes him so much like the rest of the people. They see themselves reflected in him. They also see that his impulses are not often mean. They are almost always large, fine, generous. He can't stick to one of them long enough to find out what kind of a chick it would hatch if it had a chance, but everybody recognizes the generosity of the intention and admires it and loves him for it." *

* This brilliant profile of Theodore Roosevelt — along with the Morris case and Twain's caustic summary of the world around him — was omitted in Charles Neider's later version of the *Autobiography* on grounds of "taste" or "esthetics," as Neider claimed, but really because of the prevailing Cold War theology in the American fifties whose narrow values many critics accepted so blandly, so smugly, so piously. And still do.

Mark Twain was seventy when he wrote this, but how interested he was both in his own country and the world around him when compared with some of his later critics who viewed the same material with such artistic disdain; and how this outside world, in turn, enriched and revitalized the aging artist and his work. What good prose this was, in short, which has been claimed not to be "art," and how Clemens pursued Teddy Roosevelt with the familiar satirical animosity he had shown toward some previous objects of his wrath. It was good for him, he knew, and good for his writing; and this was only a part of some further reflections on Thanksgiving, the Congo, and other world events.*

Thanksgiving Day, said Clemens, had originated in New England when the Puritans realized they had succeeded in exterminating their neighbors, the Indians, instead of getting exterminated by their neighbors, the Indians.

> Thanksgiving Day became a habit, for the reason that in the course of time, as the years drifted on, it was perceived that the exterminating had ceased to be mutual and was all on the white man's side, consequently on the Lord's side; hence it was proper to thank the Lord for it and extend the usual annual compliments.

The original reason for Thanksgiving Day had long since ceased to exist, he added, since "the Indians have long ago been comprehensively and satisfactorily exterminated and the account closed with the Lord, with the thanks due." But still the habit persisted as a national holiday, and every year the American presidents and state governors set themselves the task "to hunt up something to be thankful for, and then they put these thanks into a few crisp and reverent phrases, in the form of a procla-

* Also omitted by Neider, and by the rest of his generation of "silent" American scholars.

mation, and this is read from all the pulpits in the land, the national conscience is wiped clean with one swipe, and sin is resumed at the old stand."

The year 1906, when Mark Twain's birthday fell on Thanksgiving, was particularly noted for having very little to be thankful for. Clemens wanted to put off the whole holiday on the ground that nothing had happened during the previous twelvemonth except several vicious and inexcusable wars, and King Leopold of Belgium's usual annual slaughters and robberies in the Congo State, together with the insurance revelations in New York.

He reminisced about the Clemenses' best and oldest friend, the Reverend Joseph Twichell, and Twichell's Civil War experience under General Sickles — whose monotonous conversation reminded Clemens of Bill Nye's remark about Wagner's music. "I have been told that Wagner's music is better than it sounds." The Civil War led Twain back to his own lack of martial valor, his dislike (for such a revolutionary thinker) of any force or violence in his own life, his brilliant and comic evasions of danger, his open admission of his own cowardice. If Clemens was at all guilty about his military failure, and if this entered into his worship of General Grant (as Freudians suggest), let us remember, more importantly, that this "guilt" produced some of the greatest antiwar writing in our literature. In January of 1906 Clemens began dictating the second volume of the *Autobiography* with some discussions of Booker T. Washington's Tuskegee Institute, which he supported, and of that fashionable New York society which, lionizing Twain himself, included such figures as Joseph H. Choate, Chauncey Depew, and Colonel (George) Harvey. That February was the thirty-sixth anniversary of the Clemenses' marriage, and Livy had been dead for one year and eight months, and there followed another of those lyrical and touching passages about her. She was always cheerful, said Clemens, even in the worst of times. "During the nine years that we spent in poverty and debt she was always able to reason me out of my despairs and find a bright side to the clouds and make me see it. In all that time I never knew her to utter a word of regret concerning our altered circumstances, nor did I ever know her children to do the like."

> For she had taught them, and they drew their fortitude from her. The love which she bestowed upon those whom she loved took the form of worship, and in that form it was returned — returned by relatives, friends, and the servants of her household. It was a strange combination which wrought into one individual, so to speak, by marriage — her disposition and character and mine. She poured out her prodigal affection in kisses and caresses, and in a vocabulary of endearments whose profusion was always an astonishment to me. I was born *reserved* as to endearments of speech, and caresses, and hers broke upon me as the summer waves break upon Gibraltar.

Samuel Clemens went on to describe their early home life together, Sam and Livy and the children, and the Hartford mansion and their cherished servants — the whole domestic scene of their younger years — in one of the most tender and poignant sections of the *Autobiography*. The artist's recall is complete, the tone is touching and affectionate and entertaining; these pages of Twain's memoirs couldn't be better. It *is* a fairy tale that Mark Twain creates again of their youthful peak of fame, success, happiness, and grand living: the house that Livy's father "surprised" them with in Buffalo, the newspaper which was given to Mark Twain in part ownership, the servants including the young Irish coachman, Patrick McAleer, the housekeeper Katie Leary, the cook Ellen, and later on the other Hartford domestics who always remained part of the Clemens family. What is fascinating again is the childlike joy of the young Clemens' acceptance of all these material splendors with no qualms of conscience and no concern about his own ability to live up to this totally new (kingly) role in life. Prince and Pauper he was indeed, in about equal fashion, in another of those ingenious dualisms of his temperament.

There is in particular a loving tribute by Twain to Patrick McAleer, who had just died, and whose funeral he attended. There is the death of their first son, Langdon, for which Clemens always held himself guilty (wrongly, it would appear today), and had never spoken about until the *Autobiography*. There is Susy's death again, which now Mark Twain almost regarded as a kind of sacrificial atonement for the success of his world-wide lecture tour. The details of her meningitis attack and suffering are so blunt here as to be harrowing, and Clemens went on to talk about her childhood and her character — "she that had been our wonder and our worship." As a little child she was already oppressed and perplexed, said Clemens,

> by the maddening repetition of the stock incidents of our race's fleeting sojourn here, just as the same thing has oppressed and perplexed maturer minds from the beginning of time. A myriad of men are born; they labor and sweat and struggle for bread; they squabble and scold and fight; they scramble for little mean advantages over each other. Age creeps upon them; infirmities follow; shames and humiliations bring down their prides and vanities. Those they love are taken from them, and the joy of life is turned to aching grief. The burden of pain, care, misery, grows heavier year by year. At length ambition is dead; pride is dead; vanity is dead; longing for release is in their place. It comes at last — the only unpoisoned gift earth ever had for them — and they vanish from a world where they were of no consequence; where they achieved nothing; where they were a mistake and a failure and a foolishness; where they have left no sign that they

have existed — a world which will lament them a day and forget them forever. Then another myriad takes their place, and copies all they did, and goes along the same profitless road, and vanishes as they vanished — to make room for another and another and a million other myriads to follow the same arid path through the same desert and accomplish what the first myriad, and all the other myriads that came after it, accomplished — nothing!

And here indeed was the classical statement, in almost the same words as the later novelist Theodore Dreiser was to say it in, of the tragic view of life for modern man. A tragic view, let us note, which lay at the base of all Mark Twain's humor and gave it that remarkable and complex tone and shading; a tragic view of man's destiny which joined inexorably the high individuality of Mark Twain's genius (as it did Dreiser's) with the struggling, suffering obscure hordes of mankind. And a view of life which, moreover, for just this reason — this loss of mutual affinity, this lack of bond and union between the individual and the community — is almost completely lacking in contemporary American literature.

For this view of Sam Clemens', and this bond of the great and the little, the exalted and the lowly, the special and the general, is at the base of all great art. When the artist is too removed, or society too oppressive, no great art is possible — as we can see from all the high renascences of art; and from all the bleak and sterile periods like our own, when literary fads and fashions are mistaken for literary achievement; when both artists and critics alike are ignorant of their true literary heritage in the United States, and the real horizons and boundaries of literature itself.

In a sense Susy now dominated the second volume of the *Autobiography,* and in one of those remarkable intuitions of Mark Twain, it is she who gives shape to the remaining events of his own life, and to the soft and loving memories of life in Hartford. He proceeded by using extracts of Susy's "Biography" of her father written when he was in his fiftieth year and she in her fourteenth. "We are a very happy family. We consist of Papa, Mamma, Jean, Clara and me. It is Papa I am writing about, and I shall have no trouble in not knowing what to say about him, as he is a *very* striking character." And then Clemens went off into a scathing denunciation of the herdlike tendencies of the literary critics of his own time, and a shameless explanation of how he had always let Howells set the tone of the reviews of his new books.

He pointed out that his critics had gone so far in describing his personal appearance as to create the impression that he was distinctly and distressingly unhandsome. "That description floated around the country in the papers, and was in constant use and wear for a quarter of a century. It seems strange to me that apparently no critic in the country could be found who could look at me and have the courage to take up his pen and destroy that lie. That lie began its course on the Pacific coast, in 1864, and it likened me in personal appearance to Petroleum V. Nasby, who had been out there lecturing. For twenty-five years afterward, no critic could furnish a description of me without fetching in Nasby to help out my portrait. I knew Nasby well, and he was a good fellow, but in my life I have not felt malignantly enough about any more than three persons to charge those persons with resembling Nasby."

It is Mark Twain presenting Susy's biography of Mark Twain which incites Mark Twain to further memories. (This reflection of a reflection which Clemens apparently just stumbled on, was to become a familiar technique in a later and more sophisticated age of writers such as Virginia Woolf and Gide.) "That burglar alarm which Susy mentions," said Clemens, "led a gay and careless life, and had no principles." And there follows an episode of Livy, Sam, the burglars, and the burglar alarm in the Hartford house that I can only touch on. As the burglar advanced from one floor to another in the house, Clemens kept turning off the alarm for that floor and "explaining" to Livy just what the burglars were doing and how he (Sam) could be of no help to them. "Suppose he comes up here!" Livy exclaims at last. "I said: 'It is all right. He will give us notice.' She said: 'What shall we do then?' I said, 'Climb out of the window.' She said: 'Well, what is the use of a burglar alarm for us?' I said: 'You have seen that it has been useful up to the present moment, and I have explained to you how it will be continuously useful after he gets up here.' "

There is the episode in the Clemenses' early life when Sam, who had prided himself on keeping the secret of his obscene language and spirited profanity away from the rest of his family, made the mistake of indulging in it while the bathroom door was open. A hushed silence fell upon the house and when he returned to his bedroom, unable to meet Livy's eye, she repeated his terrible vocabulary in her cultivated voice, and they broke up in laughter together. Echoes of Tom Sawyer and Huck Finn were in this marriage too, and Clemens' memory of that exercise in "censorship" was still vivid after all the years. "Against the white pillows I saw the black head — I saw that young and beautiful face; and I saw the gracious eyes with a something in them which I had never seen before. They were snapping and flashing with indignation. I felt myself crumbling; I felt myself shrinking away to nothing under that accusing gaze. I stood silent under that desolating fire for as much as a minute, I should say — it seemed a very, very long time. Then my wife's lips parted, and from them issued — *my latest bathroom remark.* The language perfect, but the expression unpractical, apprentice-like, ignorant, inexperienced, comically inadequate, absurdly weak and unsuited to the great language. In my lifetime I had never heard anything so out of tune, so inharmonious, so incongruous, so ill suited to each other as were those mighty words set to that feeble music. I tried to keep from laughing, for I was a guilty person in deep need of charity and mercy. I tried to keep from bursting, and I succeeded — until she gravely said, 'There, now you know how it sounds.'

"Oh, then I exploded! I said, 'Oh, Livy, if it sounds like that, God forgive me, I will never do it again.' Then she had to laugh, herself. Both of us broke into convulsions, and went on laughing until we were exhausted." Clemens also discovered that the children were perfectly familiar with his profanity since they hung over the hall balcony listening while he conversed with the butler George. So much for Mark Twain and language; and the language problem in his work; and for the type of Puritanical and Victorian "censorship" which Livy reputedly, according to many scholars, starting with Van Wyck Brooks, exercised over his behavior, his talk, his writing.

He went on to discuss the game he played with Livy and the children in deliberately inserting passages of writing which he knew would draw their violent protests. "For my own entertainment and to enjoy the protests of the children, I often abused my editor's innocent confidence. I often interlarded remarks of a studied and felicitously atrocious character purposely to achieve the children's delight and see the pencil do its fatal work. I often joined my supplications to the children's for mercy, and strung the argument out and pretended to be in earnest. They were deceived, and so was their mother. It was three against one, and most unfair. But it was very delightful, and I could not resist the temptation."

One could ask, furthermore, if Mark Twain's language was

as severely censored as it has been said to be, by both Livy and
Howells, how could it remain so perfectly embedded in our literature, so solid, so fresh, so right, and so definitive? If these
things are true, then, somewhat as Lincoln suggested about
Grant's drinking, perhaps we could use a little more of
that brand of "censorship" in contemporary American writing. It is still true that as regards sex, Sam Clemens maintained
a perfect facade of silence — though the *Autobiography* shows
some key passages of sexual freedom — about his own views
and temperament. The public reasons for this (his popular audience) he openly acknowledged; perhaps the private reason,
Livy herself, was worth the price. From the Hartford home
Clemens moved backwards to the first meeting of "Mr. Clemens
and Miss Langdon" and the whole story of Livy's invalidism,
which Clemens himself sensed to be psychological as well as
physical. A famous doctor of the period first enabled her
to walk, after that curious disabling "accident" (or crisis) of
adolescence which in her case, as in Henry James', kept her
bedridden for some years. This famous psychological healer
Dr. Newton, along with Dr. John Brown of Scotland, were beloved
figures in the Clemens household, and from here derived one of
the sources of Mark Twain's continuing interest in all phases
of spiritualism, faith healing, and psychic phenomena.

There is also the episode of Samuel Clemens' own "accident"
which resulted in a prolonged stay in the Jervis Langdon fairy-
tale household (to the young provincial ruffian of the 1860s),
and then the marriage to the sheltered, cultivated, enchanting,
and invalided young eastern heiress of that time. Almost a typical Jamesian romance, but with what a difference! For Livy
was not *that* crippled. Sam Clemens remembered Livy's ministrations to his wounded scalp with great clarity. "That was very
pleasant. I should have been obliged to recover presently if it

hadn't been for that. But under Livy's manipulations — if they had continued — I should probably be unconscious to this day. It was very delightful, those manipulations. So delightful, so comforting, so enchanting, that they even soothed the fire out of that fiendish successor to Perry Davis's 'Pain-Killer.' "

Which Livy's sister, Susy Crane, had poured on Clemens' injured head. And there is the familiar story told all so freshly again of the engagement, marriage, and their early years together almost as part of the Langdon household, and of Livy's remarkable physical endurance in times of crisis or illness in the family.

Then there is a section . . . Another section? By now, in the reading of this remarkable book of free association and stream of (unconscious) consciousness, it hardly bothers us that Twain may be repeating himself, or amplifying an earlier theme, or adding a new section to a previous section. It is almost all fresh; and what we wait for is the sudden turns of his mind, the twist of phrase, the surprise passages, the way he will suddenly repeat an older section and make it appear completely new. Just as when he went back, once more, to lecturing days and that "new and devilish" invention of the period called an Authors' Reading. "This witch's Sabbath took place in a theater, and began at two in the afternoon. There were nine readers on the list, and I believe I was the only one who was qualified by experience to go at the matter in a sane way." Clemens believed that nine times ten are ninety and therefore the average time allotted to each author should be ten minutes, but "There would be an introducer, and he wouldn't understand his business — this disastrous fact could be counted upon as a certainty. The introducer would be ignorant, windy, eloquent, and willing to hear himself talk. With nine introductions to make, added to his own opening speech — well, I could not go on with these harrowing calculations; I foresaw that there was trouble on hand." And most of these authors, like Howells, were ignorant of the speech business. "He couldn't seem to learn it. He was a bright man in all other ways, but whenever he came to select a reading for one of these carousals his intellect decayed and fell to ruin." At the Longfellow memorial in Boston he had brought along a reading selection of seven thousand words which would have taken him an hour and ten minutes to read, said Clemens, not allowing for interruptions such as applause — "for the reason that after the first twelve minutes there wouldn't be any."

Howells' excuse was that he never could find a short enough selection that would be good enough to stand exposure before an audience. "I said: 'It's no matter. Better that than a long one — because the audience could stand a bad short one, but couldn't stand a good long one.'

"We got it arranged at last. We got him down to fifteen minutes, perhaps. But he and Doctor Holmes and Aldrich and I had the only short readings that day out of the most formidable accumulation of authors that had ever thus far been placed in position before the enemy — a battery of sixteen. I think that was the occasion when we had sixteen. It was in the afternoon, and the place was packed, and the air would have been very bad, only there wasn't any. I can see that mass of people yet, opening and closing their mouths like fishes gasping for breath. It was intolerable.

"That graceful and competent speaker, Professor Norton, opened the game with a very handsome speech, but it was a good twenty minutes long. And a good ten minutes of it, I think, were devoted to the introduction of Dr. Oliver Wendell Holmes, who hadn't any more need of an introduction than the Milky Way. Then Doctor Holmes recited — as only Doctor Holmes could recite it — 'The Last Leaf,' and the house rose as one individual and went mad with worshiping delight. And the house stormed along, and stormed along, and got another poem out of the Doctor as an encore; it stormed again and got a third one — though the storm was not so violent this time as had been the previous outbreaks. By this time Doctor Holmes had, himself, lost a part of his mind, and he actually went on reciting poem after poem until silence had taken the place of encores, and he had to do the last encore by himself."

An entertaining glimpse of the New England literary circle; and one may note in passing that Clemens' tone of genial comedy about them and about Howells himself is far different from his first and early awe and admiration, his adulation of them, and that altogether excessive shame and horror over the Whittier dinner, now long forgotten. There is a section in the *Autobiography* devoted to Twain's friendship with President Cleveland and his wife — "the young, the beautiful, the good-hearted, the sympathetic, the fascinating" Mrs. Cleveland. And talking of women, Clemens recalled one of their German nurses with an innocent penchant for obscenities. "It brings that pretty little German creature vividly before me — a sweet and innocent and plump little creature, with peachy cheeks; a clear-souled little maiden and without offense, notwithstanding her profanities, and she was loaded to the eyebrows with them. She was a mere child. She was not fifteen yet. She was just from Germany, and knew no English. She was always scattering her profanities around, and they were such a satisfaction to me that I never dreamed of such a thing as modifying her. For my own sake, I had no disposition to tell on her. Indeed, I took pains to keep her from being found out. I told her to confine her religious expressions to the children's quarters, and urged her to remember that Mrs. Clemens was prejudiced against pieties on week days."

Still reminiscing along, the later Mark Twain recalled a Vassar
lecture where his annoyance at his cavalier treatment by the
college president did not quite spoil his pleasure in addressing
"that great garden of young and lovely blossoms." Girls are
charming creatures, he went on to say. "I shall have to be twice
seventy years old before I change my mind as to that. I am to
talk to a crowd of them this afternoon, students of Barnard College (the sex's annex to Columbia University), and I think I
shall have just as pleasant a time with those lassies as I had
with the Vassar girls twenty-one years ago." The pagan and
plenary strain in this artist still lingered on apparently despite
all the "censorship" and "repression" and neurotic "frustration"
which we have been told so often were exercised upon him or
existed within him. And directly after this episode appears the
Mark Twain essay on the killing of six hundred Moros, as authorized by General Wood, and approved by President Roosevelt
in the treacherous acquisition of the Philippines. I have already
quoted this at some length as one of Twain's most brilliant polemical pieces; it is hardly a surprise that it was omitted in Charles
Neider's later and emasculated edition of the *Autobiography*.

There is an interlude in which Clemens described the various
letters sent to him (because he represented the conscience of the
United States during his lifetime). Among these were letters
written to "Mark Twain, Somewhere"; to "Mark Twain, God
Knows Where"; to "Mark Twain, Somewhere, Try Satan"; and
perhaps the bitterest pill of all, to "Mark Twain, c/o President
Roosevelt, The White House, Washington, America, U.S.A."
Talking to Howells about the plan of the *Autobiography*, Clemens was prompted to add: "I told Howells that this autobiography of mine would live a couple of thousand years without
any effort and would then take a fresh start and live the rest of the
time . . . He said he believed it would, and asked me if I meant

to make a library of it." Both Twain and Howells were not too far off in their estimates, and then Howells, so Clemens added, was "full of praises and indorsement which was wise in him and judicious. If he had manifested a different spirit I would have thrown him out of the window. I like criticism, but it must be my way."

Nor, in the older tradition of literature, was Mark Twain averse to sentiment or pure sentimentality, in some of these episodes, along with his polemics, his parodies, his touching sense of comedy, and of tragedy. Talking of the Vanderbilts and Mr. Carnegie and of the Roosevelt children, who were distinctly "princely," he remarked that "the things they say are rather notably not worth while." He pointed out that in the remote western villages of his youth, the same attention was paid to the local celebrities. "We recognize that there are *no* trivial occurrences in life if we get the right focus on them. In a village they are just as prodigious as they are when the subject is a personage of national importance." Mark Twain, in the central tradition of American literature, was again binding himself to the aspirations of the masses of men in his central vision of his art; was as interested in the "little" as in the "big" in this *Autobiography,* and in the small things of life as well as in the large. And who knows what is big and what is small, what is great and what is trivial in the end, since, as he asserted, "there are *no* trivial occurrences in life" if we get the right focus on them.

He parodied this grand theme immediately in his account of "The Swangos" — the Swango family riding, visiting, attending auctions, raising cattle, growing turkeys — in Hazel Green, Kentucky. Shades of Sherwood Anderson, who was perhaps the last modern writer to stress this theme in particular. There was the story of Ed Marsh, his wife's counsin, a Civil War hero, and of Calvin H. Higbie, a figure in *Roughing It,* and a silver-mining friend of Twain's from Nevada. (There is more of this invaluable material about frontier life and customs.) Then comes the remarkable sketch of Orion Clemens, the eccentric and shiftless brother of Sam's, whose history of wild schemes and terrible failures was the underside of Mark Twain's own success. Orion's was a curious personality, as Clemens said. "In all my seventy years I have not met the twin of it." And perhaps here in this brilliant ne'er-do-well, who was a complete parody of Sam Clemens while he dogged his heels and lived on Sam's generosity, was another *personal* source of the twin-fixation or Twain Myth — which had, in Mark Twain's case, a much larger generic, communal, and cultural meaning. But Orion was Sam's unfortunate twin indeed, and contributed to the pattern; and what curious insight made this artist use the twin-like phrase for his pen name? Orion is another fascinating figure among Clemens' portraits, volatile, fragmentary, contradictory, self-defeating, unbearable, and yet oddly charming and appealing. Clemens was pursued by his dark failure. For Orion it was always the American dream in fantasy, and always the American nightmare in reality; and from this grimmer picture of the frontier life the *Autobiography* moved to Clemens' meeting with the celebrated Russian revolutionary, Tchaykoffsky,* who old and grizzled as he was still had a Vesuvius inside of him. "He is so full of belief in the ultimate and almost immediate triumph of the revolution and the destruction of the fiendish autocracy that he almost made me believe and hope with him. He has come over here expecting to arouse a conflagration of noble sympathy in our vast nation of eighty millions of happy and enthusiastic freemen. But honesty obliged me to pour some cold water down his crater."

* Or Tchaikovsky, Nikolai Vasilevich, as spelled today; and not the composer, but the revolutionary populist who founded the St. Petersburg party, lived in London, returned to Russia in 1905, and became an opponent of the Bolsheviks' Revolution of October, 1917.

I told him what I believed to be true: that our Christianity which we have always been so proud of — not to say, so vain of — is now nothing but a shell, a sham, a hypocrisy; that we have lost our ancient sympathy with oppressed peoples struggling for life and liberty; that when we are not coldly indifferent to such things we sneer at them, and that the sneer is about the only expression the newspapers and the nation deal in with regard to such things; that his mass meetings would not be attended by people entitled to call themselves representative Americans, even if they may call themselves Americans at all; that his audiences will be composed of foreigners who have suffered so recently that they have not yet had time to be Americanized and their hearts turned to stone in their breasts; that these audiences will be drawn from the ranks of the poor, not those of the rich; that they will give and give freely, but they will give from their poverty and the money result will not be large. I said that when our windy and flamboyant President conceived the idea, a year ago, of advertising himself to the world as the new Angel of Peace, and set himself the task of bringing about the peace between Russia and Japan and had the misfortune to accomplish his misbegotten purpose, no one in all this nation except Doctor Seaman and myself uttered a public protest against this folly of follies.

When Tchaykoffsky said that Mark Twain's talk depressed him profoundly and he hoped Twain was wrong, Twain said that he hoped the same. When Tchaykoffsky pointed out that the United States had sent millions of dollars to help the suffering Russians, and didn't that modify Mark Twain's opinion, Twain said it did not. "That money came not from Americans, it came from Jews; much of it from rich Jews, but the most of it from Russian and Polish Jews on the East Side — that is to say, it came from the very poor. The Jew has always been benevolent. Suffering can always move a Jew's heart and tax his pocket to the limit. He will be at your mass meetings. But if you find any Americans there put them in a glass case and exhibit them. It will be worth fifty cents a head to go and look at that show and try to believe in it.*

Now can you really say that Mark Twain was anti-Semitic, anti-alien, anti-poor people, and in particular against the new urban masses (as Henry James was, and so many other American writers of the period) when he attributed to these new Americans all the traditional old-fashioned American values which he cherished and mourned. But in truth he was correct in realizing that the great American tradition had descended underground, as it were, to the minority groups who nourished and kept it alive during those turbulent years, until a few decades later it would be the young, the students, and the black Americans who carried on the same struggle, under perhaps less hopeful circumstances, and a different historical period, but with great vitality and spirit.

Clemens reached toward the other complementary peak of his temperament when his social concern — or social protest, social polemics, social satire — was directly followed by a late-blooming period of his sexual pleasure. The two human poles of civilizational restraint and biopsychic urges, the outer and inner worlds at war or at peace, agreeing, dissenting, probing, fusing, but always intensely intertwined and creative by the fact of their polar opposition and their polar necessity, were, as I say, at the core of this artist's temperament much more clearly than with most writers.

"Day before yesterday all Vassar, ancient and modern, packed itself into the Hudson Theater, and I was there," Clemens wrote

* This whole passage in the *Autobiography* has been omitted again both in Mr. Neider's modern edition of the book, I am sorry to repeat, and in Mr. Kaplan's modern biography of Mark Twain, just as it has been thought unworthy of mention in contemporary scholarship on Twain; not perhaps so much for its Russian sympathies as for its dim view of the American scene in 1906 — or its prophetic and discerning view?

in that peculiarly affectionate, tenderly comic, mock-ironic tone
he used about himself and the ladies. "The occasion was a benefit
arranged by Vassar and its friends to raise money to aid poor
students of that college in getting through the college course. I
was not aware that I was to be a feature of the show, and was
distressed and most uncomfortably inflamed with blushes when
I found it out. Really the distress and the blushes were manufactured, for at bottom I was glad. I held a reception on that
stage for an hour or two, and all Vassar, ancient and modern,
shook hands with me. Some of the moderns were too beautiful
for words, and I was very friendly with those. I was so hoping
somebody would want to kiss me for my mother, but I didn't
dare to suggest it myself. Presently, however, when it happened,
I did what I could to make it contagious, and succeeded. This
required art, but I had it in stock. I *seemed* to take the old and
the new as they came, without discrimination, but I averaged
the percentage to my advantage, and without anybody's suspecting, I think."

There were half a dozen pretty old girls, also, he added, whom
he had met in their bloom at Vassar when he and Susy had
visited there so long ago. But then, "Yesterday at the University
Club, almost all the five hundred were of the young and lovely,
untouched by care, unfaded by age." He had delivered a "moral
sermon" to the Barnard girls a few weeks earlier — if they had
only realized the true nature of such moral sermons on Mark
Twain's part — and now it was like being among old friends.
One sweet creature wanted to whisper in his ear and he was
nothing loath. "She raised her dainty form on tiptoe, lifting herself with a grip of her velvet hands on my shoulders, and put
her lips to my ear and said, 'How do you like being the belle of
New York?' It was so true, and so gratifying, that it crimsoned
me with blushes, and I could make no reply."

An old man's vanity, yes; a slightly old-fashioned Victorian touch in Twain's language that is not present elsewhere than when dealing with these adoring and delicious maidens — yet it is also remarkably open, tender, and humorous on the part of the aging Mark Twain, play-acting out the sexual comedy to the end. There is a reminiscence here of Ellen Terry as queen of the English stage for fifty years, and Clemens' cable to her:

> Age has not withered, nor custom staled, the admiration and affection I have felt for you so many, many years. I lay them at your honored feet with the strength and freshness of their youth upon them undiminished.

And no doubt Mark Twain was well aware of the intent of the original verses dedicated to the dusky Egyptian Queen:

> Age cannot wither her, nor custom stale
> Her infinite variety; other women cloy
> The appetites they feed; but she makes hungry
> Where most she satisfies.

There followed a brief account of Tom Sawyer's and Huck Finn's trials and tribulations at the hands of libraries and public institutions. These books, one or the other, or both, had been banned in Concord, Massachusetts, in Denver, Colorado, and by the Brooklyn Public Library in 1905. Just recently, as I say, further attempts have been made to censor *The Adventures of Huckleberry Finn,* without doubt the great epic of childhood in our literature, and whose hero is the old Negro slave, on the grounds that this figure is called "Nigger Jim," rather than "Negro Jim" or "Black Power Jim." When Clemens was informed by the librarian of the Sheepshead Bay Branch of the Brooklyn Library that the familiar discussion had ensued about

Huck's deceit, lies, immoral behavior, and, perhaps worst of all, improper language, Clemens wrote to Asa Don Dickinson, his informant. "I am greatly troubled by what you say. I wrote Tom Sawyer and Huck Finn for adults exclusively, and it always distresses me when I find that boys and girls have been allowed access to them. The mind that becomes soiled in youth can never again be washed clean; I know this by my own experience, and to this day I cherish an unappeasable bitterness against the unfaithful guardians of my young life, who not only permitted but compelled me to read an unexpurgated Bible through before I was 15 years old. None can do that and ever draw a clean sweet breath again this side of the grave. Most honestly do I wish I could say a softening word or two in defence of Huck's character, since you wish it, but really in my opinion it is no better than those of Solomon, David, Satan, and the rest of the sacred brotherhood."

If there was an unexpurgated Bible in the Children's Department of the Brooklyn Library, Clemens concluded, "won't you please help that young woman remove Huck and Tom from that questionable companionship?" There was a newspaper storm a little later about Mark Twain's letter, but he remained comfortably in bed. "Of course I was in bed. I am always in bed." There is another account of Frank Fuller's enthusiastic launching of Mark Twain's first New York lecture, an enormous debacle at the time which was nevertheless a steppingstone to Twain's future success. By now Twain had almost concluded his reminiscences; his mind kept moving around to include last-minute memories of present and past, but his job, his great *Autobiography,* was almost finished, as he thought, and he could not even bear to go back through the mass of material. "I am not glancing through my books to find out what I have said in them. I refrain from glancing through those books for two reasons: first — and this reason always comes first in every matter connected with my life — laziness. I am too lazy to examine the books. The other reason is — well, let it go. I had another reason, but it had slipped out of my mind while I was arranging the first one. I think it likely that in the book called *Roughing It* I have mentioned Frank Fuller. But I don't know, and it isn't any matter . . ."

Such were the ending words of *Mark Twain's Autobiography*, in its first, 1924, edition as edited by Albert Bigelow Paine; the ending that Paine thought Sam Clemens preferred. But this was only the *first* appearance of one of our great books of personal memoirs. There were to be volumes of appendices containing new material, and material omitted by the sometimes over-prudent Paine; there were to be new editions of the *Autobiography* itself, continuing up to the 1960s and no doubt after that. For Clemens had left a huge mass of still undigested, unedited, unprinted material to fill up this book and to make others which were contingent upon it. Ending on the note of laziness, indifference, casualness, even carelessness, viewing the world now from the resting place of his bed, this great voice of our letters would not stop so easily, this great spirit would hardly subside into the silence it pretended to seek.

As a matter of fact, while the last date in the first edition of the *Autobiography* was Wednesday, April 11, 1906, the Autobiography "Dictations" to Paine and a secretary would continue through 1906 at 21 Fifth Avenue, New York, and Dublin, New Hampshire; through 1907 at 21 Fifth Avenue; through 1908 in New York City and Redding, Connecticut; through 1909 when he began what was in effect an extension of his last book, a volume called *Letters from the Earth*.

Letters from the Earth would also appear in due course, when the time was ready for it; but meanwhile there was another postmortem supplement to Mark Twain's autobiography, *Mark Twain in Eruption,* published in 1940.

But here we have to discuss what might be called the Ordeal of Bernard DeVoto.

TWELVE

SPY IN THE HOUSE
OF THE OLIGARCHY

AFTER A LAPSE of over ten years, during which appeared, among other critical studies, the famous study by Van Wyck Brooks, *The Ordeal of Mark Twain,* 1920, revised in 1933, which set the style for a whole school of Mark Twain criticism; which in a different Freudian form has been revived and refurbished in the contemporary period; and during which Brooks, incidentally, moved over toward Bernard DeVoto's "defense" of Twain, while DeVoto in turn moved murkily toward Brooks' original analysis; after this whole period of critical maneuvering, Sam Clemens spoke again in his own voice.

I am also omitting here William Dean Howells' famous eulogy, *My Mark Twain,* 1910, which was partly the focus of Brooks' attack, in a period when this famous and admirable historian of our literature was liquidating all the great talents he was afterwards to rehabilitate in his "usable past." I am also forced to omit *Mark Twain's Notebook,* in 1935, in this discussion for somewhat the same reason that we had to skip *Mark Twain's Letters.* Both of these volumes, fascinating in themselves, are source books of material which is discussed here in other forms.

If in a sense it is true that Mark Twain's life and work comprised one great Autobiography — in a Whitmanesque sense which embraced the world within the soul of the artist, or rather projected the *selfless* soul of the artist upon a boundless outside experience; if Mark Twain is one of those writers whose repetitions never repeat themselves or can be read afresh each time with a new sense of discovery and pleasure — well, there is a certain limit even to this law of non-limits.

Or to put it even more truthfully, I *would* have discussed both *Mark Twain's Letters* and *Mark Twain's Notebook* with great pleasure, surely, if only I had had the patience and the time to do so. And I regret that I can't. Meanwhile still another book, *Mark Twain in Eruption,* edited by Bernard DeVoto in 1940, takes precedence in our discussion. The Albert Bigelow Paine two-volume edition of the *Autobiography,* as DeVoto told us, used "something less than half of the typescript in which everything that Mark wanted in his memoirs had been brought together. This book uses about half the remainder." So the *Eruption* volume is either a sequel or a new edition of the *Autobiography,* and Mr. DeVoto's implication is that the material was too explosive for the earlier Paine edition. This is partly, but only partly true; and while Mr. DeVoto boldly opens the book with another section of Twain's radical social criticism — more boldly, as we've seen, than the intimidated critics of the 1950s — both the new material and DeVoto's appraisal of it deserve some close consideration. DeVoto is not satisfied with either Twain's sense of "formless form" for the *Autobiography,* or Paine's own rendering of this. He has put his selections into related blocks of material, and omitted the "trivialities, irrelevancies, newspaper clippings," the disconnected and planless form of the original book which he had always found "annoying."

He had also, said DeVoto, left out of the new version of the *Autobiography* passages which were "fantastic and injurious," those which contained "violent animosities," and which were crowded with "inaccuracies, distortions, and exaggerations." And very likely this was done at the cost of some of Twain's best passages of writing; since toward the rages and furies and polemical outbursts of genius, DeVoto shows all the cautious and fearful "moderation" of the respectable mind. Twain would hardly be Twain without those distortions, exaggerations, and animosities, as we know — those lurid rages leading into irony, satire, parody, farce, and high comedy. The description of Twain's relationship with the American Publishing Company and Elisha Bliss; with his own publishing company which Clemens entrusted to his nephew-in-law, Charles Webster; the description of Bret Harte — we are cautioned about all these classic sections of the *Autobiography* by the meticulous Mr. DeVoto.

Apart from these superficial "instructions" about reading Mark Twain (which apparently every leading critic of Twain has felt it necessary to impart to Twain's readers: the feeling, in short, that humor is too dangerous a thing to be accepted as humor), DeVoto has several more severe prohibitions about Twain and the *Autobiography* which have colored a large part of modern criticism.

He warns us, for example, that the *Autobiography* is not so much an autobiography as "a kind of table-talk" about the men and events which Sam Clemens was interested in. He took this from Twain's ironical self-deprecatory description of his book. Now this may be true of DeVoto's book, which being an appendix to the *Autobiography* (rather than a new edition) lacks all the marvelous range and depth of the original memoirs. And DeVoto points out that Twain, while being "the most autobi-

ographical of writers," does not ever even try to reveal himself
— forgetting the basic assumption that Mark Twain, like Walt
Whitman, was one of those pantheistic poets whose "I" was
the world's "I," whose rare temperaments reflected universal
life, and could not be separated from it. "I contain multitudes,"
said Walt. Moreover the whole *Autobiography*, according to
DeVoto, was written under the shadow of Twain's financial
bankruptcy and domestic sorrow and was a dark and obsessional
and phobic document — whereas we have just seen that in fact
it is one of the great *daylight* books of the world! Bearing indeed
all the scars of a wide, high, and full life, as Mark Twain did,
always touching the opposite extremes of great success and deep
failure, of intense joy and the depths of sorrow, of happiness
and misery — and forgetting nothing, with that total recall which
extended most vividly back to his earliest years — he was perhaps
the most open of all the major writers in North America. Aware
of the vicissitudes of human experience, the complex interaction
of a life force which is continually in flux, never to be counted on,
always variant but with the one certain element of change and
surprise and final loss, as Twain well knew, he yet, in the final
period of his work, was able by the sheer touch of his genius to
transcend and to re-create his whole life in that one last book,
that one last illuminating and enchanting chronicle.

The rages, furies, and searing indictments of Mark Twain;
the long-remembered and even intensely treasured scores to be
evened up; the curses and maledictions that brighten these pages;
the exaggerations and obsessions that DeVoto scolds Twain for
and points his reproving finger at — what are these but the marks
of that open-ended genius whom we have been describing in this
book? Of that Mark Twain to whom love and hate were equally
valid, and to whom perhaps only one thing in the world — the
"moderation" which Mr. DeVoto advocates; or the "consensus"

which Twain himself so violently decried; or the conformity and "normalcy" of life; or the sensible and "reasonable" thing — was despicable and tedious.

It is quite true that DeVoto corrects some dates and titles that in the range of his inimitable narrative Sam Clemens guessed at, forgot, didn't care about, or, as he frankly said, was too lazy to check. It is here also, in the famous Introduction to *Mark Twain in Eruption* (a lecture or essay which DeVoto spent much time in writing and revising as one of his own major critical documents), that we come upon the source of another central error of contemporary Mark Twain criticism. I mean the silly notion that Mark Twain's whole creative life and his best literary work were confined to the narrow limits of his frontier childhood in Hannibal. "When he wrote fiction," adds Mr. DeVoto, "which is to say when the bases of his personality were finding instinctive expression, the human race was the race he had known in Hannibal. Life was confined within the circumstances of his boyhood. There is a profound difference between Tom Sawyer and Huck Finn, but one or the other of them is holding the pen in the best, the deepest, and the truest of Mark's work."

Now Mr. DeVoto is treading on very subtle and mysterious ground here — a deep and profound quagmire of misunderstanding into which he then plunged over his head. This is a half-truth which, getting at the cause of Twain's greatness which has been described in these pages, mistakes its true nature only to end up in total error. "His artistic creativeness, his phantasy-making, was rooted in his boyhood," says Mr. DeVoto. "Why this should be so is a question not germane to this Introduction; one, furthermore, which could be answered only speculatively and only in analytical psychology." But it is indeed germane not only to Mr. DeVoto's introduction, but to Mark Twain's work as a whole, as we have described it. It is the essence of

Mark Twain's genius. And it is clearly perceived not indeed in "analytical" or Freudian psychology, but in the cultural psychology of Otto Rank who continually related the Artist — remembering human nature in all its plenitude, its generosity, its happiness, its sense of love and affection and play — to that "Fall" which was the beginning of civilization, with all its repressions and discontents.

Mr. DeVoto is so close to the truth at times, it is depressing to see him always reach the wrong conclusion. Mark Twain's memory of his childhood was indeed lyrical, as "a memory of freedom, irresponsibility, and security, islanded in a countryside and a society as pleasant as any in the American past." But this unique vision of pagan splendor and ease in the Sam Clemens of Hannibal was not at all beaten down by his memories of "anxiety, violence, supernatural horror" so much as it was always present in his vision of maturity and society. His vision of human life was hardly restricted to these childhood environs so much as it was always compared with it. The lost Eden was the shining remembrance in, so to speak, man's everlasting day of atonement. In fact, what happened was just the reverse of Mr. DeVoto's concept. The remarkable thing about Mark Twain's work is not that it stopped with childhood, but that *he carried his childhood* — his sense of play and pleasure, ease and irresponsibility, humor and affection — throughout his maturity.

All big artists do this; this is just what makes them artists — but never perhaps so clearly as in the case of Sam Clemens. In the fiction itself, it is quite true that he balanced off the early Tom Sawyer–Huck Finn parables of "innocence" (a satanic innocence to be sure) with the dark fables of *Pudd'nhead Wilson, Hadleyburg,* and *The $30,000 Bequest* in a kind of polar opposition of evil within the same familiar setting. But this duality, so familiar also in Melville and other writers, found its ironic

resolution in *The Mysterious Stranger*; just as Clemens' own deep
conflicts and wounds in life were resolved in the final complex
but essentially satirical and comic tone of the *Autobiography*
itself. By contrast, and through sheer error, one must infer,
Mr. DeVoto links together *What Is Man?, The Mysterious
Stranger,* and the *Autobiography* as examples of Mark Twain's
defeat and despair. (We have seen just how *The Mysterious
Stranger* used the raw material of *What Is Man?* for a much
more sophisticated and fulfilled artistic purpose.) Mr. DeVoto
claims that the crisis period in Twain's life broke his career in
two, and left him only with a shattered talent at the end.

But the plain fact is, as I hope the pages of this book illustrate,
that Mark Twain not only survived and surmounted life's worst
things, but that his later work far surpassed his earlier in knowledge and insight, in its range and complexity of artistic vision.
It too is a celebration of life but with all its tragic depths; much
more aware and complex than the rather simplistic innocence
of Huck and Tom. The Fallen Angel in Mark Twain himself
is still the supreme and satanic observer of the world; and all the
better for his fall from that innocence he always cherished and
never quite lost.

Even in fiction one might put *The Mysterious Stranger* in the
same literary category as *Huck Finn.* But of course Mr. De-
Voto's fatal mistake, from which all his other errors spring,
is the insistence about Mark Twain "that fundamentally he was
a novelist." Only a critic unaware of a novelist's temperament
could say that. Fundamentally Mark Twain was *not* a novelist
or a fiction writer at all. As I am forced to repeat, he was a
poet-prophet on the model of Walt Whitman even more than
that of Melville. And he used the fiction form, carelessly in
many instances, as a kind of parable dumb show for certain aspects of his temperament and vision that could best be described
in that medium. But even as to Twain's bardic role, as the ac-

knowledged prophet and conscience of his country at the end of the Old Republic, a role no writer has since assumed with Twain's singular splendor, Mr. DeVoto is curiously critical.

The merit of *Mark Twain in Eruption* is that it brings together another collection of Mark Twain's brilliant socio-historical commentary. In precisely that late, or last period of Mark Twain's work which he had just finished depreciating, Mr. DeVoto assembled enough important material to refute his own thesis. But was this captious critic aware of this, was he pleased with his own book? Not completely. "What is added to the portrait of Mark Twain by this book is the citizen of the first Roosevelt Era looking toward our own time with a strong foreboding. I have said elsewhere that when *The Adventures of Huckleberry Finn* is examined from a point of view much recommended to criticism since I wrote, that of social implications, it may be seen as the American democratic hope colliding with a realization of the limits implicit in American democracy." Mr. DeVoto writes as though he had pioneered in the "social implications" of literature. And isn't this a narrow and pedestrian view of a literary work whose larger and deeper theme is that of the pagan splendor of life confronted by the prejudices, superstitions, and repressions of *all*, not merely democratic forms of civilization? And Mr. DeVoto continues with an even more surprising evaluation of Mark Twain's social criticism.

"In what Mark has to say about the government and the plutocracy at the moment when the American empire is achieved he typifies his generation's confused surprise at finding contradictions in the American axioms. The man of good will, the Mugwump, not only perceives that there is something wrong but wonders, against his belief, whether something may not have been wrong from the beginning."

Now it is hard to imagine a more numerous and profound series of misconceptions about Mark Twain than that contained in these two sentences of DeVoto's. Mark Twain certainly did not belong to "his generation" in this sense at all — a generation indeed of financial barons and titans who felt not "confused surprise" but active pleasure in contradicting all the hitherto accepted axioms of American democracy and the American Dream. (Twain *did* belong to that artistic hierarchy of Melville and Whitman, and Thoreau and Emerson, as we've seen, who before and during his own time had discovered these contradictions.) Nor was Mark Twain any longer "surprised" at such fatal contradictions in the democracy which he had been writing about directly since the mid-nineties, and implicitly long before that. Nor were his marvelous polemical essays directed only at the "plutocracy," as DeVoto implies here; long before the *Autobiography* he had discovered the far worse evils of imperialism, both in the old world and the new. Imperialism is a key word of modern history from the nineteenth to the end of the twentieth century, at least — and a word that DeVoto never once mentions! Nor was Sam Clemens, finally, a "man of good will" in that conventional sense; but an edenic-satanic genius, as we know, on a far more complex level of human feeling; and his Mugwump period was really the sign of a very youthful and provincial phase before his true literary education began.

Let us remember the brilliant and eloquent defense of the French Revolution that runs through Mark Twain's work before and after *A Connecticut Yankee*. The man who could, after each rereading of Carlyle's apoplectic history of that revolution, declare himself more of a Jacobin than ever, and not just an ordinary Jacobin, but a Sansculotte and Marat Jacobin — can hardly be classified as a Mugwump. The artist who was attacking imperialism in 1895; and who in the 1900s was proclaiming the advent of the "American Empire," while he brilliantly attacked its colonialism and its racism alike, could hardly have been so naive and confused as was stated in the introduction to *Mark Twain in Eruption.*

It seems more likely that Mr. DeVoto himself was poorly prepared either to recognize the radical depths of Mark Twain's social criticism, or, more important, to accept it. It was this same western critic, first approaching Mark Twain as the epitome of "Frontier Individualism" — that Turneresque American Frontier which has since become subject to so much qualification — who had just a little earlier rebuked the major American writers of the twenties and thirties for having lost hope in the American Dream itself. For if DeVoto had really understood and accepted Mark Twain's revolutionary premises about the end of old-fashioned American democracy, about the advent of "Monarchy" and the imminence of a native dictatorship in one form or another, then his own literary values and his work would have had to undergo a deep change. It was easier to blame Mark Twain's confusion and ignorance than to accept Twain's profound insights — as a later generation of more radical critics would do. It was easier to focus the criticism on Mark Twain's "broken career" and the "diminution" of his talent in just those areas where Twain's prophetic genius would go beyond his personal life, and would achieve its final triumphs.

Perhaps indeed it was DeVoto's own confusion and ignorance and frustration that this critic attributed to the great master whose custodian he had become. But that is not to say there were not some confusions and contradictions in Twain's description of the oligarchy and the monarchy which opens *Mark Twain in Eruption* — and perhaps this came out most sharply in the commentary on Theodore Roosevelt which DeVoto chose to begin with. It was true that Clemens' friendship with Rogers, even his adoration of Rogers, made him defend the Standard Oil trust at times even while he was attacking it. His attitude was

ambiguous here, but hardly mute, as Justin Kaplan claims. And
the attack on Roosevelt veered from seeing him as the figurehead
of the great corporations which he was ostensibly attacking —
though Clemens caught this *at the time,* long before the historians recorded it — to seeing him as the villainous creator of the
business panic of 1907. The Roosevelt commentary was another example of Twain's compulsive hatreds but — perhaps because he was too close to his subject and too angry — one of
the least engaging. Nor was Twain altogether right in evaluating
the great corporation and the finance capitalism which Thorstein Veblen was more accurately describing during the same
period. But this is hardly the same as accusing him of a blind
ignorance in this field, some aspects of which he spotted so
acutely, and some personalities among the oligarchy whom he
described so intimately, in terms that no merely "proletarian"
author would have known about.

And just here, despite his abiding affection for his financial
savior, Rogers, Sam Clemens was not diffident about pointing
out some facts concerning the Standard Oil trust. "Mr. Roosevelt is easily the most astonishing event in American history, if
we except the discovery of the country by Columbus. The details of Mr. Roosevelt's purchase of the Presidency by bribery of
voters are all exposed now, even to the names of the men who
furnished the money and the amounts which each contributed.
The men are great corporation chiefs and three of them are
Standard Oil monopolists. It is now known that when the can-
vass was over a week before election day and all legitimate uses
for election money at an end, Mr. Roosevelt got frightened and
sent for Mr. Harriman to come to Washington and arrange measures to save the State of New York for the Republican party.
The meeting took place and Harriman was urged to raise two
hundred thousand dollars for the cause. He raised two hundred

and sixty thousand and it was spent upon the election in the last week of the campaign — necessarily for the purchase of votes, since the time had gone by for using money in any other way."

Now that is a pretty well-informed and precise account of a typical American election, and despite the irregularities of the Roosevelt commentary as literature it is still useful to have it in print as history. And DeVoto underestimated — for once — the depths of Mark Twain's bitterness and despair about the new American empire when Twain closed this essay by saying he would vote for Taft and the continuation of the "monarchy." "The monarchy is here to stay. Nothing can ever unseat it . . . Things will go along well enough under this arrangement so long as a Titus succeeds a Vespasian, and we shall best not trouble about a Domitian until we get him. All in good time he will arrive. The Lord will provide — as heretofore. My humble vote is for Titus Taft, inherited insane policies and all, and may it elect him! I do not believe he will appoint a Domitian to succeed him; I only know that if he shall disappoint us and appoint Domitian, Domitian will be elected. But I am not personally concerned in the matter; I shall not be here to grieve about it."

To later historians the comparison with the early Roman emperors would seem a very apt reference as delivered by Mark Twain in 1906. On Andrew Carnegie, Clemens was even more vitriolic; on Carnegie's unabashed, unconscious, unblushing egoism, Clemens was murderous.

"He never has any but one theme, himself . . . He is himself his one darling subject, the only subject he for the moment — the social moment — seems stupendously interested in. I think he would surely talk himself to death upon it if you would stay and listen . . . He talks forever and ever and ever and untiringly of the attentions which have been shown him. Sometimes they have been large attentions, most frequently they are very small ones; but no matter, no attention comes amiss to him and he likes to revel in them. His friends are coming to observe with consternation that while he adds new attentions to his list every now and then, he never drops an old and shopworn one out of the catalogue to make room for one of these fresh ones. He keeps the whole list, keeps it complete; and you must take it all, along with the new additions, if there is time and you survive. It is the deadliest affliction I know of. He is the Ancient Mariner over again; it is not possible to divert him from his subject; in your weariness and despair you try to do it whenever you think you see a chance, but it always fails; he will use your remark for his occasion and make of it a pretext to get straight back upon his subject again."

Never mind Carnegie's ethics and ideology, which are fair game for the social historian; this was a glimpse of the man, the great philanthropist and immortal iron master. "He has bought fame and paid cash for it," Clemens added. "He has deliberately projected and planned out this fame for himself; he has arranged that his name shall be famous in the mouths of men for centuries to come. He has planned shrewdly, safely, securely, and will have his desire." And so much for the bulk of what is called American philanthropy, if you add the tax-dodging devices of the contemporary American foundations. But Clemens was just warming up to the subject of his friend Andrew Carnegie in an essay from which I can give only a few highlights. He envisioned Carnegie libraries thicker than churches. "It is a long-headed idea and will deceive many people into thinking Carnegie a long-headed man in other and larger ways. I am sure he is a long-headed man in many and many a wise small way — the way of the trimmer, the way of the smart calculator, the way that enables a man to correctly calculate the tides and come in with the flow and go out with the ebb, keeping a permanent place on the top of the wave of advantage while other men as intelligent as he, but more addicted to principle and less to policy, get stranded on the reefs and bars."

He mentioned Carnegie's meeting with the German Kaiser, and the Kaiser's bold big face. "And I could see that other face turned up toward it — that foxy, white-whiskered, cunning little face, happy, blessed, lit up with a sacred fire, and squeaking without words: 'Am I in Heaven or is it only a dream?' " And the point was that Carnegie had absolutely no self-comprehension. "Mr. Carnegie is not any better acquainted with himself than if he had met himself for the first time day before yesterday. He thinks he is a rude, bluff, independent spirit, who writes his mind and thinks his mind with an almost extravagant Fourth of July independence; whereas he is really the counterpart of the rest of the human race in that he does not boldly speak his mind except when there isn't any danger in it. He thinks he is a scorner of kings and emperors and dukes, whereas he is like the rest of the human race: a slight attention from one of these can make him drunk for a week and keep his happy tongue wagging for seven years."

So much for another of the nineteenth-century industrial barons, ignorant of the Republic's origins, principles, and history, and of our great scholars, philosophers, and statesmen of the eighteenth and early nineteenth centuries; financiers and industrialists whose power and whose greed alike had changed the whole texture of Mark Twain's America. Clemens mentioned that the name of God himself had been left out of the Constitution "but was furnished a front seat on the coins of the country." The motto "In God We Trust" had recently been removed from American coins by Roosevelt because it was a profanation of the Holy Name. That was not the right reason, said Clemens, but there was, indeed, an unassailably good reason

— the fact that the motto stated a lie. "If this nation has ever trusted in God, that time has gone by; for nearly half a century almost its entire trust has been in the Republican party and the dollar — mainly the dollar."

Now it is true that in several of these late essays, embittered and disenchanted by the moral corruption of the American democracy of which he had himself been a leading chronicler, speculating darkly about the nature of the new Empire and the "monarchy," Clemens, forgetting his previous belief in the French Revolution, the Russian Revolution, the liberation of colonial China; ignoring his whole lifetime stress on radical democratic institutions and values, fell back upon his familiar assessment of the damned human race. "The human race was always interesting, and we know by its past that it will always continue so. Monotonously. It is always the same; it never changes. Its circumstances change from time to time, for better or worse, but the race's *character* is permanent, and never changes."

Here he was lapsing, momentarily and perhaps with some reason, from his earlier stress on "change" and "conditions," and on radicalizing social *institutions;* a belief which was eloquently stressed in the great social commentary of his later period. In stressing the unalterable *character* of the human race, he was forgetting that this same character was molded into completely different forms in the four or five great periods of evolutionary development from primitive man and pagan man to Christian man and so-called "rational man." And there was no reason to suppose this evolutionary development would stop with finance capitalism; that indeed human nature, this same "character" of the race, had proved over and over again, sometimes alarmingly so, to be infinitely malleable. But that is no reason also for Mark Twain scholars, like Mr. DeVoto, to concentrate on this single aspect of Clemens' thought — which was itself reacting to a given social environment, or an environmental shift — as being the main burden of his thought when it was precisely the opposite of that. It was a desperate end prodduct of his thinking; and sometimes it does seem to be true about the damned human race.

Oddly enough, this rather negative (if also entertaining) side of the later Mark Twain is placed at the front of the book, perhaps as a "key insight," and yet, even so, the main stress of *Mark Twain in Eruption* refutes and disproves the blacker strain in these memoirs. Reverting to the central theme of the forthcoming American Monarchy, Clemens added:

> Republics have lived long but monarchy lives forever. By our teaching we learn that vast material prosperity always brings in its train conditions which debase the morals and enervate the manhood of a nation — then the country's liberties come into the market and are bought, sold, squandered, thrown away, and a popular idol is carried to the throne upon the shields or shoulders of the worshipping people and planted there in permanency. We are always being taught — no, formerly we were always being taught — to look at Rome and beware . . .

And this parallel with the Roman Empire as announced by Mark Twain in the early 1900s would become, as I say, a staple of twentieth-century thinking about the United States.

He went on to list some vivid examples of his thesis. And despite Mr. DeVoto, an artist's "examples," his detailed and concrete descriptions of life, are always more important than his "ideology." Very often, as in the case of Mark Twain, the actual writing contradicts the schematic thinking of an artist. He often thinks what he thinks he should think, but he writes what he sees and feels; and it's a poor critic who takes the artist's credo above the artist's art. While Clemens was willing to waive

moral rank and associate with the moderately criminal among
the United States Senators, even including Platt and his friend
Chauncey Depew, "I have to draw the line at Clark of Montana.
He is said to have bought legislatures and judges as other men
buy food and raiment. By his example he has so excused and
so sweetened corruption that in Montana it no longer has an
offensive smell. His history is known to everybody; he is as rotten a human being as can be found anywhere under the flag; he
is a shame to the American nation, and no one has helped to
send him to the Senate who did not know that his proper place
was the penitentiary, with a chain and ball on his legs. To my
mind he is the most disgusting creature that the republic has
produced since Tweed's time."

And of course he went to the dinner in honor of the "Montana jailbird," just as he went to the dinners for Carnegie and
the Rockefellers, in order to gather new material for his "anec-
dotes." In this sense Mark Twain was the most notorious spy in
the house of the American oligarchy. He, more than any other
writer, historian, scholar, politician or statesman, surely deserved the fame and the honor of being the greatest traitor to
his class.

For Clark of Montana led naturally to the archetypal figure
of all these corrupting and corrupted new American ruling class
financial barons. Clark's dinner reminded Twain of "the only
instance of benevolence exploded upon the world by the late
Jay Gould that I ever heard of.* When that first and most in-

---

* It is curious, in what is still the classical work on this lurid period of American
history, Matthew Josephson's *The Robber Barons,* a book which in turn leads
back to Gustavus Meyers and Thorstein Veblen, that there is such small
mention of the Mark Twain writings which, from an entirely different source,
confirm all the other historians. But then the hard core of Twain's social
criticism was still unpublished at the time of the Josephson book; and in turn
Twain was apparently ignorant of his fellow historian Veblen; while even
today most biographical dictionaries omit Meyers' name.

famous corrupter of American commercial morals was wallow-
ing in uncountable stolen millions, he contributed five thousand
dollars for the relief of the stricken population of Memphis,
Tennessee, at a time when an epidemic of yellow fever was raging in that city. Mr. Gould's contribution cost him no sacrifice; it was only the income of the hour which he daily spent in
prayer — for he was a most godly man — yet the storm of wor-
shipping gratitude which welcomed it all over the United States
in the newspaper, the pulpit, and in the private circle might have
persuaded a stranger that for a millionaire American to give five
thousand dollars to the dead and dying poor — when he could
have bought a circuit judge with it — was the noblest thing in
American history, and the holiest."

Upon Senator Clark's personal behavior Clemens lavished
some of his finest venom:

> A miracle followed. I have always maintained that no man could
> make a speech with nothing but a compliment for a text but I
> know now that a reptile can. Senator Clark twaddled and twad-
> dled and twaddled along for a full half-hour with no text but those
> praises which had been lavished upon his trifling generosities; and
> he not only accepted at par all these silly phrases but added to them
> a pile — praising his own so-called generosities and magnanimi-
> ties with such intensity and color that he took the pigment all out
> of those other men's compliments and made them look pallid and
> shadowy. With forty years' experience of human assfulness and
> vanity at banquets, I have never seen anything of the sort that
> could remotely approach the assfulness and complacency of this
> coarse and vulgar and incomparably ignorant peasant's glorifica-
> tion of himself.

That was almost as good as the Carnegie description, and
H. L. Mencken got his text here, it would seem, in his later descriptions of a generation of coarse and vulgar and ignorant

American peasants elevated to high financial status or high political office. And yet it was Jay Gould to whom Clemens reverted as the prime mover of them all. "Jay Gould was the mightiest disaster which has ever befallen this country. The people had *desired* money before his day, but *he* taught them to fall down and worship it. They had respected men of means before his day, but along with this respect was joined the respect due to the character and industry which had accumulated it. But Jay Gould taught the entire nation to make a god of the money and the man, no matter how the money might have been acquired. In my youth there was nothing resembling a worship of money or of its possessor, in our region. And in our region no well-to-do man was ever charged with having acquired his money by shady methods.

"The gospel left behind by Jay Gould is doing giant work in our days. Its message is 'Get money. Get it quickly. Get it in abundance. Get it in prodigious abundance. Get it dishonestly if you can, honestly if you must.'" Now also, Sherwood Anderson would repeat the same gospel with the same aversion in such an early novel as *Windy McPherson's Son*; Dreiser would repeat it in the Cowperwood Trilogy and *An American Tragedy*. In small or large degree every American writer would repeat it after Mark Twain; at least until the 1950s and 1960s, when it ceased to become a matter of literary importance perhaps because it was taken for granted. And there were other reasons. What is the use of going back to *that?* . .

And was this vast sea change in our history — the end of the Old Republic, the advent of American Empire, American Dynasty, and American Imperialism — a sea change and land change so well documented, recorded, and lamented by three generations of American writers after Howells and Mark Twain — was this a simple matter of Marxist economic determinism? Given the vast wealth of the American frontier, were the Rockefellers, the Vanderbilts, the Carnegies, the Senator Clarks, and the Jay Goulds simply inevitable? If there had been no Jay Gould, would the American destiny have invented one?

The point is that there was a special class of men, whether by nature and temperament, circumstance and fortune, luck or cunning, who were well equipped to handle and to exploit those vast powers which nature and their society had handed to them so freely. Another society, another culture more deeply ingrained, might have regulated and tempered their use and their abuse of this fantastic wealth in such a thoroughly primitive fashion. Historical or economic determinism can minimize but never can dispense with the role and part of individuals, of human will, in historical crisis. What is seen as "inevitable" has only become inevitable because of the clash of those heroic wills, which, as Marx himself said, produced by the clash itself a historical consequence which was not inevitable, sometimes never foreseen. The Old Republic of Mark Twain's youth was not prepared for and could not contain the fabulous wealth and power of the frontier and the particular type of cunning, ruthless, and unprincipled American entrepreneurs who came to exploit and dominate it. And now we see that the frontier, whose illusion of "freedom" was expounded so eloquently by the conservative historian Frederic Turner, and after him, DeVoto, was in fact a drama of infinite corruption.

It was that event which Sam Clemens was describing just about as accurately and eloquently as an artist could; and those men — whose personal presence he was so fortunate, in one sense, to know — whom he was pillorying. The new gospel of getting rich by any means, by abandoning all the ethical-moral restraints which had governed the older American mercantile-

agrarian community from the days of the Founding Fathers and
the heroic Revolution (despite the shadow of the Indian genocide, the uneasy presence of slavery which to some have appeared to doom the Republic from the start) — was not merely
confined to those figures Clemens had described. It had in-
fected the whole business community. "The gospel does seem
to be almost universal. Its great apostles, today, are the Mc-
Curdies, McCalls, Hydes, Alexanders, and the rest of that robber gang who have lately been driven out of their violated positions of trust in the colossal insurance companies of New
York. President McCall was reported to be dying day before
yesterday. The others have been several times reported, in the
past two or three months, as engaged in dying. It has been
imagined that the cause of these death strokes was sorrow and
shame for the robberies committed upon the two or three million
policy holders and their families, and the widow and the orphan
— but every now and then one is astonished to find that it is not
the outraged conscience of these men that is at work; they are
merely sick and sore because they have been exposed."

And what handsome prose Sam Clemens fashioned to expose
this lurid material. What shades of irony, parody, satire he invoked in these polemics, these burning hot passages of invective. How his spirit leaped at the challenge and rejoiced at the
response! Innocence, human and communal, was being betrayed; his own innocent spirit was outraged — but it was not
an altogether innocent spectator who was flaying this villainy.
It was again that special brand of the edenic-demonic artist
who was at work here. And Mark Twain had caught something
else in this whole scene which Mr. DeVoto seems not to have
noticed. I mean the ceremonies and ceremonials, the hypocritical obsequies of old-fashioned American religious observ-
ance which these financial robber-bandits used to disguise the

true nature of their activity: the vulgar show of devout religiosity which was put forth to camouflage their amoral characters and corrupt social functioning.

Meanwhile Clemens continued his lecture about the defaulting insurance magnates. "Yesterday — as I see by the morning paper — John A. McCall quite forgot about his obsequies and sat up and became impressive, and worked his morals for the benefit of the nation. He knew quite well that anything which a prodigiously rich man may say — whether in health or moribund — will be spread by the newspapers from one end of this continent to the other and be eagerly read by every creature who is able to read. McCall sits up and preaches to his son — ostensibly to his son — really to the nation. The man seems to be sincere, and I think he *is* sincere. I believe his moral sense is atrophied. I believe he really regards himself as a high and holy man. And I believe he thinks he is so regarded by the people of the United States. He has been worshipped because of his wealth, and particularly because of his shady methods of acquiring it for twenty years. And I think he has become so accustomed to this adulation, and so beguiled and deceived by it that he does really think himself a fine and great and noble being, and a proper model for the emulation of the rising generation of young men. He snivels owlishly along and is evidently as happy and as well satisfied with himself as if there wasn't a stain upon his name, nor a crime in his record. Listen — here is his little sermon —"

"Work, Work, says McCall. Tells of His Last Cigar in a Talk with His Son." And Clemens proceeded to quote from the rest of this inspiring and transparently deceitful Horatio Alger sermon in the New York *Times* of February 16, 1906. The sons and daughters of these monsters, Clemens added, moved in what was regarded as the best society. Jay Gould's daughter

had married a titled Frenchman who turned out to be a noisy
and silly ruffian, a gambler with debts of a million dollars and
more; and she was presently suing "for a separation from her
shabby purchase." Indeed the political and commercial morals
of the United States were not merely food for laughter, "they are
an entire banquet." He mentioned the old saying that the American press was the palladium of our liberties. "It was a serious
saying and it was a true saying, but it is long ago dead and has
been tucked safely away in the limbo of oblivion. No one would
venture it now except as a sarcasm."

So to the Yellow Press which both he and Howells had
already excoriated, Clemens now added the so-called American free press. And to the list of corrupt business leaders —
those new heroes of the American Dream, for whom the Horatio
Alger myth was the most brilliant act of camouflage ever to be
invented by a society which badly needed such a literary mask
to hide its true nature — he included the name of Colorado's
Simon Guggenheim. "Mr. Guggenheim has lately been chosen
United States Senator reputedly by a bought legislature in
Colorado — which is almost the customary way, now, of elect-
ing United States Senators. Mr. Guggenheim is said to have
purchased his legislature and paid for it. By his public utterances it is plain that the general political rottenness has entered
into him and saturated him, and he is not aware that he has
been guilty even of an indelicacy, let alone a gross crime.
In many instances the palladium of our liberties has nothing but
compliments for him, and justification . . . Mr. Guggenheim,
in buying what an obsolete phrase called senatorial 'honors,'
did not buy the entire legislature but practiced the customary
economy and bought only enough of it to elect him. This has
been resented by some of the unbought; they offered a motion
to inquire into the methods by which his election was achieved,

but the bought majority not only voted the motion down but actually *sponged it from the records.* It looks like sensitiveness but it probably isn't; it is human nature that even the most conscienceless thieves do not like to be pilloried in the Rogues' Gallery."

In this Rogues' Gallery of American financiers, Clemens had hardly any need to resort to whatever anti-Semitism might have lingered in him. Mr. Guggenheim belonged to the new class of robber barons, and worse Clemens could say of no man. And this profile was followed by that of the Rockefellers themselves. "One of the standing delights of the American nation in these days is John D. Rockefeller, Junior's, Bible Class adventures in theology. Every Sunday young Rockefeller explains the Bible to his class. The next day the newspapers and the Associated Press distribute his explanations all over the continent and everybody laughs.

"Young Rockefeller, who is perhaps thirty-five years old, is a plain, simple, earnest, sincere, honest, well-meaning, commonplace person, destitute of originality or any suggestion of it. And if he were traveling upon his mental merit instead of upon his father's money, his explanations of the Bible would fall silent and not be heard of by the public. But his father ranks as the richest man in the world, and this makes his son's theological gymnastics interesting and important. The world believes that the elder Rockefeller is worth a billion dollars. He pays taxes on two million and a half. He is an earnest, uneducated Christian and for years and years has been Admiral of a Sunday school in Cleveland, Ohio. For years and years he has discoursed about himself to his Sunday school and explained how he got his dollars; and during all these years his Sunday school has listened in rapture and has divided its worship between him and his Creator — unequally. His Sunday-school talks are telegraphed about the country and are as eagerly read by the nation as his son's."

Here Clemens digressed a moment from the whole gaudy farce of these cunning financiers using the Christian ethics to shield and disguise their own social behavior. (And what a grand farce it was; and what a great witness Mark Twain proved to be; since his account of this phase of finance capital's "morality" is unique in the national letters.) He went on to discuss the hypocrisy of the Christian Church itself.

For the young Rockefeller was simply repeating all the conventional Christian parables and explications. "Young John's methods are the ordinary pulpit methods. His deductions of golden fancy from sordid fact are exactly the same which the pulpit has traded in for centuries. Every argument he uses was already worn threadbare by the theologians of all the ages before it came in its rags to him. All his reasonings are like the reasonings of all the pulpit's stale borrowings from the dull pulpits of the centuries . . . Young John has never studied a doctrine for himself; he has never examined a doctrine for any purpose but to make it fit the notions which he got at secondhand from his teachers." Apparently these financial titans, brilliant at their own trade, were not religious scholars. Yet Sam Clemens thought that young John Rockefeller would do well in the church if only he had been allowed to. "I have known and liked young John for many years and I have long felt that his right place was in the pulpit. I am sure that the fox fire of his mind would make a proper glow there — but I suppose he must do as destiny has decreed and succeed his father as master of the colossal Standard Oil Corporation."

How could DeVoto miss these passages? And Clemens followed this with his own interpretation of young John's version of Christ's injunction, "Sell all thou hast and give to the poor," and with an economic interpretation of the Joseph story in the Bible. He played with different endings for a story of a clergyman who discovered a first-edition Shakespeare folio in an ignorant farmer's house, and decided he would have sent the farmer an encyclopedia in return, "for this would be the way of the human race, and I am the human race compacted and crammed into a single suit of clothes but quite able to represent its entire massed multitude in all its moods and inspiration." This was Mark Twain in his most exalted and Whitmanesque mood of the great "I" which is you and us; but not the "Big Me" which is Me alone. This was the fusion of the individual with the human race in all its grandeur and all its crimes and follies. But Clemens' view was essentially tragic or tragicomic; the laughter proceeding from the crimes and follies. One wonders at those critics who see, in his embracing of all human weakness, only a form of personal self-deprecation.

Oh, no, Sam Clemens is never to be explained in such personal terms, but only in terms of personal transcendence, or of that universality which Whitman himself borrowed from Eastern mysticism, but Sam Clemens seemed to inherit from the air, and from his native grounds. And then there is the account, at the very start of Twain's literary career, of Elisha Bliss and the American Publishing Company of Hartford, Connecticut. Mr. DeVoto again cautions us that this memory is biased and inaccurate. Very likely so, but it is the Dickensian Elisha Bliss who flowers in these pages as an immortal scoundrel — and a most credible one.

Discussing Bliss, Clemens sidetracked his reminiscences to include another publisher, Webb, who had done the *Jumping Frog* book. "Webb believed that he was a literary person. He might have gotten this superstition accepted by the world if he had not extinguished it by publishing his things. They gave him away. His prose was enchantingly puerile, his poetry was not any better, yet he kept on grinding out his commonplaces at intervals until he died, two years ago, of over-cerebration. He was a poor sort of creature and by nature and training a fraud. As a liar he was well enough and had some success but no distinction, because he was a contemporary of Elisha Bliss and when it came to lying Bliss could overshadow and blot out a whole continent of Webbs like a total eclipse." And how many scoundrels, frauds, liars, to whom the credulous Clemens entrusted his books, his money, his name and patronage, stalk through the pages of the *Autobiography*! The "innocent" Mark Twain was no stranger to the human frailty and gullibility and deviousness, to say the least, which he described so brilliantly in these dramas which are full of malice, wrath, invective — and a kind of final, forgiving sunlight comedy.

For the episodes about his early publishers were followed by a meticulous account of his investments in all kinds of inventions which promised so much and failed so quickly, except the Bell telephone in which he had wisely refused to invest. In *Mark Twain in Eruption* DeVoto published a slightly different version of Twain's relationship with Grant. It is equally interesting as the tribute of one nineteenth-century genius to another, whether or not the twentieth century would see in it the pattern of a "father surrogate," or the worship of a military strong man by a confessed military coward and shirker. Nonsense, as we know. Grant was one of those extraordinarily great men thrown up by the early Republic in its hour of need, and Sam Clemens was great enough to appreciate greatness — while Grant in turn had an unusual but not unexpected admiration for the great artist and man of peace who satirized violence and warfare.

Speaking, indeed, of the line of American humorists whom

he derived from and capped, Clemens gave his own reasons. "I have always preached. That is the reason that I have lasted thirty years. If the humor came of its own accord and uninvited, I have allowed it a place in my sermon, but I was not writing the sermon for the sake of the humor . . . I should have written the sermon just the same, whether any humor applied for admission or not. I am saying these vain things in this frank way because I am a dead person speaking from the grave. Even I would be too modest to say them in life. I think we never become really and genuinely our entire and honest selves until we are dead — and not then until we have been dead years and years. People ought to start dead, and then they would be honest so much earlier."

Marvelous words, which to a certain degree contradict the argument of Mark Twain's own preaching and "sermons," for this artist was omitting his own central sense of luxury, ease, and "play," from which the natural humor came. But both statements are true; and one can only regret that Charles Neider, the next editor of the *Autobiography*, did not pay more attention to Clemens' own belief in his moral preachings. There is another interesting account of the writing of "1601" and its subsequent history as an underground classic. "So I contrived that meeting of the illustrious personages in Queen Elizabeth's private parlor, and started a most picturesque and lurid and scandalous conversation between them. The Queen's cupbearer, a dried-up old nobleman, was present to take down the talk — not that he wanted to do it but because it was the Queen's desire and he had to. He loathed all those people because they were of offensively low birth, and because they hadn't a thing to recommend them except their incomparable brains. He dutifully set down everything they said, and commented upon their words and their manners with bitter scorn and indignation. I put into the Queen's mouth, and into the mouths of those other people, grossnesses not to be found outside of Rabelais, perhaps. I made their stateliest remarks reek with them, and all this was charming to me — delightful, delicious — but their charm was as nothing to that which was afforded me by that outraged old cupbearer's comments upon them."

Again Clemens showed his pleasure in the rich body of the language, in the most colorful kind of obscenity, in all the words that "good taste" decried and that Livy had tried so hard to censor from his writings sometimes, but never from his heart. And here in *Mark Twain in Eruption* is the violent and tragic and tragicomic portrait of Bret Harte which Paine did not dare to use in the first edition of the *Autobiography*.

Was Clemens entirely too vitriolic and wrathful and brutally honest about Harte (who had also made the mistake of insulting Livy's hospitality in Hartford), as Mr. DeVoto claimed, and did DeVoto himself have still another conflict about the propriety of publishing the full version even in modern times? Like the picture of Elisha Bliss, that of Harte is a little masterpiece in satiric and not in the end entirely unsympathetic, portraiture. Describing his first meetings with his fellow chronicler of frontier life, Clemens started with Harte's writing. It was in the California mining towns like Yreka and Jackass Gulch that Harte had learned to observe the scenery, the inhabitants, the customs which had brought him such early acclaim. "It was in those places that he also learned how to fascinate Europe and America with the quaint dialect of the miner — a dialect which no man in heaven or earth had ever used until Harte invented it. With Harte it died, but it was no loss. By and by he came to San Francisco. He was a compositor by trade, and got work in *The Golden Era* office at ten dollars a week."

Harte's writing was hardly as interesting as his personality, which to a large degree was reflected in his literary work itself. "Bret Harte was one of the pleasantest men I have ever known. He was also one of the unpleasantest men I have ever known. He was showy, meretricious, insincere; and he constantly advertised these qualities in his dress. He was distinctly pretty, in spite of the fact that his face was badly pitted with smallpox. In the days when he could afford it — and in the days when he couldn't — his clothes always exceeded the fashion by a shade or two. He was always conspicuously a little more intensely fashionable than the fashionablest of the rest of the community. He had good taste in clothes. With all his conspicuousness there was never anything really loud nor offensive about them. They always had a single smart little accent, effectively located, and that accent would have distinguished Harte from any other of the ultra-fashionables. Oftenest it was his necktie. Always it was of a single color, and intense. Most frequently, perhaps, it was crimson — a flash of flame under his chin; or was it indigo blue and as hot and vivid as if one of those splendid and luminous Brazilian butterflies had lighted there. Harte's dainty self-complacencies extended to his carriage and gait. His carriage was graceful and easy, his gait was of the mincing sort, but was the right gait for him, for an unaffected one would not have harmonized with the rest of the man and the clothes.

"He hadn't a sincere fiber in him. I think he was incapable of emotion, for I think he had nothing to feel with. I think his heart was merely a pump and had no other function. I am almost moved to say I *know* it had no other function . . ." It is a pity that we cannot escape from life when we are young, Clemens remarked, conscious of the pain and suffering in his own life, and ignoring the fact that some of his best writing was written in old age. "When Bret Harte started east in his newborn glory thirty-six years ago, with the eyes of the world upon him, he had lived all of his life that was worth living. He had lived all his life that was to be respectworthy. He had lived all of his life that was to be worthy of his *own* respect. He was entering upon a miserable career of poverty, debt, humiliation, shame, disgrace, bitterness, and a world-wide fame which must have often been odious to him, since it made his poverty and the shabbiness of his character conspicuous beyond the power of any art to mercifully hide them." Clemens also thought the sense of shame had been left out of Harte's character; and such was the opening profile of the writer whose subsequent career is delineated in these pages with equal verve; while Critic Clemens, always an astute observer of his craft, was accurate in his estimate of "The Heathen Chinee," "The Luck of Roaring Camp," and *Gabriel Conroy,* as the earliest and perhaps the only interesting works of Harte.

Harte had no feeling, Clemens repeated, "for the reason that he had no machinery to feel with." But in the end he summarized this notorious career in compassionate tones, since Harte was after all only following the laws of his own nature as every creature must; and was helpless before the demands of his own temperament. In fact Clemens hated the successful and rich Mrs. Thomas Bailey Aldrich much more devoutly, and the account of his visit to the Thomas Bailey Aldrich Memorial Museum in Portsmouth, New Hampshire, is another high point of malice and laughter. Mrs. Aldrich was opening this shrine with her own money, at the expense of other more deserving literary figures, so Clemens felt, and for a dubious purpose. "The justification for an Aldrich Memorial Museum for pilgrims to visit and hallow with their homage may exist, but to me it seems doubtful. Aldrich was never widely known; his books never attained to a wide circulation; his prose was diffuse, self-con-

scious, and barren of distinction in the matter of style; his fame
as a writer of prose is not considerable; his fame as a writer of
verse is also very limited." Nevertheless Mrs. Aldrich was going to have her museum.

"The late Thomas Bailey Aldrich was born in his grandfa-
ther's house in the little town of Portsmouth, New Hampshire,
seventy-two or seventy-three years ago. His widow has lately
bought that house and stocked it with odds and ends that once
belonged to the child Tom Aldrich, and to the schoolboy Tom
Aldrich, and to the old poet Tom Aldrich, and turned the
place into a memorial museum in honor of Aldrich and for the
preservation of his fame. She has instituted an Aldrich Memorial
Museum Corporation under the laws of the State of New Hampshire, and has turned the museum over to this corporation
which is acting for the City of Portsmouth, the ultimate heir of
the benefaction, and she has injected the mayor of Portsmouth
and other important people into that corporation to act as advertisement and directors. A strange and vanity-devoured, de-
testable woman! I do not believe I could ever learn to like her
except on a raft at sea with no other provisions in sight."

Thus the later Twain continued to break all the Victorian
sanctities, in this case, womanhood. Following after the portrait of Mrs. Eddy, compounded of admiration and outrage; following the tender, touching, lyrical, and adoring account of
Livy, the profile of Mrs. Aldrich was remarkable in its candor
and its ridicule. She was the first of a series of women whom
the later Mark Twain despised as openly as he could love others.
And Mrs. Aldrich's vanity had been fed by her husband's.
Thomas Bailey Aldrich had "very nearly as extensive an appreciation of himself and his gifts as had the late Edmund Clarence
Stedman, who believed that the sun merely rose to admire his
poetry and was so reluctant to set at the end of the day and lose

sight of it, that it lingered and lingered and lost many minutes diurnally, and was never able to keep correct time during his stay on earth." *

Yet Clemens admitted he *was* prejudiced. "It is possible that I would never be able to see anything creditable in anything Mrs. Aldrich might do. I conceived an aversion for her the first time I ever saw her, which was thirty-nine years ago, and that aversion has remained with me ever since. She is one of these people who are profusely affectionate, and whose demonstrations disorder your stomach . . ." Even the feminine sex, or as Clemens called them in the gallantry of the times, "the sex," contained its quota of hypocrites. And he was just warming up. There followed an account of the long hard trip by train to Portsmouth, for which Mrs. Aldrich had hired two special cars from Boston, which disappointed Clemens. "It was not for Mrs. Aldrich to do such a thing; it was not for Mrs. Aldrich to squander money on politeness to guests, eleemosynarily rich as she is . . . It irritated me, disappointed me, affronted me, to see her rising above herself under the elevating influence of a high family occasion; in my malice I wanted to find some way to account for it that would take the credit out of it, and so I said to myself that she, the great advertiser, the persistent advertiser, the pushing and scrabbling and tireless advertiser, was doing this gaudy thing for the sake of spreading it around in the newspapers and getting her compensation out of it as an advertisement. That seemed a sort of plausible way of accounting for it, but I was so deeply prejudiced that it did not pacify me . . . However, in my animosity I said to myself that I would not allow her to collect glory from me at an expense to

* Thus, toward the end of his life, Sam Clemens also gave his true opinion of the mainly mediocre and stuffed-shirt Victorian writers who comprised his circle of friends but with whom, in truth, he had few spiritual ties. With the exception of Howells, of course.

her of two dollars and forty cents, so I made Paine buy tickets to Portsmouth and return. That idea pleased me; indeed there is more real pleasure to be gotten out of a malicious act, where your heart is in it, than out of thirty acts of a nobler sort."

It turned out, however, that Mrs. Aldrich had merely *secured* the special cars. All her guests, as well as Mark Twain, had to pay the regular fare, and he was content. "The incident restored my Mrs. Aldrich to me undamaged and just the same old thing she had always been, undeodorized and not a whiff of her missing . . . I realized that I had gotten back my lost treasure, the real Mrs. Aldrich, and that she was 'all there,' as the slang-mongers phrase it."

Now while Paine could hardly include Mrs. Aldrich among the treasures of the original *Autobiography,* it must be said that Mr. DeVoto, to his credit, and despite some polite demurring, did include it in *Mark Twain in Eruption,* just as he included the remarkable scene with Elinor Glyn. "Two or three weeks ago Elinor Glyn called on me one afternoon and we had a long talk, of a distinctly unusual character, in the library." Clemens went on to describe the plot and theme of her *Three Weeks.* "The hero's feeling for the rector's daughter was pale, not to say colorless, and it is promptly consumed and extinguished in the furnace fires of his passion for the mysterious stranger — passion is the right word, passion is what the pair of strangers feel for each other, what they recognize as real love — the only real love, the only love worthy to be called by that great name."

The queenlet and the Englishman flit away privately to the mountains and take up sumptuous quarters in a remote and lonely house there — and then business begins. They recognize that they were highly and holily created for each other and that their passion is a sacred thing, that it is their master by divine right, and that its commands must be obeyed. They get to obeying them at once and they keep on obeying them and obeying them, to the reader's intense delight and disapproval, and the process of obeying them is described, several times, almost exhaustively, but not quite — some little rag of it being left to the reader's imagination, just at the end of each infraction; the place where his imagination is to take up and do the finishing being indicated by stars.

The unstated argument of the book, said Clemens, "is that the laws of Nature are paramount and properly take precedence over the interfering and impertinent restrictions obtruded upon man's life by man's statutes." This "unstated argument" was also, of course, very familiar to Mark Twain; very natural, very deeply and profoundly personal with him, since it was the unstated argument of his own temperament and literary work. This is the same conflict of man's natural instincts with all the civilizational restraints and inhibitions contained in what he called "man's statutes." Those "statutes" of our discontents!

This was coming very close, as we realize, to Mark Twain himself: the "divided soul" which was in fact the double soul of man under civilization; and which Sam Clemens embodied so purely in his own temperament, as I say, in a *racial* rather than a personal conflict; and in a Rankian rather than a Freudian concept of art and culture. Elinor Glyn's book brought this out clearly in him; and then there is the famous lady herself.

"Mme. Glyn called, as I have said, and she was a picture! Slender, young, faultlessly formed and incontestably beautiful — a blonde with blue eyes, the incomparable English complexion, and crowned with a glory of red hair of a very peculiar, most rare, and quite ravishing tint. She was clad in the choicest stuffs and in the most perfect taste. There she is, just a beautiful girl; yet she has a daughter fourteen years old." But she wasn't really winning, Clemens realized, she had no charm "but the charm of beauty, and youth, and grace, and intelligence and vivacity," he insisted, as if that were not enough. "She *acts* charm," and her fictional English hero would only have admired and left her, "with his purity in good repair," and yet she was remarkable.

"I talked to her with daring frankness, frequently calling a spade a spade instead of coldly symbolizing it as a snow shovel; and on her side she was equally frank. It was one of the damndest conversations I have ever had with a beautiful stranger of her sex, if I do say it myself that shouldn't. She wanted my opinion of her book and I furnished it. I said its literary workmanship was excellent and that I quite agreed with her view that in the matter of the sexual relation man's statutory regulations of it were a distinct interference with a higher law, the law of Nature. I went further and said I couldn't call to mind a written law of any kind that had been promulgated in any age of the world in any statute book or any Bible for the regulation of man's conduct in *any* particular, from assassination all the way up to Sabbath-breaking, that wasn't a violation of the law of Nature, which I regarded as the highest of laws, the most peremptory and absolute of all laws — Nature's laws being in my belief plainly and simply the laws of God, since He instituted them, He and no other, and the said laws, by authority of this divine origin taking precedence of all the statues of man. I said that her pair of indelicate lovers were obeying the law of their make and disposition; that therefore they were obeying the clearly enunciated law of God, and in His eyes must manifestly be blameless."

And here of course the gloomy and dogmatic and harsh "determinism" of *What Is Man?*, so often attacked by the critics, was flowering madly and joyously and correctly. And here too, one suddenly realizes why Sam Clemens was so early and deeply and personally involved with the Bible itself. Not for any reasons either of religious guilt, indeed, nor of a superficial atheis-

tic defiance — but simply because the Bible is the first great
textbook in Western European culture of both man's natural
origins — the Garden, the Fall, and Mark Twain's inimitable
first lovers, Adam and Eve — and of man's "statutory regulations": work, morality, the pain and suffering and loss involved
even in the primitive beginnings of civilization. For, of course,
the Bible is not only the haunting story of pagan man in all his
animal glory and virtue and innocence; it is the story of primitive man's confrontation with the first authoritarian, jealous
and demanding God of Wrath, of Monotheism, of Culture. And
Satan, the rebellious angel, is the pagan spirit of primitive man
which will not, which will never, accept the "regulations" and
statutes of Judeo-Christian culture.

Moreover, if Clemens was apparently ambiguous in describing God as both the God of Nature and of Culture, isn't that
the central conflict of Western man himself? We see God in
both lights, as a Double God indeed, who in His great book
represents precisely both the instincts of nature and the repressions which the first primitive social order devised to curb man's
natural instincts. The meeting with Elinor Glyn brought up all
of this again from Mark Twain's unconscious. And that is to
say, the *Autobiography* is such a great book because, in Twain's
last years, it crystallized and made articulate his whole life and
career; the central thrust and meaning of his art. And did he
not half consciously or more, genius that he was, feel this himself when he made such great claims and sweeping grandiose
statements about the future life of His, like God's, primal book?

And didn't Sam Clemens embody the whole profound conflict in himself — and yet still retain his natural soul and con-
trive to defeat and to triumph over the cultural restraints of his
own period — when after all this he told Madame Glyn that
absolutely she could not publish such heretical sentiments on his
part?

"Of course what she wanted of me was support and defense — I knew that but I said I couldn't furnish it. I said we were servants of convention; that we could not subsist, either in a savage or a civilized state, without conventions; that we must accept them and stand by them, even when we disapproved of them; that while the laws of Nature, that is to say the laws of God, plainly made every human being a law unto himself, we must steadfastly refuse to obey those laws, and we must as steadfastly stand by the conventions which ignore them, since the statutes furnish us peace, fairly good government, and stability, and therefore are better for us than the laws of God, which would soon plunge us into confusion and disorder and anarchy, if we should adopt them. I said her book was an assault upon certain old and well-established and wise conventions, and that it would not find many friends, and indeed would not deserve many.

"She said I was very brave, the bravest person she had ever met (gross flattery which could have beguiled me when I was very very young) and she implored me to publish these views of mine, but I said, 'No, such a thing is unthinkable.' I said that if I, or any other wise, intelligent, and experienced person, should suddenly throw down the walls that protect and conceal his *real* opinions on almost any subject under the sun, it would at once be perceived that he had lost his intelligence and his wisdom and ought to be sent to the asylum."

But of course Mark Twain *was* publishing his opinions if only for the posterity which he knew would cherish them, in this curious and entertaining double game with Madame Glyn, while she in turn would make sure that the interview would be published from her side of it, with Clemens not really objecting since he could not be held responsible for it.*

* According to DeVoto "there is a brief note on this interview in Elinor Glyn's autobiography, *Romantic Adventure,* in 1937"; but Twain also points out in

There was a touch of Tom Sawyer's slick double-talking in Mark Twain's account of this remarkable interview — along with the central theme of Huck Finn's primary, pagan, and outlawed sensuousness. Indeed, from the very start of Mark Twain's career these two "boyhood" characters had embodied the deeper content of his literary vision which he was now finally clarifying and articulating in his last book. So much for the critics who claim that Twain's childhood vision of life in Hannibal was all in all; that his work never developed beyond that simplistic and essentially naive opening to his career. The truth about Twain is in fact the reverse of this statement: the mature Twain had created the "childhood" characters, with great literary care and precision of craft, in order to convey a profound and beautiful view of life.

Did he then agree with Freud's harsh dictum that all civilization is developed at the price of human repression? That is true — except for art and the artist which, as Otto Rank perceived, and as Sam Clemens intuitively knew, are based on the edenic pleasure principle always conjoined, always in conflict with man's "statutes." So that even Twain's final injunction to Madame Glyn that we live by convention not by instinct, by hypocrisy and not by truth, was expressed here with a kind of mocking laughter. In this episode of the *Autobiography,* Twain was also playing a double game with himself: that is, he was publishing in full what he was commanding Elinor Glyn never to publish. And the glowing portrait of Elinor Glyn was followed by the angry sketch of Marie Corelli.

---

his *Autobiography* that she had written down the whole interview "without any softening and purifying modifications, and that it was 'just splendid, just wonderful.' She said that she had sent it to her husband, in England. Privately I didn't think that that was a very good idea, and yet I believed it would interest him. She begged me to let her publish it and said it would do infinite good in the world, but I said it would damn me before my time and I didn't wish to be useful to the world on such expensive conditions."

As the last of the feminine portraits in *Mark Twain in Eruption,* Marie Corelli's is also the most animated; it makes Mrs. Aldrich's look almost beneficent. "I met Marie Corelli at a small dinner party in Germany fifteen years ago and took a dislike to her at once, a dislike which expanded and hardened with each successive dinner course until when we parted at last, the original mere dislike had grown into a very strong aversion." And the rising tide of Sam Clemens' wrath was due at least partly to the fact that the conniving lady novelist had taken advantage of his weakness for the sex. "When I arrived in England, I found a letter from her awaiting me at Brown's Hotel. It was warm, affectionate, eloquent, persuasive; under its charm the aversion of fifteen years melted away and disappeared. It seemed to me that that aversion must have been falsely based; I thought I must certainly have been mistaken in the woman, and I felt a pang or two of remorse. I answered her letter at once — her love letter I may say — answered it with a love letter."

Clemens quoted the homely old adage: supposing is good, but finding out is better . . . or worse. Marie Corelli had invited him for lunch at her home in Stratford-on-Avon while he was en route to London. His English agent discovered that it was impossible for him to keep this date and still speak at the Lord Mayor's dinner that evening without exhausting himself. Despite all of Clemens' impassioned pleading of age and poor health and weariness, Marie Corelli was adamant about his keeping the date with her — for her purposes of displaying him to her friends and neighbors. Clemens kept the engagement — and described it — and described her. He put upon her that "unobstructed eye" we have mentioned; that painter's eye for scene, surface, and texture; that hard, direct, unflinching, and uncompromising gaze which he directed at the realities, rather than the appearances, illusions, and deceptions of the world

around him. Poor Marie Corelli! when he began to describe her
physical appearance too — for not even with Mrs. Aldrich had
Mark Twain used this look and these words upon the ladies
who surrounded him. "She is about fifty years old but has no
gray hairs; she is fat and shapeless; she has a gross animal
face; she dresses for sixteen, and awkwardly and unsuccessfully and pathetically imitates the innocent graces and witcheries
of that dearest and sweetest of all ages; and so her exterior
matches her interior and harmonizes with it, with the result —
as I think — that she is the most offensive sham, inside and
out, that misrepresents and satirizes the human race today. I
would willingly say more about her but it would be futile to try;
all the adjectives seem so poor and feeble and flabby, this morning."

So Marie Corelli had her triumph over Mark Twain, and exhibited him not once but several times in Stratford to demonstrate her prize and her power and her place in the world. But
he was no gentleman about it; and as a result the shabby and
scheming little lady-romancer of the Victorian epoch dwells
immortally in the pages of the *Autobiography*. After Marie
Corelli (Mary Mackay), who managed to outlive Twain at least,
he reverted to another leading figure in the whole line of pious
financiers or merchant-preachers. Although chronologically
the portrait of John Wanamaker had been written around 1886,
Clemens did not add anything to it in the final draft. Perhaps he
did not need to. "When a United States Court has convicted a
man of being a pirate — that is to say, a thief — it is perhaps
time for him to resign the superintendency of his Sunday school
and tone down some other of his lurid pieties; unless, as is more
than likely in Mr. John Wanamaker's case, he uses these arts
and offices merely as advertisements for his mercantile business.
It is now time — and also just and right — to secure to this

odorous pilgrim this extra distinction, which he has laboriously and indisputably earned — to wit: that he is the only individual in a population of 60,000,000 who is known to have picked the pockets of the heirs of the dead General Grant. The soldier fought death, hour by hour, in pain and weariness, to earn money to leave behind as a livelihood for his family; and before they had got a penny of it, this occasional moral instructor of youth in the Philadelphia Business College had his scrofulous hands on it. John Wanamaker helped himself first; the family had to wait. Whenever he prays from the platform of his Sunday school hereafter, it will be a good idea for him to always fetch out this incident and explain it to the Throne. It may not do any real good, but it will amuse the angels."

It also amused the satanic Mark Twain, who signed this little moral sermon of his own as Samuel L. Clemens of the firm of Publishers of General Grant's Personal Memoirs; and had actually brought suit against Wanamaker on this score, as De-Voto tells us, in the late 1880s. In another early section of the *Autobiography,* written about the same time, Clemens gave a bright and funny description of a visit paid to a New England village tavern by himself and the Reverend Twichell where they found themselves surrounded by rustic obscenities of speech which could have come straight out of Tom Jones' eighteenth-century England. This language did not shock the women of the house, as Clemens noticed, including the landlady and her little daughter, when an eloquent, warm-blooded ostler discoursed at length. And this village was barely a half-day's journey from the Bostonian citadel of literary refinement.

This pleasant old-fashioned rural interlude was a kind of prelude to, and a sharp contrast with, what was in effect the closing satire of *Mark Twain in Eruption*; which was an answer to the religious optimism of the period which considered man as the darling of the universe, the pearl of God's eye. He quoted a religious publication, the Chicago Presbyterian *Interior*: "For ourselves we do thoroughly believe that man, as he lives just here on this tiny earth, is in essence and possibilities the most sublime existence in all the range of non-divine being — the chief love and delight of God."

"Land," he said, "it is just for the world the way I feel about it myself, sometimes, even when dry. And when not dry, even those warm words are not nearly warm enough to get up to what I am feeling, when I am holding on to something, and blinking affectionately at myself in the glass, and recollecting that I'm it . . . And when I am feeling historical, there is nothing that ecstatifies me like hunting the Chief Love and Delight of God around and around just here on this tiny earth and watching him perform. I watch him progressing and progressing — always progressing — always mounting higher and higher, sometimes by means of the Inquisition, sometimes by means of the Terror, sometimes by eight hundred years of witch-burning, sometimes by help of a St. Bartholomew's, sometimes by spreading hell and civilization in China, sometimes by preserving and elevating the same at home by a million soldiers and a thousand battleships; and when he gets down to today I still look at him spread out over a whole page of the morning paper, grabbing in Congress, grabbing in Albany, lynching the innocent, slobbering hypocrisies, reeking, dripping, unsavory, but always recognizable as the same old Most Sublime Existence in all the range of Non-Divine Being, the Chief Love and Delight of God; and then I am more gladder than ever that I am it."

This was the difference between the official, conventional, religious and social "morality" of the period, and the true morality of his culture as embodied in the spirit of Samuel Clemens. This was in effect the ending note of *Mark Twain in Eruption*, the peroration of the book, of the time, and of the greatest author of the time. And despite the fact that Mr. DeVoto's collection must be viewed as an appendix or supplement to Mark Twain's *Autobiography*, rather than a "new edition," and the fact that some of this material is familiar or repetitious, and some of it should have been edited down (the harangues on Teddy Roosevelt in particular), and some of it is now irrelevant to Mark Twain's true import: still this book has enough new, fresh and valuable material in it to constitute a solid contribution to Mark Twain's writing. And so we reach the central puzzle of the volume again. Why, just when Mr. DeVoto was presenting this important material, did he feel it necessary to introduce it with a major essay which is both patronizing and denigrating to the book's real value? Which is inaccurate in its premises and conclusions alike about Mark Twain's work, which is really most misleading about Mark Twain himself, and which has become a source of so much misleading Mark Twain criticism in our own period? It is a question: when we see a critic and editor and a Mark Twain literary executor, who has devoted his life to establishing or re-establishing Mark Twain's literary position, suddenly devaluing his own life's work as well.

Well, not all of it, because DeVoto, like many other Mark Twain scholars, stressed the early books of Twain, the idyllic childhood theme, the trauma of middle life, the career broken in half. The later works, including the *Autobiography* itself, and particularly the later social commentary, are thus viewed as having only a minor, incidental, and psychologically oriented meaning — or failure of meaning. The thesis of the present book is of course just the opposite; and this book's documentation from the writings of Mark Twain himself would seem to prove that thesis substantially and without doubt. My good-

ness! Just in terms of prose style, Clemens' writing was never
more eloquent and acute than in the radical phase of his later
social criticism. There was no breakdown of communication
here, but rather an abundant and delightful amplification, clari-
fication, and impact. To the historian, this material comes directly from the center of the period and from an observer
uniquely qualified to report on it. Direct from the horse's
mouth, or from Satan's rebellious and penetrating account, this
is invaluable material for any historian of the period and of
American culture in general. And how much of it can you read
without bursting into laughter? And how much of it is simply
brilliant commentary on human life, and man's universe?

Since the "failure" which DeVoto described so eloquently
was not remotely that of Mark Twain, it is clearly that of Mr.
DeVoto himself. As indeed it was. For Bernard DeVoto had
re-established Mark Twain's position as a great writer, after Van
Wyck Brooks' curious attack — but only in terms of the frontier, of frontier humor, of frontier "bounce," verve, imagination, action, and optimism. DeVoto himself had come east with
much the same vision of American society and culture. His
early novels reflected this view of life; and his career, outside
of his work on Mark Twain, was mainly journalistic, and conventional in values. But let me quote from the jacket of *The
Literary Fallacy,* published in 1944. "All Mr. DeVoto's work,
whether fiction, history, or literary criticism, has explored the
realities of American culture. He has been a persistent, brilliant
opponent of the school of American thought, dominant during
the 1920's, which repudiated American life and American literature as barren and vulgar, without color or worth, a wasteland
of unimaginative materialism fatal alike to individuality, talent,
and hope." And this book itself — actually a collection of lectures — attacked all the major writers of the 1920s and 1930s
for their "false view" of their own culture. But how could

such writers as H. L. Mencken, Sinclair Lewis, Ernest Hemingway, John Dos Passos, William Faulkner, Thomas Wolfe —
to list only a few of the writers whom Mr. DeVoto attacked —
how could such a group of writers *all* be wrong about their own
period, not to mention the sharp differences among them?

Mr. DeVoto was confusing cultural analysis with his own
moral peptalks. He argued in effect, and in fact, that one should
not use the writers of a culture to try to understand the culture;
and that the major writers of twentieth-century American culture were deliberately falsifying their period. The point really
was, however, that you could discern different weaknesses or
blind spots or emotional blocks in each of these writers, but you
could hardly ignore the main burden of their complaint. And
these followed after such other figures as Dreiser, Sherwood
Anderson, Ellen Glasgow, Jack London, Edith Wharton, Willa
Cather, etc., who had been saying the same thing before the
1920s but whose work Mr. DeVoto ignored or denied.

Mr. DeVoto's own background and personal experience,
moreover, were so *un*typical and so atypical of both the glamor-
ous and expatriated Jazz Age and the Depression epoch of the
1930s that one would have thought an elementary caution and
modesty would have prevented him from defending "the American way of life" against the social critique not merely of the
writers he mentioned but of even another generation of American writers which opened with Stephen Crane and Frank Norris
in the 1890s. Not to mention the same disenchantment with
the promise of American society voiced as far back as Melville,
as the later and darker Whitman, as Howells, and as Mark Twain
himself. But this was precisely the problem faced by DeVoto
when he discovered in his own favorite author, the author upon
whom DeVoto's whole career was based — when he discovered
in perhaps the best and most prophetic strain of Mark Twain's
work the very same themes he had been attacking in the "de-

cadent" writers of the twenties and thirties. And in Twain, moreover, even more than in the generations of modern American writers from Frank Norris to Thomas Wolfe and the early John Steinbeck, this whole radical critique of American democracy was perhaps even more openly and vividly described. And it was actually written as early as the turn of the century — not to mention *Following the Equator* in 1897, which Mr. DeVoto does not mention.

Yes, Twain was propounding just those ideas which Mr. DeVoto had been attacking so violently in his own period. These themes, insights, descriptions of the newly available Mark Twain material destroyed all of Mr. DeVoto's own central assumptions as historian and critic. His biggest book on the frontier outside of his writings on Mark Twain, *The Year of Decision: 1846,* was based on the same "wholesome" optimistic and patriotic view of the frontier's impact on American life, following along what we have already described as Turner's ambiguous theory.

In sober fact, moreover, Mark Twain's work had *always* refuted DeVoto's western virility and optimism. Let us remember that Huck Finn's Mississippi sojourn was already an *escape* from the binding and ugly restraints and conventions of the western towns, including that of slavery. As early as *The Gilded Age,* in 1873, Twain had given us an unpleasant picture of the raw, crude, materialistic frontier society. The later and darker fables revolved around the same scene with almost a polar emphasis of slavery, crime, and all the other human weaknesses. *Pudd'nhead Wilson, The Man That Corrupted Hadleyburg, The $30,000 Bequest,* and *The Mysterious Stranger* may be construed as a logical development of what the earlier Twain had felt and had not quite dared to express — rather than as a complete reversal and rejection of his earlier belief. Once again, *Life on the Mississippi* was another chronicle of a special kind of fairy-tale *release* from the frontier's grim reality (that is the source of the book's charm). And *Roughing It,* where Twain assuredly did not tell all he knew, was hardly a visionary picture of the western mining towns.

To his credit, Mr. DeVoto gives Twain much praise for *The Mysterious Stranger* — as a comeback after long years of crisis and depression: just those very years which we have seen to be filled with vital books. But in a deep sense he had earlier falsified (or given a false color to) Mark Twain's real meaning. Twain's was also — wasn't it? — a very tough and realistic talent underneath all its glamor and glitter. And when it came to the same realistic appraisal, in Twain's later years, of the democracy's capture by the oligarchy during the last quarter of the nineteenth century; of democracy's decline, and the return of the "monarchy" which Mr. DeVoto correctly described as dictatorship and fascism; when it came to the theme of Christendom and imperialism which Mr. DeVoto could not quite bring himself to mention — what *was* he to do?

Yet this is a familiar dilemma in literary history: that of a critic, biographer, or historian who discovers that his whole work has been based on a "literary fallacy" indeed. And Mr. DeVoto's response was predictable. Since he could hardly deny that Mark Twain's work in the area of social commentary was valuable, and that it had indeed by 1940 influenced DeVoto's own belated movement from an early conservatism to almost a kind of liberalism — the simplest thing would be for him, DeVoto, to assume the position that Mark Twain had discovered, to assume it as fact, and then to point out Mark Twain's alleged "ignorance" in this area of history. At least that is the only possible sense I can make out of DeVoto's famous essay which with one and the same gesture introduced some of Mark Twain's best examples of social criticism and denied their importance, and even Twain's competence to produce them.

In fact, in DeVoto's desperate straits he was forced almost

to return to that psychological thesis of Twain's frustration as a mature artist which he had earlier forced Van Wyck Brooks to recant. Only this time DeVoto reinforced his own view by "outside authorities," and that is to say orthodox Freudian psychoanalysts whom he had consulted about Mark Twain's conflicts. But a critic is in a bad way when he is forced to rely not upon his own psychological knowledge and instincts, but upon such outside sources. And the Freudians are notorious for imposing rigid, orthodox schemata upon a writer whose *total* orientation and true literary vision they have not the slightest sense of.

It is possible, too, that under the tensions of World War II, of the Nazi-Soviet pact which preceded our entrance into the war in 1941, that DeVoto's own patriotic presence obliged him to muffle and divert some of the most searching and damaging of Mark Twain's comments on the decline (or conversion) of the American democracy. All critics, all writers, all historians are subject to such historical and social pressures which, just recently, the school of "New Criticism" based on pure esthetics has vainly tried to ignore. Despite the wrongness of Bernard DeVoto's final devaluation of Mark Twain, and the trend it has created about this area of Twain's work, one might feel a certain sympathy for a critic who is caught in such a dilemma. In order to escape from it he had to try to negate a master writer upon whom, in effect, his own career was based. He had to denigrate and deny what he knew was correct and true in Mark Twain in order to defend what he had come to know was false in his own career. Worse, he must have known that Twain's work would survive his critique of it, just as it would survive all its critics, good and bad, to flourish again, through its own inner power and grace, and needing no voice but its own.

THIRTEEN

THE ANECDOTIST
OF THE FIFTIES

IN VIEW of what followed, however, DeVoto's strictures appear rather more beneficial than not. At least DeVoto *presented* the best aspects of Twain's social commentary even while he devalued them. Charles Neider, in 1959, simply repressed and deleted this whole area of Mark Twain's work for the most dubious reasons. Moreover, while DeVoto's *Mark Twain in Eruption* was clearly a kind of supplement to the *Autobiography,* Neider's *The Autobiography of Mark Twain* claimed to be, and was in certain aspects, a new edition of the famous book.

In his introduction Neider pointed out that "for the first time the whole manuscript is being used as the source, not parts or selections of it." But he neglected to say that his new version was the most severely streamlined edition of the *Autobiography* to appear yet. (Neider also describes DeVoto's *Mark Twain in Eruption* as a new edition of the *Autobiography,* which it surely is not.) More accurately, Neider rejects DeVoto's psychologizing on the "failure" of the *Autobiography*: "When he invoked Hannibal [that is, his early years] he found there not only the idyll of boyhood but anxiety, violence, supernatural horror, and an uncrystallized but enveloping dread. Much of his fiction, most of his masterpiece [*Huck Finn*], flows from that phantasy-bound anxiety." So Neider quotes DeVoto, and surely Sam Clemens was no stranger to these psychic states which he himself described so openly in the *Autobiography*.

But we have seen how Mark Twain's laughter could wash away those somber strains of his temperament which any great writer must be aware of; laughter which Mr. DeVoto did not seem to appreciate or understand. Nor is *Huck Finn* the *only* masterpiece of Twain's, as DeVoto and his successors have continually proclaimed, not realizing the "broken childhood" of Mark Twain was never broken, and is the key element, indeed, of his temperament and work. But I have reverted to Mr. DeVoto only because Mr. Neider quotes another key passage of the supposed "indictment" of Twain's later, and obviously more interesting, mature and complex work. Neider correctly sees that Twain wrote the *Autobiography* for his own pleasure, which is always the secret of a writer's best writing, and not out of some impulse to examine his own deep core of dread . . . that DeVoto invented.

Neider goes on to examine Twain's various reasons for writing the *Autobiography* the way he did, and Paine's reasons for selecting or editing out various sections of the book, and for keeping Clemens' stream-of-consciousness form. And he (Neider) describes his own method of editing the *Autobiography*. "Working with the autobiographical manuscript as a whole, both unpublished and published parts, I weeded out a variety of material. I did this for several reasons: in order to make a wieldy volume which would meet certain requirements of the general reader (for whom this book is designed); in order to unburden the excellent parts of the dated, dull, trivial and journalese sections of the work; and in order to concentrate less on opinion and second-hand recollection amd more on the truly autobiographical, the more purely literary and the more characteristically humorous material. My volume is to a high degree anecdotic, but I believe this to be a virtue rather than a defect in that it correctly represents the creative slant of Mark Twain's mind."

Neider continues with a more or less detailed selection of what he has used in his version of the *Autobiography*, and what has been omitted. But isn't this a curious kind of general statement about the book — which becomes much more curious after we have read the book. A wieldy volume, yes, of course; by all means omit the dated dull and trivial journalese; although it is not so often that Sam Clemens, and especially the later Clemens, wrote any purely dated and dull stuff. But to do this "in order to concentrate less on opinion and second-hand recollections and more on the truly autobiographical." Are we then to omit Twain's *ideas,* and opinions about life, and that is to say, the central core of Mark Twain's writing? Are we to equate this equivocal "opinion" with "second-hand recollections," as Neider seems to imply — and opinion and recollections of *what?* And finally, are we to assume in Mark Twain's case that the truly autobiographical parts of his last book are the "more purely literary" (whatever that means); are *only* the "characteristically humorous" material, and to a high degree "anecdotic"?

What a medicinal-sounding word Mr. Neider uses instead of the more familiar "anecdotal," and as we read along in his version of the *Autobiography* the real import of his introduction becomes clear. Now let me say at once that he has performed a valuable service in arranging the *Autobiography* in chronological order, and that his edition is highly readable. It is even, within its arbitrary limits, another good book by Mark Twain; it surely serves as an obvious refutation of DeVoto's thesis that the later Mark Twain was crushed and broken and full of dark forebodings which the *Autobiography* tried to deal with and failed. Nonsense! We have already demonstrated that just as Sam Clemens was a "daylight writer" of the Old Republic, despite all those darker elements of temperament and experience every major writer must have, so the *Autobiography* itself is a "daylight book," a triumphant conclusion to Twain's human existence and literary career, a celebrating of life despite all of life's tragedies. In Neider's pages is the whole chronicle of Clemens' boyhood and youth in Hannibal, again. Neider has put it all together, instead of the original broken form of Twain's reminiscences, and the whole experience of Twain's rebel youth is even more impressive.

There is the complete account of Sam's childhood friends and games, his early life on the Mississippi, his apprentice printing days and the self-taught printer-philosophers who gave him his first intellectual experiences. There is the great open loving tribute to his mother; the death of his brother Henry in the steamboat explosion; the account of Nevada mining days with Orion; and Neider has added to the *Autobiography* some material on Clemens' pool and billiard life. There is the account of his first famous book, *The Innocents Abroad,* in 1869; the early lecture life; and, among all these scintillating literary sketches, a new profile of the master of the lecturing circuit, James Redpath. "The chief ingredients of Redpath's make-up were honesty, sincerity, kindliness and pluck. He wasn't afraid. He was one of Ossawatomie Brown's right-hand men in the bleeding Kansas days; he was all through that struggle. He carried his life in his hands and from one day to another it wasn't worth the price of a night's lodging. He had a small body of daring men under him and they were constantly being hunted by the 'jayhawkers,' who were pro-slavery Missourians, guerrillas, modern free-lancers."

I quote this at random among all the things in the *Autobiography* which are such a pleasure to read over; and because Twain's view of Ossawatomie Brown is so different from that of those modern historians who have labeled Brown an insane fanatic. (There are also interesting photographs of Twain in the Neider volume.) There is the familiar story of his marriage to Livy; the chronicle of their early married life and the children — the wealth, the fame, the elegance, and the affection of their family life. Neider has cut most of Susy's Diary which Clemens recalls with such pride in Paine's edition, and used as the takeoff for his earlier associations. But the account of Livy and Sam remains as warm and touching and affectionate as ever; and there is the same tale of the burglar alarm that Clemens installed in the Hartford mansion to "warn him" of illegal activities. There is the whole chronicle of the publishing house; Grant's Memoirs; the bankruptcy — though for some curious reason Neider omits the perhaps stranger, and more crucial story of the Paige typesetter. And Neider does add the important concluding comments to the Bret Harte affair which summarize Twain's central vision of life, if so much else of his commentary has been edited out of this new version of the *Autobiography*.

After all his scorn and anger and burning fury about Bret Harte's behavior, Sam Clemens still avoided a final judgment, or rather made one: "The human family cannot be described by any one phrase; each individual has to be described by himself. One is brave, another is a coward, one is gentle and kindly, another is ferocious; one is proud and vain, another is modest and humble. The multiferous traits that are scattered, one or two at a time, throughout the great animal world, are all con-

centrated, in varying and nicely shaded degrees of force and
feebleness in the form of instincts in each and every member of
the human family. In some men the vicious traits are so slight
as to be imperceptible, while the nobler traits stand out conspicuously."

> We describe that man by those fine traits and we give him praise
> and accord him high merit for their possession. It seems comical.
> He did not invent his traits; he did not stock himself with them;
> he inherited them at his birth; God conferred them upon him;
> they are the law that God imposed upon him, and he could not
> escape obedience if he should try.

Sometimes a man is a born murderer, or a born scoundrel —
like Stanford White, Clemens continued. "And upon him the
world lavishes censure and dispraise; but he is only obeying the
law of his nature, the law of his temperament; he is not at all
likely to try to disobey it, and if he should try he would fail. It is
a curious and humorous fact that we excuse all the unpleasant things that the creatures that crawl and fly and swim and
go on four legs do, for the recognizably sufficient reason that
they are but obeying the law of their nature, which is the law of
God, and are therefore innocent; then we turn about and with
the fact plain before us that we get all our unpleasant traits by
inheritance from these creatures, we blandly assert that we did
not inherit the immunities along with them, but that it is our
duty to ignore, abolish and break these laws of God. It seems
to me that this argument has not a leg to stand upon and that it
is not merely and mildly humorous but violently grotesque."

Now one should note here that in his last period of writing, Sam Clemens, far from being haunted, frustrated, and totally cynical, had extended even to *man* — that beast! and momentarily ignoring the hypocrisy he had condemned as man's

"moral sense" — the natural innocence of edenic and animal life. This total indictment of man's "weakness" was in a deeper sense a final acceptance of life, even a farewell blessing to that human race which Twain had damned and vilified and beaten and scourged. This was even a strange benison which held mysteriously and wordlessly within it some promise of man's hope and man's faith.

As for Bret Harte himself whom Twain described as mercilessly and satirically as he had the scoundrelly inventor Paige and his scoundrelly relative and publisher, Charles Webster — why was he, Harte, after all, any different from the common lot?

> By ancient training and inherited habit, I have been heaping blame after blame, censure after censure, upon Bret Harte, and have felt the things I have said, but when my temper is cool I have no censures for him. The law of his nature was stronger than man's statutes and he had to obey it. It is my conviction that the human race is no proper target for harsh words and bitter criticisms, and that the only justifiable feeling toward it is compassion; it did not invent itself and it had nothing to do with the planning of its weak and foolish character.

Thus the larger benediction of the artist who had, perhaps more than any other artist of his time, indulged in just those harsh words and bitter criticisms of the human race in all "its weak and foolish character." And by adding these words freshly to the Bret Harte section of the *Autobiography*, Neider, of course, reminds us again of the final light and luminosity of Twain's last book, and the remarkable wrongness of Mr. DeVoto's description of it. Neider also, after the account of Susy's death, includes, for the first time, the full and detailed description of Livy's death; a description, a transcription, which is again so eloquent and affectionate — so open in its candor, so aware of human

frailty, so patient and devoted in all its sorrow and suffering —
as almost to draw a tear from the stoniest of Freudian
hearts.

At the final moment of her illness, Livy was infused by an appearance of new health and vitality. "I was deceived by her in-
spiriting life and animation, and far over-stayed my privilege.
Only a word and a kiss were permissible, but I stayed a full half
hour. Then I blamed myself and said I had done wrong; but
she said there was no harm, and lavished caresses upon me in
her old natural way, the way which has been hers for thirty-four
years, and she said 'You will come back?' and I said 'Yes, to
say good-night' — meaning at half-past-nine, as usual these
many, many months. As usual, I stood a minute in the door,
bending inward and throwing kisses, she throwing kisses in response, and her face all bright with that new-found smile —
I not dreaming that I was looking upon that dear face for
the last time in life. Yet so it was."

Clemens sat in his room musing, filled with a deep contentment at the experience. "My heart-burdens strangely gone, my
spirit at peace for the first time in so many heavy months." He
was uplifted, exalted and he did a thing he had done rarely
"since we lost our incomparable Susy eight years ago, whose
death made a wound in her mother's heart which never healed."
He went to the piano and began to play the "old songs," the
Negro hymns and spirituals which he had always loved, but
which, as he said, nobody else had cared for except Livy and
Susy. "When I sang them Susy always came and listened; when
she died, my interest in them passed away; I could not put
force and feeling into them without the inspiration of her approving presence. But now the force and feeling were all back,
in full strength, and I was all alive, and it was as if eight years
had fallen from me. In the midst of 'My Lord He call me! He

call me by the thunder!' Jean crept into the room and sat down, to my astonishment and — embarrassment; and I stopped, but when she asked me to go on, only the astonishment remained, and it was a pleasant one and inspiring." Clemens sang the almost forgotten words of many songs for Jean until quarter past nine when he returned to Livy's room and found her dead, still sitting upright on the bed, supported by the nurse and their housekeeper Kate Leary.

"It was twenty minutes past nine. Only five minutes before, she had been speaking. She had heard me and had said to the nurse, 'He is singing a good-night carol for me.' They had had no idea that she was near to death. She was happy and was speaking — and in an instant she was gone from this life. How grateful I was that she had been spared the struggle she had so dreaded. And that I, too, had so dreaded for her. Five times in the last four months she spent an hour and more fighting violently for breath, and she lived in the awful fear of death by strangulation. Mercifully she was granted the gentlest and swiftest of deaths — by heart failure — and she never knew, she never knew!

"She was the most beautiful spirit, and the highest and the noblest I have known. And now she is dead."

The death of Livy is one of the valuable new entries in Neider's edition of the *Autobiography,* and the full account of her last moments contained in these pages should persuade anybody except the most obtuse critic — still seeking evidence of their spiritual separation and deathbed hostility! — about the true nature of their relationship. Even an artist like Mark Twain could hardly invent such an account. To Neider's credit also, this touching and illuminating episode of their private lives is followed directly by one of Twain's most biting indictments of Anglo-Saxon culture:

"For good or for evil we continue to educate Europe. We have held the post of instructor for more than a century and a quarter now. We were not elected to it, we merely took it. We are of the Anglo-Saxon race. At the banquet last winter [1905] of that organization which calls itself the Ends of the Earth Club, the chairman, a retired regular army officer of high grade, proclaimed in a loud voice, and with fervency, 'We are of the Anglo-Saxon race, and when the Anglo-Saxon wants a thing *he just takes it.*'

"That utterance was applauded to the echo. There were perhaps seventy-five civilians present and twenty-five military and naval men. It took those people nearly two minutes to work off their stormy admiration of that great sentiment; and meanwhile the inspired prophet who had discharged it — from his liver or his intestines or his esophagus or wherever he had bred it — stood there glowing and beaming and smiling and issuing rays of happiness from every pore, rays that were so intense that they were visible and make him look like the old-time picture in the Almanac of the man who stands discharging signs of the zodiac in every direction, and so absorbed in happiness, so steeped in happiness, that he smiles and smiles and has plainly forgotten that he is painfully and dangerously ruptured and exposed amidships, and needs sewing up right away."

The soldier man's great utterance, interpreted by the expression which he put into it, meant in plain English, 'The English and the Americans are thieves, highwaymen, pirates, and we are proud to be of the combination.'

Out of all the English and Americans present, there was not one with the grace to get up and say he was ashamed of being an Anglo-Saxon, and also ashamed of being a member of the human race, since the race must abide under the presence upon it of the Anglo-Saxon taint.

Nor could he himself do so, Clemens added, speaking for the public figure of Mark Twain. "I could not perform this office. I could not afford to lose my temper and make a self-righteous exhibition of myself and my superior morals that I might teach this infant class in decency the rudiments of that cult, for they would not be able to grasp it; they would not be able to understand it."

It was an amazing spectacle, he continued, "that delighted outburst of enthusiasm over the soldier prophet's mephitic remark."

> It looked suspiciously like a revelation, a secret feeling of the national heart surprised into expression and exposure by untoward accident, for it was a representative assemblage. All the chief mechanisms that constitute the machine which drives and vitalizes the national civilization were present — lawyers, bankers, merchants, manufacturers, journalists, politicians, soldiers, sailors — they were all there. Apparently it was the United States in banquet assembled, and qualified to speak with authority for the nation and reveal its private morals to the public view.

The ecstatic enthusiasm over the strange sentiment of Anglo-Saxon imperialism, Clemens continued, was repeated throughout the performance. "Whenever during the rest of the evening a speaker found that he was becoming uninteresting and wearisome, he only needed to inject that great Anglo-Saxon moral into the midst of his platitudes to start up that glad storm again."

But he put Anglo-Saxon morality within a larger framework. "After all, it was only the human race on exhibition. It has always been a peculiarity of the human race that it keeps two sets of morals in stock — the private and real, and the public and artificial." And then he reversed his argument to show how the nature of the human race in general was even perhaps best illustrated in the so-called most advanced part of it, the Anglo-Saxon part. "Our public motto is 'In God we trust,' and when we see those gracious words on the trade-dollar (worth sixty cents) they always seem to tremble and whimper with pious emotion. That is our public motto. It transpires that our private one is, 'When the Anglo-Saxon wants a thing *he just takes it.*' Our public morals are touchingly set forth in that stately and yet gentle and kindly motto which indicates that we are a nation of gracious and affectionate multitudinous brothers compacted into one — '*e pluribus unum.*' Our private morals find the light in the sacred phrase, 'Come, *step* lively!' "

Clemens went on to trace the relationship of America and Europe in respect to this new (modern) national morality. "We imported our imperialism from monarchical Europe, also our curious notions of patriotism — that is, if we have any principle of patriotism which any person can definitely and intelligibly define. It is but fair then, no doubt, that we should instruct Europe in return for these and the other kinds of instruction which we have received from that source." He proceeded to list the lessons that America had given Europe after our early notions of liberty had helped to bring on the French Revolution. (And vice versa.) "But for us, Europe might never have known the interviewer; but for us certain of the European states might never have experienced the blessing of extravagant imposts; but for us the European Food Trust might never have acquired the art of poisoning the world for cash; but for us her Insurance Trusts might never have found out the best way to work the widow and orphan for profit; but for us the long delayed resumption of Yellow Journalism in Europe might have been postponed for generations to come. Steadily, continuously, persistently, we are Americanizing Europe, and all in good time we shall get the job perfected."

Prophetic words as seen from the vantage point of the 1970s. And it is both revelatory and entertaining to compare Mark Twain and Henry James again as brother-authors of the same historical period. Because their discussion of similar ideas offers such a fascinating example of polarity in American literature, it is almost impossible *not* to compare them. James' central thesis was, of course, that Europe must educate America, which was gross, vulgar, materialistic, and uncultivated; and that America, as his novels always assume, would gladly accept this submissive role. That the truth was quite the opposite, as Mark Twain saw, and that Henry James made a hopeless error in his central esthetic assumptions must be attributed to that absolute disdain for history, in any true sense, which is so obvious both in the "Master" and his disciples.*

Infatuated by the "Dream of Europe" in his notion of the international novel, Henry James was absolutely ignorant, of course, of the real forces — social, economic, political, cultural, and historical — which were operating in the England and the America of his own period. And obsessed by his esoterical literary vision, which no breath of real life, culture, and history could ever touch, or could ever blemish, the "art" of James (as later with Nabokov) could only result in a realm of unique literary fantasy. These were entertainments, games, baroque and bizarre "romances" of human souls whose whole charm results from the fact that they are unlike any other human souls ever produced by society, culture, and history. Or by a "pure" human psyche, let us say, which always in the end reflected

---

* After Twain, and excluding James, it was Theodore Dreiser who knew (in the Cowperwood Trilogy especially) that America was in fact "teaching" Europe through the process of financial infiltration and control; and that is to say, through material power rather than any "esthetic" or "cultural" process. America has in fact almost destroyed Europe by Americanizing it, while James' hallowed England is our colony in all but name.

only the insulated and embedded psyche of Henry James himself; and whose only recognizable trait was its talent for ownership, control, and manipulation; and, ultimately, of psychic or psychological *profit*.

Only in this way did Henry James, quite unconsciously, reveal the values of his own culture; while, by contrast, Mark Twain, scouring and castigating the property-and-profit motive, and the debased morality of finance capitalism and its contemporary extension of imperialism, was the artist of the full human soul. This brilliant summary of Anglo-Saxon "virtue" was in effect the concluding section of Neider's *Autobiography*; and these final pages, so full of anger, scorn, and outraged eloquence, suddenly remind us of how few other pages like this Mr. Neider has selected for this new edition of Twain's famous book. The index of Neider's *Autobiography* is almost an index of missing persons. And of absent social causes. Neider's index, when compared with Paine's or DeVoto's or almost any other Mark Twain index, is notable mainly for its lapses, its open spaces, its whole vacant and desert-like quality in the central area of Mark Twain's social criticism. Where, for example, is there any mention of or any real reference in Mr. Neider's shifting, ambiguous introduction to this volume to the whole series of brilliant essays, many of them composed originally for the *Autobiography,* or along with it, and printed around the 1900s or in the later volume called *Europe and Elsewhere?* I mean of course Twain's early descriptions of the imperialism which was destroying whole countries and cultures in Asia and Africa; or Twain's fascination with the diabolical Cecil Rhodes in South Africa; or Twain's late and last elevation and exaltation of Satan himself, versus the moral hypocrisy of Western European Christianity — "Christendom."

Where is there any mention of Clemens' eloquent exhortation to our "Blushing Exiles" to defend proudly the American land-grabbing of Cuba when compared with the bloody and shameful history of Spain? Where is there any footnote, even, on Twain's celebrated essay, "The United States of Lyncherdom" — or reference to Twain's remarkable self-education on the vital problem of racism? Both European and American racist cultures, which became so important to Clemens himself, are not remotely conjured up in Neider's complacent Cold War version of the *Autobiography*. Where is there any allusion to another famous essay, *To the Person Sitting in Darkness,* or to China, or to Twain's subsequent rejoinder "To My Missionary Critics." Where is there any reference, in short, not merely to these specific issues and essays but to that whole central vein of Twain's social-cultural rebellion and protest from the time of Huck Finn and the primitive frontier to the time of King Leopold, the Russian Czar, and our own Teddy Roosevelt? As we know, Paine's original *Autobiography* had much of this material; DeVoto's supplement, much more.

The closing selection on the Anglo-Saxon race, in Neider's *Autobiography,* intended perhaps as a sop or a solace, really gives the whole game — and the book — away. Neider's Mark Twain is indeed a folklorist, a genial satirist, a patriot, an anecdotal teller of tall tales. But that is all. Why, Paine himself, cautious and conformist Victorian that he was, had more respect for Twain's central values and vision of life than to omit this whole side of Twain's genius. Possibly Paine overdid, in the first and what is still the standard edition of the *Autobiography,* the running account of "the Morris case" which Clemens used as an indictment of the haughty arrogance and disdainful manner of the new American oligarchy. But the Morris case (which Neider also omitted) led into Mark Twain's further commentary on the state of affairs which the United States, as a whole, had arrived at.

Now that is the real key to all of Neider's omissions of Twain's social criticism, and also of Justin Kaplan's negation of Twain's achievement in this area. During the Cold War period of the 1950s which conditioned the thinking of both Neider and Kaplan, there was to be very little criticism, in effect none, of a democracy which was considered to be struggling for its very survival against the so-called Russian Frankenstein. As revealed in a series of sensational disclosures in the year 1968, this intellectual stance was formulated by the CIA-funded "Congress for Cultural Freedom," — which dominated the cultural activities of both Europe and the U.S., and became the prevailing ideology for the "Free World's" leading intellectuals. And as further revealed in a series of books by young revisionist historians of the 1960s, the whole concept of the "Cold War" and the "Free World" was highly ambiguous, if not totally erroneous, and simply another ideological product of our own CIA's Frankenstein monster. Its real effect was to enslave *American* culture.

From Paine's original edition of the *Autobiography,* we remember that the Morris case led directly into the great insurance company scandals of the period; into the Standard Oil Corporation, into the Panama Canal Commission scandal; into the Russian revolution and the mystery of why American troops were being dispatched to China; into General Funston and the Philippines; and into Twain's blistering attack against the arrogant, ruthless, deceitful Theodore Roosevelt himself — the imperialistic, blustering, and warmongering President of the new American Empire.

None of this is in what we may now call Neider's censored version of Mark Twain's *Autobiography,* as I have already suggested in discussing Paine's *Autobiography.*

Nor does Neider include Clemens' famous satirical essay on Thanksgiving as printed in the Paine edition. To satirize a national holiday might be construed, in the Fatal Fifties, as giving comfort and aid (and classified information?) to the monolithic conspiracy of atheistic communism organized to destroy the very center of democracy — which in the 1900s Mark Twain was already having those dark doubts about. Better to simply ignore that little gem on the genocide of the American Indian. Far better not to remember that in 1906 Clemens had himself wished to ignore Thanksgiving on the grounds that nothing had happened to be thankful for except several vicious and inexcusable wars, and King Leopold's usual slaughters and robberies in the Congo, and the resurgence of the Russian Czar. Far far better for Charles Neider to omit *all* of Mark Twain's antiwar polemics and parodies which the naive and unpoliticized Paine had so innocently included in the book of an earlier, an older American world; not realizing that such literary gems were not "art" and were merely "tasteless and transient journalism."

The revival of this material in the radical resurgence and reaction against the Cold War period during the American sixties, and the emergence of the "New Left" in our universities did of course indicate a certain permanency and lasting relevance in Twain's old-fashioned social satire. Some of the essays we have discussed here have appeared almost continuously in New Left periodicals and programs, and were clearly among the best-written and freshest sounding satires, parodies, and polemics of the new period. And a period which was in fact only reverting to an older and major strain of social criticism and social justice in American literature and culture alike. It was the Cold War period which was the exception in our history — with the exception of the fact that at times the Cold War threatened to be the norm in our future history. What was the real future, indeed, of the Old Republic and the Democracy, which in those later essays Mark Twain himself saw as reverting to a proto-fascist "monarchy"?

In Paine's "antiquated" edition of the *Autobiography* also, there was the now-famous essay on "The Killing of 600 Moros" in our treacherous acquisition of the Philippines: another unflattering event in the New World's history deemed to be invidious, and doomed to exclusion by the Cold War historians, scholars, and biographers. We remember Clemens' direct statement of his real position in his period as the *conscience* of America; and what indeed he himself considered his true role as social prophet: a theme one hardly meets in the "anecdotal" Neider book. Where is the account, again, of Nikolai Vasilevich Tchaykoffsky, the revolutionary populist who came to visit Clemens, as did radical and revolutionary figures from the whole outside world where Twain's name was perhaps even more revered than in his own country? Tchaykoffsky's (or Tchaikovsky's) name is as absent from Mr. Neider's index as the event is from his narrative. And Twain's response, so vivid, clear, eloquent, that I will just reproduce it here again for the sake of the *style,* the writing craft that Mr. Neider says is the true base of his omissions:

> I told him what I believed to be true: that our Christianity which we have always been so proud of — not to say, so vain of — is now nothing but a shell, a sham, a hypocrisy; that we have lost our ancient sympathy with oppressed peoples struggling for life and liberty; that when we are not coldly indifferent to such things we sneer at them, and that the sneer is about the only expression the newspapers and nation deal in with regard to such things.

But it is obviously quite true that such a description of the American spirit would hardly be consoling to a nation whose national psyche was being constrained again to the so-called Christian struggle of "containing" (or suppressing) an international surge of communism and "atheism." It might just arouse the Americans; it would not be consoling to our allies in the Cold War consortium; it might give away our true view of those mainly non-Christian Asian and African peoples who were adopting various (and non-monolithic) forms of native communism and socialism in their liberation struggles against the Western European and American "Free World." A Free World just then obsessed by spiritual censorship and demonology.

Twain concluded (we know) by saying that Tchaykoffsky's only real support would come from the immigrants, the poor, and the Jews: those who had not yet had time to become "Americanized." What heresy! Unspeakable; unprintable! and surely unprinted in the Mark Twain material published in the 1950s. Now, as we know, if it was Bernard DeVoto who started this contemporary trend of denigrating Mark Twain's social criticism in the *Mark Twain in Eruption* of 1940 — for whatever personal reasons we have suggested — at least DeVoto *published* the Twain material which he was so niggardly in praising. But in Neider, once more, where are the glowing personal portraits of Carnegie, Roosevelt, the Rockefellers, and the other members of the new American oligarchy? From this whole firsthand view of his own country and society, which had changed so much for the worse in Clemens' own lifetime, a change which he was in the center of and which he recorded so intimately and eloquently — from this whole rich historical treasure in *Mark Twain in Eruption,* there is not a single selection in Mr. Neider's later version of the *Autobiography.*

It has been said that the reason for such a startling omission was simply that the DeVoto volume was so lately published; and Neider had stated (or pretended) that his edition was altogether "new." But what was the purpose of such originality when there was already one well-established version of this famous book, and one recent and almost invaluable supplement to it? What was the need — and what was the cost of such "originality"?

We have just come from the description of *Mark Twain in Eruption*: there is hardly any reason to recall the virtues that shine out from beneath the curious editorial assumptions of Mr. DeVoto. But it was Mr. Neider who carried DeVoto's directives to the final and logical conclusion of liquidating this whole area of Mark Twain's work. Was the latest editor of the *Autobiography* altogether blind about such Twain essays as the description of Andrew Carnegie's ego? Or on Carnegie as the epitome of the whole new oligarchy of industrial barons and titans who had so radically changed the nature, the being, the essence of the old democracy into the portentous and ominous shadow of the new "monarchy"? Or the prophetic comparison of American monopoly capitalism and ancient Roman decadence? Or the savagely brilliant description of the "Montana jailbird," Senator Clark? Or the profile of Jay Gould as the worst robber baron of them all; Jay Gould as "the mightiest disaster which has ever befallen this country." How could any editor omit such choice items of Mark Twain's literary achievement? And the analysis of Jay Gould's "gospel," in rather the same literary tone that Clemens had used for Mary Baker Eddy's gospel?

Not to mention those corrupt magnates like the McCurdies, the McCalls, the Hydes, and Alexanders — "and the rest of that robber gang who have lately been driven out of their violated positions of trust in the colossal insurance companies of New York" — whom Sam Clemens had pilloried so magnificently in his letters from the grave. Not to mention Clemens' blistering strictures on the American press as "the palladium of our liberties," in the course of his vivid profiles of Colorado's Senator Simon Guggenheim, and then the Rockefellers, father and son, as Christian ministers and teachers of the young. And then Clemens' wholehearted and hilarious attacks on the Bible itself as the source of Christian morality and Christian culture, and indeed of Western civilization.

But enough. What is missing in Charles Neider's "modern" edition of Mark Twain's *Autobiography* is not merely what I have been describing as Twain's "radical social criticism" as a central theme in his work. What is missing in Neider's book is, in effect, the whole *public aspect* of an artist whose chief interest, whose whole value, whose true literary position was exactly in such public utterances, as expressed through the various modes of his own writing from the satirical essay or the sardonic parable to the realm of fiction itself and back to his genius for direct reportage. If Mark Twain was the acknowledged conscience of his nation — to the outside world its great literary and almost religious prophet in Tolstoyan terms — how can this version of his autobiography dare to reduce him to the simplistic status of a "humorist." And quote mainly, almost exclusively from his "anecdotic" or autobiographical passages! The most social of all our writers, as should be clear by now; the most "public" — to the point of having almost no psychic core that was not entwined with all of nature, and all of the culture surrounding him; and the most "open" — to the world surrounding him, to all of human experience — has been reduced to a purely private raconteur.

Mr. Neider is trying to make another Simon Wheeler ("The Celebrated Jumping Frog of Calaveras County") out of the artist whose career started with the famous parody of a garrulous narrator. But it won't work. It can't work with Mark Twain. Even the most personal reminiscences in Neider's *The*

Autobiography of Mark Twain carry with them all the flavor
and color of an age and a culture and a public personality beyond compare. And what is needed obviously is still another
edition of this book — now really becoming the "whole library"
that Clemens prophesied it would be — using Mr. Neider's
chronological structure (which is the contribution of his edition)
but including in its scope the whole central matrix of Mark
Twain's temperament and career which Mr. Neider chose to
exclude. In this sense Neider's is hardly so much a new "edition," again, as another kind of appendix to the original Paine
edition. And what is really needed is a comprehensive *Autobiography,* based on the central material of Paine and using both
Neider's and particularly DeVoto's supplementary material.

Even without the central flaw which makes the latest edition
of the *Autobiography* so incomplete as to be misleading and useless in any full evaluation of Mark Twain, there is something just
too slick and streamlined in Mr. Neider's presentation. It should
really be described as an "Introduction" to Mark Twain's *Autobiography.* Everything is just a bit too neat, clear, logical, and
efficient; not to mention such other serious omissions, apart
from the socio-historical sections, as the whole Dostoevskian
episode of the Paige typesetter. One returns to Paine's earlier
version with a kind of relief and delight; as if revisiting an earlier
American age when existence was less urgent and life so much
more leisurely and larger — an earlier age whose civilizational
constraints, for all that, were still less constraining. When one
could, with pleasure, take the time — or maybe, as Huck said,
"put in the time" — to follow Sam Clemens' explorations of his
own memories.

Yes, to follow along those free and far-ranging and uncon-
ventional, and eloquent, and heartbreaking, and sometimes
wrathful and angry and ironical and hilarious associations and

sensations and speculations and sermons and dissertations and prophecies and condemnations, just as they came to him in that inimitable literary voice which was apparently so casual, natural, and artless.

FOURTEEN

ETERNAL LIFE,
LIGHT AND LAUGHTER

Our story is almost over, but there was an entertaining post-script to Neider's version of Mark Twain's *Autobiography,* which this indefatigable disciple made into still another Mark Twain book.

On August 18, 1959, the official Russian magazine, the Moscow *Literary Gazette* (*Literaturnaya Gazeta*) published a severe criticism of his edition, which left Neider in a dilemma. "Normally I do not reply to criticisms of my books," he says. "This particular one, however, offered a special and complex challenge. It was obviously 'protected'; it struck through me at the society of which I am a part; and it seemed to discount the possibility of free literary endeavor in my country. Consequently I decided to take some action to bring my views to the attention of those readers who had been exposed to the article defaming me."

What he did was to appeal directly to Premier Khrushchev who had recently visited the United States to initiate the first thaw in the frozen or landlocked Cold War epoch. Now follows a curious statement: "Being uncertain what it cost to send an airmail letter to Moscow, I had to experience the embarrassment of taking my letter to the post office (I had to go there anyway), where I hoped that the clerk would not notice the name on the envelope. He did notice it, however. 'What? Khrushchev? Are you crazy?' he exclaimed. I couldn't blame him."

In the first place why was Mr. Neider so embarrassed about sending a letter to Russia? Secondly, he must have known that it is against postal regulations for any "clerk" to make any observation about any letter. It is the business of the Post Office to carry the mail, not to comment on it. And thirdly, he should have known that not only in Russia but from all over the world, a whole range of people, from peasants to intellectuals, were in the habit of writing directly to Mr. Khrushchev, just as in the American democracy every American citizen has the right to appeal directly to the President. But anyway he soon received a letter from the foreign editor of the *Literary Gazette* saying that they would open their pages for his answer to their criticism. And this event was so unusual, Mr. Neider adds, that it merited front-page stories in the leading American newspapers and news services.

Well, maybe so; but what Mr. Neider doesn't seem to realize is that through the darkest years of the Cold War period, the Russian scholars were particularly interested in the American literary scene, that they continued to publish reviews, extracts, digests of American books, and were in fact very well informed about American cultural events. Perhaps it was the American press and American scholarship that was so surprised by this; but in any event Mr. Neider now went directly into the debate itself. "These recent criticisms in the *Literary Gazette* are of course not isolated ones, nor are they new. The attacks followed

an old Soviet line on Mark Twain, which consists in general of
this: Mark Twain is of primary significance as a social and political observer; his objects of attack are chiefly aspects of the
American scene; and the United States officially and unofficially
suppresses or distorts his attacks against itself. This notion of
America's being a monolithic structure with control stemming
from the top, naturally strikes most Americans as a curious one."

But this Soviet "attack" was in fact a very accurate description, not indeed of the whole range or meaning of Mark Twain's
art, but of just that part of it which Charles Neider had omitted
or suppressed. It was an accurate statement, not indeed of the
great tradition of American culture and art, but of the modern
epoch which existed under the blight of Cold War culture, and
of which Mr. Neider's own "taste" was the obvious product.
Not only Russia but the whole late nineteenth century world had
worshiped Mark Twain not merely as a humorist, but as a social and moral voice of justice and humanity whose humor
made the lesson more effective. How many times had Sam Clemens himself said that this was the true basis of his art? And how
clearly had Mr. Neider reduced that universal and immortal
humor to a kind of personal "anecdotage." (I mean "anecdotic.") Just as Neider now fell back upon DeVoto's notion that
Mark Twain was "primarily a writer of fiction," when in fact
Twain was a social, moral, and metaphysical prophet, poet,
and fabulist who used the fictional mode, along with other
modes, to convey his complex and shifting vision of life.

Perhaps the Russian critic was narrow and dogmatic in his
view of Twain, but he was not quite as inaccurate as the rather
complacent Mr. Neider imagined — and which of these critics
was in effect the narrower of the two? In his reply Mr. Neider
asserted that "what I am interested in primarily are psychology,
humor, emotions, reflections, and reminiscences," rather than

the "didactic" side of Mark Twain; and that he had selected the unpublished sections of the *Autobiography* "from the aesthetic, not the social view." He was speaking chiefly of language, and to him "the journalistic and didactic Mark Twain seemed too often strident or flat." (He is speaking of all those marvelously eloquent, impassioned passages and essays which we have already quoted and discussed.) Neider even said that perhaps these essays were better in Russian translation than in their native American (!), and —

> For me — and there are many novelists and critics with the same orientation — there is a beauty of language, a nobility or harshness of language, which is closely bound to great work and that is inseparable from it. A thought or an emotion or a bit of psychology does not exist in itself but through and with the language which it forms and which forms it. The aesthetic element for me is a primary one when it comes to literature.

One might be curious to know what Mr. Neider means by "a bit of psychology," but all one can say to this bit of critical pomposity and simple-minded estheticism is, well now, Mr. Neider: However did you discover *that?* Meanwhile in 1962, there appeared still another DeVoto volume of Mark Twain's writing, called *Letters from the Earth,* with another curious bit of background history. In the book's introduction, Henry Nash Smith, who was then literary editor of the Mark Twain papers, and a leading Twain scholar, explains that DeVoto, before his sudden and tragic death, had recommended that three volumes be published from the balance of Mark Twain's unpublished work. These were: one, further selections from the autobiography (*Mark Twain in Eruption*); two, a volume of letters; and three, a collection of essays and sketches.

DeVoto actually began work on the third volume first, and

had it ready for the printer in March, 1939, when Clara Clemens objected that certain parts of the manuscript presented a distorted view of Mark Twain. "The project was accordingly dropped," says Mr. Smith, "and the work has lain unpublished for more than twenty years in the successive depositories of the Mark Twain papers, at Harvard, the Huntington Library, and the University of California, Berkeley." Since 1960, the fiftieth anniversary of Twain's death, we are told, at least a dozen books about him had been published; and Clara Clemens (Gabrilowitsch Samossoud) withdrawing her objections, the book was published in 1962 in its original 1939 form.

Perhaps that is why, and certainly when compared to the glittering and spectacular social commentary of *Mark Twain in Eruption,* this "new" volume appears slightly old-fashioned and slow-moving at first. It is a collection of early and late essays and fragments, of good and bad things, and of some innocuous material that Mark Twain never published, with good reason, during his own lifetime. The opening chapters of religious satire may or may not include the "finest didactic chapters of the *Autobiography*" which a little earlier Charles Neider was not able to reprint because of Mark Twain's daughter's objections. It seems reasonable to suppose that these chapters were Clara's main concern; but they are really very unimportant in a modern context, and rather tedious. It is still interesting to notice that Neider refers to them as "good" didacticism, while Twain's social satire is "bad" didacticism; and DeVoto himself attempts to enclose Twain's social and moral radicalism within his religious radicalism. What is it there at the core of Sam Clemens that so terrifies these commentators and obliges them to indulge in such verbal gymnastics?

It could be the plain truth which is always so hard to face. In any case the opening of *Letters from the Earth* includes ten letters from Twain's Satan who has been exiled again and has chosen to reside upon the earth. This was a work which Clemens had initiated for his own pleasure during the last period of his life. Within its loose framework of religious fantasy and irony (some of it reminiscent of *The Mysterious Stranger*) he poured a random selection and a loose summary of all his familiar ideas.

Satan was being punished, to be sure, for "his too flexible tongue," a trait he shared with Tom Sawyer and Sam Clemens. And again Satan and Twain waxed lyrical about the human race. "This is a strange place, an extraordinary place, and interesting," Satan wrote to Saint Michael and Saint Gabriel. "There is nothing resembling it at home. The people are all insane, the other animals are all insane, the earth is insane. Nature itself is insane. Man is a marvelous curiosity. When he is at his very very best he is a sort of low grade nickel-plated angel; at his worst he is unspeakable, unimaginable; and first and last and all the time he is a sarcasm. Yet he blandly and in all sincerity calls himself the 'noblest work of God.' . . . Moreover — if I may put another strain upon you — he thinks he is the Creator's pet. He believes the Creator is proud of him; he even believes the Creator loves him; has a passion for him; sits up nights to admire him; yes, and watch over him and keep him out of trouble. He prays to Him, and thinks He listens."

In this sense "Letters from the Earth" (from which DeVoto took the title for the book) was the explication for some — though not all — of the mysteriousness in *The Mysterious Stranger*. It contains both man's view of God and God's view of man. "For there is nothing about man that is not strange to an immortal. He looks at nothing as we look at it, his sense of proportion is quite different from ours, and his sense of values is so widely divergent from ours, that with all our large intellectual powers it is not likely that even the most gifted among us would ever be quite able to understand it." And now man is a mystery in truth, rather than God; and Clemens went on to describe man's notion of heaven in his familiar way — but with an unfamiliar twist. For here heaven, unlike that visionary scene of sardonic horrors in *Captain Stormfield,* consisted not merely of psalm singing, praying, church-going, removable wings and halos, but concerned itself with both the biological and social aspects of man. "For instance, take this sample: he has imagined a heaven, and has left entirely out of it the supremest of all his delights, the one ecstasy that stands first and foremost in the heart of every individual of his race — and of ours — sexual intercourse."

This was a new note in all of Twain's reflections on man, God, and heaven. It was to be amplified in "Letters from the Earth," and perhaps it was the outspoken sexual content of these letters, as much as the religious satire, which caused Clara Clemens to hesitate so long about having them published.

To leave out the notion of sexual intercourse in heaven, said this Satanic Twin of Twain's, was as if "a lost and perishing person in a roasting desert should be told by a rescuer he might choose and have all longed-for things but one, and he should elect to leave out water!" And this later Satan went to further extremes in depicting the role of the sexual passions in mortals, and even more so in immortals. "First of all, I recall to your attention the extraordinary fact with which I began. To wit, that the human being, like the immortals, naturally places sexual intercourse far and away above all other joys — yet he has left it out of his heaven! The very thought of it excites him; opportunity sets him wild; in this state he will risk life, reputation, everything — even his queer heaven itself — to make good that opportunity and ride it out to the overwhelming climax. From youth to middle age all men and all women prize copulation above all other pleasures combined, yet it is actually, as I have said: it is not in their heaven; prayer takes its place."

Now this is not altogether as ironical as it sounds, since sexual intercourse *is* placed at the center of certain more ancient, more pagan, and perhaps wiser religious thinking. But this is certainly the most direct, overt, and illuminating — perhaps almost astonishing — statement of Mark Twain's about the most taboo subject in what still amounted to the end of the Victorian epoch. And note that Sam Clemens included women equally as man's *partner* in sexual desire — another unheard of concept in Victorian culture — and there was still more to follow on this subject.*

Pausing to observe that this Christian heaven hadn't a rag of intellectuality in it, Clemens returned to his favorite historical couple, Adam and Eve, and their sin. "Very well, Adam and Eve now knew what evil was, and how to do it. They knew how to do various kinds of wrong things, among them the one principal one — the one God had his mind on principally. That one was the art and mystery of sexual intercourse. To them it was a magnificent discovery, and they stopped idling around and turned their entire attention to it, poor exultant young things!"

What Twain was really writing, in these fragmented and uneven pages which still contained such brilliant things, was his own newly revised version of the Bible; and such a book would have been a sensation. In his reconstruction of our primal myth, Clemens pointed out that "Adam and Eve entered the world

---

* I am reminded of Leslie Fiedler's notion of a homosexual love affair between Huck and Jim on the Mississippi River. Readers of this book will have long ago concluded that Fiedler's "thesis," if it deserves that name, is both sensational and silly; but perhaps if Mr. Fiedler had known about the later statements of Sam Clemens about sexual matters, he would hardly have dared to formulate such an absurd hypothesis.

naked and unashamed — naked and pure-minded; and no descendant of theirs has ever entered it otherwise. All have entered it naked, unashamed, and clean in mind. They have entered it modest. They had to acquire immodesty and the soiled mind; there was no other way to get it. A Christian mother's first duty is to soil her child's mind, and she does not neglect it. Her lad grows up to be a missionary, and goes to the innocent savage and to the civilized Japanese, and soils their minds. Whereupon they adopt immodesty, they conceal their bodies, they stop bathing naked together."

But Twain's "New" Testament was also a stirring attack upon Christianity itself and upon Western Christian civilization in its entirety — despite all of Mr. Neider's involuted rationalizing on this subject, and the complete expunging of this aspect of Twain's work in Neider's *Autobiography*. For there followed a savage denunciation of the Judeo-Christian Jehovah himself, whom Clemens, incidentally, never identified by name.

And, after further commentary on the flourishing of sexuality in the pagan period of the Bible, and the visitations upon the lovely sex by the primitive gods, and the multiplying of the human race, we are treated to Mark Twain's version of the Flood. "By help of those visiting foreigners [the pagan gods] the population grew and grew until it numbered several millions. But it was a disappointment to the Deity. He was dissatisfied with its morals; which in some respects were not any better than his own. Indeed they were an unflatteringly close imitation of his own. They were a very bad people, and as he knew of no way to reform them, he wisely concluded to abolish them. This is the only really enlightened and superior idea his Bible has credited him with, and it would have made his reputation for all time if he could only have kept to it and carried it out. But he was always unstable — except in his own advertisements — and his good resolution broke down."

For some strange reason God still took pride in man, Twain said. "Man was his finest invention. Man was his pet, after the housefly, and he could not bear to lose him wholly, so he finally decided to save a sample of him and drown the rest . . ." Nothing could be more characteristic of God, Twain said, and he proceeded with a meticulous analysis of Noah's Ark; and a description of certain things not commonly known. "All these facts were suppressed in the Biblical account. You find not a hint of them there. The whole thing is hushed up."

There is a description of God's small-mindedness, including jealousy as one of his central traits; and of the microbes, who in this version actually constituted the main population of the Ark. Shem was full of hookworms, and God was especially generous in contributing his disease to the poor. "It is wonderful, the thorough and comprehensive study which the Creator devoted to the great work of making man miserable. I have said he devised a special affliction-agent for each and every detail of man's structure, overlooking not a single one, and I said the truth. Many poor people have to go barefoot, because they cannot afford shoes. The Creator saw his opportunity. I will remark, in passing, that he always has his eye on the poor. Nine-tenths of his disease-inventions were intended for the poor, and they *get* them. The well-to-do get only what is left over. Do not suspect me of speaking unheedfully, for it is not so; the vast bulk of the Creator's affliction-inventions *are* specially designed for the persecution of the poor."

Thus spoke Twain's Satan in "Letters from the Earth" — a Twainish Satan, however, who made some social discriminations in describing man's earthly condition, unlike the totally sardonic Satan of *The Mysterious Stranger*. And so much for the "anecdotic" and purely personal Mark Twain whom Charles Neider created out of Cold War fantasy and aberration. Published just three years after Neider's "new" version of the *Auto-*

biography, the volume called *Letters from the Earth* completely refutes every aspect of Mr. Neider's narrow and blinkered vision of Mark Twain himself.

I repeat these statements for the sake of history and Mark Twain scholarship rather than for my own interest, but I think Sam Clemens is entitled to the pleasure of seeing such a swift and ironical case of historical retribution. (History was always awarding such entertainments to this favorite child.) And here Twain began alternating his satire between the Deity and the Pulpit. His main point was that God never invented a single human or social reform, but immediately rushed to get the credit for any good deed that men achieved. The Creator was indeed "the one that never sleeps when there is a chance to breed sorrow for somebody." Speaking of the sleeping sickness in Africa caused by the tsetse fly, and the Pulpit's praise of science as being god-given, Clemens concluded: "He is surely a curious Being. He commits a fearful crime, continues that crime unbroken for six thousand years, and is then entitled to praise because he suggests to somebody else to modify its severities. He is called patient, and he certainly must be patient, or he would have sunk the pulpit in perdition ages ago for the ghastly compliments it pays him."

Man, commented Clemens again, is without any doubt the most interesting fool there is. Also the most eccentric. He went on to describe the central civilizational conflict in human evolution: the conflict between the laws of God and those of man. But in this case he viewed God as pagan and plenary nature, the true source of all animal and human temperament and drives, which "man" (society, civilization) had attempted to suppress and inhibit. (Perhaps the reverse is true; or rather God obviously embodies both strains of the human temperament.) He traced his argument to its central core of sexuality, again. "Temperament is the law of God written in the heart of every creature by God's own hand, and *must* be obeyed, and will be obeyed in spite of all restricting or forbidding statutes, let them emanate whence they may." He compared the sexual temperaments of the goat and the tortoise. "The excitable goat, the emotional goat, that has to have some adultery every day or fade and die; and the tortoise, that cold calm puritan, that takes a treat only once in two years and then goes to sleep in the midst of it and doesn't wake up for sixty days. No lady goat is safe from criminal assault even on the Sabbath day . . . whereas neither the gentleman tortoise nor the lady tortoise is ever hungry enough for the solemn joys of fornication to be willing to break the Sabbath to get them. Now according to man's curious reasoning, the goat has earned punishment, and the tortoise praise."

More boldly still, Clemens asserted the sexuality of the (Victorian!) woman when compared with the often limited and unreliable male sexuality; and the fact that female sexuality had been repressed to conform to man's view of it — that women were in fact the sexual slaves and sexual property of a "master" who could hardly compete with them. In these pages of sexual comparison Clemens was frank and funny to the point of obscenity; he was convulsed by the notion of female sexuality all but overcoming the inadequate and restricted male. "Now there you have a sample of man's 'reasoning powers,' as he calls them. He observes certain facts. For instance, that in all his life he never sees the day when he can satisfy one woman; also, that no woman ever sees the day that she can't overwork and defeat, and put out of commission any ten masculine plants that can be put to bed to her. He puts these strikingly suggestive and luminous facts together, and from them draws this astonishing conclusion: The Creator intended the woman to be restricted to one man."

Perhaps women were even more of a damned fool to Clemens than man was. But certainly this was open and frank and remarkably bold sexual commentary on the part of an artist who has been so often, so continually, so tediously described as "censored" and "neurotic" and "frustrated" and "repressed" at the very core of his being. This "core" remained constant with Clemens, as we've seen, from his youth to his age, during poverty and wealth, success and failure, sickness and health, joy and tragedy. And it actually flourished and grew freer and bolder and more luxurious in the final phase of his life. He described a buxom royal princess of the Sandwich Islands whose harem included thirty-six splendidly built young native men. By comparison he thought that Solomon's harem of seven hundred wives and three hundred concubines was poorly serviced. "To save his life he could not have kept two of those young creatures satisfactorily refreshed, even if he had fifteen experts to help him. Necessarily almost the entire thousand had to go hungry years and years on a stretch. Conceive of a man hardhearted enough to look daily upon all that suffering and not to be moved to mitigate it. He even wantonly added a sharp pang to that pathetic misery; for he kept within those women's sight, always, stalwart watchmen whose splendid masculine forms made the poor lassies' mouths water but who hadn't anything to solace a candlestick with, these gentry being eunuchs. A eunuch is a person whose candle has been put out. By art."

From time to time, Clemens concluded, "I will take up a Biblical statute and show you that it always violates a law of God, and then is imported into the lawbooks of the nations, where it continues its violations. But those things will keep; there is no hurry." This was in all ways a brilliant view of the long tradition of Judeo-Christian morality which lay at the base of man's development in Western European culture. It was a view whose essential soundness, if not the entertaining and deliberately ludicrous details, has been supported by modern depth psychologists searching for the key to culture and civilization, to evolutionary progress and/or societal reversion. The key to a fuller and happier human existence, and a less tortured and sickly life, *within* society.

The Old Testament, continued Clemens, gave us the Deity as he was before he got religion. "The other one gives us a picture of him as he appeared afterward. The Old Testament is interested mainly in blood and sensuality. The New one is Salvation. Salvation by Fire." The first time the Deity came down to earth, said Clemens — excuse me, I mean the Satan of these "Letters from the Earth" said, or Satan-Twain — he brought life and death. "When he came down the second time, he brought hell." And Clemens embarked upon another of his passages about the meaning of life in death.

Life was not a valuable gift, but death was. Life was a fever-dream made up of joys embittered by sorrows, pleasure poisoned by pain; a dream that was a nightmare-confusion of spasmodic and fleeting delights, ecstasies, exultations, happinesses, interspersed with long-drawn miseries, griefs, perils, horrors, disappointments, defeats, humiliations, and despairs — the heaviest curse devisable by divine ingenuity; but death was sweet, death was gentle, death was kind; death healed the bruised spirit and the broken heart, and gave them rest and forgetfulness; death was man's best friend; when man could endure life no longer, death came and set him free.

Thus Twain in the tragic mood; and hard upon it Twain in the ironic mood. For in time the Deity perceived that death was a mistake. "A mistake in that it was insufficient; insufficient for the reason that while it was an admirable agent of the inflicting of misery upon the survivor, it allowed the dead person himself to escape from all further persecution in the blessed refuge of the grave." This was not satisfactory to the Deity, said Clemens, and a way must be contrived to pursue the dead beyond the tomb. "The Deity pondered this matter during four thousand years unsuccessfully, but as soon as he came down to earth and became a Christian his mind cleared and he knew what to do. He invented hell, and proclaimed it."

Thus Jesus Christ, who replaced the jealous and cruel Jehovah of the Old Testament, and became a symbol of all that was gentle, merciful, and forgiving, was in Mark Twain's eye, a crueler and more malign figure. It was in Christ's name, not Jehovah's, that hell was invented and proclaimed. But there was not that much difference between the two Deities, and the chronicle continued with a detailed account of Jehovah's crimes against mankind. "The Biblical law says: 'Thou shalt not kill.' The law of God, planted in the heart of man at his birth, says: 'Thou shalt kill.' The chapter I have quoted shows you that the book-statute is once more a failure. It cannot set aside the more powerful law of nature . . . According to the belief of these people, it was God himself who said: 'Thou shalt not kill.' Then it is plain that he cannot keep his own commandments. He killed all those people — every male. They had offended the Deity in some way." And Clemens went on to illustrate all of the possible offenses to the Deity that he could imagine, except that of being guilty. "The Lord slew Onan for that, for the Lord could never abide indelicacy. The Lord slew Onan, and to this day the Christian world cannot understand why he stopped with Onan, instead of slaying all the inhabitants for three hundred miles around — they being innocent of offense, and therefore the very ones he would usually slay. If he had a motto, it would have read, 'Let no innocent person escape.' "

In these passages indeed Sam Clemens was pursuing the Lord himself with the same fascinated concern, and almost obsessional curiosity, and wrathful malice which he had used in the case of Mary Baker Eddy; who herself had had some thoughts of replacing the Virgin Mary.

There followed a sort of bawdy exchange with the Lord, developing from Onan's sin in sexually withdrawing from his brother's wife. And again there was the related commentary on God and the Pulpit. "Human history in all ages is red with blood, and bitter with hate, and stained with cruelties, but not since Bible times have these features been without a limit of some kind. Even the Church, which is credited with having split more innocent blood, since the beginning of its supremacy, than all the political wars put together have spilt, has observed a limit. A sort of limit. But you notice that when the Lord God of Heaven and Earth, adored Father of Man, goes to war, there is no limit. He is totally without mercy — he, who is called the Fountain of Mercy. He slays, slays, slays! All the men, all the beasts, all the boys, all the babies; also all the women and girls, except those that have not been deflowered."

This was in connection with the campaign against the Midianites in the Old Testament. And Clemens, in wrathful tones reminiscent of King Leopold's Congo — for injustice and cruelty five thousand years ago were just as fresh and searing to him as yesterday's event — went into another savage discourse on the Lord's treatment of the 32,000 Virgins and their induction into sexual slavery under the divine guidance. "It was the Father that inflicted this ferocious and undeserved punishment upon those bereaved and friendless virgins, whose parents and kindred he had slaughtered before their eyes. And were they praying to him for pity and rescue, meantime? Without a doubt of it . . . These virgins were 'Spoil,' plunder, booty.

He claimed his share and got it. What use had *he* for virgins? Examine his later history and you will know."

Clemens concluded once again — like Beethoven he had so many chances to end his compositions which he ignored — by comparing the peaceful moral preachings of the Judaic-Christian Biblical God with his actual behavior. "Would you expect this same conscienceless God, this moral bankrupt, to become a teacher of morals; of gentleness; of meekness; of righteousness; of purity? It looks impossible, extravagant; but listen to him. These are his own words." And then Clemens-Twain suggested that the Beatitudes and the chapters from Numbers and Deuteronomy which he had just been quoting should always be read from the pulpit together. "Then the congregation would get an all-round view of Our Father in Heaven. Yet not in a single instance have I ever known a clergyman to do this."

There is no doubt that if Mark Twain had ever completed and published his satanic version of the Bible, it would have been a remarkable book. Meanwhile we are glad that Mr. DeVoto rescued these fragments for publication, and they were much better than the next section of *Letters from the Earth*, called "Papers of the Adam Family." These were "translated from the Adamic," according to Clemens and Paine and DeVoto, throughout Twain's career, starting as early as the 1870s, and were obviously intended as another testament of Biblical times. The first translations were extracts from "Methuselah's Diary," which preceded the publication of "Adam's Diary" by some fifteen years, and, according to Paine, there was an even earlier version of "Shem's Diary" which has been lost.

How Clemens enjoyed conversing with primitive and edenic human nature in the Bible before the Fall — or the first coming of morality, society, and civilization — as DeVoto remarks here, concerning Twain and the Adam Family, but without recognizing the source or true meaning of this communion. DeVoto did realize the analogy in Twain's mind between the Flood and the imminent destruction, as he (Twain) felt, of his own American democracy. "In Methuselah's time as in Mark Twain's time, a great civilization had reached the point when the destructive forces it contained were beginning to dominate. He appreciated its greatness; he also appreciated the inevitability of its collapse. He and Methuselah lived in eras which they both loved and hated but in which they were never quite at home, eras with a doom on them, eras when the world was spinning toward the abyss."

Here indeed DeVoto, under the guise of analyzing the historical crisis in Mark Twain's religious chronicle, was himself far more direct and open in the analysis of his own society than anywhere else in his public writings — although the lingering traces of his belated frontier optimism persisted in the generalized vagueness of his statements; in the romantic use of Twain's formulations; and in the addition of some rather peculiar social commentary of his own. Now we know that from the very start of his career, Sam Clemens had been critical of many of those democratic institutions which so much later DeVoto still supported without doubt and without question. But it was only in the mid-nineties, as we have seen, that he met at first hand the conditions and consequences of western imperialism upon those "backward" and "pagan" and "pigmented" countries whose great champion in America (and for the whole world) Mark Twain became.

The breaking point in Clemens' personal career, to which DeVoto earlier had attributed the deterioration in his talent, was in fact the dividing line which gave a new force, power, eloquence to Twain's later writings — which now, quite belatedly, and still in another (religious) guise DeVoto paid tribute to. For

he does note that around 1906, the "Father of History" became
the "Mad Prophet" — as Twain's social discontent persisted and
increased. "The year 920 After Creation was fateful for
Adamic society," so DeVoto paraphrased Twain, "and he saw
the same forces at work round him, the same softened people, the same corrupt plutocracy, the same venal and bewildered
government, the same chaos." That *was* the symbolic content
which Twain intended to convey in "Papers of the Adam Family" — even though a more sophisticated historian would not
use DeVoto's description of a "bewildered government" —
as Twain did not — a "softened people" (softened from or by
what?) and the almost meaningless word "chaos."

The twentieth-century United States Government of the mili-
tary-industrial-scientific complex, of world monopolies and
super-conglomerates; this corporate state of armed imperialism
and colonial wars of extermination was not "bewildered."
Only its own people (and some historians) were. What Mark
Twain was describing in both his direct social commentary and
his religious parables was much more accurate, pointed, and
particularized than DeVoto acknowledged. I only wish I could
say as much in favor of the Adam Family papers as literature as
has been said about their meaning and purpose. Despite De-
Voto's inclusion of them as such a large block of *Letters from
the Earth,* they are really quite boring to read. Partly because
Clemens had started them so early as the 1870s as a desultory
sort of self-entertainment, they are difficult and confusing to
read, and some of them are written in a falsely archaic style.
Maybe DeVoto used them to *obscure* Twain's direct social criticism; or at least they were more congenial to him.

In the 1900s Clemens also wrote a variation on "Eve's Diary"
called "Eve's Autobiography," which was much more theoretical and pseudo-scientific and even pseudo-historical than the

published version of "Eve's Diary" already discussed in these pages. It is true that Twain was writing of the world's rising birthrate which would concern the thinking of the twentieth century; and that he Swiftianly proposed war as the only solution for the population explosion. And it was here he developed the notion of the "Shoemaker-Dictator" who would sweep "the Double Continent with fire and sword" to purge its commercialism and moral corruption. But his descriptions of the North American nation's final phase had been done better before. (These papers were probably the false inspirations or first drafts or poorer formulations of what Mark Twain said more forcefully elsewhere.) And his elaborations of the "Law of Periodical Repetition" and the "Law of Intellectual Averages" were not only historically untrue but monotonous.

These were mainly either preliminary or repetitious fragments of Mark Twain's best work which were gathered together in *Letters from the Earth*; yet they still contained such brilliant passages as Twain's indictment of the Philippines war (once again) in phrases completely appropriate to the Vietnam war of the 1960s. "I pray you to pause and consider. Against our traditions we are now entering upon an unjust and trivial war, a war against a helpless people, and for a base object — robbery. At first our citizens spoke out against this thing, by an impulse natural to their training. Today they have turned, and their voice is the other way. What caused the change? Merely a politician's trick — a high-sounding phrase, a blood-stirring phrase which turned their uncritical heads: *Our Country, right or wrong!* An empty phrase, a silly phrase. It was shouted by every newspaper, it was thundered from the pulpit, the Superintendent of Public Instruction placarded it in every schoolhouse in the land, the War Department inscribed it upon the flag. And every man who failed to shout it or was silent, was proclaimed a traitor — none but those others were patriots. To be a patriot, one had to say, and keep on saying, 'Our Country, right or wrong,' and urge on the little war. Have you not perceived that the phrase is an insult to the nation?"

In the early years of the Nixon Administration — just as in the epoch of President Theodore Roosevelt — when the inglorious "little" war in Vietnam (which had turned out to be larger and longer than the Pentagon had estimated) was still being pursued under the deceitful guise of making peace; and when so many replicas of the American flag had blossomed forth in every area of the Empire as to make the lack of showing the flag very conspicuous — those words *were* appropriate. And Clemens' prophetic words applied directly to those who claimed it was "impossible" to end the war without honor. "Only when a republic's *life* is in danger should a man uphold his government when it is in the wrong. There is no other time. The Republic's life is not in peril. The nation has sold its honor for a phrase. It has swung loose from its safe anchorage and is drifting, its helm is in pirate hands. The stupid phrase needed help, and it got another one: 'Even if the war be wrong we are in it and must fight it out: *we cannot retire from it without dishonor.*' Why, not even a burglar could have said it better. We cannot withdraw from this sordid raid because to grant peace to those little people upon their terms — independence — would dishonor us. You have flung away Adam's phrase — you should take it up and examine it again. He said, '*An inglorious peace is better than a dishonorable war.*' You have planted a seed, and it will grow."

The source of Mark Twain's "compulsive" hatred for Theodore Roosevelt is thus tracked down. It was Roosevelt whom he blamed for the collapse of the Old Republic; the advent of the American Empire which was to lead to the Monarchy, and to the Dictatorship. Now this process of the Oligarchy and Imperialism — after the American heartland had been exploited, despoiled, and enchained by the new breed of financial barons and titans in the post-Civil War epoch — had started long before, as Clemens knew and described. But it was during the Rooseveltian era that Mark Twain saw the *outward* expansion of this process until it did in fact lead to something like the American world imperium in the 1950s and 1960s. Twain saw the brutal and ruthless beginnings of this right at home in the 1900s, and he foresaw how it would destroy the democracy.

"But it was impossible to save the Great Republic. She was rotten to the heart. Lust of conquest had long ago done its work; trampling upon the helpless abroad had taught her, by a natural process, to endure with apathy the like at home; multitudes who had applauded the crushing of other people's liberties, lived to suffer for their mistake in their own persons. The government was irrevocably in the hands of the prodigiously rich and their hangers-on; the suffrage was become a mere machine, which they used as they chose. There was no principle but commercialism, no patriotism but of the pocket. From showily and sumptuously entertaining neighboring titled aristocracies, and from trading their daughters to them, the plutocrats came in the course of time to hunger for titles and heredities themselves. The drift toward monarchy, in some form or other, began; it was spoken of in whispers at first, later in a bolder voice."

And from monarchy, the lost republic called upon the Shoemaker-Prodigy from the Deep South to take control. The standing army — another innovation of American democracy — refused to obey the Congress, and the Dictatorship set in.

This apocalypytical vision was at the center of the posthumous DeVoto volume called *Letters from the Earth;* and its publication was another service from a badly harassed critic, even though he only allowed Twain's social criticism to filter through the religious parables.

The rest of the collection included stray and casual pieces of minor interest; yet, as always with Mark Twain's prose, there were some other interesting or entertaining passages to be noticed. There was another children's story ("A Cat-Tale") he had invented for Susy and Clara whose main distinction was the hilarious Mark Twain line drawings and his "analyses" of these works of art. (A special volume should be published of Mark Twain's drawings and his descriptions of them.) The front end of one of his cats, for example, was peacefully asleep, the rear end was ferociously active. There was another essay on "Cooper's Prose Style" adding some further remarks on that early American master's craft. "I beg to remind you that an author's way of setting forth a matter is called his Style, and that an author's style is a main part of his equipment for business. The style of some authors has variety in it, but Cooper's style is remarkable for the absence of this feature. Cooper's style is always grand and stately and noble. Style may be likened to an army, the author to its general, the book to the campaign. Some authors proportion an attacking force to the strength or weakness, the importance or unimportance of the object to be attacked; but Cooper doesn't. It doesn't make any difference to Cooper whether the object of attack is a hundred thousand men or a cow; he hurls his entire force against it. He comes thundering down with all his battalions at his back, cavalry in the van, artillery on the flanks, infantry massed in the middle, forty bands braying, a thousand banners streaming in the wind; and whether the object be an army or a cow you will see him come marching sublimely in, at the end of the engagement, bearing the more preferable fragments of the victim patiently on his shoulders, to the stopping-place. Cooper's style is grand, awful, beautiful; but

it is sacred to Cooper, it is his very own, and no student of the
Veterinary College of Arizona will be allowed to filch it from
him."

Menckenesque? One might add that while the New Criticism
of the mid-twentieth century has made important discoveries in
respect to the technique of writing, it hasn't yet approached the
effects of Mark Twain's studies of his own craft. There was a little postscript to the Gorky incident in which Clemens attempted
to rationalize his and Howells' behavior in terms of human custom as the rock of society, and law as the only pure reason.
But the fact remains that these two American writers had be-
haved badly in cutting Gorky because he had arrived for a
tour of revolutionary lectures with his mistress. (The fact
was that this "mistress" was Gorky's common-law wife; and the
Russian embassy had spread the slander.) But then Clemens
followed this with a remarkable little essay (originally meant
for the *Autobiography*) written in 1908 and called "Something
About Repentance." It was curious, he said, about the misasso-
ciation of certain words:

"For instance, the word Repentance. Through want of reflection we associate it exclusively with Sin. We get the notion
early, and keep it always, that we repent of bad deeds only;
whereas we do a formidably large business in repenting of good
deeds which we have done. Often when we repent of a sin,
we do it perfunctorily, from principle, coldly and from the head;
but when we repent of a good deed the repentance comes hot
and bitter and straight from the heart. Often when we repent of a sin, we can forgive ourselves and drop the matter out
of mind; but when we repent of a good deed, we seldom get
peace — we go on repenting to the end. And the repentance
is so perennially young and strong and vivid and vigorous! A
great benefaction conferred with your whole heart upon an

ungrateful man — with what immortal persistence and never-cooling energy do you repent of that! Repentance of a sin is a pale, poor, perishable thing compared with it.

"I am quite sure that the average man is built just as I am; otherwise I should not be making this revelation of my inside." And note again perhaps the most original spirit of them all drew all his faith and strength and power — in that older tra-dition of nineteenth-century American writing from Emerson and Thoreau, Whitman and Melville — from an absolute iden-tification with the people, the masses, and that "average man" who was both the mask and the true source of strength for Clemens' art. This was the source of our literature's great-ness in its high period; and the lack of this was the cause of con-temporary American literature's failure. "I say the average man," Clemens continued, "and stop there; for I am quite cer-tain that there are people who do not repent of their good deeds when the return they get for them is treachery and ingratitude. I think these few ought to be in heaven; they are in the way here. In my time I have committed several millions of sins. Many of them I probably repented of — I do not remember now; others I was partly minded to repent of, but it did not seem worthwhile; all of them but the recent ones and a few scattering former ones I have forgotten. In my time I have done eleven good deeds. I remember all of them, four of them with crystal clearness. These four I repent of whenever I think of them — and it is not seldomer than fifty-two times a year. I repent of them in the same old original furious way, undiminished, al-ways. If I wake up in the night, they are there, waiting and ready; and they keep me company till the morning. I have not committed any sin that has held me like this save one; and have not repented of any sin with the unmodifying earnestness and sincerity with which I have repented of these four gracious and beautiful good deeds.

"Possibly you who are reading these paragraphs are of those few who have got mislaid and ought to be in heaven. In that case you will not understand what I have been saying and will have no sympathy with it; but your neighbor will, if he is fifty years old."

This is surely one of the best and shortest of all informal essays. Not a word is wasted, not a word could be cut, not a word is wrong; this is implacable prose, riding high with mature wisdom. (Twain the frustrated adolescent!) One is reminded of those pages in the *Autobiography* concerning Clemens' earlier sense of sin and doom — at night in the dark hours — which somehow never survived the light of day. What has happened to Mr. DeVoto's thesis of the split Twain, the frustrated Twain, the tragic and dark Twain who was so unresolved and tormented, unfulfilled to the end of his life? As we said originally, the *Autobiography* is not such a work. Full of torment, tragedy, sorrow about the human lot, it is still one of the great *daylight* documents of literature (I repeat) where the artist is immersed in the communal experience, and where finally all of the pain and suffering of human experience is recognized and acknowledged in beautiful art — and dissolved by the laughter of genius.

A rare thing even in the upper brackets of literature, for Twain was not being merely entertaining, either. What was being described in "Repentance" was the consuming vanity of the human heart, so much larger than conventional morality. And what Clemens was celebrating was his own release from conventional worldly obligations — the free soaring of spirit in the very last of his years. Talking of form, this barely page-and-one-half sermon must be counted among his best things. There followed a purely Dadaistic extract from the earlier days of Clemens' repudiation of the Victorian taboos; an unfinished burlesque of the etiquette books of the period which preached "good manners" — refinement, gentility, sexual repression —

to a supposedly crude and ignorant American audience. Apparently Clemens worked on this unfinished book from the 1880s on; and I have space only to quote a little from still another collection of essays of philosophical speculations about man's nature. This was called *The Damned Human Race* and written mainly in the years from 1900 to 1909, and could just as well have been included in the *Autobiography*.

Twain devoted a good deal of time to proving that if the Lord had intended the earth only for man's use, he had certainly taken his time about it, and tried many other experiments and failures before reaching this conclusion. This essay was notable for the range of his thought and knowledge in geology, astronomy, biology. Darwinism was at the center of these speculations, and pulpit religion was the target. In a section titled "In the Animal's Court" he showed again that none of the lower animals could escape the law of his own makeup. The lion was bold because he was bold, the wolf was savage, the sheep was tame and sacrificial, the fox was cunning, the machine was a machine. And what was Man, Clemens wondered, if not a mixture of all these elements, along with the pretense of free will. But in "The Lowest Animal" he was even more direct and sardonic; and one remembers Clemens' affinity, from the very start of his career, with the animal world. "I have been studying the traits and dispositions of the 'lower animals' (so-called) and contrasting them with the traits and dispositions of man. I find the result humiliating to me. For it obliges me to renounce my allegiance to the Darwinian theory of the Ascent of Man from the Lower Animals; since it now seems plain to me that that theory ought to be vacated in favor of a new and truer one, this new and truer one to be named the *Descent* of Man from the Higher Animals."

In brief space Clemens then went on to catalog his familiar

complaints about man, and the familiar virtues of the higher animals. Perhaps because his space was shorter, his complaints more varied and vivid, his comparisons with the animal world so generously in their favor, this becomes almost one of his unbearably savage — Swiftian — essays. And so we come to the last section of *Letters from the Earth,* in the last — well, almost — of Mark Twain's books we can discuss here. This was another fragment of narrative, written in the late nineties, at the peak of Sam Clemens' domestic troubles, which DeVoto titled "The Great Dark," and to which he gave so much editorial study and analysis.

Perhaps too much. This was an interesting fragment of work, at best, illuminating as to the depths of Clemens' despair, to the point where he felt he could no longer distinguish between illusion and reality in life (as other works of this period also recorded) — to the point that he believed his whole lifelong domestic idyll of love and pleasure with Livy and their children was in fact an illusion; an illusion which the Livy figure in "The Great Dark" does not remember as a fact.

But the central point of the present book is that Samuel Clemens was not a major talent frustrated at midpoint. Not in the least; not at all; not possibly so. And I think that we have more than amply refuted the old and recurrent thesis of Twain's "frustration," his "failure," his final "bitterness." On the contrary we have seen just how Clemens recovered his talent intact from the pit and quagmire of disaster. The whole point is that he surmounted the crisis of mid-life; he survived it and he transcended it.

He entered his mature and later periods of writing quite triumphantly indeed, with all his old powers enhanced, rather than broken or diminished, by his own central tragic experience; by his depth realization of life's pain and evil. He retained to the end the central source of his artistic virtue: that untouched spring of pagan, plenary, and edenic innocence, that full sense of joy and pleasure in life, which sprang up even more freely in his final decades — which came to a second and later flowering despite all those civilizational discontents which he, perhaps more than any other American writer, also felt so directly and personally at the center of his being.

It was only certain Twain critics, from the youthful Van Wyck Brooks, who came to change his mind, to Bernard DeVoto and Charles Neider and Justin Kaplan, as we've seen, who refused to acknowledge — or who were perhaps ignorant of — the value of his later writing. Mark Twain was more correct in his own estimate of that work, his joy in writing it, and yes, his pleasure in receiving the world's acclamation then (and yet again today) for having written it. The last periods of his writing were indeed younger in spirit if wiser in essence than much of his earlier and middle periods of work. *Huck Finn* as his single great classic — what nonsense! His whole career was a classic. He was not merely the artist of American youth and the past; he was surely our most mature and wisest of artists whose acerbity and profundity alike were ringed about with the imperishable comic spirit. In his age he only became freer, bolder, more open and honest, more emancipated both socially and sexually, from the taboos of his epoch which, at base, his spirit had never accepted.

To the critics' discomfort at times (and perhaps this was the true cause of their discontent), he became even more satanic and savage in the social commentary of his last period. But was he not also, as we have seen during the same period of his work, more touching, tender, and lyrical, bringing forth our tears when he wielded that magical wand; this genius who was wedded to both the tragic deeps and the great peaks of the human comedy.

Presently, even more Mark Twain material is being opened up

for public inspection — the bonanza of his genius is still being tapped. Sponsored by the Modern Language Association, the University of California Press is publishing some fourteen volumes of Twain's hitherto unpublished papers. While most of this material has already been studied by Mark Twain scholars, and while some of it — like the dreadful extract of Huck Finn and Tom Sawyer "Among the Indians," published for no good reason in *Life* magazine in 1969 — was rejected for publication by Sam Clemens himself, or by his subsequent literary editors, still, I have no doubt that out of these fourteen volumes of unpublished papers at least one more valuable Mark Twain book will emerge. And perhaps, as one must hope, another one. And maybe another.

Nobody should discount anything that Samuel Clemens wrote, as I said earlier, and as I hope this book has demonstrated. At least it has presented the various levels of Mark Twain's art in all its range, scope, depth, and variety — of a talent which seems as fresh and sharp and enchanting today as when the ink first flowed from its inspired pen. It is with some sense of personal loss (at least momentarily) that I write these closing pages about such an unearthly, yes, and divine spirit which was so firmly rooted in the earth. These notes and letters and parables and commentaries from the older world of the American democracy, which appear so often as if written by some visitant from another planet . . . and concerned above all with the mysterious soul of man. And that old-fashioned bardic and runic American artist who now belongs to all the world, to the history which he meditated upon, to whatever future, uneasy, dark or dubious as it appears from here, may still hopefully prevail.

SELECTED READINGS

BESIDES THE MARK TWAIN BOOKS mentioned in the text of this book, I should like to acknowledge my debt, first of all, to *Sam Clemens of Hannibal,* written by my early friend Dixon Wecter whose sudden and tragic death stopped a career full of promise. Also by Wecter as editor, *Mark Twain to Mrs. Fairbanks* and *The Love Letters of Mark Twain.* Of much value to any student of Mark Twain is *Mark Twain: The Development of a Writer,* by Henry Nash Smith, the former literary editor of the Mark Twain papers. Also by Bernard DeVoto is *The Portable Mark Twain,* a useful if now somewhat antique volume, and DeVoto's *Mark Twain at Work.* I must mention two useful short studies, *Mark Twain* by Stephen Leacock, and *Mark Twain: Man and Legend* by DeLancey Ferguson, although both these volumes subscribe to the familiar and "received" legend of Mark Twain which the present book does not accept. The indefatigable Charles Neider has to his credit also: *Mark Twain* (a study); *The Complete Short Stories of Mark Twain*; and *The Travels of Mark Twain.* Among books on or by the Clemens family are *My Father Mark Twain* by Clara Clemens and *Awake to a Perfect Day* by Clara Clemens (Gabrilowitsch Samossoud). Also *My Cousin Mark Twain* by Cyril Clemens (With Introduction by Booth Tarkington) and *Mark Twain, Family Man* by Caroline Thomas Harnsberger. Also *Mark Twain, Business Man* by Clemens' great-nephew, Samuel Charles Webster, and *Susy and Mark Twain: Family Dialogue,* by Edith Colgate Salsbury. A pamphlet called *Nook Farm* and published by the Stowe-Day Foundation is of interest as to the community life of the Clemenses. See also *Nook Farm: Mark Twain's Hartford Circle,* by Kenneth R. Andrews; and *Mark Twain Himself,* by Milton Meltzer, is an attractive picture-book history.

Among many essays and shorter studies of Mark Twain, Matthew Josephson's essay in *Portrait of the Artist as American* is of particular interest. (The same writer's *Robber Barons* almost anticipated, if it could not include, Mark Twain's invaluable first-hand material on that epoch just recently published.) Other major studies of Twain, discussed in the text of this book, as I say, are listed in the Index. For the rest, there are scores of studies, critiques, introductions, analyses, and critical and biographical studies which are of particular interest about one aspect or another of Mark Twain, but about which I cannot do more than to make a general acknowledgment of my indebtedness.

Index